Lloyd George
and the Generals

Frontispiece. David Lloyd George: his hair, which he allowed to grow long, rapidly turned white during the war.

Lloyd George and the Generals

David R. Woodward

Newark: University of Delaware Press
London and Toronto: Associated University Presses

Associated University Presses, Inc.
4 Cornwall Drive
East Brunswick, NJ 08816

Associated University Presses Ltd
25 Sicilian Avenue
London WC1A 2QH, England

Associated University Presses
2133 Royal Windsor Road
Unit 1
Mississauga, Ontario L5J 1K5, Canada

Library of Congress Cataloging in Publication Data

Woodward, David R., 1939–
Lloyd George and the generals.

Bibliography: p.
Includes index.
1. Great Britain—Politics and government—1910–
1936. 2. World War, 1914–1918—Great Britain.
3. Lloyd George, David, 1863–1945. I. Title.
DA577.W66 1983   941.083   81-52983
ISBN 0-87413-211-8

Printed in the United States of America

Contents

List of Illustrations

Preface

The British victory in World War I, achieved at immense human and material cost, failed to create a better world and led to widespread disillusionment. Had victory been worth the ghastly slaughter, and of equal importance, had the war been conducted along right lines? Scapegoating flourished in Britain as both civil and military leaders censured their rivals about their alleged blunders. Chief among the combatants were David Lloyd George and the generals, who resumed their wartime disputes in the publishing houses. This war of paper bullets had begun almost as soon as the guns fell silent, with the liberal editor A. G. Gardiner initiating the fray on November 30 with an article in the *Daily News* headlined "MR. LLOYD GEORGE AND UNITY OF COMMAND: A LEGEND AND THE TRUTH," which attempted to strike down the notion that Lloyd George had "won the war." The generals and their sympathizers soon followed Gardiner into print with polemical accounts of Lloyd George's role in the war. The view that the generals had won the war in spite of Lloyd George was canonized in the British official history of the war compiled by Brigadier-General James E. Edmonds. To be sure, Lloyd George had his defenders. None proved more one-sided than the Welshman himself, who portrayed the generals in his memoirs as inept and stupid. Nor has time stilled the passions aroused by Britain's deadliest war. Witness the angry reaction to the simplistic musical, *Oh, What a Lovely War,* which characterized the military authorities as callous butchers, and the running battle between John Terraine, the staunch defender of the "Westerner" Sir Douglas Haig, and the late Captain Liddell Hart and his disciples, apostles of indirect strategy.

Too rarely have these often partisan accounts added to our understanding of the how and why of decisions affecting the lives of tens of thousands of British soldiers. Considerable literature exists on both Lloyd George and the higher direction of the Great War, yet access to many private and official papers sealed until the mid-1960s or later permits a fresh and more balanced look at Lloyd George's controversial role in military affairs and his frequently antagonistic relationship with the British high command, which his "Eastern" or indirect strategy exacerbated. The wealth of new material makes possible a detailed description of how civil and military authorities grappled with the problems of fighting a world war which centered around a great land war against Germany. That misjudgments abounded is understandable. The magnitude and complexity of events often overwhelmed the participants. Lloyd George, his civilian colleagues, and the generals were no exception. The record underscores their fallibility and reaffirms that the war posed few questions with simple, easy answers.

That record has largely been reconstructed from diverse primary sources: the contemporary press, *Parliamentary Debates,* the private papers, published diaries and memoirs of those involved in formulating and executing military policy, and the voluminous records of the Cabinet Papers. For the first time, an important chapter in the distinguished and often turbulent career of one of Britain's greatest prime ministers can be given the comprehensive study it deserves. Also, new evidence unearthed either clarifies or answers persistent questions concerning the Calais conference, the Maurice debate, Lloyd George's Balkanite strategy, the government's commitment to the Somme and Passchendaele offensives, Sir William Robertson's downfall, the government's manpower policies, the creation of a Supreme War Council and generalissimo, and other important topics. The story, as it unfolds, examines the influence of the monarchy and press on the decision-making process, and, from a wider perspective, weighs the difficult relationship between the civil and military authorities in a democracy at war. Where did the responsibility of the British civil authorities end in the conduct of a total war which involved all elements of the nation? Where did the authority of the soldiers begin?

This is narrative history for which I make no apologies. As A. J. P. Taylor once observed, "After all, the distinguishing mark of history is that events happen in order of time. How else can you present them?"

I am very much in the debt of the many individuals who assisted me in the researching and writing of this book. The staffs of British libraries and archives in which I worked and Miss Josephine Fidler, the acquisitions librarian of Marshall University library, could not have been more helpful. Mrs. Margaret Gerke and Mrs. Juanita Harold assisted me in typing the manuscript. Dr. Alan Gould, Dr. Robert Maddox, Dr. Donna Spindel, and Dr. Michael Galgano, colleagues of mine in the History Department at Marshall University, read and commented on some of the chapters. Dr. Trevor Wilson of the University of Adelaide must be singled out for special recognition. His extensive comment on my manuscript saved me from some embarrassing gaffes and prodded me to rethink some of my conclusions. The same can be said of Dr. Stuart Kaufman of the University of Maryland, who read the entire manuscript. Fred Woodward, the director of the Regent's Press of Kansas, counseled me in various important ways. Any errors in fact or interpretation, of course, are my responsibility. I am also most appreciative of the summer grants-in-aid, sabbatical, and funds for typing given me by Marshall University. Finally, I am grateful to my wife, Martha, for her encouragement, understanding, and keen proofreading eye, and to my daughter, Catherine, for her ready acceptance of a new environment in an English school and a flat in Wimbledon while I completed my research.

Facets of the manuscript have previously been published in *Albion, The Historian,* and the *Canadian Journal of History* and appear here by permission. I have made every effort to avoid infringing upon the copyright of any individual or institution and regret any possible oversight in this regard. For permission to quote materials to which they hold copyright, I wish to thank the following: the government archives, Pretoria, South Africa; the British Library; the Public Record Office; the India Office Library and Records; the Trustees of the Liddell Hart Centre for Military Archives; the New College Library; the House of Lords Record Office; the Imperial War Museum; the Beaverbrook Foundation; the Bodleian Library; A. J. P. Taylor; representatives of the Spears and Robertson families; Lord Scarsdale; Her Majesty Queen Elizabeth II; Mark Bonham Carter; Vice Admiral Sir Ian Hogg; Lord Hankey; Lord Haig; Lord Esher; Andrew Rawlinson; Lord Derby; and Major C. J. Wilson.

I also acknowledge my indebtedness to Anthony Sheil Associates, Ltd., in respect of quotations from *The Fifth Army* by General Sir Hubert Gough; to David Higham Associates, Ltd., in respect of quotations from *Lloyd George: A Diary by Frances Stevenson,* edited by A. J. P. Taylor; to Wells Gardner, Darton & Co., Ltd., which currently holds the copyright for Ivor Nicholson & Watson, Ltd., in respect of quotations from *Lord Riddell's War Diary, 1914–1918;* and to William Collins Sons & Co., Ltd., in respect of quotations from *Politicians and the War, 1914–1916* and *Men and Power, 1917–1918* by Lord Beaverbrook.

Finally, I thank the Imperial War Museum for permission to reproduce the photographs that appear on these pages.

Lloyd George
and the Generals

1

Birth of an "Easterner"

IT was growing late on the evening of August 4, 1914. David Lloyd George, the chancellor of the exchequer, sat with a few other anxious ministers around the green table in the historic cabinet room. Prime Minister Herbert W. Asquith sat "with darkened face and dropped jowl." Sir Edward Grey, the foreign secretary, held his head in his hands. All were silent. They were waiting for Germany's response to the British ultimatum. Would Great Britain soon be at war over the German violation of Belgian neutrality? The deadline for Germany's response was midnight in Berlin, eleven o'clock by British time. The silence was broken by the loud chime of Big Ben. To Lloyd George, as he later noted in his memoirs, the clock seemed to strike "'Doom!' 'Doom!' 'Doom!'" eleven times.[1]

On the surface Lloyd George was as ill prepared for the test of war as were most of the other members of Asquith's ministry. His only military experience had been an undistinguished stint in the pre-Haldane militia. He had enjoyed the comraderie of the barracks and the annual camps at Morfa Conway in northern Wales. But he had learned little of warfare. Once, he had suffered a great embarrassment. As he later related the story to his private secretary and whiskey-drinking companion, Albert J. Sylvester:

> I very nearly lost my reputation. We were engaged in a mock battle over the hills, and the company to which I was attached was ordered to charge the "enemy." Shouting at the top of our voices, we broke from cover and charged wildly over the hill side. I was racing along when to my horror I felt something snap. My braces had broken and my trousers commenced to drop down. It was a most uncomfortable moment. I couldn't fall out of the charge, for I was in the first row of men. As I ran, my trousers came lower and lower, till I was forced to hold 'em up with one hand and grip my rifle in the other.[2]

The generals were later to have a similar mental picture of Lloyd George—the Welshman holding his pants up with one hand as he stormed their citadels of power and influence.

Before the assassination of Archduke Ferdinand, Lloyd George's reputa-

15

tion was generally that of a left-wing radical in the Liberal party who was primarily interested in social reform. The popular image of this "cottage-bred boy" was that of a pacifist and isolationist, a reputation he had gained, in part, because of his opposition to the Boer War.

The view that Lloyd George was a pacifist and isolationist was incorrect. At least since Britain's confrontation with Germany during the second Moroccan crisis in 1911, he had shown an interest in international affairs and a surprising grasp of strategic questions on the Continent. In his famous Mansion House speech, on July 21, he had rebuked Berlin over its aggressive action in Morocco. With the arrival of the German warship *Panther* at Agadir still fresh on his mind, Lloyd George, at Asquith's request, had attended an important meeting of the Committee of Imperial Defence on August 23, 1911. In an all-day session, he had observed with intense interest a showdown between the Admiralty's "Blue Water" and the War Office's "Continental" schools of British strategy. General Sir Henry H. Wilson, the director of military operations, spoke first on Britain's role in a European war. With a pointer and a large map, one of Britain's most articulate officers skillfully outlined and defended the general staff's plan to send six regular divisions of the British Expeditionary Force to France. Admiral A. K. Wilson, the first sea lord, countered with the Admiralty's maritime strategy. He was unconvincing.

During the discussion Lloyd George did not hesitate to speak out. In fact, he was the first to ask what the general staff's response would be to a French retreat, an event he discovered that the generals had not even considered. He also looked beyond the Western theater, asking questions about Russia's role in the war.[3]

A few days after this meeting Lloyd George sent Winston Churchill, who had also participated in the discussion, a memorandum. He wrote:

> We ought to know what R[ussia] is capable of before we trust the fortunes of Europe to the hazard. We are even now almost at the point whence we cannot recede.
>
> Here is another position we ought to reconnoitre. What about Belgium? 150,000 British troops supporting the Belgian army on the German flank would be a much more formidable proposition than the same number of troops extending the French line.
>
> It would force the Germans to detach at least 500,000 men to protect their lines of communication. The Anglo-Belgian army numbering 400,000 men would pivot on the great fort at Antwerp. The command of the sea would make this position impregnable.[4]

There is no evidence that Lloyd George questioned the essential correctness of the general staff's "Continental" strategy in 1911 which pushed Britain toward a war in Europe which she was ill prepared to fight with her small professional army. To the contrary, the Welshman showed a surprising eagerness to go to war with Germany. According to Peter Rowland, a recent biographer of Lloyd George, "he was actually convinced that the sooner a war was fought the better."[5]

Austria's declaration of war against Serbia on July 28, 1914, forced Lloyd

George to confront once again the prospect of Britain's involvement in a European war. This time his position was to be much less bellicose and more ambivalent.

As the country edged towards a war he had not anticipated he was "filled with horror at the prospect." It was, as he wrote to his wife, Margaret, as if he were "moving through a nightmare world."[6] Many of his countrymen and colleagues placed him with the noninterventionists in Asquith's ministry. As chancellor of the exchequer and second-in-command to Asquith, he was a key figure in the debate over Britain's involvement in the war. If Lloyd George chose to resign in opposition to Britain's participation, he would almost certainly wreck Asquith's ministry and be responsible for a divided government stumbling into war.

But Lloyd George did not attempt to lead a mutiny against his country's involvement in the Continental struggle. Cameron Hazlehurst, who has made the most thorough investigation of the Welshman's position on the eve of war, concludes that "the recollections and contemporary records of those who were present show conclusively that he neither organized nor directed the thinking of the waverers."[7] Still, until Germany rejected the British ultimatum of August 4, Lloyd George's colleagues were uncertain of his position. He talked of peace, resignation, and even of accepting Germany's violation of Belgian neutrality. On a map he had traced with his finger the extreme southerly route the Germans might take through Belgium. "You see," he explained, "it is only a little bit, and the Germans will pay for any damage they do."[8]

Lloyd George's ambiguous statements and understandable hesitancy belie his true position during the anxious days of early August. Although his heart rebelled against war, his mind was prepared to accept the consequences of German aggression.[9] His willingness to fight perhaps is explained by his understanding of German strategy and the results of British inaction. He had a better appreciation of the military situation than many of the other members of the cabinet. During the earlier crisis with Germany in 1911, as we have seen, he had shown a real understanding of the war plans. More recently, on August 1, 1914, he had been given a memorandum on the military situation in Europe which had been prepared for him by the general staff at Winston Churchill's request. This appreciation of the strategic situation in Europe had warned: "The German plan of operations is clearly deducible. The German forces must crush France with as strong and swift a succession of blows as possible before Russia can assist her, leave some Reserve troops to hold her, and then turn Eastwards with their main forces to defeat, detach, or frighten away Russia, with the assistance of Austria." Furthermore, "there is reason to suppose that the presence or absence of the British army will determine the action of the Belgian army. It will very probably decide the fate of France."[10]

On August 2, the evening of the German ultimatum to Belgium demanding the right of way to invade France, Lloyd George's mind was fixed on military developments. While dining at the home of Sir George Riddell, a newspaper proprietor and his frequent golfing companion, he placed a large official war map which had been circulated to the cabinet on the table. He then regaled those present with a discussion of the position of the German and French divisions. "As he munched his cutlets Lloyd George kept talking and pointing to the map, "dabbing at it" with his fork—as Napoleon is said to have done."[11] At this dinner Lloyd George insisted that he "would rather resign" than accept war over anything but the violation of Belgian neutrality. But since a German invasion of Belgium seemed almost a foregone conclusion, "he was in effect, if not in appearance, a war man."[12]

As he pored over the war map, word reached London of the German ultimatum. The headlines in the *Times* the next morning, August 3, vividly depicted the situation across the Channel:

FIVE NATIONS AT WAR
FIGHTING ON THREE FRONTIERS
GERMAN DECLARATION TO RUSSIA
INVASION OF FRANCE
GERMAN TROOPS IN LUXEMBURG

On August 4, the massive German right wing began its march across Belgium in a giant enveloping move of the French army. "Necessity knows no law," the German chancellor declared in the Reichstag. Five hundred trains a day arrived at the Belgian frontier, flooding that small country with German troops. Some German soldiers had left Berlin with the words "Pleasure trip to Paris" written on their transport cars. The chancellor of the exchequer, like most of his contemporaries, was caught up in the excitement of war. He wrote his comrade Alick Murray: "In a week or two it might be good to be the advance guard of an expeditionary force to the coast of France, and run the risk of capture by a German ship!"[13]

Germany's violation of Belgian neutrality enabled Lloyd George to side with the overwhelming majority of the cabinet without doing great violence to his image as a man of peace. Frances Stevenson, his private secretary, mistress, and later wife, has astutely observed: "My opinion is that L.G.'s mind was really made up from the first, that he knew we would have to go in, and that the invasion of Belgium was, to be cynical, a heaven-sent excuse for supporting a declaration of war."[14]

Lloyd George's acceptance of war was made easier by his belief, which was widely shared, that the war would be short. Almost without exception, Europe's leaders believed that the boys would be "home by Christmas." Grey's famous speech to the House of Commons on August 3 tended to reassure the nation: "For us, with a powerful Fleet, which we believe able to protect our commerce, to protect our shores, and to protect our interests, if we are engaged in war, we shall suffer but little more than we shall suffer even if we stand aside."[15] Economic activity and even sports continued as usual. Plans were made to start the football season on schedule and cricket matches continued to be played in the counties.

As Europe descended into war, Lloyd George's immediate responsibilities were in the treasury. His attention focused initially on the monetary crisis caused by the war rather than on official war maps. He was, in fact, not included when Asquith convened a council of war in the cabinet room at

4:00 P.M. on August 5. The heads of the Admiralty and the War Office along with Britain's leading soldiers were there. The crucial question was: should the British Expeditionary Force immediately be dispatched to fight on the left flank of the French armies? The general staff, solidly in the grip of the "Continentals," had previously made arrangements with the French military authorities to assist France.[16] No other war plan really existed, and Britain's war leaders gave no serious consideration to falling back on a maritime or "blue water" strategy.[17] The decision of this "rather motley gathering,"[18] as Asquith called it, unwittingly involved the British Empire in a long and costly war of attrition with the German army on the desolate and shell-pocked battlefields of France and Flanders. To keep her most important ally from being overwhelmed, Britain, then and later, had no choice but to fight a land war in the West. The extent of Britain's commitment to the western front, however, remained an open question; and an intense strategical debate revolved around this issue until the end of the war.

On August 7 the British Expeditionary Force began to embark and within the next few days four infantry divisions and one cavalry division secretly crossed the Channel. By August 22, the British Expeditionary Force had taken up a position on the French left near Maubeuge at Mons, a mining area covered with smoking slag heaps. Britain's professional force of less than 90,000 men was now directly in the path of the German offensive. The next day the British army went into action in western Europe for the first time since Waterloo. Although the British Expeditionary Force inflicted heavy casualties on the attacking Germans during the Battle of Mons, it had to retreat the following day because of the general retirement of the French on their right.

As fierce battles waged along the frontiers, Britain's civilian and military leaders began to wrestle with the problems of fighting a great war. Parliament quickly sanctioned 500,000 men for the army. To mold these recruits into a mass force, Asquith selected as secretary of state for war Lord Kitchener of Khartoum, who had to be abruptly summoned to London from Dover, where he was about to depart for Egypt. Asquith's choice for the leadership of the War Office was overwhelmingly popular with the British public. Tall and aloof, with sculpted features, Lord Kitchener projected determination. He was Britain's most distinguished soldier. Soon his impressive visage, with the message "Your Country Needs You," appeared on the hoardings in an extensive poster campaign. The British people responded in great numbers. Kitchener—even more than the king or Asquith—became a symbol for the unity of the nation.

Although the public viewed Kitchener as Britain's greatest soldier, his appointment was almost certainly a mistake. The new head of the War Office was a foreigner to the give and take of politics and was incapable of working effectively with his civilian colleagues. He thought little of their opinions and suspected their ability to keep secrets. It was, he noted, "repugnant and unnatural to have to discuss military secrets with a large number of gentlemen with some of whom he was but barely acquainted."[19] He was especially concerned about the ministers' gossipy wives, once remarking that "if they will only all divorce their wives . . . I will tell them everything."[20] Kitchener had a point. The ministers often revealed state secrets to their wives—*and* to their girl friends! Asquith and Lloyd George were both notorious in this latter respect.

Kitchener ran a one-man show in the War Office, refusing to delegate authority. Wearing the blue dress uniform of a field marshal, he worked alone from precisely nine o'clock in the morning to dusk. His awesome military reputation, combined with his civil authority as secretary of state for war, made him dominant in the military realm. His greatest contribution to the war effort was his realization that the war would be a long one and that Britain must build a great army. But he had serious liabilities as a strategist. The general staff, which had lost many of its most capable officers when they accompanied the British Expeditionary Force to the Continent, was headed by General Sir James Wolfe Murray, who was old and out of touch with the new forms of warfare. Cowed by Kitchener's forceful personality, Murray kept the general staff in the background and it did not play its proper role of planning military operations and assessing their strategical significance. Hence Britain had no strategical rudder during the opening months of the war.

In the first weeks of the war, as the British and French forces were being shoved back by the German army, Lloyd George and the other ministers had little knowledge of what was happening at the front. Lord Kitchener "in his loud staccato voice" did give brief reports to the cabinet. But, according to Lloyd George, "His main idea at the Council table was to tell the politicians as little as possible of what was going on and get back to his desk as quickly as he could decently escape."[21]

Lloyd George's first indication that the British Expeditionary Force was in peril came when Churchill interrupted his work at the treasury, informing him that the British Expeditionary Force, which was in the process of re-treating nearly 200 miles in thirteen days, was falling back from Mons. Several days later the chancellor of the exchequer and his countrymen were stunned by a special Sunday edition of the *Times* on August 30. A special correspondent, reporting from Amiens, sent waves of panic through the nation when he described the "terrible losses" of the British Expeditionary Force and the "almost incredible rapidity" of the German advance.[22] The anxious ministers were faced with the terrible prospect that Germany might deliver a knock-out blow to the Anglo-French forces.

Concern over a quick German victory evaporated during a great battle in early September on the Marne. The French, assisted by the British, launched a counterattack on September 6. As a result of this battle, the German army was pushed across the Marne. Paris was saved. Of greater significance, the Allied victory at the First Battle of the Marne destroyed the German war plan—the Schlieffen Plan—to defeat France within the first weeks of the war.

The German setback was cause for rejoicing. A sobering thought, how-ever, was that the war would be longer and would entail greater sacrifice than almost anyone had realized. Lloyd George clearly had mixed feelings about the great adventure upon which he and his poorly prepared country had embarked. But he now shed publicly his pro-Boer image and committed himself totally to the conflict, first in a little-noticed speech to a deputation from the Association of Municipal Corporations on September 8 and then in a speech to London Welshmen at the Queen's Hall on Saturday, September 19, which guaranteed extensive coverage in the Sunday papers. Believing that his September 19 speech was a "landmark in his career," he was filled with apprehension.[23] Shortly before speaking, he lay on a sofa, "yawning and stretching himself in a state of high nervous excitement."[24]

At the Queen's Hall, Lloyd George was composed. Standing before a large crowd, he stressed Britain's obligation to defend the "five-feet-high" nations against the "road hog of Europe."[25]

Lloyd George's subsequent actions gave support to his fighting words. He began to deal with questions beyond his departmental responsibilities. He was especially concerned about the shortage of munitions. He saw that the demands of the battlefield were outstripping production. This interest in munitions production gave him his first opportunity to go to the front.

On October 16, he crossed the Channel at night to discuss munitions production in France. He found Paris guarded by old men with obsolete rifles. From the capital he motored to Amiens near the front. For the first time in his life, he listened to "the crack of shells fired with murderous intent against human beings."[26] General Castelnau, one of France's most tactful and urbane generals, took him on a tour of the French lines beyond Douleens. As they drove through war-scarred territory, General Castelnau, who had already lost two sons in battle, talked about the war. He was disturbed. Like other generals, he had thought that the conflict would be a war of movement. The other war leaders with whom Lloyd George talked were equally at a loss in dealing with trench warfare. "It is *stalemate*. We can not turn them out of their trenches," he wrote his wife, "& they cannot turn us out."[27]

By the time of Lloyd George's visit to France the mobile phase of the war in the West was over. Soldiers were digging in where their advances had been halted. From the Belgian North Sea coast to the border of Switzerland, an almost continuous system of fortifications was being constructed. Crude at first, these earthworks were to be vastly improved in the months and years ahead. By the end of 1915 there were perhaps twenty miles of trench for every mile of front line. And this figure continued to climb. Before 1914, the British army required annually 2,500 shovels and spades. During the war, however, 10,638,000 digging implements were produced.

The defenses consisted of parallel trenches dug in a zigzag pattern to provide for a better field of fire. The first line, which was usually within rifle range of the enemy but beyond the range of grenades, was where casualties were the greatest. Not far behind the foremost breastworks was a second line of trenches, where the bulk of the troops were housed in dugouts to protect them during bombardment. Some of these dugouts were lined with boards and protected by large beams and sandbags. Communications trenches connected the first trench to the second. Beyond the trenches to the rear were fortified points in villages or woods or even a reserve line. Supplies and reliefs were usually brought up at night in the open. Soldiers had to operate below the surface of the ground because of the new fire weapons, especially the improved artillery and machine gun.

Between the trenches of the belligerents was no-man's-land. This shell-pocked area was crisscrossed with barbed wire in double and treble thickness strung on trestles and stakes to a height of between three and five feet. At night no-man's-land was often a beehive of activity as patrols reconnoitered in the darkness broken only by flares.

A section of the Hindenburg Line, the most formidable defensive line on the western front.

For soldiers at the front, life was muddy, cold, and wet. Only the large rats, which shared the soldiers' quarters and food, seemed to prosper. Despite the frequent rotation of troops, most of the armies had broken or were near the breaking point before the war was over.

In 1914, the British army held a short section of the line—about twenty-one miles—on the Flemish plain. On the British left toward the sea, the line was held by the French and Belgians. On their right, the French, who held over 400 miles of the line, had their forces stretching to Switzerland.

After the First Battle of the Marne, both sides attempted to envelop the other in what has been called the "race to the sea." The British Expeditionary Force, strengthened by reinforcements, was soon locked in a bloody struggle with the German army. The First Battle of Ypres (called "Wipers" by British soldiers) was just getting underway as Lloyd George was returning to London. It was the British army's first experience with trench warfare. When this indecisive battle came to an end the old British army had been practically destroyed. Less than half of the first soldiers sent to France were still on their feet.

When the opposing forces reached the sea, there were no more flanks to attempt to turn. General Joseph-Jacques Césaire Joffre, the commander in chief of the French army and the commander of the British Expeditionary Force, Sir John French, a former cavalry officer, then turned to frontal assaults against well-defended German positions. They believed that a breakthrough was possible. Yet until 1918 all efforts to break into the open failed on the western front. Why did these "siege-offensives," as Churchill aptly called them, miscarry? The attackers did not have the means to maintain the momentum of their attack. "The assault could never be driven through into the open country fast and cleanly enough," Cyril Falls has written, "to prevent new lines of resistance being established and the defense congealing about the bulge, as skin reestablished itself about a wound. The break-*in* could not be converted into a break-*through*."[28] Additional points that could be made are: the railroad enabled reserves to be brought quickly to the front to plug any hole; and the new rapid-fire weapons strengthened the defense more than the offense.

The last days of the First Battle of Ypres found Lloyd George in a deep depression. He told Frances Stevenson, to whom he often bared his soul, that he feared that he would be overwhelmed by it all. "War is not his work," she recorded in her diary, "and he feels that he has not the heart to deal with it. It is all so horrible."[29]

There was little if any war news to lift one's spirits. Turkey had come into the war in early November, slamming shut the Straits, Russia's best outlet to her allies. The Russian army had suffered staggering losses. The myth of the Russian "steam roller" had been exposed. It could roll backwards as well as forwards. Elsewhere in the East, Serbia was fighting for survival against an Austrian invasion. On December 2, the Austrians occupied Belgrade. Although the Serbian capital was quickly liberated and the Austrians thrown back, there was great concern in the cabinet that this "five-feet-high" nation—standing alone—could not long defend herself.

As these momentous events occurred in Europe and the Near East, the war began to spread to other parts of the world. Although Britain sent the bulk of her available forces to France, she also used her imperial position, supported by her sea power, to strike at Germany's overseas possessions in the Pacific and Africa. When Turkey joined the Central Powers, a tiny imperial force quickly occupied Basra near the Persian Gulf, the opening move of what eventually developed into a great campaign up the Tigris toward Baghdad. Also, the British began to strengthen their defenses in Egypt to protect the Suez Canal from Turkish attack.

As the war map expanded, Lloyd George began to look beyond the western front. The slaughter in France horrified him. Although he was as perplexed as the military authorities about trench warfare, he blamed the heavy Anglo-French casualties on inept generalship. Running hot and cold on Kitchener, he referred to him among his friends as "just a big figurehead."[30] He told Miss Stevenson that "our soldiers are the best in Europe, but they are being wantonly sacrificed because those in authority do not know how to make the best use of them."[31]

Lloyd George's lack of experience did not deter him. Never in awe of the "expert," he believed that the civilians could not afford to leave the conduct of the war exclusively in the hands of the military. Whatever he lacked in formal training, he believed that he made up for in imagination and boldness, qualities which he thought were in short supply in the British high command. His knowledge of warfare was gained from reading books and memoranda written for him and especially through conversations with soldiers, both high and low.

Lloyd George's understanding of the revolution in warfare caused by the new rapid-fire weapons played a major role in his opposition to hurling men against barbed wire and machine guns. With the erection of formidable defenses in the West, he concluded that large-scale, plodding, and prolonged offensives there were senseless slaughter, resulting in a human holocaust. Protective of British blood, he never accepted the generals' battles of attrition. He found support for this view in the Warsaw banker I. S. Bloch's important six-volume work, *The War of the Future,* which was published in French in 1898. Bloch's final volume, *Is War Now Impossible?,* published in English in London in 1899, argued that the new military technology gave the advantage to the defense and led to indecisive siege warfare.[32]

Convinced by his reading of Bloch and his tour of the western front that there was little likelihood that the Allies could obtain decisive results in the West in the foreseeable future, Lloyd George began to focus his attention on the Balkans. Concern for Serbia's precarious position and the opportunities he saw there for both the soldier and the diplomat galvanized him into action. As December came to an end, he began his long, acrimonious, and controversial campaign to influence British strategy.

NOTES

1. David Lloyd George, *War Memoirs of David Lloyd George,* 2 vols. (1938), 1:47, and entry of March 29, 1915, A. J. P. Taylor, ed., *Lloyd George: A Diary by Frances Stevenson* (1971), p. 37.

2. Albert James Sylvester, *The Real Lloyd George* (1947), p. 11.

3. Committee of Imperial Defence (114), August 23, 1911, CAB 38/19/49.

4. Lloyd George to Churchill, August 25, 1911, Lloyd George MSS, C/3/15/6; also see Churchill to Lloyd George, August 31, 1911, Lloyd George MSS, C/3/15/7. For a recent account of Lloyd George's and Churchill's support of intervention on the Continent, see K. M. Wilson, "The War Office, Churchill and the Belgian Option: August to December 1911," *Bulletin of the Institute of Historical Research* 50 (November 1977):218–28.

5. Peter Rowland, *David Lloyd George: A Biography* (1975), p. 251.

6. Lloyd George to Margaret Lloyd George, August 3, 1914, quoted in Kenneth O. Morgan, ed., *Lloyd George Family Letters, 1885–1936* (1973), p. 167.

7. Cameron Hazlehurst, *Politicians at War, July 1914 to May 1915: A Prologue to the Triumph of Lloyd George* (1971), p. 63.

8. Lord Beaverbrook, *Politicians and the War, 1914–1916* (1960), p. 23. It has been suggested that Lloyd George made this statement at lunch on August 2. Don M. Creiger, *Bounder from Wales: Lloyd George's Career Before the First World War* (1976), pp. 249–50. Lloyd George also repeated these sentiments to C. P. Scott, the editor of the *Manchester Guardian*, on August 4. But my reading of Scott's diary is that he was at that time referring to his position of the preceding days. See Trevor Wilson, ed., *The Political Diaries of C. P. Scott, 1911–1928* (1970), pp. 96–97. The genesis of this idea may have been a General Staff appreciation which suggested that "it seems to be likely that the Belgians will not treat a German advance across her country as a violation of her territory." Major A. H. Ollivant, "A Short Survey of the Present Military Situation in Europe," August 1, 1914, Lloyd George MSS, C/16/1/14.

9. Hazlehurst, *Politicians at War, July 1914 to May 1915*, pp. 54–65. Michael G. Fry aptly characterizes Lloyd George's position with his chapter heading, "Understandable Emotions, Predictable Decisions." *Lloyd George and Foreign Policy*, vol. 1: *The Education of a Statesman: 1890–1916* (1977), pp. 183–213.

10. Ollivant, "A Short Survey of the Present Military Situation in Europe," August 1, 1914, Lloyd George MSS, C/16/1/14, and Wilson Diary, August 1, 1914.

11. Entry of September 30, 1931, Lord Hankey, *The Supreme Command, 1914–1918*, 2 vols. (1961), 1:161, and *Lord Riddell's War Diary, 1914–1918*, pp. 3–5.

12. Hazlehurst, *Politicians at War, July 1914 to May 1915*, p. 108.

13. Lord George to Murray of Elibank, August 4, 1914, quoted in ibid., p. 117.

14. Frances Lloyd George, *The Years That Are Past* (1967), pp. 73–74.

15. *H. C. Deb.*, 5th series, vol. 65 (August 3, 1914).

16. For prewar planning, see Samuel R. Williamson, Jr., *The Politics of Grand Strategy: Britain and France Prepare for War* (1969), John Gooch, *The Plans of War: The General Staff and British Military Strategy c. 1900–1916* (1974), Nicholas d'Ombrain, *War Machinery and High Policy: Defence Administration in Peacetime Britain 1902–1914* (1973), and Paul Kennedy, ed., *The War Plans of the Great Powers, 1880–1914* (1979). Also see Michael Howard, *The Continental Commitment; The Dilemma of British Defence Policy in the Era of the Two World Wars. The Ford Lectures in the University of Oxford* (1972).

17. "Secretary's Notes of a War Council Held at 10, Downing Street, August 5, 1914," CAB 42/1/2.

18. The Earl of Oxford and Asquith, *Memories and Reflections, 1852–1927*, 2 vols. (1928), 2:30.

19. Philip Magnus, *Kitchener: Portrait of an Imperialist* (1959), p. 284.

20. Hankey Diary, September 11, 1915, 1/1.

21. Lloyd George, *War Memoirs*, 1:51.

22. See the illuminating article by John Terraine which touches on press coverage of the British retreat from Mons, "The Impact of Mons, August 1914," *History Today* 14 (August 1964):521–31.

23. Frances Lloyd George, *Years That Are Past*, p. 75.

24. Entry of September 19, 1914, *Lord Riddell's War Diary*, p. 32.

25. *Times* (London), September 20, 1914. Earlier Lloyd George had made his first speech on the war to a deputation from the Association of Municipal Corporations, *Times* (London), September 9, 1914. For an analysis of this speech, see Hazlehurst, *Politicians at War, July 1914 to May 1915*, pp. 175–76.

26. Lloyd George, *War Memoirs*, 1:92.

27. Lloyd George to Margaret Lloyd George, October 20, 1914, quoted in Morgan, *Family Letters*, p. 173.

28. Cyril Falls, *The Great War* (paperback edn., 1959), p. 83.

29. Entry of October 30, 1914, *A Diary by Frances Stevenson*, p. 8.

30. Entry of October 25, 1914, *Lord Riddell's War Diary*, p. 36.

31. Entry of December 16, 1914, *A Diary by Frances Stevenson*, p. 17.

32. Lloyd George was influenced by I. S. Bloch in preparing his famous January 1, 1915, memorandum which advocated the diversion of British military power to the eastern Mediterranean. See Lloyd George MSS, C/16/1/3.

2

Balkanite

ON December 31, Lloyd George wrote the prime minister:

> I am uneasy about the prospects of the war unless the Government take some decisive measures to grip the situation. I can see no signs anywhere that our military leaders and guides are considering any plans for extricating us from our present unsatisfactory position. . . . Could we not have a series of meetings of the War Committee of the C.I.D. at an early date? Occasional meetings at intervals of a week or a fortnight will end in nothing.[1]

By this time Lloyd George had very bold and specific views on strategy, which he circulated on New Year's Day to his colleagues in the War Council, a small body created by the cabinet to deal with general matters of war policy. Great Britain was rapidly putting a splendid fighting force in the field, he noted, and this new army should not be sent to France to be flung "against impregnable positions" in "futile enterprises." The Welshman's alternative strategy to the western front involved *"two independent operations"* on opposite sides of the Mediterranean, one against Austria in the Balkans and the other against the Ottoman Empire in Syria, which would isolate the Turkish troops moving against the Suez Canal.[2]

Dearest to his heart was a political-military thrust in the Balkans. Since the beginning of the war he had been encouraged by his contacts with the brothers Noel and Charles Buxton, who headed a British mission to the Balkans in August, to believe that the Balkan states could be easily mobilized against Austria-Hungary.[3] He was convinced that Britain's failure to create a Balkan confederation was largely due to excessive caution and timidity by British diplomacy and the absence of a strong British military presence in the area. He did not hesitate to infringe upon the Foreign Office's domain. In mid-December, he lobbied Rumanian representatives who were seeking a British loan, believing that he had " 'roped Roumania in.' "[4]

If Britain made the Balkans her principal theater of military operations, he was confident that Rumania and Greece, and perhaps even Bulgaria, would join forces with Serbia and Montenegro. Austria, already suffering heavily at the hands of the Russians, he argued, would then be confronted with a sizable Allied force on her southern flank. Germany would be faced with the unhappy choice of either abandoning her primary ally or attempting to keep entact "an enormous front, in the aggregate of 1,200 miles." Trench warfare, he hopefully noted, might be avoided because the new front "would be much too lengthy for the Austrian forces to entrench and hold."[5]

Political considerations were a dominant theme in Lloyd George's January 1 memorandum. He stressed the psychological advantage of a "dramatic victory" somewhere to keep his countrymen united behind the war effort, and warned his colleagues that the volunteers who were eagerly lining up before the recruiting offices were "vastly superior" in "intelligence, education and character" to earlier soldiers. They would not tolerate senseless bloodletting on the western front.[6] And, of course, he contended that the fence-sitting Balkan nations would be brought into the war on the side of the Entente.

To his credit, the chancellor of the exchequer emphasized the need for an early decision by the government in order to begin preparations for opening a new front in the Balkans. "Expeditions decided upon and organised with insufficient care and preparation," he prophetically warned, "generally end disastrously."[7]

Lloyd George's proposal for an alternative strategy was not the only one put forward. The competition, in fact, was brisk. Maurice Hankey on Boxing Day (December 28) had first broached the subject of concentrating British power in the East because of the stalemate in the West. Hankey had one of the keenest and most active military minds in the government. A career officer, he had served in the Royal Marine Artillery at sea and the Department of Naval Intelligence in the Admiralty. Prior to the war, he had been a central figure in strategic planning as the secretary of the Committee of Imperial Defence. Now he was at the very center of policy making as the secretary of the War Council. Although he had not talked with Lloyd George, there were striking similarities between the two proposals. Both a Balkan offensive and an attack on Syria were discussed by Hankey.[8] Hankey's indirect strategy formed the basis for a very close relationship between himself and Lloyd George for the rest of the war.

Another entry into the realm of grand strategy was the forceful and imaginative Winston Churchill, the first lord of the Admiralty. "Are there not other alternatives than sending our armies to chew barbed wire in Flanders?"[9] Churchill asked the prime minister on December 29, 1914. Although Churchill considered Germany's "northern flank the primary and most vulnerable objective"[10] as the new year began, he was quickly to shift his attention to the Dardanelles. Thus were born the "Easterners," who were united by their distaste for the huge losses on the western front and the political advantages of military operations in the Near East. Fabulous prospects seemed in the offing as they cast their eyes toward Turkey and the Balkans. Russia might be relieved through the conquest of the Straits and the defeat of Turkey, the Balkans mobilized against the Central Powers and

Austria-Hungary brought to her knees. Germany would stand weakened and alone. If Germany continued to concentrate on the western front, so much the better. "We should ask nothing better," Hankey had written, "than he should hurl fresh masses to destruction on our impregnable position."[11]

On January 7, the War Council began an important examination of Britain's future strategy. Lord Kitchener opened the discussion by bringing up a proposal by Churchill and Sir John French to turn the German flank at Zeebrugge along the Flanders coast by land and amphibious operations. To ensure success, French wanted fifty Territorial battalions dispatched to the Continent. Fearing that this would drastically disrupt his attempt to create a new army, Kitchener was hostile to the proposal.

This breach in the ranks of the army gave the "Welsh Wizard" an opportunity to introduce his Balkan strategy. Before a final decision on the Zeebrugge operation was made, he wanted to

consider the large question of the future employment of the new Armies. If our army on the Continent was to be thrown away and shattered in an operation which appeared to him impossible, the war might continue indefinitely, or at any rate for two or three years more. Was it impossible, he asked, to get at the enemy from some other direction, and to strike a blow that would end the war once and for all? If some new plan should be decided on, every man would be required for it in April or May, and the loss of some fifty battalions of Territorial troops would be very severely felt.[12]

The following day at noon, when the War Council resumed its deliberations, Lloyd George attempted once again to guide the discussion. With "great ability and persuasiveness,"[13] according to Hankey, he lobbied for an attack on Austria. Having talked with Hankey since his New Year's Day memorandum, he was prepared to admit that his bold scheme had a weakness—lines of communication.[14] One route to Austria was by way of Salonika. From that Greek city an army could move over the top of the Balkans on the Salonika-Nish-Belgrade railway. But, Lloyd George confessed, "the Salonica railway, though a good railway of German construction, had only a single line of track, and it would be difficult to supply a large army along it, particularly if the Greeks also had to be supplied by it." In his next breath, he attempted to overcome this deficiency. Ragusa (or Dubrovnik) on the Dalmatian coast, he argued, "might be used to supplement the Salonica line, giving two lines of communication."[15]

Lloyd George was actually too quick to accept the alleged deficiency of communications from Salonika to Serbia. True, the present carrying capacity of the railway to Belgrade was low. But with Greek support the number of trains going both ways could easily have been doubled from six to twelve. Access to Serbia by road was indeed limited. But this, too, could have been vastly improved if the Allies had acted with energy and determination.[16]

By introducing Ragusa into the discussion, Lloyd George weakened his case. Asquith, who had visited Ragusa the previous year immediately made objections. "The railway was of narrow gauge, and there was only one road, which, though a good one, ran through difficult and mountainous country," he said. Kitchener, the oracle of high strategy, was even more trenchant in his comments. "Ragusa," he bluntly proclaimed, "was an impossible sea base." As for Salonika, "it could only be used if Greece were an ally; the single line of railway leading to Serbia could only support, at the outside, an army of 200,000 men." The Dardanelles, rather than Austria, Kitchener argued, "appeared to be the most suitable objective, as an attack here could be made in co-operation with the Fleet."

Another blow to the Welshman's Balkan strategy was a letter from Sir John French which Kitchener summarized for the War Council. French denied "the impossibility of breaking through the German lines." French also warned the civilians that "a crushing defeat, however, of the French would be very dangerous and embarrassing to our safety, and must be made impossible. . . . not a man could be diverted from France to any other theatre of operations without the consent of the French, and this would never be obtained."[17]

Lloyd George's initial attempts to redirect the war effort thus ended in failure. His considerable powers of persuasion had gone for naught. The commander in chief of the British Expeditionary Force was hostile, and logistical arguments which Lloyd George was in no position to refute had been raised by Kitchener. Churchill, who was at this time interested in land and sea operations at Zeebrugge or especially in the Baltic, had given him no support. Furthermore, the prime minister had raised objections. Lloyd George could only take comfort in the War Council's opposition to an increased British effort on the Continent at Zeebrugge and in Hankey's mind-boggling suggestion that a successful attack on the Dardanelles would "give us the Danube as a line of communications for an army penetrating into the heart of Austria, and bring our sea power to bear in the middle of Europe."[18]

Lloyd George's response to this setback was to redouble his efforts. His advocacy of Balkan operations had one great strength. The strongest and most influential voices in the War Council—himself, Churchill, and Kitchener—were all unhappy with the frontal attacks on the western front. If the support of Kitchener and Churchill could be gained, his Balkan plans had a chance of being implemented. Caught between the "Easterners" and "Westerners," who wanted to concentrate almost exclusively on the German army in the West, the prime minister was characteristically irresolute. If he leaned in one direction, it was toward the "Westerners." Asquith's indecision might be ended, however, if support among the professional soldiers could be found for a Balkan thrust.

The War Council's opposition to the proposed Zeebrugge operation and its growing interest in military operations in the eastern Mediterranean created anxiety at general headquarters. On January 12, Sir John French hurried across the Channel to present the views of the "Westerners." Lloyd George was waiting for him. In a long interview the persistent and persuasive Welshman attempted to convert French. Lloyd George, who was intrigued by statistical data, had fresh War Office figures to show that Berlin had a superiority in numbers and was sending additional soldiers to the West. Lloyd George was often to note—only partly in fun—that the "soldiers must be ignorant of simple arithmetic."[19] The soldiers, if given a chance to respond, would have replied that Lloyd George placed an amateur's emphasis on numbers, overlooking the quality and leadership of the troops involved.

Having stressed German strength, the chancellor of the exchequer wanted to know what would happen if the British did break through. Would they really be any better off? French, Lloyd George later told Stevenson, admitted that general headquarters had not really considered its next move. Lloyd George then repeated his views on the advantages of a Balkan offensive. When he left French, Lloyd George, carried away by the force of his own convictions, believed that he had won the field marshal over to his strategic views.[20]

On the next day the War Council held an important discussion with French leading off. The field marshal—supported by Churchill—was initially optimistic about the chances of clearing the Belgian coast. But, Lloyd George wanted to know, would the Zeebrugge operation result in decisive results? "How," he asked, "did Sir John French think that the German resistance was to be finally broken?"

The discussion then turned to the relative strength of the armies on the western front. Brigadier-General G. M. W. Macdonogh, the able chief intelligence officer of the British Expeditionary Force, argued that the Germans did not enjoy a superiority on the western front. To the contrary, the Entente enjoyed an advantage of 500,000 rifles. Lloyd George listened in amazement. Figures furnished him by the War Office told a different story. The discrepancy between various sets of figures supplied by the military was "extraordinary," he noted. During the lunch break he visited with Macdonogh in an attempt to reconcile the different figures.

When the War Council resumed its deliberations, Lloyd George announced "that it would not be safe to base our calculations on a superiority of the Allies of 100,000 men. This, he suggested, was not a sufficient superiority to justify the taking of the offensive." His figures were not challenged by the soldiers. Thus the Allies seemed strong enough to withstand any attack, but too weak to attempt one of their own.

The Welshman then attempted to get his colleagues to look at the war as if there were a single front. The proposed Zeebrugge operation must not "be discussed by itself. The question was, did it contribute towards the main object of defeating the enemy? What he feared was that we should sustain very heavy losses, and become so entangled in this secondary operation as to prevent us from exercising a decisive influence elsewhere when the opportunity presented itself." As for the French, what was Joffre's plan for "overcoming Germany?" Kitchener replied "that, so far as he knew, General Joffre had no big conception for terminating the campaign." French then volunteered that "General Joffre hoped to achieve some success by his offensive, but relied on the Russians to finish the business." He then flatly admitted that Joffre "was not strong enough to break down the German resistance."

After this damaging admission by the military and with the discussion now taking a favorable turn for his Balkan project, Lloyd George said that he "was quite prepared to support General Joffre in any offensive movement which gave reasonable prospects of success." If Joffre, however, failed "to achieve success" and it, of course, seemed obvious from French's and Kitchener's previous remarks that little could be expected from his offensive, Lloyd George wanted the government "to try some entirely new plan."

With the War Council now in favor of putting off a decision on the Zeebrugge operation, attention turned to the East. " We ought also to consider," Grey noted, "what we should do in the event of a complete stalemate. For this purpose we should study the possibilities of (a) co-operation with Serbia and (b) an attack on the Gallipoli Peninsula."

It was now quite late in the day. The blinds had been drawn to blot out the approach of a winter evening. With the British leaders tired and ready for adjournment, Churchill made a dramatic announcement which was to undermine Lloyd George's Balkan scheme even though this did not become apparent until later. The first lord of the Admiralty revealed a plan by Vice-Admiral Carden, the commander in chief in the Mediterranean, to launch a naval assault against the Dardanelles, that narrow strip of water separating Europe and Asia Minor which had been called the Hellespont in antiquity. "The idea caught on at once," Hankey notes in his memoirs. "The whole atmosphere changed. Fatigue was forgotten."[21]

Since no troops were involved and the Admiralty's plan appeared to complement his scheme, Lloyd George gave his approval. The army also gave its assent, with Sir John French, in response to a query by Lloyd George, admitting "that complete success against the Germans in the Western theatre of war, though possible, was not probable." Sir John also uttered words which were dear to the Welshman's heart. "If we found it impossible to break through, he agreed that it would be desirable to seek new spheres of activity—in Austria, for example." A delighted Lloyd George then emphasized that there must be no delay in taking the initial steps for a Balkan assault. "Not only should the question be studied," he said," but actual preparations should be made. For example, rolling-stock would have to be manufactured for the Salonica railway, and perhaps barges built for the Danube." Churchill, who had expressed opposition to Balkan operations, "agreed that preparations should be made. At the worst they would be a good feint."

The War Council then decided: "That if the position in the Western theatre becomes in the spring one of stalemate, British troops should be despatched to another theatre and objective, and that adequate investigation and preparation should be undertaken with that purpose, and that a Sub-Committee of the Committee of Imperial Defence be appointed to deal with this aspect of the situation."[22]

The War Council's conclusion appeared to represent a great personal triumph for Lloyd George. Within a week, he had played the dominant role in reversing the War Council's thinking. Even the generals had expressed some support for his ideas. Kitchener's hostility to trench warfare especially pleased Lloyd George. It was now his view that "Kitchener was a big man and the best for the job."[23] Only Churchill appeared dead set against the project; and Lloyd George was naturally much put out with him, even unfairly accusing him privately of seeking personal glory with his naval schemes.[24]

The War Council's actions up to this point were sufficiently indecisive and nebulous that almost everyone involved in the deliberations believed that his way of thinking had been approved. The "Easterners" were happy with the War Council's tilt toward operations on the periphery. But this was deceiving for the civilians did not really comprehend the ultimate consequences of other decisions made by them at the same time. Although a final decision had been put off, the War Council okayed preparations for the Zeebrugge operation. Of even greater import, the War Council agreed to support offensive action in the spring in league with the French. To be sure, this was made conditional. If the offensive failed, British troops would be sent elsewhere. But this still left the initiative in the hands of the generals on the western front. Would they admit failure? Almost certainly not. Faced with stubborn German resistance, they would request more men and equipment. This would drastically limit the number of British soldiers available for action elsewhere. Closer to home, Kitchener alone decided what British troops were available. His estimate of British reserves was colored by his opinion of the large reserve force in Great Britain—the Territorials. Kitchener's stuffy professionalism led him to exclude the Territorials from any proposed expeditionary force to the Balkans. "A Town Clerk's Army"[25] was his contemptuous dismissal of it. Kitchener was wrong. When sent into action on the western front, they fought well. As French had informed the War Council, "They had proved a great success, and had behaved very well in the trenches."[26]

To seize the initiative from the generals in the West, Lloyd George wanted to send Allied troops to the Balkans as soon as possible. If the British delayed until after the spring attacks, it might be too late. The War Office furnished him with exactly the ammunition he needed—a paper warning of an imminent renewal of the Austro-German attack against Serbia.[27] With the members of the cabinet expressing great concern about Serbia, Lloyd George made his case as strongly as possible for the immediate dispatch of a British force to the Balkans with the political purpose of getting Rumania and Greece to commit themselves to the Entente.[28] Following this cabinet meeting on the twentieth Lloyd George met with Kitchener and Asquith. The prime minister was now obsessed with helping Serbia, noting: "The main point at the moment is to do something really effective for Serbia. . . . I am sure that this is right and that all our side-shows, Zeebrugge, Alexandretta, even Gallipoli, must be postponed for this. The troops must come either from those that we already have in France, or from those which we were going to send there."[29] After Kitchener promised to come up with the necessary troops, Lloyd George then sent for the Greek Minister in London and informed him that Britain was prepared to send an army corps to the Balkans if Greece and Rumania threw in their lot with the Entente.[30]

With momentum building in London for immediate intervention in the Balkans, Lloyd George brought his powers of persuasion to bear against the French. Sir John French had warned the government that the French government "would not like it if we were to divert troops to some theatre of war other than France."[31] But Lloyd George was not so sure. Perhaps Sir John's "Western" prejudices colored his views. On January 22, Lloyd George attempted to win over the French war minister, Alexandre Millerand, at a dinner attended by, among others, Kitchener, Churchill, Grey, and Asquith. Millerand, although he could not (or would not) speak a word of English, made it clear that Joffre was committed to big attacks in the West in 1915, which would require all possible British assistance. Any attempt to help Serbia would have to wait until after the military results from the western front were in.[32]

Millerand was hostile to an expeditionary force being sent to the Balkans because his government had already discussed and rejected this idea. Before the "Easterners" had asserted themselves in London, Aristide Briand, the minister of justice, had suggested in November that an Anglo-French force of 400,000 men should be sent to Salonika to assist Serbia and open up a new front, an idea that was supported by Franchet d'Espèrey, the commander of the Fifth Army, and Joseph Galliéni, the governor of Paris. The French cabinet, then and later in early January, however, had drawn back from challenging Joffre, who had achieved dictatorial control over strategy.[33]

Unknown to Lloyd George, Kitchener had decided to support Millerand against the British ministers. Although Kitchener saw merit in Lloyd George's proposal for military-political action on Austria's southern flank, he was not willing to quarrel with Joffre. The night after Lloyd George talked with Millerand, Kitchener dined with the French war minister at the French embassy. The Frenchman was assured by Kitchener that "he would not press the Serbian scheme just now."[34]

The consequences of Kitchener's understanding with Millerand were soon apparent. On January 28 the newly created subcommittee of the Imperial Defence Committee met in the War Office. Kitchener was in the chair. Churchill, Lloyd George, and Arthur Balfour, who had been attending War Council meetings as the unofficial representative of the Unionist opposition, were the other members. Sir James Wolfe Murray, the chief of the Imperial General Staff, and Major-General C. E. Callwell, the director of military operations, were included to give professional advice.

Assistance to Serbia dominated the discussion. The approach of better weather might herald an attack on that isolated and beleaguered state. Those present were optimistic about overcoming any difficulties, technical or otherwise, in assisting Serbia. The Serbian army was short of mounted troops, but Kitchener said that "this was a deficiency which it would not be very difficult for us to make up." Also, according to Kitchener, Serbian roads "were all right" and the Danube was not a formidable military obstacle. Lloyd George, with his plan to open up communications with Serbia via Ragusa in abeyance, suggested for the first time that the Bulgarian port of Dedeagatch in Thrace could be utilized. "This," he argued, "would have the double effect of drawing Bulgaria into the war and of opening up a second line of railway to Nish." Lloyd George's statement speaks volumes about his reading—or rather misreading—of Balkan politics. He thought that the Balkan states would quickly fall in line if Britain resorted to force. The British occupation of Dedeagatch would almost certainly have brought Bulgaria into the war, but on Germany's rather than Britain's side.

As was his bent, Balfour attempted to sum up: "The conclusion to draw from this and previous discussion was that the Adriatic should be ignored; that the naval bombardment of the Dardanelles should be attempted; and that at any case a force should be landed at Salonika." Lloyd George responded "that he was very anxious to send an army to the Balkans in order to bring all the Balkan States into the war on our side and settle Austria. M. Venizelos had recently offered to come into the war without conditions provided that Roumania did likewise."

Kitchener agreed that it was "very desirable" to send troops to Serbia. He even "expressed the view that ultimately we might send an army of 500,000 men to Serbia, and if the Dardanelles were open we could maintain it there." Then, because of his pact with Millerand, Kitchener added an ominous "however." The government's chief military adviser said that "he was not quite sure that the right moment had arrived." And then there was the question of troops. "It was difficult to get British troops out of France, and he was sending his last man to France."

Lloyd George was horrified by Kitchener's casual attitude. A week earlier the head of the War Office had been prepared to send an army corps to the Balkans. The Welshman attempted to commit Kitchener to a specific date when troops would be sent. Kitchener hedged: "There was no pressing necessity," he said, "as an Austro-German invasion was impossible owing to the snow." But what of the political role of these troops? Were not they also to be sent out to mobilize the Balkans against Turkey and the Central Powers? If troops were not sent immediately, perhaps they could be promised. "We ought to offer an army corps to Serbia at once," said Lloyd George, "naming the probable date of arrival." The discussion then veered away to the dispatch of two Territorial divisions to France to participate in the proposed Zeebrugge operation. Should these troops not be held back for possible use in the Balkans? The subcommittee decided to bring this matter to the immediate attention of the War Council.[35] At this point prospects for Lloyd George's project seemed bright. If troops could be found, the sentiment was to send them to Salonika rather than the Dardanelles. To be sure, Lloyd George's colleagues viewed the dispatch of troops to the Balkans solely in political terms and were cool toward a major military effort against Austria. But Lloyd George believed that once Britain made a troop commitment to the Balkans, expanded Allied operations would inevitably follow.

At 6:30 that evening the War Council took up the question, with Kitchener summarizing the position of the subcommittee. "They had," he said, "discussed the different theatres of war in which troops could be used." Salonika had been the first choice. In his next breath, however, Kitchener pointed out that there was no need for haste and, besides, he had no troops to spare for the present. This would be equally true in the future if Britain continued to send fresh divisions to France.

Balfour suggested that at least a brigade could be found to send to Salonika. But he admitted, as Kitchener had pointed out, that British intervention would do no good in the long run unless it was backed with sufficient force.

Broad concern was expressed about Britain's open-ended commitment to France. With Joffre insisting that every available man be sent to the barbed wire and trenches of the western front, Britain's hands were tied. Lord Crewe, the secretary of state for India, suggested "that the French had probably magnified their danger, and wanted to make our flesh creep in order to obtain future reinforcements."

Despite the obstacles posed by coalition warfare, Lloyd George's colleagues in the War Council remained enthusiastic for limited military intervention in the Balkans for political purposes. Churchill, now the motivating force behind an attack on the Dardanelles, gave Lloyd George's strategy a boost by arguing in favor of the dispatch of the first available soldiers to Salonika as a political move to influence the Balkan states.

The climax of the War Council's meeting came when Churchill announced that the Admiralty was now prepared to carry out the plan to attack the Dardanelles. Rear-Admiral H. F. Oliver, the chief of the war staff, then told the ministers that "the first shot would be fired in about a fortnight."[36]

At the conclusion of his busy day, Lloyd George was almost certainly relieved that the government had at long last displayed some firmness of purpose. British battleships would soon swing into action at the Dardanelles. His pet project, however, remained at dead center. His efforts had been largely responsible for the War Council's general approval of intervention in the Balkans. Even Churchill agreed that the first available soldiers should go to Salonika—not to the Dardanelles. But it was obvious that as long as Kitchener counseled delay and the French opposed the venture no decisive action to win over the wavering Balkan states would be taken.

A telegram from the British minister to Sofia, the capital of Bulgaria, both alarmed the chancellor of the exchequer and gave him leverage with the secretary of war. A note was quickly dispatched to Kitchener:

> You will I am sure have seen Telegram Number 14 in last night's sections from Sofia. It is so obviously the German interest to crush Serbia in order to detach Bulgaria from the Triple Entente and to free a way to Constantinople that it is risky to doubt the accuracy of the telegram. The French delayed assistance to Antwerp until it was too late. This time the responsibility is ours and we shall not be held blameless if a catastrophe occurs.[37]

Kitchener's response was that he could only spare a brigade for intervention. He then repeated what he had told the War Council. "To go there," he wrote, "with a small force such as a brigade would be useless unless followed up by others as we should be laughed at as soon as it was discovered that we were only an Army *pour rire*."[38]

Lloyd George's rejoinder was to emphasize the link between military operations and diplomacy. "I am fairly confident you will not get these Balkan States to decide until they see khaki!"[39]

To pry some troops away from the western front, Churchill was sent by the War Council to France to persuade Sir John to divert at least two divisions to Salonika. Churchill found French hostile to any military operations "on strategic grounds" in southeast Europe. As usual, however, he proved malleable when confronted with strong arguments from an "Easterner," agreeing to hold two divisions at the government's disposal "from the middle of March onward."[40]

More important than the stance of the British generals was the position of France. Britain was best suited for peripheral operations. But would her most important Continental ally allow her to limit her commitment to the western front? On January 29, Lloyd George had written Churchill: "Are we really bound to hand over the ordering of our troops to France as if we were her vassal? . . . It would be criminal folly if we allowed it to compel us to look on impotently while a catastrophe was being prepared for the Allies in the Balkans."[41] To force the French high command to consider all fronts, Lloyd George began to consider for the first time some joint military authority to coordinate the Entente military efforts.

On February 1, with a new suit bought for the occasion, Lloyd George departed for Paris to break down French resistance. Ostensibly, the purpose of his trip was to attend a meeting with the French and Russian finance ministers. His mind, however, was fixed on the Balkans—not the finances of the Triple Entente. To his surprise and annoyance, he discovered when he talked to Alexandre Ribot, the minister of finance, that Millerand had returned from London without mentioning his discussions with the British ministers about an expeditionary force to the Aegean. Lloyd George wasted no time in rectifying this situation. Without instructions from his government, he took his case to the French government, talking with President Raymond Poincaré, the foreign minister Theophile Delcassé, the prime minister René Viviani, and the influential Briand, one of France's shrewdest and most able ministers.

Briand could not have been more enthusiastic about an Allied expeditionary force to the Balkans, but Poincaré was doubtful that Joffre would approve of French participation. The French president warned Lloyd George that "the diplomatic and political considerations must be very strong to justify the French Government in disregarding the views of the military authorities." Joffre's narrow concern for the western front gave Lloyd George an opportunity to suggest for the first time the creation of an Allied council to force the Entente generals to treat the war as a single front. He urged upon Poincaré "the desirability of instituting a council to sit in France with representatives from the Russian commander in chief, the French commander in chief and the British commander in chief so that those commanders in chief may be kept respectively informed of the intention and operations of their colleagues; there being at present a want of coordination between the armies of the Allies which is an advantage to the German commander."[42]

Lloyd George's whirlwind diplomacy resulted in a special meeting of the French cabinet on February 4. An Allied expeditionary force to Salonika "to assist Serbia" was accepted in principle. But important qualifications were added: the British must not renege on their promise to send four more divisions to France and French participation would be delayed until Joffre was prepared to release the necessary troops.[43]

Lloyd George was cock-a-hoop with delight. Overlooking Poincaré's uncertainty about Joffre's position he wrote Sir Edward Grey:

> Briand was of opinion and so was the President, that if a joint note were addressed to Roumania and Greece asking them whether they would be prepared to declare war immediately if an Expeditionary Force of two Divisions were sent to Salonika, and if they replied in the affirmative, then no doubt General Joffre would gladly spare the necessary force. Briand said it was too preposterous to imagine that if 40,000 men from the West brought in 800,000 from the East, thus withdrawing German pressure on the West, that any general could possibly object to such a plan.[44]

On his way back to London, Lloyd George stopped by British general headquarters. Sir John French, who was entertaining his second prominent "Easterner" in several days, remained unenthusiastic about giving up any troops. Lloyd George then asked what Sir William Robertson, French's new chief of staff, thought of the proposed Salonika expeditionary force. French said, " 'He is here. Would you like to see him?' " Lloyd George answered in the affirmative and soon he and Robertson were face to face for the first time. Their conversation gave no hint of the bitter and explosive relationship that they were to have later. Sir John presented Lloyd George's proposal. Before Robertson could respond Lloyd George butted in, " 'Before you answer, let me put the question in my way.' "[45] After hearing him out, Robertson, according to Lloyd George, proclaimed the plan " 'good strategy.' "[46] Given the future battle over grand strategy between these two men, Robertson's alleged statement is extraordinary.[47]

"My experience yesterday," Lloyd George wrote Grey of his interview with French and Robertson, "shows that the Generals if properly taken in hand can be persuaded." With the French ministers accepting an Allied expeditionary force to the Balkans in principle and with the British generals apparently in line, Lloyd George hoped that khaki would be on the way to the Balkans within a fortnight. It could not come any sooner. Reports from the Balkans were ominous. German soldiers were reported on the borders of Rumania and Serbia; and Bulgaria was apparently on the verge of joining the Central Powers.

Lloyd George's dynamism and persuasiveness had had a considerable impact in London and Paris. But it should not be exaggerated. Moreover, there was an element of opportunism that can not be overlooked. In his discussions with French politicians and British generals, Lloyd George tended to hear only what he wanted. Every positive response was eagerly seized upon; every negative response was ignored or discounted.

On February 9, Britain's war leaders gathered once again to discuss intervention in the Balkans. The unity and clearness of purpose which Lloyd George sought was absent. The War Council's debate was long and contradictory, with the generals, especially Sir John French, who had been invited to sit in, placing many mines in the path of the proposed expeditionary force to southeast Europe.

Grey opened the discussion with a report that the French foreign minister, Delcassé, who had followed Lloyd George to London to coordinate France's and Britain's Balkan policy, had agreed to send a division to Salonika. But he had added an important qualification—the French military authorities had to give their approval. The Russians, who had been asked to participate in the venture, had told Grey that they could provide only 1,000 Cossacks. Where, then, could the troops come from?

Kitchener, who did not speak against the project, insisted that only first-line troops should be sent, suggesting the 29th Division, the last remaining regular division in Britain. Its place in the trenches of the West could be taken by the North-Midland Division, the best of the Territorial divisions in Kitchener's opinion. This suggestion provoked an immediate response from French, who argued against using Territorials in the front lines.

An exasperated Churchill then reminded French that "the original object in sending four divisions to France was to enable Sir John French to undertake an offensive operation against Zeebrugge." But this on-again, off-again operation was once again postponed. "Nevertheless," Churchill stressed, "it was still intended to send out the four divisions which were to be utilized for the purpose of taking over a larger front from the French army, and so releasing French troops. . . . He would receive the original number of reinforcements, the only difference being that a Territorial division instead of a Regular division would be sent."

French continued to raise objections to the proposed expeditionary force. He pointed out that as recently as six days ago General Joffre had opposed the idea. He also argued that the Germans posed no immediate threat to Serbia and were not in a position to influence events in the Balkans. Their forces, he argued, were tied down by the Russians. Furthermore, if only Greece were coaxed to join the Triple Entente by the presence of Allied troops, it was not worth the effort. In a final hit at Lloyd George's scheme, French suggested that conditions were so primitive in Serbia that British soldiers would have a difficult time adjusting.

Lloyd George spoke often and forcefully during the discussion. He wanted immediate action. The War Council had given its approval "in principle some weeks ago." Now the French government had also "expressed approval in principle." Yet nothing was being done while the Germans acted.

The political advantages of an Allied force being sent to Salonika seemed so overwhelming that the War Council overruled the commander of the British Expeditionary Force. Grey was instructed to draft a note to Athens as the first step of the dispatch of the 29th Division to Salonika. The delivery of the British note, however, was to be delayed until the French ambassador in Athens received instruction from Paris.[48]

When the Anglo-French proposal was presented on February 15 to Venizelos, the pro-Ally Greek premier, he turned it down. The limited intervention for political purposes which the Allies envisaged had little attraction for the Greeks. Rumania's hesitancy also figured in Venizelos's calculations. If Rumania had been willing to commit herself to the Entente, the Greeks were prepared to do likewise. Bad luck was another factor in the unsuccessful Anglo-French *démarche*. The proposal was not backed up by the booming of Allied guns at the Dardanelles as had been planned. Because of bad weather and other difficulties, the naval assault had been delayed from the eleventh to the fifteenth, and finally to the nineteenth.

Greece's refusal to join the Entente until conditions were more favorable effectively destroyed the momentum for intervention at Salonika. As Asquith put it, "our eyes are now fixed on the Dardanelles."[49] On February 16, the War Council made the important decision to send the 29th Division to the Dardanelles instead of Salonika.[50] From now on if troops could be scraped together, they were to be sent to Turkey rather than the Balkans. Thus the Dardanelles campaign—which had gained Lloyd George's support because it originally involved only great ships—completely undercut his plan to invade the Balkans.

At nine minutes to ten on the morning of February 19, the long-awaited naval attack on the Dardanelles began. The large Allied armada of battleships which had been assembled before the outer forts opened fire at long range. There were delays caused by bad weather, but by the beginning of March the Turkish defenses had been destroyed. A telegram from Athens offering immediate Greek aid added to the confident mood of Britain's war leaders. Discussion of an expeditionary force to follow up the apparent success of the navy took on a new urgency.

The military and diplomatic events of the next few weeks, however, demonstrated that the optimism of the War Council was premature. Russia, fearing Greek designs on Constantinople, vetoed Greek participation and that country once again drew back from intervention in the war. Meanwhile, as the Allied fleet slowly and hesitantly continued its campaign, the Turks strengthened their intermediate and inner defenses. The next major obstacle for the great ships was the intermediate forts at the Narrows. On March 18, in brilliant sunshine on calm waters, the Allied armada attempted to pound its way through the narrow passage of water across which Lord Byron had once swum.

As the attack progressed, two British battleships and one French battleship were sunk by mines in the dangerous waters. Three more warships were disabled. Although Britain had suffered only sixty-one casualties, the loss of six capital ships was ominous. The commander of the fleet, Vice-Admiral de Robeck, who had replaced the ailing Carden, called off the attack and informed London that the forts had to be taken by soldiers. It is now known that the Turkish defenders were running out of ammunition and that another vigorous assault might have destroyed the forts and placed Constantinople under the guns of the Allies.

It was against this background that the tireless Lloyd George fought on for his Balkan strategy throughout February and into early March. Usually inclined to look on the dark side of news from the front, he was anxious about developments in the East. In early February, utilizing poison-gas shells, Germany had begun its successful Masurian "Winter Battle." Lloyd George was convinced that the poorly equipped Russian army was in danger of imminent collapse.[51] If Russia went under, he was certain that Berlin would concentrate on Serbia to secure her communications to Turkey.

To stave off a disaster for the Entente, he wanted to concentrate all available men in the eastern Mediterranean. The Mesopotamian campaign—a "side issue" he argued—should be abandoned and the troops involved should be sent to the eastern Mediterranean to strengthen the Allied force being assembled there.[52] Realizing that the Dardanelles for the moment commanded the field, he was willing for this force in the East to be used to follow up a successful naval attack. As he wrote in a memorandum on February 22 for the War Council: "If we have a large force ready, not merely to occupy Gallipoli, but to take any other military action which may be necessary in order to establish our supremacy in that quarter, Roumania, Greece, and I think, very probably, Bulgaria will declare for us."[53] But, standing alone in the War Council, he opposed turning the Dardanelles campaign into a sea *and* land operation. Only if the navy succeeded should troops be employed. On February 24, he told the War Council that he "hoped that the army would not be required or expected to pull the chestnuts out of the fire for the Navy. If we failed at the Dardanelles we ought to be immediately ready to try something else."[54] Everyone present, of course, understood the direction of thought of Britain's leading Balkanite.

Lloyd George's impatience grew as Britain's political leaders awaited the fate of the naval attack on the Dardanelles. At the very least preparations for an Allied expeditionary force could be made. But the War Office did nothing. In Lloyd George's mind the Foreign Office was just as dilatory. The opportunity to coordinate military and diplomatic policy might be lost forever. In his February 22 memorandum to the War Council, the Welshman urged "that a special diplomatic mission, based on our readiness to despatch and maintain a large expeditionary force in the Balkans, should immediately be sent to Greece and Roumania to negotiate a military convention."[55] On February 26, Lloyd George reiterated this suggestion in the War Council. Obviously relishing the thought of going himself, Lloyd George argued in favor of sending "a special envoy" to the Balkans.[56] But Grey was "dead opposed to anything of the kind."[57] Nor was the foreign secretary willing to go himself. A disgusted Lloyd George sarcastically told Hankey that Grey should meet with the French and Russian foreign ministers at Salonika "instead of going fishing for a holiday."[58]

It is interesting to speculate what might have been the result if Lloyd George, that great wheeler-dealer, had gone himself to the Balkans. With the western front and the Dardanelles operation having first call for British men and guns which Kitchener deemed available, he would have been forced to try to win over the Balkan states with promises of territory and money. In all likelihood, he would have enjoyed no better luck than Grey in finding his way through the thicket of Balkan politics. The Allies could not agree on what concessions to offer the Balkan states to entice them into their corner; and the intense Balkan rivalries meant that if Greece and Rumania joined the

Allies, Bulgaria, who commanded the principal communication lines between Germany and Turkey, would almost certainly join the Central Powers.

It would be convenient at this point to evaluate the Welshman's Balkan strategy. His strategical views have received scathing comment from the professional soldier. Typical of this criticism would be the recent statement of Brigadier-General Sir Edward Spears: "The ideas that Lloyd George put forward on military matters outraged all the teachings of military experience and history, concerning which the Prime Minister was as ignorant as he was about French poetry or the French language."[59] The reaction at general headquarters to an invasion of the Balkans was just as trenchant, if more earthy.

Any analysis of Lloyd George's strategical views must consider both its political and military aspects. As Lloyd George maintained, British diplomacy in the Balkans had a fatal weakness: the failure to coordinate military operations with diplomacy. Eustace Percy, a member of the Foreign Office, later asked a fundamental question in a memorandum: why were military operations in Gallipoli initiated when it was obvious that this commitment would make it impossible to send an adequate force to the Balkans? Also, there had been "no *General* Staff work in regard to the Balkans."[60] In short the one hand, the Foreign Office, did not know what the other hand, the War Office, was doing. The Germans did not make this mistake. To a considerable degree, Erich von Falkenhayn, the chief of the German general staff, concentrated on the East in 1915 for political purposes. He was determined to protect his southern flank and bolster Germany's allies.[61]

Although Lloyd George was right in principal about the necessity of coordinating military and diplomatic moves, he can be faulted for his facile assumptions about creating a Balkan confederation. He argued that boldness and decisiveness would overcome all political difficulties. But the intervention at Salonika contemplated by the War Council was almost certainly inadequate for its purposes. With the Germans throwing their weight against Russia and in support of Austria, two divisions (about 38,000 men) were unlikely to sway Balkan opinion. To Lloyd George, of course, limited involvement was better than no involvement at all; he hoped that Balkan operations once under way would grow substantially and rapidly. But there was a great element of uncertainty about this.

It is important to keep in mind that Lloyd George, unlike his colleagues, had military as well as political objectives in mind. He wanted to make what he considered the soft underbelly of the Hapsburgs a major theater, shifting Britain's emphasis away from the stalemate in the West. Putting aside the political difficulties of mounting a Balkan offensive for the moment, was this militarily feasible in 1915? Sir William Robertson, who later became the chief spokesman for the "Westerners" as chief of the Imperial general staff (hereafter abbreviated C.I.G.S.), has expressed a major criticism of the military toward opening a great campaign in the Balkans. Having made a tour of the Balkans in 1906, he was convinced that "of all countries in Europe none was defensively stronger, and therefore none less favourable to the offensive, than the Balkan Peninsula."[62] Liddell Hart, the apostle of indirect strategy, however, reminds us in reference to the Balkans that "the acceptance of topographical difficulties has constantly proved preferable to that of a direct attack on an opponent firmly posted and prepared to meet it."[63]

Logistics were another important consideration. Conveying men and supplies to the East was actually not a serious impediment in early 1915. British shipping tonnage (due to the capture of many enemy ships) was greater than it had been at the outbreak of war. With undersea assault by the submarine in its embryonic stage, the ships would have gotten through. Getting the men and material away from Salonika was another matter. But Lloyd George's critics have exaggerated the difficulties here. As the British official history of the Macedonian campaign notes:

With regard to the communications, their deficiencies were emphasized in many reports and appreciations; but, after all, for a Near Eastern port, Salonika, with its good harbour easily made secure against submarines, with three broad-gauge railways—that to Constantinople via Dorjan, that to Belgrade, and that to Monastir—radiating from it, must be admitted to have been unusually favorable to a great military enterprise.[64]

The general staff was virtually invisible during the planning of military operations in the Near East. Its head Sir James Wolfe Murray incredibly occupied a seat in the highest councils of war without ever opening his mouth. Kitchener's gnomic and terse comments were no substitute for staff work. In fact, professional strategic advice was so weak that Hankey became the government's most important adviser on strategy by default. Although sympathetic to Lloyd George's Balkan plans, Hankey believed that the Dardanelles campaign, once launched, should be supported to the exclusion of the proposed Salonikan expedition.[65]

If Lloyd George had had his way and preparations had begun as early as January, C. R. M. F. Cruttwell points out, a Balkan campaign "could have begun in earnest in June, when Italy [which joined the Entente in April 1915] would also have begun to knock on the Isonzo. Austria's position throughout the spring was so critical that she could not have forestalled such an expedition by another attack on Serbia, where she had already failed three times with severe loss."[66]

Another serious objection to Lloyd George's strategy has been succinctly stated by Robertson: "We could not alter the geography of Europe which conferred upon the enemy the advantage of a central position, and thereby enabled him to keep one of his opponents in check with a part of his armies while he threw the bulk of them into a decisive blow against another."[67] Lloyd George was to have this interior versus exterior lines argument thrown in his face many times. And it carried great force. But it was not so valid an argument in 1915 as it was to be later for a simple reason: with the start of its great spring offensive in Russia, Germany was in no position to transfer her troops elsewhere. As Cruttwell writes:

From May onwards the Central Powers were committed to a great campaign with the object of crippling Russia. An analysis of that campaign shows clearly that it could not have been broken off before September. . . . Therefore the West could have been organized defensively for that year without serious risk. It could have been thoroughly insured in (say) the proportions of 5 to 4, while allowing for the employment of large forces elsewhere. For in fact during this year Allied superiority in France amounted to nearly 7 to 4.[68]

In retrospect, a case can be made for Lloyd George's Balkan strategy. If the War Council in January had chosen the Balkans over the Dardanelles and had been able (a very big if) to enlist the support of the British and French generals for a large Anglo-French expeditionary force, the war might have been fought to a conclusion sooner. The armies of Greece, Rumania, Serbia, and Montenegro would have swelled the Entente forces, and a thoroughly demoralized Austria-Hungary might have been driven from the war. Isolated, Turkey might have sued for peace. Russia, on the other hand, would have been greatly encouraged by its link to the West. With help on the eastern front (Russia, after all, had to take on Germany, Austria, and Turkey all at once) and with fresh supplies flowing to her army, she might have remained in the war for the duration.

The above, obviously, is hypothetical. Despite the attraction of the Balkans to Lloyd George in World War I and some British strategists in World War II, it can not be proven that military operations there were a better route to victory over Germany. What happened in the West in 1915, on the other hand, is history. The French high command's strategy of winning the war in twelve months prevailed, resulting in the calamitous loss of life. When the slogging matches of the spring and autumn were over, the French had suffered nearly 1,300,000 casualties, inflicting upon the enemy some 506,000 casualties.[69] The relatively small British Army, in support of the French strategy, suffered casualties even higher in proportion. Nowhere was the front moved more than a few miles.

By March, when the most promising moment for intervention in the Balkans had passed, Lloyd George's Balkanite sentiments were being ignored by the war leaders who mattered. Grey, a strong "Westerner," believed that military considerations should shape diplomacy rather than the reverse. He never favored anything more than limited intervention at Salonika, and he steadfastly resisted what he considered the Welshman's unwarranted intrusions into the realm of diplomacy. Kitchener placed primary emphasis on the western front and had enough difficulty gathering troops he believed fit for combat for the Dardanelles—let alone Lloyd George's Balkan strategy. Meanwhile, Asquith continued his leisurely direction of the War Council. Lloyd George, amazed that the prime minister did not share his view of the urgency of the situation in the Balkans and elsewhere, became increasingly critical of his leadership. As he once told Sir George Riddell: "The P.M. is treating the war as if it were Home Rule or Welsh Disestablishment. He does not recognise that the nation is fighting for its life."[70] Perhaps it was Churchill who delivered the cruelist blow to Lloyd George's offensive strategy in the Balkans. On March 3, when the Dardanelles campaign seemed assured of success, Churchill told the War Council that "we ought not to employ more troops in this theatre of war than are absolutely essential in order to induce the Balkan states to march. He was still of opinion that our line of strategy was an advance in the north through Holland and the Baltic. . . . The operation in the East should be regarded merely as an interlude."[71] Without any support in the War Council or from the military authorities, Lloyd George diverted his energy into other areas, especially the production of munitions. His Balkan designs, it appeared, seemed destined to be ignored even if the Dardanelles campaign succeeded.

NOTES

1. Lloyd George To Asquith, December 31, 1914, Lloyd George MSS, C/6/11/24.

2. "Suggestions as to the Military Position," January 1, 1915, quoted in Lloyd George, *War Memoirs*, 1:219–22.

3. For Lloyd George's correspondence with Noel Buxton, an important backbench Liberal MP, see file C/6/7 in Lloyd George MSS. Also see Fry, *Education of a Statesman*, pp. 279–86, and H. H. Asquith to Venetia Stanley, August 21, 1914, quoted in Martin Gilbert, ed., *Winston S. Churchill*, vol. 3: *Companion, Part 1, Documents: July 1914–April 1915* (1972), p. 49.

4. Entry of December 16, 1914, *A Diary by Frances Stevenson*, p. 18, and War Council, December 16, 1914, CAB 42/1/6.

5. Lloyd George, *War Memoirs*, 1:223.

6. Ibid., p. 220.

7. Ibid., p. 226.

8. Memorandum by Hankey, December 28, 1914, Kitchener MSS, W.O. 159/2.

9. Churchill to Asquith, December 29, 1914, quoted in Winston S. Churchill, *The World Crisis*, 4 vols. (1923–28), 2:30–31.

10. Martin Gilbert, *Winston Churchill*, vol. 3: *The Challenge of War, 1914–1916* (1971), p. 337.

11. Memorandum by Hankey, December 28, 1914, Kitchener MSS, W.O. 159/2.

12. War Council, January 7, 1915, CAB 42/1/11.

13. Hankey, *Supreme Command*, 1:261.

14. Ibid.

15. War Council, January 8, 1915, CAB 42/1/12.

16. Captain Cyril Falls, *Military Operations, Macedonia from the Outbreak of War to the Spring of 1917* (1933), 1:83.

17. War Council, January 8, 1915, CAB 42/1/12.

18. Ibid.

19. Hankey, *Supreme Command*, 1:258.

20. Entry of January 21, 1915, *A Diary by Frances Stevenson*, p. 21.

21. Hankey, *Supreme Command*, 1:265.

22. War Council, January 13, 1915, CAB 42/1/16.

23. Entry of January 17, 1915, *Lord Riddell's War Diary*, p. 52.

24. Entry of January 17, 1915, *A Diary by Frances Stevenson*, pp. 20–23.

25. Magnus, *Kitchener*, p. 290.

26. War Council, January 13, 1915, CAB 42/1/16.

27. War Office, "Indications of a New Austro-German Offensive Against Serbia," January 21, 1915, Lloyd George MSS, C/16/4/1.

28. Asquith to George V, January 21, 1915, CAB 37/123/33.

29. Asquith, *Memories and Reflections*, 2:67–68.

30. Greek Minister to M. Venizelos, January 21, 1915, Lloyd George MSS, C/8/7/1.

31. War Council, January 13, 1915, CAB 42/1/16.

32. Asquith, *Memories and Reflections*, 2:68–69, and Esher Diary, January 22, 1915, 2/13.

33. George H. Cassar, *The French and the Dardanelles: A Study of Failure in the Conduct of War* (1971), pp. 35–40.

34. Esher Diary, January 24, 1915, 2/13.

35. Subcommittee of Imperial Defence Committee, January 28, 1915, CAB 42/1/27.

36. War Council, January 28, 1915, CAB 42/1/28.

37. Lloyd George to Kitchener, January 29, 1915, Lloyd George MSS, C/5/7/14.

38. Kitchener to Lloyd George, January 29, 1915, Lloyd George MSS, C/5/7/12.

39. Lloyd George to Kitchener, January 29, 1915, Lloyd George MSS, C/5/7/13.

40. Churchill to Kitchener, January 31, 1915, quoted in Churchill, *World Crisis*, 2:176–77.

41. Lloyd George to Churchill, January 29, 1915, quoted in Gilbert, *Companion, Part 1, Documents: July 1914–April 1915*, p. 472.

42. Michael Palairet to Lloyd George (British Ambassador Sir Francis Bertie's account of Lloyd George's conversation with Poincaré inclosed), February 5, 1915, Lloyd George MSS, C/3/6/2.

43. Note, "Decision at Council Meeting this Morning," February 4, 1915, ibid.

44. Lloyd George to Grey, February 7, 1915, Lloyd George MSS, C/4/1/16; also see entries of February 3–4, 1915, Lady Algernon Gordon Lennox, ed., *The Diary of Lord Bertie of Thames, 1914–1918*, 2 vols. (n.d.), 1:107–9.

45. Entry of February 7, 1915, *Lord Riddell's War Diary*, p. 61.

46. Entry of February 8, 1915, *A Diary by Frances Stevenson*, p. 29.

47. Robertson has written: "Mr. Lloyd George once said that he had explained his plan to me when on a visit to G.H.Q. in France . . . and that I had agreed with it. If so, I must have entirely misunderstood the account he gave me of it. . . ." Sir William Robertson, *Soldiers and Statesmen, 1914–1918*, 2 vols. (1926), 2:88.

48. War Council, February 9, 1915, CAB 42/1/33.

49. Asquith, *Memories and Reflections*, 2:75.

50. War Council, February 16, 1915, CAB 42/1/35.

51. Ibid., February 26, 1915, CAB 42/1/47.

52. Ibid., February 24, 1915, CAB 42/1/42.

53. Lloyd George, "Some Future Considerations on the Conduct of the War," February 22, 1915, CAB 42/1/39.

54. War Council, February 24, 1915, CAB 42/1/42.

55. Lloyd George, "Some Future Considerations . . ."

56. War Council, February 26, 1915, CAB 42/1/47.

57. Asquith to Venetia Stanley, February 26, 1915, quoted in Gilbert, *Companion, Part I, Documents: July 1914–April 1915*, pp. 577–78.

58. Hankey Diary, March 6, 1915, 1/1.

59. Nancy Maurice, ed., *The Maurice Case from the Papers of Major-General Sir Frederick Maurice*, with an appreciation by Major-General Sir Edward Spears (1972), p. 5. Spears is wrong. Lloyd George knew some French, enough anyway to compose love notes in that language to Miss Stevenson.

60. Memorandum by Eustace Percy, October 11, 1915, F.O. 800/95.

61. C. R. M. F. Cruttwell, *A History of the Great War, 1914–1918* (1936), p. 140, and C. J. Lowe and M. L. Dockrill, *British Foreign Policy, 1914–1922*, vol. 2: *The Mirage of Power* (1972), pp. 169–207.

62. Robertson, *Soldiers and Statesmen*, 2:88.

63. B. H. Liddell Hart, *The Real War, 1914–1918* (paperback edn., 1930), p. 120.

64. Falls, *Military Operations, Macedonia from the Outbreak of War to the Spring of 1917*, 1:83.

65. For the most succinct and revealing discussion of how military policy was formulated during this period, see Gooch, *Plans for War*, pp. 299–330.

66. C. R. M. F. Cruttwell, *the Role of British Strategy in the Great War* (1936), p. 39.

67. Robertson, *Soldiers and Statesmen*, 2:87.

68. Cruttwell, *British Strategy in the Great War*, p. 38.

69. These are Churchill's calculations, and the difference between Allied and German losses in his account may be on the high side. But, whatever figures one accepts, it seems obvious that French and British losses were considerably higher than those suffered by the Germans. Churchill, *World Crisis*, 3:41.

70. Entry of August 20, 1915, *Lord Riddell's War Diary*, p. 118.

71. War Council, March 3, 1915, CAB 42/2/3.

3

Munitions, Compulsion, and the Fall of Serbia

IN 1915, Lloyd George's daily life had not been much altered by the great war. To be sure, like many of his countrymen, he glanced nervously at the sky. In January, Berlin had first sent her rigid airship, the Zeppelin, against Britain, bombing Yarmouth on the Norfolk coast. In the months to come, these huge and menacing gas bags struck terror in the hearts of many civilians. When these sky raiders appeared, workers fled factories and railways were thrown into confusion. Lloyd George shared his countrymen's concern about the Zeppelin, spending many nights away from 11 Downing Street, the official residence of the chancellor of the exchequer. He commuted to a modest house at Walton Heath, which had been given him by his friend and confidant, Lord Riddell. A frequent passenger in his car was his dog, Zulu. Once his pet had been stunned by a passing car; but much to Lloyd George's relief and amusement, Zulu had first been revived and then befuddled by a dose of brandy. Lloyd George's commuting was the occasion for one of his favorite stories. Returning to Walton Heath after dinner in London, his car broke down and his chauffeur got out to make repairs. Without the chauffeur's knowledge, Lloyd George also left the car. To the Welshman's dismay, the chauffeur made the necessary repairs and then drove away without noticing that his passenger was missing. Lloyd George—or so he alleged—then made his way in the dark to a great house which turned out to be an asylum. Attired in an evening cape and opera hat, he explained his predicament to a man who answered his knock at the door and then identified himself as the chancellor of the exchequer. The man's response was: "Certainly. Do come in. The rest of the cabinet have been expecting you."

Lloyd George was often joined at Walton Heath by his private secretary and mistress, Frances Stevenson. A graduate of the University of London in Classics, Miss Stevenson had fallen "under the sway of his electric personality" the first time she saw him.[1] She became his private secretary at the treasury in 1912 "on his own terms, which were in direct conflict with my essentially Victorian upbringing."[2] Bright, efficient, sensitive, and attractive, she was a loyal and warm companion to Lloyd George, who was over twenty-five years her senior. Their relationship took an alarming turn in February 1915, when Frances became ill and believed that she was pregnant.[3] Lloyd George placed her at Walton Heath under the care of a faithful servant. Either it was all a mistake or she suffered a miscarriage. There was to be no politically embarrassing child.

This relationship was kept from the general public by a protective press and his friends accepted it. Some of his political foes, however, believed that this affair was proof that he was unfit for membership to decent society. To them, he was the "Goat." Stories about his womanizing had followed him throughout his political career. Though exaggerated, these stories were real enough. In defense of his wayward ways, Lloyd George once brazenly put the following rationalization to his wife:

> You say I have my weakness. So has anyone that ever lived & the greater the man the greater the weakness. It is only insipid, wishy washy fellows that have no weaknesses. . . .
> You must make allowances for the waywardness & wildness of a man of my type. What if I were drunk as well? I can give you two samples you know of both the weaknesses in one man & the wives do their best under these conditions. What about Asquith & Birkenhead? I could tell you stories of both—women & wine.[4]

His wife, Margaret, made allowances. Passionately Welsh and uncomfortable in the hustle and bustle of London, she spent much of her time in her beloved Wales away from her adulterous husband. There was never a formal separation, which might have damaged his political career.

At fifty-two, Lloyd George's appearance was impressive. Although of moderate height, he had a powerful build which exuded strength. His eyes were blue and his hair, which he allowed to grow long, was rapidly turning white. Of a sociable disposition, he was relaxed and charming. With a drink and pipe (or cigar) in hand, he could dominate any social gathering with his wit, dynamism, and genius as a storyteller. What is sometimes overlooked is that he was an excellent listener as well. He constantly pumped his friends and associates for ideas and seldom acted without consulting others. His outgoing and personable ways were a great asset for they often enabled him to lower the guard of his most bitter enemies. There were few British politicians who could be better company.

His tastes were, for the most part, thoroughly middle class. He shunned ceremony and preferred simple food—beans and bacon were among his favorites. For relaxation, he liked drives through the countryside, long walks, singing, and golf. Britain had many better golfers, but few who were more avid. Neither the war, winter, nor the king were allowed to interrupt his golfing routine. Once the king requested an interview with him at Buckingham Palace on a Saturday morning. " 'Damn the King!' " he exploded, " 'Saturday is the only day I have to play golf. I can't play on Sunday for I mustn't shock my Nonconformist friends on too many points at the same time!' "

Lloyd George's dynamism and zest for winning the war discomforted some of his Liberal colleagues. Although he deplored the unprecedented death and destruction of the war, he did not draw back from committing himself to the unlimited conflict. If more men and high-explosive shells were needed, they must be obtained. Nothing must stand in the way. If necessary, the state must play an ever-increasing role in mobilizing the country for war. New weapons as well as new forms of warfare were readily considered by him. A suggestion in the War Council that a blight might be spread over Germany's crops got his enthusiastic support. When Churchill opposed what he termed "poisoning" food, Lloyd George ingeniously riposted that "a blight did not poison but merely deteriorated the crop."[5] German civilians would starve nonetheless.

Lloyd George's drive and his quick and flexible mind involved him in a bitter clash with the professionals in the War Office over the production of munitions. Having shown an interest in munitions as early as September 1914, Lloyd George was convinced that the hidebound and unimaginative approach of the soldiers to the production of munitions might lose the war. The War Office's policy, he later noted, "seemed even to be that of preparing, not for the next war, but for the last one."[6] When he paid a visit to Woolwich Arsenal shortly after the war began, he "found stacks of empty shells which were being slowly and tediously filled, one at a time, with ladles by hand from cauldrons of seething fluid."[7]

The War Office's initial failure to deliver an adequate supply of munitions could hardly be blamed on Kitchener, who inherited a system incapable of keeping up with the demands of modern war. But Kitchener was reluctant to accept what he considered interference by Lloyd George in the War Office's domain; and he consequently became the target for Lloyd George's aggressive and unrelenting efforts to reorganize and increase the production of munitions. Earlier, Lloyd George had thought that Kitchener was Britain's most able soldier because he had given support, indecisive and muddled though it had been, to "Eastern" ventures. Now, however, he thought him "without imagination" and "distrustful of all civilian interference."[8] A showdown occurred in this civil-military struggle in early March. In a "truly royal row," as Asquith described it, neither Kitchener nor Lloyd George would bend. Both threatened resignation.[9]

The thunder and lightning in Whitehall abated somewhat in early April. Asquith appointed a cabinet committee under Lloyd George's chairmanship to deal with munitions. Kitchener, however, created an Armaments Output Committee within the War Office. Continued conflict was inevitable as the professional soldier learned to cooperate with the civilians under Lloyd George. However, Kitchener's acceptance that Lloyd George had a role to play in munitions, limited though it might be, did improve relations between the two men. On April 21, Lloyd George even defended the War Office's delivery of munitions before the House. Within three weeks he was to regret these words of praise.

Lloyd George's renewed anger at Britain's dominant war lord is explained by two unexpected visitors whom Lloyd George received on May 12. They were Sir John French's secretary, Brinsley Fitzgerald, and one of his aides de camp, Captain Frederick Guest. Their commander had sent them to talk with Lloyd George and the Unionist leaders Arthur Balfour and Bonar Law. Armed with documents from general headquarters to the War Office requesting more ammunition, especially high-explosive shells, they told the chancellor of the exchequer that Kitchener had ignored Sir John's urgent pleas for months. Lloyd George was profoundly shocked. It had been rumored earlier that the British army was running short of shells, but Kitchener had assured the government that the supply of munitions was adequate. It now appeared that the head of the War Office was guilty of criminal deception. No civilian knew of Sir John's plight. As Lloyd George later wrote, "This was the first communication on the shell question that I had received from the Commander-in-Chief."[10]

Lloyd George apparently believed that French's intrigue against Kitchener was perfectly justified under the circumstances. He would not have been so tolerant of this internecine struggle among the "brass hats" if he had known that he was being used, in part, in an attempt to reverse the government's "Eastern" strategy. Sir John French hoped to destroy Kitchener because of the latter's support of strategy which threatened to take men and shells away from the West.[11]

Sir John French also gave his one-sided views on the shell shortage and the meager reinforcements the British Expeditionary Force was receiving to the most influential military correspondent of the day, Colonel Charles à Court Repington of the *Times*. On May 14, Repington discussed the recent British offensive, the Battle of Festubert, under the provocative headline: "NEED FOR SHELLS. BRITISH ATTACKS CHECKED. LIMITED SUPPLY THE CAUSE." It is the contention of Max Aitken (Lord Beaverbrook) that Lloyd George immediately saw the "potential political dynamite" in this report from the front.[12] Furious with Kitchener's apparent incompetence and his secretiveness, he seized upon Repington's account in the *Times* to undermine the secretary of state for war and gain control of munitions. As was often his method, he chose an indirect approach. According to Aitken he went to the most powerful press lord in Britain, Lord Northcliffe, the owner of the *Times* and *Daily Mail,* and urged him to launch a press campaign against Kitchener.[13] The megalomaniac Northcliffe apparently needed little encouragement.[14] Lloyd George also met secretly with Repington and was given incriminating material to be used against the head of the War Office.[15]

Lloyd George's use of the press was hardly unusual. With Parliament's role considerably diminished and with partisan party politics generally in abeyance because of the war, Fleet Street, with its hold on the British public, served as the opposition to the government. Rather than deliver a direct attack on an opponent, politicians leaked stories and material to their supporters in the press, a practice which is certainly not unknown today. Lloyd George was a master at planting stories. No British politician was better connected with the press lords. Riddell, owner of *News of the World,* C. P. Scott, the owner and editor of the *Manchester Guardian,* Robertson Nicoll, the editor of the *British Weekly,* Robert Donald, the editor of the *Daily Chronicle,* and Lord Burnham, the owner of the *Daily Telegraph,* among others, were frequently in his company. With Lord Northcliffe, however, he enjoyed a very uneasy relationship. Perhaps it was his realization that he was likely to be used by Northcliffe rather than the reverse.

As Northcliffe moved to launch his press campaign on munitions to discredit Kitchener, an unguided missile emerged from the Admiralty—Lord Fisher. Seething with discontent with Churchill over the Dardanelles and determined to win control of the Admiralty, "Jacky" Fisher decided to resign. Lloyd George, quite accidentally, was one of the first to learn of his intentions. As he was passing the entrance lobby of 10 Downing Street on Saturday morning, May 15, he saw a glum first sea lord who blurted out: "I have resigned!"[16] With a munitions scandal brewing and with the nation's most famous naval figure determined to resign, Asquith's Liberal ministry was in serious trouble.

Fisher's resignation had a decisive impact on Bonar Law, the leader of the Unionists, who telephoned Lloyd George and told him that the government was faced with either a rebellion of the Unionists in the House or the acceptance of a coalition government. The chancellor of the exchequer agreed that coalition was the only solution and invited Bonar Law to visit him at the treasury. When Bonar Law arrived, Lloyd George excused himself and went down the corridor to 10 Downing Street to see the prime minister.[17] In a matter of minutes, the decision was made to include the Unionists in a coalition government to preserve the party peace in Parliament. Lloyd George then collected Bonar Law and the three men met in the cabinet room. During the discussion of a reconstructed government, Asquith and Lloyd George agreed that it was "absolutely necessary to get rid of Kitchener."[18] Who would replace him? Asquith suggested Lloyd George.

On the same day, May 17, an excited Lloyd George told an astonished Miss Stevenson, "Well Pussy, I'm leaving this place!" Asquith, he informed his secretary, had offered him the War Office and he was going to accept it.[19] In the next three days, however, he clearly had second thoughts. "He does not want to leave this place," Stevenson recorded in her diary on the eighteenth.[20] By the nineteenth, he still had reservations and Stevenson believed that he would "leave it in the hands of the Prime Minister to decide."[21] On May 20, Lloyd George was no longer equivocable. "Tories want me in the War Office—*but I will not go,*" he wrote his wife.[22]

One can only guess what was going through Lloyd George's mind during these days. He apparently had no idea of undermining Asquith. If he was involved in a conspiracy, it would seem to be directed against Kitchener rather than the prime minister.[23] Supplanting Kitchener at the War Office would enable him to have his way on munitions. On reflection, however, he must have perceived many disadvantages. His amateur standing and lack of support from his Liberal colleagues would allow him no influence over British strategy. The generals would fight him tooth and nail; Asquith was certain not to back him; and the press would recoil in horror if he attempted to interfere with the strategic direction of the war. His strongest support came from the Unionists and they were not opposed to the generals' "Western" strategy. Even a friend and fellow opponent of the Western offensives such as Churchill wrote Asquith, "I am sure LG will not do for WO."[24]

There was also the very serious problem of occupying Kitchener's shoes. Kitchener's standing had fallen within the government, but he was still held in high esteem by the public. A small crowd gathered every day at the War Office just to see the nation's hero. Surely, some of the public outrage at his dismissal would be directed at his successor.

Remaining at the treasury, the second most important position in the government, seemed preferable, especially if Lloyd George were given the authority he wanted to reorganize munitions production. On May 19, Northcliffe's mass-circulation paper, the *Daily Mail*, fired a shot across the bow of the War Office. "THE TRAGEDY OF THE SHELLS. LORD KITCHENER'S GRAVE ERROR," screamed the heading of its leading article.

On that same day, Lloyd George wrote a very strong letter to Asquith. Under the circumstances, it came close to being an ultimatum.

> If these facts [shell shortage] are approximately correct, I hesitate to think what action the public would insist on if they were known. But it is quite clear that the proceedings of a Munition Committee from which vital information of this character is withheld must be a farce. I cannot therefore continue to preside over it under such conditions. . . .
> A Cabinet Committee cannot have executive power: it can only advise and recommend. It is for the department to act. They have not done so, and all the horrible loss of life which has occurred in consequence of the lack of high-explosive shell is the result.[25]

As Asquith mulled over Lloyd George's request for an independent Ministry of Munitions, Northcliffe continued to pile on the pressure. On May 24, the *Daily Mail*'s leading article asserted: "Within the next few days the War Office will be reorganized. It is to be hoped that Lord Kitchener will remain the gatherer of armies. . . . It is equally to be hoped that the whole question of shells and other munitions of war will be put into the hands of another Cabinet Minister, who will take into his confidence some of the leading business men of the country." Who else but the present chancellor of the exchequer would fit this description? In fact, Northcliffe and Lloyd George had discussed the munitions situation at Walton Heath the day before this leading article appeared.[26]

Northcliffe's press campaign may indeed have helped Lloyd George get his Ministry of Munitions. But the attack against Kitchener had unexpected consequences. There was a violent reaction from the public. Copies of the *Daily Mail* and the *Times* were burned at the London Stock Exchange and elsewhere. A sign, "The Allies of the Huns," was placed over the plate of the *Daily Mail*'s office on Throgmorton Street. Angry letters poured in, and the paper suffered a large temporary circulation loss. The national clamor helped convince Asquith to keep Kitchener at the War Office.[27]

When the new coalition government was announced on May 26, there was a Ministry of Munitions headed by Lloyd George. The treasury was given to Reginald McKenna with the understanding that Lloyd George could reclaim it later. The Welshman had gained one of his greatest victories over the military hierarchy. His direction of the production of munitions in the next

Lloyd George at Wormwood Scrubbs watching a Killen-Strait tractor fitted with torpedo wire-cutters.

months gave abundant proof that he was the right man for the job. He understood the requirements of modern war better than most of the generals. The new technology of war, especially if it offered hope of breaking the stalemate, excited him. He immediately grasped the value of the heavily armored vehicle or tank when Kitchener viewed this clanking contraption as " 'a pretty mechanical toy.' "[28] Kitchener was equally remiss about the machine gun, believing that at the very most four machine guns per battalion were sufficient. Lloyd George's response to Kitchener's figures was: "Take Kitchener's maximum (four per battalion); square it, multiply that result by two; and when you are in sight of that, double it again for good luck."[29] This produced sixty-four machine guns per battalion, which actually fell a bit short of eventual requirements. Another important new weapon which Lloyd George rescued from oblivion was the Stokes light mortar, which had been rejected by the soldiers.[30]

Lloyd George's involvement in delivering the sinews of war kept him away from the inner councils of war. Throughout June, he was absent from the Dardanelles Committee, which had replaced the War Council. The committee's new name accurately reflected the dominant interest of the politicians. On April 25, beachheads on Gallipoli had been established by an amphibious assault at dawn. Once ashore, however, the British, Australian, and New Zealand troops were unable to move beyond the beaches and capture the high ground. Reinforcements were sent but the troops remained on their precarious beachheads. The conflict assumed the depressing character of the stalemated trench warfare of the West.

Lloyd George, with his Balkan plans stymied by this operation, was profoundly pessimistic about the British effort at the Dardanelles. Without any khaki in the Balkans, he also was convinced that it was only a matter of time before the Germans and Austrians would overrun Serbia, seduce Bulgaria, and establish a direct line of communications with Turkey. He told his friend C. P. Scott in mid-June that Berlin was toying with London in the Near East: "When it suited them they could drive us into the sea."[31]

On June 19–20, Lloyd George chaired a conference on munitions at Boulogne. Since that French city "was crowded up to the attics," the only space available for the discussion was a dirty and ill-smelling room at a second-rate hotel. During the talk it became obvious to the British delegation (which included military representatives) that there would not be enough big guns and high-explosive shells to justify a big British effort on the western front until 1916.[32]

Lloyd George returned to London with his opposition to a large-scale British attack in the West in 1915 reinforced by the technical arguments of this munitions conference. His country's continued subordination to French strategy alarmed him more than ever. The British Expeditionary Force had more than doubled in size since the beginning of the year and he feared that Joffre, despite the gigantic losses suffered by the French in the spring and the British failure at Festubert, would insist that these fresh but poorly equipped forces should be hurled against machine guns and barbed wire. Without adequate artillery support, Lloyd George believed, this would be tantamount to the murdering of thousands of British soldiers. At his first Dardanelles Committee meeting (July 5) he emphasized that "it would be the greatest mistake to send out any reinforcements to the Army in France until it could be fully supported with heavy guns and ammunition."[33] Caught between Joffre, who desired a big offensive, and the British ministers, who did not, Kitchener hedged. He "said that he would do his best, but the French said that the offensive is vital to them. They provided most of the men and were defending their own territory, and we therefore considered them entitled to do what they liked."[34]

In fairness to Kitchener, there is no question that he was in a difficult position. After the Battle of Festubert had begun poorly for the British, he had wired Sir John French that the dispatch of the new army to France was contingent upon breaking through the German lines.[35] On the other hand, with the Russian army in full retreat in the East, there might be merit in Joffre's argument that the Anglo-French forces had to launch a big attack in the West to take the pressure off the Russians. Perhaps Kitchener's belief that the French had to be supported because of their predominant military role in the West is the best explanation for his actions.

After the July 5 Dardanelles Committee meeting, Kitchener and other British leaders (Lloyd George was not among them) crossed the Channel to Calais for the first inter-Allied conference to coordinate war policy. Although Kitchener was genuinely in favor of delaying a great offensive in the

West until 1916, he was more inclined to support Joffre than the British civilians. Sir Henry Wilson recorded this revealing conversation he had with Kitchener just before the latter departed for France: "He wants to see Joffre alone and to tell him of all his fears, show him his whole hand, and come to an agreement as to what he shall say in front of the politicians whom he hates and distrusts as much as, I told him, Joffre did."[36] Early in the morning on the sixth, Kitchener had his private conference with Joffre, apparently telling him that, if the French supported an expansion of the Gallipoli campaign, he would not oppose a major offensive later in the year, by which time he seems to have believed that the Turks would be flying the white flag of surrender over the Dardanelles. But he apparently made it clear that the burden of fighting would fall to the French. British support would be largely confined to taking over more line to free French soldiers for the offensive.[37]

At the conference which began at 10:00 A.M. and lasted three hours, Kitchener in fluent French presented London's case against a premature offensive. Although no formal conclusions were drawn up, Hankey succeeded in putting down some "unformulated" conclusions by talking to the British leaders who participated in the discussion. These conclusions included an agreement that no general (as opposed to local) offensive would be launched. In sum, the Anglo-French policy in the coming months was to be that of an active defensive to tie the Germans down in the West,[38] and the British politicians returned to London convinced that a large-scale attack had been ruled out for the rest of 1915. Joffre, however, as we will shortly see, placed a different interpretation on the conclusions of the conference.

Lloyd George's relations with the head of the War Office continued to deteriorate during the summer. There was considerable friction and jealousy between Lloyd George's civilians in the new Ministry of Munitions and the professionals in the War Office. Kitchener's rejection of Lloyd George's offensive plans in southeastern Europe also created a wide gulf between the two men. Earlier, Lloyd George had believed that Kitchener was Britain's greatest general because of his dislike of big and futile attacks in the West and his support of an indirect strategy. In June, however, Kitchener stated his strategical views for British arms after the Dardanelles campaign. He wrote: "Even assuming that we secure both the Dardanelles and the Bosphorus, it is now practically impossible for us to undertake a great campaign directed against Austria-Hungary during the year 1915."[39]

In August, Lloyd George latched on to the divisive issue of compulsion (or compulsory service) to use as a stick with which to beat both Kitchener and his protector, Asquith. It became a symbol for the Welshman's determination to win the war at all costs. Rejecting the Liberals' almost laissez-faire attitude toward the conflict, he sought to use state power to mobilize the country for total war. On August 18, he appeared before the War Policy Committee of the cabinet, which had been created to examine the question of compulsion. "Would you go to the point of placing every citizen at the orders of the Government?" the chairman, Lord Crewe, wanted to know. "If you ask me whether personally I think it would help the efficient conduct of the war," Lloyd George responded without hesitation, "I say at once that it certainly would. I would say that every man and woman was bound to render the services that the state required of them, and which in the opinion of the state they could best render. I do not believe you will get through this war without doing it in the end; in fact, I am perfectly certain you will have to come to it." Lloyd George, of course, did not want to seem the accomplice of Joffre, who insisted on squandering men in futile attacks. As he told the committee, "I do not feel myself that the only field of operations is in France by any means."[40]

Because of his position in the government, the most important critic of compulsion was Kitchener. His opposition is surprising, but it perhaps can be explained. He may have believed that it would be butchery to draft more men into the army before they could be properly equipped. At least, that was Hankey's conclusion from conversations he had with Kitchener on the subject.[41] In justifying his position on compulsion to the government, he displayed the dark side of his character. To be blunt, he lied and got other officers to lie for him about the military facts.[42]

Meanwhile, military developments in the East and the West combined with the fight over compulsion to bring Lloyd George's irreconcilable differences with Kitchener to a head. First, the British campaign on Gallipoli continued to miscarry. A surprise attack at Suvla Bay on August 6 was poorly executed. Initially only a brigade and a half of the Turkish defenders stood in the way. But a great opportunity was lost because of the inertia and mistakes of the generals. The troops once ashore did not immediately advance to occupy the commanding heights of the Dardanelles. The local commander, Sir William Stopford, took a nap aboard his ship; some of his troops cavorted on the beach and in the water, while others made tea. It was rather like a summer holiday at Brighton. When the fighting began in earnest, the British were unable to dislodge the reinforced Turks from their commanding position. This failure was a crushing setback to those who hoped the fresh assault would end the stalemate on Gallipoli.

The "Easterners" were dealt another blow on August 20. This time it was Kitchener rather than the Turks who delivered the punch. After a four-day conference with French and Joffre, Kitchener surprised the Dardanelles Committee with the news that he now favored a big attack on the western front. Because of Russia's precarious position, "he could no longer maintain the attitude which was agreed upon in conjunction with the French at Calais [in July], namely, that a *real* serious offensive on a large scale in the West should be postponed until all the Allies were quite ready." Perhaps echoing Joffre, he made the dubious assertion that "trench work was becoming very irksome to the French troops, and that an offensive was necessary for the *moral* of the French army, amongst the members of which there was a good deal of discussion about peace."

How an all-out attack rather than local attacks to occupy the German army would give more assistance to the Russians he could not explain. In response to sharp questioning from Churchill, he could only answer lamely that "unfortunately we had to make war as we must, and not as we should like."[43]

With profound reluctance and skepticism, the civilians bowed to Kitchener's will. Few decisions made by the government during the war were as crucial as this one. "It was with this decision," Michael Howard has written, "that the total commitment of British resources to the Western Front really began."[44] A truly astonishing aspect of this incident is that Kitchener had been deceived by Joffre's argument that Britain might break up the alliance if she withheld her support. The truth was that the French government was opposed to Joffre's plan and feared with reason that he would destroy the morale of the French army with his headlong attacks.[45] If Kitchener had stood up to Joffre, he might have given the French civilians the courage to overrule their granite-willed commander in chief.

Lloyd George, who had not been present, was informed of the government's capitulation to Joffre by Bonham Carter, the prime minister's private secretary.[46] His frustration over the direction of the war now knew no bounds. In the West, the Kitchener-Joffre combination was sponsoring an offensive in which almost no British politician believed. In the East, it was clear that the British were stalemated at Gallipoli; the campaign there was consuming men and equipment at an ever-increasing rate with no end in sight. The survival of Serbia, meanwhile, hung in the balance, with Kitchener apparently oblivious to the potential German threat to that small state. When the government's oracle on strategy was asked in the Dardanelles Committee if he had considered a Balkan thrust by Berlin to link up with Turkey, Kitchener had answered that he had, "but he thought it would be a mistake on the part of the Germans." Churchill's sarcastic comment to this bit of strategical wisdom is worth recording. He noted that "it would be a mistake we should be very sorry to see them make."[47]

To Loyd George there was no better proof of Kitchener's indifferent attitude toward Serbia and the Balkans than his failure to make any plans or preparations to deal with a German attack. In January and February, the War Council—at Lloyd George's prompting—had instructed Kitchener to make the necessary initial preparations for the sending of an expeditionary force to the Balkans.[48] Kitchener had turned a deaf ear. As Lloyd George later bitterly commented: "Not even a mule had been bought for transport when the German blow fell on Serbia."[49]

Kitchener was made to look foolish in early September when the French suddenly offered to furnish four divisions for the war against Turkey. Kitchener was completely taken aback by this unexpected development. Perhaps it meant, he told an equally puzzled Dardanelles Committee, "that the French had decided to postpone their offensive."[50] Lloyd George and Churchill were elated, with Churchill passing the Welshman a note which read, " 'I feel like a man who was about to be shot, and who instead is left a large fortune.' "[51] A few days later Kitchener had to tell the ministers that it was the dispatch of the four French divisions which had been postponed. Joffre's offensive was still on.[52] The confusing signals emanating from Paris were the result of a furious tug of war going on between the French civilians, who wanted to support the Dardanelles venture, and Joffre, who opposed any diversion of French military strength away from the West.

This comedy was not lost on Lloyd George. Britain, he believed, was certain to lose the war if Kitchener continued in the War Office. His obsessive secrecy, the contradictory opinions he often expressed in the Dardanelles Committee, and his kowtowing to Joffre appeared to make him a greater menace to the nation than the German Zeppelin and U-boat. Some of his ire at the secretary of state for war was directed at Asquith, who dared not risk the public outcry and sack Kitchener. There was little chance that Lloyd George, acting alone, would be able to have his way with the prime minister. His influence with his chief was now at its nadir, all his suggestions "pooh-poohed."[54] His relations with most of his fellow Liberals were equally bad. Only Churchill was really close to him. In desperation, he turned to the Unionists for support, especially Bonar Law, Curzon, and Sir Edward Carson.[55] They approved of his strong stand on compulsion and they shared his contempt for the head of the War Office, with Bonar Law and Curzon openly ridiculing Kitchener's direction of the Gallipoli campaign in the Dardanelles Committee.[56] This was a combination to be reckoned with.

On September 14, Lloyd George dined with Churchill and Curzon, agreeing to join with the Unionists to force Asquith to remove Kitchener and accept compulsion.[57] Lloyd George was almost certainly ambivalent about plotting with the Tories against Kitchener and especially Asquith. As he told Stevenson, he hated "going against his party."[58]

Serbia dominated Lloyd George's thinking in the latter part of September. With the Austro-German campaign against Russia drawing to a close, the enemy would soon be able to concentrate on Britain's only Balkan ally. Meanwhile, "Foxy Ferdinand," the king of Bulgaria, moved closer to the Central Powers, announcing general mobilization and armed neutrality on September 19. Serbia appeared doomed if Bulgaria launched an assault from the rear. Her only chance of survival appeared to depend upon decisions being made in London and Paris. Would her allies, Belgrade asked, be willing to send immediately a force of 150,000 men to the Balkans? This show of determination by London and Paris might stiffen Greece's backbone and cool Bulgaria's ardor for war.

Faced with a desperate situation, Britain's war leaders were forced to reconsider Lloyd George's Balkan strategy. There could not have been a more inopportune time to send an expeditionary force to the Balkans. A big attack was about to be launched in the West and British forces in the East were still locked in combat with the Turks in Gallipoli. Something had to give. Lloyd George suggested in the Dardanelles Committee on September 23 that the some 40,000 British soldiers at Suvla Bay be transferred to Salonika. Athens should be telegraphed immediately and informed that eventually a force of 150,000 would be sent. Kitchener, as usual, threw cold water on the Welshman's Balkanite ideas. He still felt that the German threat to Serbia was exaggerated and he warned that the proposed intervention "might be a greater drain than the Dardanelles operation."

To bolster his case for involvement in the Balkans, Lloyd George characteristically fell back on the political considerations involved. Always the adroit politician, the Welshman used a clever argument which was calculated to appeal to the British politician. Berlin can not "do us much harm in the West," he warned, but in the East, Britain's Asian empire was at stake. To block the road to Egypt, Persia, and India, Britain must construct a wall in the Balkans. For the most part, the bricks for this barrier would come in the form of Balkan soldiers. Once again, he emphasized that khaki in the Balkans might mean as many as 1,000,000 new soldiers for the Entente.

The Dardanelles Committee was divided and the discussion was long and heated. As was often the case, no clear plan of action emerged. Instead, it was decided to explore the situation further.[59] When the French government was sounded out, it enthusiastically endorsed the idea of sending 150,000 men to Salonika. This forced the hand of a reluctant British government, to the delight of Lloyd George. Preparations were begun to send a small Anglo-French force to Salonika.

Meanwhile, the Anglo-French armies launched their general offensive in France on September 25. In a pouring rain, mud-caked soldiers went "over the top" and advanced toward the German fortifications. The French generals were supremely confident. Ten divisions of cavalry had been brought up to exploit the anticipated breakthrough. In the British sector, there was not the same confidence. Handicapped by a shortage of big guns and shells—the French usually had twice as many—the British attack, known as the Battle of Loos, was doomed from the outset.

Kitchener had told the Dardanelles Committee that the French hoped to break the German lines within five or six days after they delivered their attack. By the end of September, however, the French cavalrymen still had their swords sheathed and their horses tethered. Lloyd George was convinced that Joffre would never admit defeat and that the fighting would drag on for weeks to no purpose while the British position in the East crumbled.[60]

On September 30, he lunched secretly with the important Unionist leader Lord Milner and Geoffrey Dawson, the influential editor of the *Times,* who was more under the influence of Milner than his employer, Northcliffe. A meeting place, incidentally, had been difficult to arrange. Dawson had first suggested his home. But Lloyd George had balked when informed that Reginald McKenna, his bitter rival, lived next door. McKenna would surely inform Asquith that Lloyd George was conspiring with the opposition. Hence Milner's residence, which was "opposite to a blank wall," was chosen. At this luncheon, Lloyd George attacked Kitchener's and Asquith's stand on compulsion, expressed his pessimism about the offensive in France, and suggested a shake-up of the government. He wanted a small committee with "full responsibility" to replace the Dardanelles Committee, which was too large a body to act decisively. Time was running out. Using the lexicon of a golfer, Lloyd George warned that the enemy was " 'four up and five to play.' "[61]

Lloyd George's stand on compulsion and his unrelenting support of Balkan intervention further weakened a government that seemed in the process of disintegration. The collapse of Britain's "Eastern" strategy in conjunction with the unsuccessful attack in the West and Russia's great retreat put almost everyone's nerves on edge. Kitchener, worn down by the responsibilities of his office, was especially affected. He cornered Hankey on September 30 and spent almost an hour venting his anger against his critics, who, of course, included most prominently Lloyd George. "He was almost in a hysterical condition; I couldn't have believed it possible; he even talked seriously of resigning,"[61] Hankey recorded in his diary.

As Anglo-French troop ships neared Salonika, Britain was still without a coherent Balkan policy. Were troops to be sent in just to influence Balkan opinion or was the expedition designed to be a military operation to save Serbia? As Lloyd George's ally, Sir Edward Carson, succinctly put it: "Were we simply going to make a demonstration or to open up a great campaign?"[62] The indecision and confusion which characterized British policy was understandable. The tangled Balkan situation contained many uncertainties. What was occurring in Greece at this juncture was typical of the whole muddled situation. Venizelos indicated that Allied troops would be welcome at Salonika. But King Constantine, who was married to the kaiser's sister, expressed opposition. Thus it was not even known if the Anglo-French force on its way to Salonika would be greeted as friend or foe.

A further brake on large-scale involvement in the Balkans was supplied by the British military. Two important memoranda were prepared by the general staff dealing with Balkan operations. The first, dated September 24, admitted that it was probably too late to do anything to save Serbia if the Central Powers attacked before November 1. The second, dated October 2, expressed concern that the German threat to Serbia might be a clever ploy "to induce the entente powers to disseminate their forces." Further, "the General Staff are of opinion that the defeat of the German Army in the Western theatre of war is still the main strategical objective and that, so long as this is so, the balance of advantage is against the employment of any Allied troops in the Balkan theater which could possibly be thrown into the scale in France, unless it can be shown that the defeat of Serbia would more than counterbalance success by the Allies in the main theatre."[63] These general staff appreciations, it should be noted, were a result of a change in late September in the way in which the civilians were informed of the strategy and progress of war. Kitchener's muddled and inconsistent strategic advice had forced Asquith to strengthen the general staff. Sir James Wolfe Murray—called a "feeble old man"[64] by Hankey—was replaced by the handsome and professional Lieutenant-General Sir Archibald Murray, who had been chief of staff of the British Expeditionary Force. On Asquith's instructions, the general staff now began to provide the government with frequent appreciations of the military situation.[65] This new arrangement helped make the "Western" stance—the view of the general staff—the dominant strategy of the government.

On October 5, the first contingents of the Anglo-French force of 13,000 men landed at Salonika. The British contribution, the 10th Division, arrived fresh from Gallipoli attired in cotton khaki shorts, clothing totally unsuited for the severe Balkan winter. Tents arrived without tent poles. After nine months of scheming and wheedling, Lloyd George finally had his khaki in the Balkans. But it was too little too late. Because King Constantine opposed his policies, Venizelos resigned on the same day that the Allied troops landed. This placed the whole operation in even greater jeopardy. In fact, if Venizelos had resigned a few days earlier, it is unlikely that the Allied soldiers would have gone ashore.

The Dardanelles Committee met in a very frustrated and anxious mood on October 6. The Balkan situation looked hopeless. Britain was even confronted with the possibility of a Balkan "Belgium." Because of Constantine's hostility, London was open to the charge of violating the neutrality of Greece. Furthermore, a potentially hostile Greek force was now placed along the Allied lines of communication to Serbia. Despite the great odds against a successful British effort in the Balkans, Lloyd George plunged ahead. "Surely it would be better to make our stand against the German eruption in the East, where we would have the co-operation of the excellent Serbian army, than elsewhere," he argued. His refusal to recognize the futility of sending aid to Serbia at this point infuriated his colleagues. Unusually strong language was directed against him. "Madness" was the way in which Churchill characterized military operations from Salonika under the circumstances. "Unthinkable" was Grey's response to Lloyd George's suggestion that Greece's neutrality should be ignored. The only support he gained was from Carson, who was smoldering with discontent over the government's previous lackadaisical attitude toward the defense of Serbia. In the end, the Dardanelles Committee decided to stop any more British troops from being sent to Salonika until the Greek political situation was in clearer focus.[66]

The next day the Dardannelles Committee continued its discussion of the deteriorating situation in the East. Telegrams just received from the military attaché at Nish made it clear that an Austro-German attack on Serbia was imminent. Lloyd George insisted that the Gallipoli campaign was now doomed because the Germans would soon be at Constantinople. But he drew back from asking that the British forces there be withdrawn at once. Perhaps fearing that such a suggestion would damage his compulsionist ties with Churchill and the Unionist leader Curzon, he asked only that "a scheme for evacuation" be developed. The Welshman also repeatedly asked for a careful study by the newly revitalized general staff of the military situation in the Near East. This was a hit at Churchill and especially Kitchener, who were both opposed to breaking off the Gallipoli operation.[67]

Lloyd George had his way. Asquith created a special committee of naval and military experts to examine the question over the weekend. The advice of this body was a cruel disappointment to Lloyd George. The generals and admirals assumed a strong "Western" stance, slamming the door on British involvement in the Balkans to save Serbia.

As the British leaders debated, the Central Powers acted. On October 6–7, Austro-German forces launched an attack against Serbia. By the eighth the enemy occupied Belgrade. Meanwhile, the Bulgarians ended their wobbly neutrality and moved to sever Serbia's link to Salonika, crossing the Serbian frontier east and southeast of Nish.

As Bulgaria massed her troops on Serbia's eastern frontier on the eleventh, the Dardanelles Committee held one of its unhappiest meetings. Largely because of French pressure, the government was still committed to sending additional troops to the East. To the dismay of Lloyd George, the prime minister suggested that these troops be used to launch a new attack in Gallipoli. Kitchener minced no words in describing the importance of Gallipoli, noting that the abandonment of that peninsula "would be the most disastrous event in the history of the Empire."

Lloyd George and Sir Edward Carson were more concerned about the abandonment of Serbia. Lloyd George "thought that if Great Britain abandoned Serbia, the whole of the East would point to the way she abandoned her friends, and that Germany was the country to be followed. . . . It seemed to him a very serious thing to abandon Serbia." In spite of his strong plea for Serbia, Lloyd George was still unwilling to break with Unionists such as Curzon, who feared that the evacuation of Gallipoli would do irreparable damage to the British position in the East. "It also seemed that it would be a great disaster to withdraw from Gallipoli," he noted, "but at the same time if we made another effort there which failed, it would double the number of men we might lose."

The last part of the meeting was taken up by a discussion of Serbia, which the majority of the British leaders were obviously prepared to write off. Serbia was not to be promised assistance. Nor were the soldiers already at Salonika to proceed through Greece north to Serbia. The only concrete decision made by the Dardanelles Committee was to send a "specially selected General" to the Near East to study the Gallipoli and Salonika operations. Later, once Joffre's offensive was over, troops would be transferred to Egypt for possible use in one or the other theaters.[68]

Lloyd George emerged from the cabinet room in a dark mood. For months he had played the role of Cassandra. But the generals who wanted to concentrate on the German army in the West and the civilians who favored the Dardanelles over the Balkans had ignored him. That evening, overwhelmed by a feeling of impotence, he paced back and forth, dictating a bitter memorandum for the eyes of his colleagues, especially Kitchener, whom he largely blamed for the Serbia catastrophe:

> It perplexes the mere civilian to find any explanation for the neglect of the military authorities to provide against so disastrous a blow to our Empire, when it was so clear to any careful observer that it was impending. It is incredible that the fifth day after the blow had actually fallen finds us without a plan—unless the sending of some general—not yet fixed upon—to the eastern Mediterranean to account for a scheme of operations can be called a plan.[69]

Ignoring the military's solid technical arguments against a British rescue mission, he continued to emphasize political considerations in support of his Balkan strategy. Both the empire and British prestige must be protected. Furthermore, the government's dilatoriness would have serious political consequences at home. He noted, "The Cabinet may depend upon it that when it becomes clear to the British public that we have been taken by surprise and that we have not made the slightest preparation to counter the German thrust, confidence will vanish in our capacity to conduct the War, and rightly so."[70]

On the twelfth he made a last-ditch effort to help Serbia. His ally was Churchill, although relations between the "heavenly twins" were strained because of Churchill's strong Dardanelles views. First, he and Churchill "swooped down" on an exhausted Kitchener with a telegram offering Greece and Rumania 150,000 men immediately if they would support Serbia.[71] With Kitchener's approval, they then descended on the prime minister, who was unable to resist their goading. In fact, the number of soldiers promised was raised to 200,000.[72]

The telegrams were sent, but Greece and Rumania remained on the fence. German actions spoke louder than British promises. Meanwhile, the small British force in Greece advanced to the Bulgarian border—but no farther. "Britain," it has been written, "like a timid bather, would not go in above her knees."[73] The French, however, appeared ready to risk drowning. They continued to push north toward Nish along the road and railway through the Vardar valley.

An explanation of French policy in the Near East is necessary. As early as February, Lloyd George, as we have seen, had discovered "Eastern" sentiment among the French politicians, especially Briand. This civilian inclination to divert French troops to the East had been reinforced by the curious case of General Sarrail, the hero of the Radical-Socialists and a potential successor to Joffre. In July, Joffre dismissed Sarrail from command of the Third Army. This provided an outcry from the left and threatened the "Sacred Union." To placate his supporters, the Viviani government appointed Sarrail to the French Eastern Expeditionary Corps, which was a "nonexistent army."[74] Later, in October, Sarrail was sent to Greece to take command of the French forces there. In Greece he served as a magnet to attract political support for a bigger Balkan effort. The French also felt it a point of honor to support Serbia. Even Joffre exclaimed, "On ne peut pas faire autrement." But the French commander in chief refused to release more than three divisions.[75] Hence Paris expected the British to bear much of the burden of sending troops to the Balkans. When a new government was formed under Briand in late October, French pressure on London intensified.

By mid-October it appeared that Lloyd George could do little more to save Serbia. But he was not without influence and resources in attacking the men he held responsible—especially Kitchener—for leaving Serbia in the lurch. He talked of resignation.[76] But, unlike Carson, who did resign, he was more inclined by his combative nature to seek the resignation of others. Kitchener was his primary target, although he felt that Asquith must share the responsibility for the failure of British arms and diplomacy in the East.[77] Working with Churchill and the Unionists, he put tremendous pressure on the prime minister over the issue of compulsion, threatening to wreck the government. Asquith's response was to draw closer to Kitchener. "I should like you to realize," he wrote the head of the War Office, who appeared to be wavering on compulsion, "that what is now going on is being engineered by men (Curzon & Ll. George & some others) whose real objection [sic] is to oust you. . . . So long as you and I stand together, we carry the whole country with us. Otherwise the Deluge!"[78]

Opposition to Kichener was now at epidemic levels within the government. At the conclusion of a cabinet meeting on October which Asquith did not attend because of illness, the members of the Dardanelles Committee stayed on with the exception of Kitchener. It was their decision that Kitchener had to go.[79] There was also wide support for Lloyd George's view that the argumentative and cumbersome Dardanelles Committee should be replaced by a smaller committee. Asquith was prepared to accept this suggestion, contemplating the creation of a small body composed of himself, and the heads of the War Office and Admirality.[80] Such a body, of course, could only serve to magnify Kitchener's influence. Lloyd George was determined that any reorganization of the government must destroy—not enhance—Kitchener's power.[81] On October 31, he wrote Asquith a blunt letter:

> . . . unless there is a complete change in the War Office the new Council will be just as impotent as the Cabinet and old Council have proved themselves to be. Our War Administration have committed every blunder that the enemy would wish them to be guilty of. . . .
> If I thought the appointment of a small Committee would put an end to all these amazing series of blunders, I should be satisfied. But I have gone on for months always thinking that every mistake must surely be the last, and finding myself constantly surprised by the capacity of our great war lords for blundering.

Lloyd George ended his letter with a threat of resignation, warning "that I can no longer be responsible for the present war direction."[82]

Lloyd George's threat to leave the government and the tidal wave of opposition to Kitchener forced Asquith to act. A master political tactician, he chose an indirect approach to evade a violent reaction from the public. Kitchener would be sent away from London on a special fact-finding mission to the Mediterranean. In his absence, the prime minister would take over the War Office. "We avoid by this method," he assured Lloyd George, "the immediate supersession of K[itchener] as War Minister, while attaining the same result."[83]

On the morning of November 4, Kitchener attended what many thought would be his last cabinet meeting. Just before adjournment, this bronzed national hero rose to leave the company of ministers who no longer had faith in him. He nodded in the direction of Asquith and then slowly walked to the door. No words were exchanged. Lloyd George, as he later confessed to Miss Stevenson, was touched by Kitchener's humiliation.[84]

Lloyd George's happiness over the fact that he might never again cross strategical swords with Kitchener was diluted by Asquith's reorganization of the government. When the new committee held its first properly constituted meeting on November 5, Lloyd George, Grey, Asquith, and Balfour, who had replaced Churchill at the Admiralty, sat around the table. The first sea lord, Admiral Sir H. B. Jackson, and the C.I.G.S. were also in attendance to offer advice on military questions.[85] On the eleventh, however, Asquith told the House that the membership of the War Committee included himself, Lloyd George, Balfour, McKenna (exchequer), and Bonar Law (colonies). The presence of his archenemy McKenna enraged the Welshman.[86] Of more concern was the size of the new War Committee. When Grey and the military advisers were included, the membership of the committee swelled to eight or more. To Lloyd George, this was further confirmation of the prime minister's irresolution.

Much of the War Committee's attention was taken up by the British position in the Near East. What made a decision so difficult was Britain's precarious political position in the East. In Hankey's words, "It resembles a line of children's bricks standing on end: all that is required is the momentum to upset the first brick, which causes the next one to upset its neighbour."[87] The first brick was Serbia and the last bricks in the line were Persia, Afghanistan, India, Tripoli, Algiers, and Morocco. If Britain were going to make a stand in the Near East, the ministers' choice was clearly Gallipoli rather than Salonika. Only Lloyd George was enthusiastic about the Balkans.

Even after all hope of saving Serbia was gone, Lloyd George clung stubbornly to his Balkan strategy. He just could not bring himself to abdicate the strategical direction of the war to the "Westerners." Believing that the British generals were "crowding troops into France"[88] in a futile effort to breach impregnable German defenses, he continued to argue in favor to a major campaign in southeastern Europe which "would mean lengthening the German line across Europe, and so attenuating it and making it weaker everywhere."[89] He remained convinced that khaki in the Balkans would eventually result in Greece's and Rumania's entry into the war on the Entente side, substantially increasing Entente numbers. He was prepared to admit that a major Balkan offensive could not be attempted in 1915. But what about 1916? Do not "lock the door" to the Balkans and "throw away the key," he impassionedly pleaded with his colleagues.[90] No longer equivocal about the abandonment of Gallipoli, he wanted British troops there transferred to Salonika. The Welshman pointedly warned the War Committee that it "would be assuming great responsibility if it came to a decision to keep our forces on the Peninsula."[91]

The fact that Britain's leading generals were united in their opposition to staying in the Balkans did not shake Lloyd George's confidence in his own views.[92] Sir William Robertson, the chief of staff of the British Expeditionary Force, whose views were now frequently before the government, argued that Germany—the main enemy—could only be defeated in France and Flanders.[93] In defense of his "Western" stance, Robertson even insisted that the recently concluded Anglo-French attacks at Loos and Champagne had "achieved brilliant tactical results" and represented "a real victory."[94] If these were "victories," Lloyd George wanted no more of them. He was convinced that the "expert" opinions expressed by the "Westerners" were parochial and consequently biased.[95] Proof of this bias was the strong support that some French and especially Russian generals in November gave to his ideas. In fact, the Russian general staff could not have been more Lloyd Georgian in its view, insisting that the Entente's best strategy was a "great turning movement in south-eastern Europe."[96]

In spite of (or perhaps because of) his usual persistence and aggressiveness, the Welshman's views were shaken off by the ministers as dew drops from the lion's mane. Only Bonar Law gave him tentative support.[97] As Balfour patiently explained: "The time for attacking the Central Powers in the South-East was over, and we should withdraw every man from Salonica to Egypt in [*sic*] the Western front. With a hostile Bulgaria, an unfriendly Greece, and a crushed Serbia, the order of things had changed. We must simplify our strategy."[98] As November came to a close, irresistible momentum built up for the complete withdrawal from the eastern Mediterranean. Weighing heavily on the minds of the British leaders was the belief that Britain was dangerously close to a war with Greece because of the presence of French and British soldiers in that country.

Before the British retreated, however, French opinion had to be changed. The surprise reappearance of Kitchener like a ghost from the grave to haunt Lloyd George helped nerve the British government to challenge Paris. Kitchener, as we have seen, was not expected to return to London. But Asquith's clever arrangement to keep him in the East had come unstuck. As Kitchener was on his way to the Mediterranean, the *Globe,* on November 5, thundered: "Lord Kitchener, acting with a single eye to the interests of his King and country, has tolerated manoeuvres and machinations which none but the patriotic soldier would have endured for a day." With the public aware of the dissension between the head of the War Office and his colleagues in the government, Asquith trembled at the prospect of keeping Kitchener in the East if he wanted to return; and he did.

On December 1, just back from the East, Kitchener took his usual place in the cabinet room when the War Committee met. He bluntly told the ministers that Britain, even if she desired, could not hold Salonika. In fact, if Germany attacked, "the Greeks would probably join in."[99] Two days later he went further. He presented an ultimatum to Asquith. If Britain did not withdraw at once, he would resign.[100]

An Anglo-French conference to resolve the difference between London and Paris was subsequently held at Calais on December 4. One British minister was conspicuous by his absence. For obvious reasons, Asquith left Lloyd George at home to enjoy a weekend with Miss Stevenson at Walton Heath. At Calais the British delegation was adamant that military considerations should determine the future of the Allied expeditionary force in the Balkans. With great reluctance the French agreed that preparations should be made to evacuate Salonika.[101]

Although it appeared that evacuationist sentiment had triumphed at Calais, appearances were deceiving. When Briand returned to Paris he was faced with a revolt by the Socialists in his government. The "Sacred Union" was threatened. On the other side of the Channel, the British delegation was greeted by a skeptical Lloyd George. After going through the telegrams between Paris and London, it was obvious to the Welshman that the Briand government still wanted to retain an Allied foothold in the Balkans.[102] This belief was soon confirmed by his friend and counterpart, Albert Thomas, the French minister of munitions, who was sent by the French cabinet to London in a desperate attempt to use Lloyd George to reverse the position of the British government. The French could not have found a more willing accomplice.

Accompanied by Bonar Law, Lloyd George had his interview with Thomas on December 6. Armed with Thomas's strongly expressed views, Lloyd George berated his colleagues in a late afternoon meeting of the War Committee in the prime minister's room at the House of Commons. He warned his government that the Calais decision threatened to destroy the Briand government and undermine the Anglo-French alliance.

Kitchener riposted with the statement that "if it were decided to reinforce the troops at Salonica and maintain that force for the whole winter, it might result in our losing the war, and he could not be responsible for such a policy." Kitchener's hysterical analysis had little impact. Pushed by Lloyd George the ministers were prepared to subordinate military considerations to political considerations. If there were "any breach in the Alliance the war would be lost," Bonar Law emphasized.

Earlier in August Kitchener had won approval for Joffre's disastrous autumn offensive by stressing Britain's obligations to support her Continental allies without regard for the merits of Joffre's strategy. Now Lloyd George was using this same argument with success to block an Allied retreat from the Balkans. These two incidents underline the haphazard manner in which critical military and political decisions were made in the anti-German coalition in 1915.

To his credit Lloyd George on this occasion pointed to the lack of coordination and planning in Entente policy. He said "that a scheme for bringing the war to a conclusion appeared not even to have been thought out, or at least shown to the War Committee. He inquired if it was still the idea to press for a decision on the West, and if it was possible to do so, or if the idea was to starve Germany out. It seemed to him that we were endeavouring to carry on the war by a piecemeal policy of action in different directions, such as Gallipoli, Salonica, Egypt." Kitchener retorted that "he had so far seen many schemes put forward that would not end the war, but he thought the time was not yet ripe to try and formulate a plan which would do so." Lloyd George's sarcastic reply was that "he was certain the German General Staff was in possession of a plan."[103]

In retrospect, Lloyd George's outburst, whatever his intentions, was directed as much against the "Easterners" as the "Westerners." As a matter of fact, the general staff had a "plan" to win the war: the concentration of British military power on the western front. In the final analysis, this approach differed little from the strategy of the German high command. To Lloyd George, however, the continued pounding of the German defenses without decisive results was a reflection of the intellectual bankruptcy of the British military.

The one-two punch of Thomas and Lloyd George resulted in the British war leaders deciding to await the decision of Allied military leaders who were meeting at Joffre's headquarters. Murray's report of the proceedings of this conference to the War Committee on the eighth seemed to vindicate Lloyd George's position. Although no important British general could be found to support the Salonika venture, the Serbian, French, Italian, and Russian military representatives were opposed to evacuation.[104] Kitchener and Grey were then sent to Paris to calm the troubled waters with the result that a decision to evacuate Salonika was put off.

Lloyd George's position during the collapse of Serbia and the debate over the evacuation of Salonika and Gallipoli further isolated him in the high councils of the government. His support of the abandonment of Gallipoli estranged him from the "Easterners." He had been proven right about the German threat to Serbia and Kitchener's incompetence and would be proven right about compulsion. But this did not improve his standing with Asquith and the Liberals. To the contrary, his refusal to bend, to go along with the majority, made him a divisive and to some even dangerous force in the government. The way in which the French had been able to use him to reverse the decision at Calais to evacuate Salonika was a case in point. Despite the hostility he provoked, Lloyd George made no effort to be conciliatory. He was not above assuming an "I told you so" posture. On December 20, he went a step further, rising in the House of Commons to deliver a biting speech which could be interpreted as an attempt to disassociate himself from the "wait and see" attitude of Asquith's government: "Too late in moving here. Too late in arriving there. Too late in coming to this decision, too late in starting with enterprises. Too late in preparing. In this War the footsteps of the Allied forces have been dogged by the mocking spectre of 'Too Late.' "[105]

It is sometimes assumed that Lloyd George's unrelenting pressure over munitions, compulsion, and grand strategy is explained by his boundless ambition to supplant Asquith. His growing disenchantment with Kitchener did indeed inevitably draw him into conflict with Asquith, who for months lacked the courage to replace, demote, or overrule the government's adviser on military policy. But there is no real evidence to suggest that it was Asquith rather than Kitchener whom Lloyd George hoped to remove.

Asquith himself finally came to realize that Kitchener must have his powers considerably diminished. But he still wanted to retain the protective umbrella that Britain's most popular soldier offered to the government. As he confided to Hankey, he desired a solution which would enable the government to "use his great name and authority as a popular idol, both here, in the Colonies, & abroad."[106] In early December, Kitchener acquiesced to making leadership of the War Office little more than a figurehead position. Earlier he had lost munitions to Lloyd George; now the strategical direction of the war was stripped from him and given to Robertson, who replaced Murray as chief of the Imperial general staff on December 23. Only recruiting and the administration of the War Office remained in his hands. Kitchener's diminished role did not cool Lloyd George's conflict with the army leadership. The future was to hold a confrontation between the Welshman and Robertson that made the former's differences with Kitchener seem minor by comparison.

NOTES

1. Frances Lloyd George, *Years That Are Past*, p. 52.

2. Ibid., p. 40.

3. A. J. P. Taylor, ed., *My Darling Pussy: The Letters of Lloyd George and Frances Stevenson* (1975), p. 5.

4. Lloyd George to Margaret Lloyd George, July 24, 1924, quoted in Morgan, *Family Letters*, p. 203.

5. War Council, February 24, 1915, CAB 42/1/42.

6. Lloyd George, *War Memoirs*, 1:75.

7. Ibid., p. 77.

8. Entry of March 15, 1915, *Diaries of C. P. Scott*, p. 120.

9. Asquith, *Memories and Reflections*, 2:83; for the exchange of letters between Kitchener and Lloyd George, see Lloyd George MSS, C/5/7/18–19.

10. Lloyd George, *War Memoirs*, 1:119–20.

11. Gilbert, *Challenge of War, 1914–1916*, p. 553.

12. Beaverbrook, *Politicians and the War, 1914–1916*, p. 88.

13. Ibid. Beaverbrook's statement is the only evidence to link Lloyd George with the initiation of the press campaign. Lloyd George's correspondence with Northcliffe over the shell crisis came *after* the press campaign against Kitchener began. See Lloyd George MSS, D/18/1/1–10.

14. It is significant that Northcliffe had earlier written Sir John French: "A short and very vigorous statement from you to a private correspondent (the usual way of making things public in England) would, I believe, render the Government's position impossible, and enable you to secure the publication of that which would tell the people here the truth and thus bring public pressure upon the Government to stop men and munitions pouring away to the Dardanelles, as they are at present." Northcliffe to Sir John French, May 1, 1915, Northcliffe MSS, vol. 7.

15. Lieut.-Col. C. à Court Repington, *The First World War, 1914–1918*. 2 vols. (1920), 1:39, and Repington to Lloyd George, May 17, 1915, Lloyd George MSS, D/18/6/1.

16. Lloyd George, *War Memoirs*, 1:134.

17. Bonar Law's and Lloyd George's accounts of this meeting agree in their essentials. See Hankey Diary, October 6, 1920, 1/5, and Lloyd George, *War Memoirs*, 1:135–36.

18. Stephen Koss, *Asquith* (1976), p. 187.

19. Entry of May 18, 1915, *A Diary by Frances Stevenson*, p. 51. "Pussy" was the nickname given Miss Stevenson by her young students when she taught at a boarding school at Wimbledon.

20. Ibid.

21. Ibid. On May 19, Lloyd George told Riddell that "Mrs. L. G. had begged him not to go to the War Office and that Mrs. Asquith had done the same. He said he did not want to go." Entry of May 19, 1915, *Lord Riddell's War Diary*, p. 89.

22. Lloyd George to Margaret Lloyd George, May 20, 1915, quoted in Morgan, *Family Letters*, p. 177.

23. Stephen Koss, "The Destruction of Britain's Last Liberal Government," *Journal of Modern History* 40 (June 1968): 257–77, argues that Lloyd George was involved with Balfour and Churchill in a conspiracy against Asquith. Also see his *Asquith*, pp. 192–94. Hazlehurst, however, has convincingly demonstrated that Koss's thesis is seriously flawed. See his *Politicians at War, July 1914 to May 1915*, pp. 240–45 and 255–60.

24. Churchill to Asquith, May 17, 1915, quoted in Gilbert, *Companion, Part 2, Documents: May 1915–December 1916*, p. 898.

25. Lloyd George to Asquith, May 19, 1915, Lloyd George MSS, C/6/11/40.

26. Entry of May 24, 1915, *A Diary by Frances Stevenson*, p. 53.

27. George V's firm support of Kitchener may also have been a consideration for the prime

minister. The king told Esher "that whatever happened he meant to support Lord K[itchener] even if it led to the fall of the Government." Esher Diary, May 15, 1915, 2/14.

28. A. J. P. Taylor, *English History, 1914–1945* (1965), p. 35; also see Lloyd George's minute on the memorandum, "A Suggestion for neutralising the power of the trench and obstacle," September 23, 1915, by Major A. I. R. Glasford, Lloyd George MSS, D/10/6/2.

29. Lloyd George, *War Memoirs*, 1:360.

30. Lloyd George's reputation has been further enhanced by a recent study of the Ministry of Munitions. See R. J. Q. Adams, *Arms and the Wizard: Lloyd George and the Ministry of Munitions* (1978).

31. Entry of June 16, 1915, *Diaries of C. P. Scott*, p. 128.

32. Lloyd George, *War Memoirs*, 1:327–32.

33. Dardanelles Committee, July 5, 1915, CAB 42/3/7.

34. Ibid.

35. Robertson to Wigram, May 16, 1915, RV GV Q2522/3/175, and Esher Diary, May 21 and June 30, 1915, 2/14.

36. Wilson Diary, July 5, 1915.

37. Hankey Diary, July 6, 1915, 1/1; Gilbert, *Challenge of War, 1914–1916*, p. 672, and George H. Cassar, *Kitchener: Architect of Victory* (1977), p. 381.

38. Hankey Diary, July 6, 1915, 1/1.

39. Kitchener, "An Appreciation of the Military Situation in the Future," June 26, 1915, CAB 37/130/27.

40. "Report of the Proceedings at a Meeting of the War Policy Cabinet, held at 11, Downing Street, on Wednesday, the 18th August, 1915, at 3:30 P.M.," CAB 37/132/28. Lloyd George, of course, was also interested in getting skilled workers for the munitions industry.

41. Hankey, *Supreme Command*, 1:426–27.

42. Victor Bonham-Carter, *Soldier True: The Life and Times of Field-Marshal Sir William Robertson, 1860–1933* (1963), pp. 132–33.

43. Dardanelles Committee, August 20, 1915, CAB 42/3/16.

44. Howard, *Continental Commitment*, p. 57.

45. Cassar, *French and the Dardanelles*, pp. 151–80.

46. Bonham Carter to Lloyd George, August 21, 1915, Lloyd George MSS, D/18/2/5.

47. Dardanelles Committee, August 31, 1915, CAB 42/3/20.

48. War Council, January 13 and February 9, 1915, CAB 42/1/16 and 33.

49. Lloyd George, *War Memoirs*, 1:308.

50. Dardanelles Committee, September 3, 1915, CAB 42/3/23.

51. Entry of September 15, 1915, *A Diary by Frances Stevenson*, p. 57.

52. Asquith to George V, September 10, 1915, CAB 37/134/8.

53. Cassar, *French and the Dardanelles*, pp. 175–89.

54. Entry of September 2, 1915, *A Diary by Frances Stevenson*, p. 56.

55. See files D/16 and D/17 in Lloyd George MSS.

56. See, for example, Dardanelles Committee, August 27, 1915, CAB 42/3/17.

57. Entry of September 15, 1915, *A Diary by Frances Stevenson*, p. 59.

58. Ibid.

59. Dardanelles Committee, September 23, 1915, CAB 42/3/28.

60. Entry of October 1, 1915, *Diaries of C. P. Scott*, pp. 139–40.

61. Hankey Diary, September 30, 1915, 1/1.

62. Dardanelles Committee, October 4, 1915, CAB 42/4/2.

63. General staff memoranda of September 24 and October 2, 1915, CAB 42/3/29 and 42/4/2.

64. Hankey Diary, May 18, 1915, 1/1.

65. Asquith to Kitchener, September 23, 1915, Kitchener MSS, P.R.O. 30/57/76.

66. Dardanelles Committee, October 6, 1915, CAB 42/4/3.

67. Ibid., October 7, 1915, CAB 42/4/4.

68. Ibid., October 11, 1915, CAB 42/4/6.

69. Memorandum by Lloyd George, October 14, 1915, CAB 37/136/9, Frances Lloyd George, *Years That Are Past*, p. 83, and entry of October 12, 1915, *A Diary by Frances Stevenson*, pp. 66–67.

70. Memorandum by Lloyd George, October 14, 1915, CAB 37/136/9.

71. Esher Diary, October 12, 1915, 2/15.

72. Hankey Diary, October 13, 1915, 1/1.

73. Falls, *Great War*, p. 138.

74. Cruttwell, *History of the Great War*, p. 226.

75. Esher Diary, October 8, 1915, 2/15, Jan Karl Tanenbaum, *General Maurice Sarrail, 1856–1929: The French Army and Left Wing Politics* (1974), pp. 57–69, and Cassar, *French and the Dardanelles*, pp. 181–235.

76. Entry of October 12, 1915, *A Diary by Frances Stevenson*, p. 67.

77. Lloyd George told Miss Stevenson that "if he [Asquith] were in the pay of the Germans he could not be of more complete use to them." Ibid., p. 68.

78. Asquith to Kitchener, October 17, 1915, Kitchener MSS, P.R.O. 30/57/76.

79. Gilbert, *Challenge of War, 1914–1916*, p. 710.

80. Ibid., p. 712.

81. Lloyd George informed Scott that he was more concerned about the military's uncertain direction of the war than he was about compulsion. Entry of November 1–2, 1915, *Diaries of C. P. Scott*, pp. 152–53.

82. Lloyd George to Asquith, October 31, 1915, Lloyd George MSS, D/18/2/11.

83. Asquith to Lloyd George, November 3, 1915, Lloyd George MSS, D/18/2/12.

84. Entry of November 15, 1915, *A Diary by Frances Stevenson*, p. 72.

85. War Committee, November 5, 1915, CAB 42/5/3.

86. Entry of November 15, 1915, *A Diary by Frances Stevenson*, pp. 72–73.

87. Hankey, "The Future Military Policy at the Dardanelles," November 29, 1915, CAB 42/5/25.

88. War Committee, November 16, 1915, CAB 42/5/14.

89. Ibid., November 20, 1915, CAB 42/5/17.

90. Ibid., December 6, 1915, CAB 42/6/4.

91. Ibid., November 16, 1915, CAB 42/5/14.

92. See, for example, A. J. Murray, "Views of the General Staff on the Present Situation at Salonica and in the Balkans, with Deductions as to our Wisest Course of Action there," November 23, 1915, CAB 42/6/4.

93. Robertson, "Memorandum on the Conduct of the War," November 8, 1915, CAB 42/5/6.

94. Robertson, "Memorandum for the Meeting of Representatives of the Allied Armies," November 25, 1915, CAB 42/5/13.

95. War Committee, December 6, 1915, CAB 42/5/13.

96. See memoranda by Hankey and A. J. Murray, November 29 and December 13, 1915, CAB 42/5/25 and 42/6/7. Also see entry of November 24, 1915, *A Diary by Frances Stevenson*, p. 79.

97. As early as June, Bonar Law had expressed sympathy with Lloyd George's desire to concentrate on the weakest link of the enemy alliance. See Bonar Law to Lloyd George, June 28, 1915, Lloyd George MSS, D/17/8/2.

98. War Committee, November 23, 1915, CAB 42/5/20.

99. Ibid., December 1, 1915, CAB 42/6/1.

100. Asquith to George V, December 3, 1915, CAB 37/139/7.

101. See D. J. Dutton, "The Calais Conference of December 1915," *The Historical Journal* 21 (March 1978): 143–56.

102. Entry of December 6, 1915, *A Diary by Frances Stevenson*, p. 84.
103. War Committee, December 6, 1915, CAB 42/6/4.
104. Ibid., December 8, 1915, CAB 42/6/6.
105. *H. C. Deb.*, 5th series, vol. 77 (December 20, 1915).
106. Hankey Diary, December 8, 1915, 1/1.

4

"Westerners" in the Ascendancy: The Somme Offensive

ASQUITH'S shakeup of the high command in late 1915 included the recall of Sir John French, whose political machinations, inept direction of the Battle of Loos, and constant bickering with Joffre and Kitchener had been his undoing. Sir Douglas Haig's appointment as commander in chief of the British Expeditionary Force on December 19, along with Sir William Robertson's selection a few days later as C.I.G.S., created one of the most formidable and important partnerships in British military history.

Haig and Robertson were very much opposites in background and demeanor. Of Norman origin, the Haigs of Bemerside went back at least to the twelfth century. Among Britain's social elite, Haig was educated at Oxford and Sandhurst, went shooting with the Prince of Wales while at Staff College, and married a maid of honor to Queen Alexandra in the private chapel of Buckingham Palace. The son of a tailor and village postmaster, Robertson's first employment had been as a domestic servant, once serving as a footman for the Cardigan family in Northamptonshire. At the age of seventeen he joined the 16th Lancers as a trooper over the opposition of his mother, who wrote, "I would rather Bury you than see you in a red coat."[1] The remarkable climb of this rugged North countryman through the ranks to field marshal found no parallel in the British army.

Handsome, dignified, and always immaculately attired, Haig seemed perfectly cast as the commander in chief of the British Expeditionary Force. Robertson, in all likelihood, would be assigned the role of the tough, steady sergeant. He was stocky and powerfully built, with a thick moustache and a prominent jaw and chin. His eyes beneath his dark and bushy eyebrows were penetrating. Haig walked with a light step. Robertson was ponderous. Their personalities were in equally sharp contrast. Haig was formal and excessively polite. Robertson, or Wully, was earthy and as discreet as a cannon shot. "I've heard different" was his blunt retort to those with whom he disagreed. When angry, his countenance took on the appearance of an approaching storm. Haig kept his temper and emotions under rigid control.

Only a rare tug at his moustache or a stiff thrusting movement of his forearm betrayed any emotion. An excitable individual would be hushed with the words, "Don't fuss."

Robertson was a round peg in a round hole. Haig, an extremely complex individual, has largely eluded his biographers. A bundle of contradictions (the same has rightly been said of Lloyd George), Haig seemed two persons. There was the public Haig, who seemed generous to a fault, and then there was the private Haig, with a petty and malicious streak which his diary reveals. He was as loyal to his subordinates as he was disloyal to his superiors. In the end even Robertson was discarded. After listening to Haig omit all reference to him in a speech to the army commanders at the Senior Service Club after the armistice, Robertson angrily told a friend, "I'll never go farting with 'aig again."[2] Harshly critical of the ungentlemanly behavior of others, Haig himself intrigued against his fellow officers, including Kitchener, Sir Archibald Murray, and French. Methodical and meticulous, he went to the extreme of drawing diagrams in his diary of the seating arrangements of an important conference. Some thought he had a clerk's mind, but he could make difficult and important decisions in a flash, proposing to the girl he married two days after he first met her.

Perhaps Haig's deeply devout nature best explains his conduct during the war. A Scottish Presbyterian, he apparently believed that he was predestined to lead the British army to victory. Before the Somme offensive he wrote his wife two very revealing letters. On June 22 he noted: "*I feel* that every step in my plan has been taken with the Divine help—and I ask daily for aid, not merely in making the plan, but in carrying it out, and this I will continue to do, until the end of all things which concern me on earth." With the guns of the British bombardment crashing in the background on the eve of the attack, he wrote: "I feel that every thing possible for us to do to achieve success has been done. But whether or not we are successful lies in the Powers above. But I *do feel* that in my plans I have been helped by a Power that is not my own.—So I am easy in my mind and ready to do my best whatever happens tomorrow."[3]

Haig's partnership with God was both a great source of strength and of weakness. It unquestionably kept him from flinching as he carried out the bloody task of fighting the German army. On the other hand, the self-assurance and optimism that flowed from his sense of divine mission led him to rely too heavily on his own judgment and instincts. His general staff, headed by his close friend Lieutenant-General Sir Launcelot Kiggell, was his servant rather than adviser. As Esher perceptively noted: "His General Staff seems to be an excellent machine, formed to carry out his ideas and intentions. They initiate nothing."[4]

Haig had made a serious study of war prior to 1914, but the result was often to reinforce preconceived notions which he was slow to alter. He was one of the first generals to recognize the importance of the tank and machine gun, but he often made poor tactical use of the new machines of warfare.[5] His greatest blind spot was his unshakable belief that the cavalry had a vital role to play in modern warfare. Five years of contact with breastworks, barbed wire, and machine guns never altered this view one iota. There is no more damning comment to be made of his leadership of the British Expeditionary Force than this. Dismayed by the failure of the cavalry at Cambrai, he ordered an investigation made for his eyes only. He minuted this report: "They [British cavalry officers] fail to realise that the horse is our weapon, that we can do anything if we use it, and that the German is the feeblest of foes if pushed. . . . Risks must never be considered & the objective must be obtained no matter what the losses are."[6] After the cavalry had gone into action in October 1918, Haig triumphantly noted in his diary: "A great advance has been made today, due greatly to the action of our cavalry."[7] The usually uncritical British official history offers a different judgment on this engagement: "The cavalry had done nothing that the infantry, with artillery support and cyclists, could not have done for itself at less cost; and the supply of the large force of horses with water and forage had greatly interfered with the sending up of ammunition and the rations for the other arms, and with the allotment of the limited water facilities."[8] Perhaps an American new to the western front said it best: "You can't have a cavalry charge 'until you have captured the enemy's last machine gun.' "[9]

The question perhaps should be asked: Was there a better man in 1915 to command the British Expeditionary Force? If it had not been Haig at this juncture, it would have been Robertson, who would have been an improvement over Haig in one respect. Cautious and realistic, Robertson was protective of British manpower and was wary of attacks aimed at a breakthrough or distant objectives. The ghastly losses during the initial stages of the Somme offensive prompted him to make an attempt (behind Haig's back!) to influence the tactics and objectives of the British army. Private letters, which implicitly criticized Haig's leadership, were sent to Kiggell and General Henry S. Rawlinson, the commander of the Fourth Army, who was in charge of executing the offensive. In his direct way, Robertson wrote Rawlinson: "The thing you have got to keep your eye on is that he [the German] does not beat you in having the better man-power policy. . . . all that is needed is the use of common-sense, careful methods, and not to be too hide-bound by the books we used to study before the war."[10]

Haig, however, was the choice of the army in 1915. No one agreed with this more than Robertson. As he told Esher, "I could not have done what he has. I knew he was the only man to command the Army. I might have had the command myself, but I knew he was the better man, and that my place is where I am now."[11] Furthermore, it must be noted that Haig's courage and tenacity were important factors in Britain's ultimate success. He was no genius but he was certainly no dunce either, as John Terraine's prolific pen has demonstrated.[12]

A common meeting ground for Haig and Robertson was their belief that Britain could only attain victory by concentrating against the German army in the West. Robertson's strategical views were those of a textbook general, cautious and conventional rather than imaginative. One can search his strategic appreciations in vain for the element of surprise in warfare. From the start of the conflict he was an unalloyed "Westerner" and his mind was closed to arguments in favor of another theater. His bible was a memorandum that he had written before becoming C.I.G.S.:

The war may end either in the defeat of the Central Powers, in the defeat of the *Entente,* or in mutual exhaustion.

The object of the *Entente* Powers is to bring about the first of these results, which can only be attained by the defeat or exhaustion of the predominant partner in the Central Alliance—Germany. Every plan of operation must therefore be examined from the point of view of its bearing on this result. If it is not, it will have a false basis, and will accordingly lead to false conclusions.[13]

Robertson and Haig also shared a common distaste for politicians in whose company their limited fluency placed them at a disadvantage. Robertson often responded with fierce grunts when questioned; Haig seldom finished his sentences. Before the war Haig had startled his audience when he had presented prizes to the interregimental winners of a cross-country race. "I congratulate you on your running," he had said. "You have run well. I hope you run as well in the presence of the enemy."[14] Lloyd George has often been given most of the blame for his antagonistic relationship with the British high command. And it is true that his aggressiveness and at times devious approach to Haig and Robertson fostered mistrust. But Robertson and Haig were equally to blame. Both men were incapable of working sympathetically with politicians who dared to question their military views. As Haig's head of the intelligence branch at general headquarters, Brigadier-General John Charteris, has written: " 'Politician' with Douglas Haig is synonymous with crooked dealing and wrong sense of values."[15]

The rise of the formidable duo of Haig and Robertson was no accident and had been preceded by backstairs intrigue. Often portrayed as the "bluff, honest soldier," Robertson was in fact a skillful wire puller. Like Haig, he had George V on his side, a fact that often has not received adequate attention. Friendly with the king since his tour of duty at Aldershot, 1907–10, Wully kept in close touch with Buckingham Palace about military policy through the king's equerry, Major Clive Wigram, and private secretary and adviser, Lord Stamfordham. Although the king was keenly aware of his position as a constitutional monarch, he believed that he had a right and a duty to play an active and forceful role in military matters. After all, the army and navy fought in his name.

The king's admiration of Kitchener and his staunch defense of him against his civilian critics did not deter the strong-willed Robertson from voicing opposition to the Dardanelles expedition and complaining about the shortage of shells. "Here we can beat the German," he wrote Wigram on March 24. "No more d——d silly eccentric Dardanelles fiascos, pretty well doomed to failure & in no circumstances likely to help in decisive result. Fancy our fighting on a front from Calais to Constantinople."[16]

As the Dardanelles ventures began to compete with the British commitment to the western front, Robertson came to the conclusion that the only way to bring Kitchener and the "Easterners" to heel was to revitalize the moribund general staff. The support of Haig was easily gained and the machinations began in June 1915.[17] The king through Stamfordham was told:

The Govt. must receive the best military advice at home (Hankey &

George V (flanked by the queen and Mrs. Poincaré) at Abbeville with Sir Douglas Haig in July 1917.

Callwell are I suppose the chief advisers. Ridiculous!) The S. of S. for War has not the time to study matters & formulate advice, in addition to his other work. The General Staff, with a trusted & competent head, should be allowed to function & do the work for which it was designed, & which it alone can do. It has been obliterated. Having the views of the different C's in C., & the advice of the General Staff at home, the Govt. will be in a position to see where they are & what they can best do. The present method of the higher conduct of the war can only lead to disaster.[18]

At about the same time Haig wrote his friend Kiggell, who was then serving as the director of home defence in the War Office: "I do hope your C.G.S. will do something to assert himself and save the Empire from disaster before it is too late."[19] Robertson's and Haig's lobbying may well have been a factor in Asquith's decision to reform the general staff in September. At any rate their criticism of the higher direction of the war was valid.

Wolfe Murray's successor as C.I.G.S., Archibald Murray, was soon in Haig's and Robertson's doghouse. The turning point came when Kitchener, over the opposition of the general staff, decided to send eight divisions from France to Gallipoli in mid-October.[20] On October 17, Robertson, fresh from discussions in London on grand strategy, paid an important visit to Haig at 2:00 P.M. Replacing French with Haig was one topic of discussion, but the two generals also discussed the strategical direction of the war. Because

Murray would not stand up to Kitchener, Haig believed that he was "quite unfit for any responsible position as military *adviser*."[21]

A week later Haig told the king when they dined together that Robertson must be brought to London as C.I.G.S.[22] Meanwhile, Robertson was reprimanding Murray for caving in to Kitchener. "It is of course no use laying down these excellent principles and expressing such entire conviction of their soundness," he wrote on October 21, "unless we are prepared to carry them to their logical conclusion and stand or fall by them."[23]

Kitchener's departure from London in early November to make a survey of the military situation in the East left Asquith in charge of the War Office. Supported by Buckingham Palace, Haig and especially Robertson stepped into the vacuum created by the absence of the government's chief military adviser. On November 15 Robertson reported to Haig from London:

Stamfordham writes that the King is quite sure of the two changes he ought to make in France & the W.O. but that *he* cannot make them. Murray is thought by Stamfordham (who of course does not understand) to be doing *very* well, & I have no doubt he suits the politician for the time being. I feel sure I know exactly what ought to be done, in fact [,] I think & feel the same as you do, but what I can really do is doubtful. . . . I see the King to-night, and the P.M. this morning when he returns from the country![24]

Two days later Robertson informed Haig:

Kitchener is still S. of S. for War and is causing much confusion by acting as such in the Mediterranean. . . . I think K. is the chief trouble. He ought to be moved on but they fear to move him and yet it is hopeless his being away so long as he is Secretary of State.

Thanks to K.'s absence the General Staff have recently made a certain position for themselves and for Murray but the latter is as wobbly as ever. . . .[25]

As Haig and Robertson stirred the pot in Whitehall, the crisis of leadership in the War Office boiled over when Kitchener announced that he was returning to London on November 30.[26] Murray wrote Robertson of Kitchener's return and warned him that the secretary of war would probably make "strong efforts to divert forces from the main theatre to Egypt."[27] Robertson responded by telling Murray to stick to his guns, but he had little hope that he would or could.[28]

At this point Robertson's and Haig's lobbying of the king bore fruit. On December 3, Stamfordham wrote Asquith:

His Majesty is thinking much about Lord Kitchener's position and hears that some people advocate his being appointed C. in C. of all the Forces overseas other than those in France and to be responsible for their operations: that Sir W. Robertson should become C.I.G.S. at the War Office. The King would deprecate the first arrangement. If Kitchener had to direct and be responsible for the operations in the various theatres of war, he would expect to be granted carte blanche as regards both the supply of men & their movement to & employment in the different localities—This would be impossible. . . .

But His Majesty does believe that important advantages would be secured by the transfer of Sir W. Robertson to the post of C.I.G.S. making him responsible only to the *War Council* for whose information and advice he and his staff would deal with all matters of strategy and conduct of war—Lord K. would as S. of S. for War be in the same position as any other member of the Council of War to criticise and collectively to accept or reject these recommendations: but *not* to interfere with the decisions of the CIGS before they reach the War Council.

P.S. The King has every reason to believe that any arrangement in the above lines would be acceptable to Lord K.[29]

Three days later the prime minister responded: "K & I both agree that Robertson should become C.I.G.S. here. What you support as to the direct relations betwen the G.S. here & the War Council would, I think, automatically follow."[30]

Robertson's exact relationship with Kitchener now had to be worked out. When Robertson had completed his delicate negotiations with Kitchener, he had achieved a position that made him virtually independent of the secretary of state for war. The War Committee was to "receive *all* advice on matters concerning military operations through one authoritative channel only"—the C.I.G.S. A sticking point initially was that Robertson also insisted that "all operation orders should be issued and signed by the C.I.G.S."—not Kitchener.[31] This left Kitchener with no executive authority and he understandably thought of resignation.

But the government could ill afford to lose Kitchener's prestige. In the end a concession was made to Kitchener's pride (and the constitution!). The wording in Robertson's conditions was modified so that orders in military operations would be issued under the authority of the secretary of state for war. This arrangement was eventually given the full force of law by an order in council issued by the king in January 1916.

Robertson was satisfied (and why not?) with the outcome of the negotiations, but he worried that Kitchener might be unable to work under this humiliating arrangement. "If he *will* but leave me to do my work & if he will confine himself to his own, all should be very well," Wully wrote Wigram. "But he *must* so behave."[32] Robertson need not have been concerned. Kitchener retired into the background without a murmur—either then or later.

On December 23 Robertson entered his new office at Whitehall determined to dictate British strategy. For the first time he was forced extensively to deal with civilians. Unlike Kitchener, he was up to the task.There was little give and a great deal of take in his relationship with the ministers. "He knew what he wanted," Hankey has written, "and he nearly always got his way."[33] Debate with the civilians was avoided at all costs. "Where the politician goes wrong," he once explained, " is in wanting to know the why and the wherefore of the soldier's proposals, and of making the latter the subject of debate and argument across a table. You then have the man who knows but who cannot talk discussing important questions with the man who can talk but does not know, with the result that the man who knows usually gets defeated in argument and things are done which his instinct tells him are bad."[34] With the lives of tens of thousands of British soldiers at stake, this position was untenable.

Secrecy was one of Robertson's most effective means of controlling the ministers. They could not argue against what they did not know or understand. Murray's practice of briefing the ministers with weekly appreciations was discontinued. Instead, Wully gave a weekly "summary" which included nothing that Britain's war leaders could not get from their daily (and heavily censored) newspapers. Hankey viewed these "summaries" as "really almost an insult to the intelligence of the War Committee and the Cabinet."[35] Robertson's orders to his commanders in the field were secret. He even went to the extreme of moving and making preparations to move divisions to the West without the War Committee's knowledge.[36]

Robertson's vast power encouraged him to want more. Fresh from a War Committee meeting in which the ministers had once again displayed in his view "an inability to govern," he wrote the following identical statement to Haig and Archibald Murray, who had been given command of the Egyptian Expeditionary Force, that hinted at a military dictatorship: "I am writing this with the object of saying that practically anything may happen to our boasted British Constitution before this war ends & that the great asset is the army—whose value will be fixed largely by the extent to which we at the top stick together and stand firm."[37]

Wully's obduracy, secrecy, and strategical views were bound to bring him into conflict with Lloyd George. Shortly after Robertson became C.I.G.S., Lloyd George gave a small dinner party at the Savoy in his honor. It was immediately obvious to Hankey, who was a guest, that the chemistry between the two men was not right.[38] Strategy, rather than opposite personalities, however, created the unbridgeable gulf between the two men.

The reader will recall that Lloyd George's early advocacy of a Balkan offensive and his position in the government as the supplier of war material to the Entente had given him a broad view of the conflict. He wanted all of the many theaters to be treated as a single front. If Russia and Italy needed guns and ammunition, they should be provided, even at the expense of home defense or the requirements of the British Expeditionary Force. Furthermore, he was always alert to any political advantages which might be gained. Robertson, however, argued that all political objectives, no matter how important, had to be subordinated to offensive operations in the West, once arguing strenuously against Lloyd George's proposal to send a few machine guns to neutral Rumania for political purposes.[39]

Robertson got the best of this argument with Lloyd George over British strategy. The Dardanelles fiasco had discredited the leading "Easterners," with the exception of Lloyd George, who had favored the Balkans over the Straits. Furthermore, Lloyd George could advance no alternative strategy which offered any chance of defeating the German army in the foreseeable future. He could argue within the War Committee—as he did in January and April 1916—that the wisest course of action was to contain Germany in the West and defeat Turkey. But he could not explain how Turkey's defeat would win the war. It was even more difficult to demonstrate how an offensive from Salonika against the Bulgarians by the relatively small and poorly equipped Allied force there would shake the foundation of the Central Powers. The most opportune time for action in the Balkans had been sacrificed to the Dardanelles venture and Joffre's cult of the offensive. If total victory remained Britain's goal, Germany had to be defeated. A great attack in the West in 1916 might not bring victory, but there was intense pressure on the civilians to make the attempt. The Allied commanders had agreed at the Chantilly military conference in early December to launch simultaneous attacks. The British Expeditionary Force, which would rise to fifty-seven divisions by the middle of the year, was expected to do its duty.

At his first War Committee meeting as C.I.G.S., Robertson came away with an important victory. The ministers accepted his position that Gallipoli must be abandoned. Wully next moved to get the civilians to accept the offensive strategy of the Chantilly military conference. In a short note to the War Committee, he sought unequivocal support for the generals' cult of the offensive.[40]

To his chagrin, he discovered that, although the "Easterners" had been weakened by their failures, they had not been silenced. Lloyd George and the slender, handsome Balfour, who had replaced Churchill as the first lord of the Admiralty, took the lead in expressing the civilian doubts about the results of a big offensive in the West justifying the cost. A bachelor in his sixties, Balfour was of a philosophical bent. He could ably state his case for a particular course of action, but his arguments were often weakened by the suspicion of some of his colleagues that he had few firm convictions and could just as easily argue the case of the other side. Still, this senior Conservative statesman was Lloyd George's most important ally at this juncture in his conflict with the military over the conduct of the war.

Robertson's second conclusion in his note to the War Committee provoked the most discussion. He had written: "Our efforts are to be directed to carrying out offensive operations next spring in the main theatre of war in close co-operation with the Allies and in the greatest possible strength."[41] Balfour pointed out "that if it were possible for the Allies *really* to pool their resources he could not imagine that they would undertake an offensive on the West. On that side the defensive positions had never been broken, and they were increasing in strength every day. . . . It seemed to him that possibly there might be a better chance of success in the South or the East." Lloyd George gave strong support to the first lord of the Admiralty: "General Joffre had always favoured this idea of a great offensive on the West: he had always been confident, and he had always been wrong. . . . Though the General Staff in their Appreciation favoured an attempt to break through the German front on the West, it was nowhere stated how this was to be done."

Bonar Law cut short these criticisms by asking the crucial question: If the general staff's view were rejected, how, then, could Britain hope to defeat Germany? Balfour lamely suggested—to Robertson's utter amazement—that "the weakest part of the German line was the Russian front." Lloyd George was silent. In the end Robertson's conclusion was accepted with the qualifying words: "Every effort is to be made to prepare to carry out the offensive."[42]

In the following days, Balfour and Lloyd George, fearing that the generals would assume that a great British offensive had been okayed, continued to make life miserable for Robertson. "Do not German theories of war, as well as German internal necessities," Balfour asked in a memorandum, "compel them, rightly or wrongly, to attempt the offensive? And is not this what, from our own point of view, we ought most to desire?" After the Teutonic force had spent itself in futile attack, it might then be defeated. Balfour also believed that the General Staff's fixation on the western front, although based on sound military principles, ignored political considerations. "Our prestige in the East has a military value, and, irrespective of political interests or national pride," he concluded, "it may therefore be worth while sending soldiers away from the 'main theatre of war' in order to support it."[43]

Largely because of Balfour's persistence, the War Committee once again discussed the proposed offensive. The "Easterners" scored a minor triumph over the General Staff. The government's position on the offensive was further amended to read: "Every effort is to be made to prepare for carrying out offensive operations next spring in the main theatre of the war in close co-operation with the Allies, and the greatest possible strength, although it must not be assumed that such offensive operations are finally decided on."[44]

Lloyd George and Balfour then forced a discussion of future British military policy. Obviously concerned that no decision by the civilians would give the initiative to the French and British generals by default, he reminded his colleagues "that it had to be remembered that we had already undertaken two offensive operations, both of which had come to nothing. We could not afford to have another of the same sort. This would amount to a defeat. Therefore we ought to delay until we were really strong enough." Later in the discussion, Lloyd George attempted to keep alive interest in Eastern operations:

. . . if it was a question of a general offensive, we should do as the Germans did—we should attack their ally so as to force the Germans to do what we had to do in Servia. If they made a big attack in France they could not do it elsewhere. He concurred in Mr. Balfour's idea [Eastern operations in early 1916]. In the main, it was our business to sit tight on the Western frontier, and then take the offensive in Egypt, Mesopotamia, or Salonica. If we attacked in either of these places, the Turk must be there, and the German must come to his assistance. We could not do both things. It meant the selection of an alternative.

Lloyd George's and Balfour's rearguard action had mixed results. The rest of the War Committee were not prepared to buck the unanimous opposition of the soldiers against expanding the British commitment in the outer theaters. On the other hand, the War Committee readily accepted Lloyd

George's suggestion that an Anglo-French conference on munitions requirements be held. This would enable the ministers to decide if and when the
offensive should be launched.[45]

After this meeting Robertson wrote Haig and singled out Lloyd George as
one of the "wobbling" ministers. The minister of munitions' opposition to an
attack before large supplies of shells had been accumulated, he warned, was
"the thin end of the wedge for deferring matters."[46]

Robertson and Haig were determined to keep the ministers on course.
Haig, the eternal optimist, was convinced that he could break through the
German lines and prove the correctness of his "Western" strategy. Unlike
Haig, Robertson was not as confident of a breakthrough in 1916. He resorted
more to the policy of attrition to justify a prolonged general offensive. "Even
if our success be no greater than that obtained in the past," he wrote in a
memorandum for the War Committee, "the attempt would appear to be
justified. The Germans are approaching the limit of their resources. . . ."[47]

Although Robertson and Haig could make an excellent case for concentrating on the West in 1916, they could advance no convincing argument that
the British attacks in 1916 would be a marked improvement on those in 1915.
Robertson's explanation of the initial Anglo-French failures was that the
generals were dealing with "conditions without precedent in war," and the
required "amount of force to break through the enemy's front . . . could only
be arrived at by experiment."[48] When asked by skeptical civilians why a
general offensive would succeed in 1916 when all others had failed with
considerably higher losses than the enemy, Wully fell back on the argument
that more men and shells were going to be used this time.[49] This line of
reasoning meant an increased emphasis on "mass" and an acceptance of
casualties unprecedented in British military annals. "The vastness of the
material and mechanical power available in modern war," Cruttwell has
perceptively written, "seemed to produce a kind of dull megalomania in
which ingenuity of execution was sacrificed to the immensity and elaboration of the preparation."[50] The single most important innovation in land war,
the tank, was thought by Wully to be "rather a desperate innovation." Even
after the tank had demonstrated its potential, he cautioned Haig not to
request too many. "Besides the men they absorb," he wrote, "they also take
up a great deal of steel, which is now rather scarce, and in general the tanks
should not be ordered unless you think they are really necessary."[51]

Following the January 13 meeting of the War Committee, the ministers'
queasiness toward the offensive subsided somewhat. This was largely due to
Kitchener's assurances that there would be no repetition of the unimaginative slaughter of Loos and Champagne. He told Balfour and others that he
favored a series of limited attacks to wear down the enemy rather than a
spectacular and prolonged general attack.[52] Kitchener's reassuring words
were worthless because he had no influence at general headquarters, which
was responsible for planning and executing the offensive.

On January 28, Lloyd George left for Paris to attend a conference on
munitions requirements. Prone to seasickness, he was more apprehensive
than usual. A letter from a psychic had warned him to beware the twenty-
eighth and twenty-ninth of the month. And indeed his trip was unusually

hair-raising. His passage across the mine-infested Channel was delayed until high tide, when the mines would be deeper in the water. The destroyer which took him across was torpedoed the next day. Safely ashore, he missed a Zeppelin attack on Paris by thirty minutes.[53] A noteworthy event of his trip was his first meeting with Haig. Although Lloyd George attempted to be ingratiating, Haig thought him "shifty and unrealiable."[54] Robertson's recent warning that Lloyd George must be watched carefully at the munitions conference so that he would not "queer our pitch" no doubt colored the commander in chief's opinion of the minister of munitions.[55]

What Lloyd George learned on his trip to France set off alarm bells in his head. Contrary to what Kitchener had been telling the ministers, it appeared that Joffre was determined to launch a general offensive along the lines of the costly attacks of 1915. When Lloyd George brought this to the attention of the War Committee, he was brushed aside.[56]

On February 21, the Germans unleashed a bombardment of unprecedented fury against the French defenses at Verdun. In all, two million shells fell upon the French defenders. The ten-month Battle of Verdun had begun. The ferocity of the German assault reinforced Lloyd George's correct belief that the generals were underestimating Germany's staying power. At a War Committee meeting the day after the Battle of Verdun began, he insisted that "the time had arrived to discuss the projected summer campaign." But before the civilians made a decision, they must know more about the strength of the respective forces: "It was impossible for us to measure the forces of the opposing sides unless we had knowledge of the resources available. . . . before the offensive could be contemplated the relative forces in men and materials should be carefully weighed. Perhaps the War Office were in possession of this information." When Robertson remarked that this matter would be taken up by the Allied commanders at a military conference in early March, Lloyd George pointedly said that the War Committee should discuss the question first. More than resources would be examined if he had his way. The civilians would also address the question of "breaking through either on the West or East." A long and muddled discussion of the respective strength of the opposing forces then ensued, with Lloyd George adhering to his position that "if we had no facts to go upon, he did not understand how we could decide on offensive action."[57]

Lloyd George's words made as much impression as a light rainfall on the desert. To Robertson he was an irritating though ineffective critic. The Welshman stood virtually alone in the War Committee. Already estranged from the Liberals, he saw his Unionist support drop away in late 1915 and early 1916. Bonar Law, who earlier had given him support, now viewed him with suspicion and often challenged his criticism of the military in the War Committee debates. Churchill accurately assessed his standing in a letter to his wife: "LG by all accounts is isolated. He has been vy foolish in his relations with me, Bonar Law, FE [Frederick E. Smith, the attorney-general, 1915–19] & Curzon. He might have combined us all. As it is he has earned the deep distrust of each."[58]

Lloyd George even had difficulty getting his dissenting views recorded in the minutes. When he received his copy of the minutes of the February 22 meeting of the War Committee, he was shocked to learn, as he immediately wrote Hankey, that "the whole of the very important discussion on this question of the offensive, and the directions given to the War Office and myself with regard to the furnishing of further information is omitted from the minutes." He also questioned a conclusion that indicated that the War Committee had ruled out an offensive in southeastern Europe for the present.[59] Hankey, with the approval of the prime minister, then inserted some qualifying remarks in the conclusion in question which served to mollify the "Eastern" sensibilities of Lloyd George. As for the pending offensive in the West, Hankey responded that the prime minister intended to take up the question at the next meeting of the War Committee.[60]

This important discussion, however, was delayed. As Hankey wrote Lloyd George:

> The original intention had been to raise the question of the offensive, as suggested by you at the last meeting. The Prime Minister is inclined to think, however, that it would be better to postpone the subject. The C.I.G.S. has represented that he cannot give any opinion worth having, owing to the events now going on at Verdun, and he considers that we cannot usefully pursue the subject until the situation has cleared up.[61]

It was not until March 21 that the ministers returned to the proposed British offensive. The catalyst for their discussion was a meeting of the Allied commanders at Joffre's home at Chantilly on March 12. As Robertson attempted to describe the results of this conference, it became clear that once again the Allies had failed to achieve a common policy. The Russians seemed inclined to attack prematurely; the Italians, not at all; and the French, tied down at Verdun, appeared to want the British to bear the burden of the offensive. "It was all very slippery and sloppy," said Asquith.

Lloyd George fumed. "both the allied armies had ammunition and we might find one evening that they were launched on a great attack without any reference to the War Committee," he said. Later he commented that we "ought to know whether the Committee were to consider the offensive or leave it to Gen. Haig; in the latter case there was nothing further for the War Committee to say."[62]

Lloyd George looked on with great foreboding as the British army moved closer to a general and possibly premature offensive. In an attempt to divine the motives of Joffre, who previously had largely determined the strategy of the British Expeditionary Force, he asked Major-General John P. Du Cane, the director general of munitions design in the Ministry of Munitions, to comment on a statement made by Joffre in mid-March on the military situation. Suspicious of Robertson and generally kept in ignorance about military questions, the Welshman, in his own words, was "groping in the dark & crying for guidance."[63]

Du Cane told Lloyd George in a private memorandum that the British army might have to launch an attack "for one of two reasons:" to bail out the French at Verdun or to participate in a counter-attack to turn the Battle of Verdun into a decisive Allied victory. If Britain did nothing while the Germans destroyed the French army at Verdun, Du Cane emphasized, it would be "a disgrace to British arms." Only if the German army exhausted itself at Verdun "without precipitating a crisis" would it be possible for the British to postpone their offensive.[64]

By the beginning of April it was clear that the ministers could no longer delay their decision on the offensive. Joffre had written Haig proposing "a joint attack on the largest possible scale." Would the civilians, Haig wanted to know, give him permission to proceed?[65] Haig's letter had a chilling effect on the civilians. It seemed clear what lay ahead. The attack was to be all out and the casualties might run into the hundreds of thousands. Lloyd George still withheld his support. Was it really wise to launch a general offensive with the objective of achieving decisive results rather than powerful though limited blows? "We must have a superiority in men and material," he told the War Committee. "He did not see how we could enter on a very great offensive *now*."

Robertson tried to encourage the civilians by promising that Haig would not allow Joffre to misuse the British army. Haig, he correctly asserted, was determined not to go off until he was convinced that the British army was prepared; and, although the British commander approved of a big attack, he "would not make a fool of himself." Kitchener chimed in with the not so reassuring words that the government "must trust that they [the French] would not make the same mistakes as before. He did not think they were such fools as to repeat them."

As the War Committee drew closer to giving the generals what they wanted, Lloyd George predictably made an attempt to get the ministers to look eastward. He "personally held to the plan of holding the Germans up, and smashing the Turks. That would be very unpleasant for Germany." Robertson quickly brought the discussion back to the central question— Haig's request for authority to attack. The minister "must say one way or the other," he emphasized.[66]

There could now be no pretense of holding back. The civilians had to either accept or oppose an offensive on the generals' terms. They agreed. Their only hope was that Haig, as Robertson had assured them, would employ his forces prudently.

Another consideration for the minister of munitions in early 1916 was that there was now talk of a compromise peace within the government. In February the British leaders had been confronted with President Wilson's dramatic offer to mediate the war on terms which were not unfavorable to the British but fell far short of total victory.[67] Only Grey expressed qualified support for American mediation when it was discussed within the War Committee in February and March, but the Welshman believed that other ministers, most notably McKenna, were sympathetic to a compromise peace.[68] If Britain were not prepared to accept the "lame peace"[69] which Lloyd George abhorred, it appeared obvious that Britain must put up a good fight in the West in 1916. As Grey had grimly warned the government at the beginning of the year: "I believe that the only chance of victory is to hammer the Germans hard in the first eight months of this year. If this is impossible, we had better make up our minds to an inconclusive peace."[70]

Lloyd George's position on two questions before the government—Salonika and general conscription—was influenced by the April 7 decision. The government's commitment to the offensive seemed to make imperative the drafting of more men into the army. Earlier, Asquith had attempted to keep his coalition government together on this explosive issue through a series of compromises. First, in the autumn of 1915, he had sought to mollify the compulsionists with an "ingenious evasion"[71]—the Derby plan, a complicated system which kept the voluntary system alive by requesting that married and unmarried men attest by a government pledge their willingness to serve. In January 1916, Asquith had been forced to retreat one step further with the Compulsory Military Service Act which applied to bachelors. This gave Asquith and the anti-compulsionists only temporary relief. By mid-April Lloyd George and the Unionists were manning the ramparts again. Having gotten the single men, they wanted the married ones, too. The corridors of Whitehall were rife with rumors. Everyone seemed on the verge of resignation. One day it was Lloyd George and the Unionists. The next day it was Asquith. Indeed, the prime minister wrote on May 19 that he was "preparing to order my frock-coat to visit the Sovereign this afternoon."[72] Lloyd George and the Unionists had the upper hand in this war of nerves because of the military's support. For once, the minister of munitions was full of praise for Wully. Stevenson recorded in her diary, "He thinks a lot of Sir William Robertson who has written a very able memorandum on the need for men, and saying that nothing but compulsion for all will be of any use; and D. [for David] feels that with this document behind them they can make a firm stand."[73] Asquith soon caved in, extending conscription to both married and single men between the ages of eighteen and forty-one.

Lloyd George's wholehearted support of the War Office's position on conscription was not without its opportunistic and paradoxical side. Although he opposed the "Westerners," he fought to give them the men to support their strategy. He even used arguments which he knew to be false, once telling Stamfordham that if the British at Ypres and Loos " 'could have pushed in a fresh division we should probably have won.' " Although no one in the government believed more strongly that the civilians must not leave the conduct of the war exclusively in the hands of the generals, he bluntly told Stamfordham that he preferred turning the war completely over to the military to Asquith's lackadaisical leadership. " 'I would rather see old Derby (sic) with a strong General Staff conducting the War than that it should continue to be run as it now is by the present Government,' " he asserted.[74] It is no wonder that the prime minister believed that "the only really difficult person in the Cabinet was Mr. Lloyd George who he was afraid *did* wish to destroy the Govt."[75]

As for Salonika, with the British course firmly charted in the West, Lloyd George believed that little, if anything, could be done in the Balkans for the present. He was alive to the possibility that a premature and feeble assault from Salonika might result in a Dardanelles-like fiasco, thereby rendering impossible any future attack in southeastern Europe. Recently, another "side show" had resulted in an unmitigated disaster for British arms. In the

Mesopotamian theater, a British army had surrendered unconditionally to the Turks on April 29 at Kut-el-Amara after a 143-day siege. The beaten force had then been "herded like animals across the desert, flogged, kicked, raped, tortured, and murdered."[76]

The French, however, to the intense displeasure of the British government, continued to pressure London, with Joffre writing Robertson on April 25, urging a Balkan offensive against Bulgaria.[77] When the War Committee discussed Joffre's request, strange sentiments were uttered by Britain's leading Balkanite: "He was not in favour of it because General Joffre simply asked for it. . . . 300,000 was not enough to make an impression in the Balkans."[78] Britain's shipping crisis was one powerful argument against this "side show," but Lloyd George resisted raising it with the French. His motive, in all likelihood, was that once this argument was accepted, it would make difficult any further operation on the periphery. "If the necessity was great," he argued, "we could conceivably find the ships. If the country was prepared to cut down their supplies, they could find them."[79]

The upshot of the Salonikan discussions was an usually firm stand by the War Committee. A memorandum was prepared which stated that "the War Committee are therefore definitely and unanimously opposed to any offensive operations from Salonica."[80]

As usual, the French refused to bend and a special Anglo-French conference met in London on June 9 to continue the debate. At the last moment Lloyd George hesitated in his unfamiliar role as an opponent of a Balkan attack. He thought of not attending and when the conference began at 10 Downing Street he was absent. After an hour passed, however, he appeared, eventually delivering one of the most dramatic speeches of the day. "To attempt the operation with inadequate strength," he emphasized, "was to discredit it." Furthermore, "an unsuccessful offensive would prejudice any further offensive on this flank. No government after the failure would try it a second time. This indeed was the main reason for his opposition."[81] In spite of Lloyd George's surprising opposition, the French remained adamant and it was only agreed that the offensive should be postponed until conditions were more favorable. This compromise suited Lloyd George, and he almost immediately began lobbying within the War Committee for the strengthening of the offensive potential of the Allied force at Salonika.

It should not be assumed that Lloyd George's support of Robertson on compulsion and Salonika put him in the general staff's camp. Along with Hankey, he was in fact instrumental in leading a revolt of the ministers against the general staff's secrecy and high-handedness. On Monday, May 22, Hankey had a lengthy talk with Lloyd George about the paucity of information the general staff was furnishing the ministers. The minister of munitions readily agreed that something must be done.[82] After all, the prime minister, at his urging, earlier had to force Robertson to tell him how many battalions there were in the British army, information which was obviously essential to the Ministry of Munitions.[83] At Lloyd George's request, Hankey placed the question of military information on the agenda of the May 24 War Committee meeting. Hankey also wrote the prime minister an unusually strong letter:

The War Committee is the Commander-in-Chief in commission of all the forces and resources of the British Empire; the Members of the Committee and not the General Staff are responsible to Parliament, the country, and the Empire for the conduct of the war; and I would submit that the information they at present receive, both from the Admiralty and the War Office, is utterly inadequate for the proper discharge of their great responsibility.[84]

A "frightful row"[85] occurred when the War Committee met on the twenty-fourth. The astonishing arrogance of the Army Council, the governing board of the army, rather than the military's secretiveness was the issue. On May 19, Washington had made a fresh effort to revive its peace plan: the so-called House-Grey Memorandum. When word of this reached the Army Council, its members, which included Kitchener and Robertson, threatened resignation "if the War Committee insisted on an inquiry into the peace question."[86]

At the start of the War Committee's meeting, Hankey and the military advisers were excused while the ministers discussed American mediation. No record was kept, but McKenna told Hankey as they walked to lunch "that he, the P.M., Grey, and Balfour had been in favour of accepting President Wilson's good offices owing to the black financial outlook, while Bonar Law and Ll. George were averse, as they did not admit of the seriousness of the financial situation."[87] In the end the government once again backed away from a compromise peace. The military's opposition, along with Lloyd George's and Bonar Law's stand, made the exploration of peace political suicide for Asquith's government.

When the War Committee resumed its meeting after lunch, the ministers vented their anger at the soldiers. No reference was made in the minutes to peace discussions. Instead, the discussion focused on the high command's insistence that a vast number of horses must be maintained in France, many being used, it should be emphasized, for transport rather than for the cavalry. (During the war, the feeding of these horses, according to A. J. P. Taylor, took up "more shipping space than was lost to German submarines."[88]) The government had been exploring ways to lessen the shipping crisis, with Haig's cavalry catching its eye. Haig, who envisaged his cavalry chasing the defeated Germans, was greatly offended and opposed any government investigation of the British Expeditionary Force's utilization of horses. He wrote Robertson: "It appears that the War Committee have overlooked the fact that I am responsible for the efficiency of the armies in France."[89] Robertson needed no prodding. He had already decided that he and the Army Council must put "our foot down" to stop the civilians from meddling in military questions.[90] Hence the Army Council's support of Haig was belligerent and unyielding:

The Council therefore cannot but regard the recommendation of the War Committee as a serious reflection on the manner in which they have discharged their dues, and one which if carried into effect would undermine their responsibility and impair their authority with the army. If His Majesty's Government decide to proceed with a special investigation under a Minister of the Crown—that is, if they feel themselves unable to

rely upon the judgment and advice of the Army Council in this matter—
the Council respectfully submit that it will not be possible for them to
continue to be responsible either for economical administration or for the
efficient conduct of the war.[91]

With feeling running high in the committee, the Welshman's cup of indignation overflowed.

> *Mr. Lloyd George* agreed that it was most surprising to receive such a
> letter which amounted to the Army Council setting itself up against the
> Government. After referring to somewhat similar transaction in connec-
> tion with the Admiralty, he said that he considered it a perfectly insolent
> letter from Sir. D. Haig. The letter talked about his responsibility—to
> whom was he responsible? He was responsible to them, to the Govern-
> ment, and through the Government to Parliament, and through Parliament
> to the people. The effect of this letter was to tell the War Committee "to
> mind their own business" and not interfere with his. He thought that the
> documents of the Army Council and of Sir D. Haig were most improper.
> There was another matter to which he wished to direct their attention.
> That was the way the War Committee was treated in the matter of infor-
> mation, which was withheld from them. They had a perfect right to inves-
> tigate any matter connected with the war that they pleased. If they said
> they wished to investigate anything, no one had the right to say that they
> objected, and to tell them to mind their own business.[92]

Several days later, on May 30, the War Committee finally discussed Lloyd
George's agenda item on military information. The minister of munitions
emphasized once again the supreme responsibility of the War Committee,
expressing concern about the movement of divisions without the ministers'
knowledge, and suggesting "that there had been decisions which they might
have modified had they known all that the War Office knew."[93]

Robertson promised to do better about providing the ministers with information and the civil-military crisis quickly subsided with the C.I.G.S.'s
power intact. Robertson and Haig's conduct of the war was about to be put
to a severe test—the long-awaited Somme offensive. Haig had been biding
his time while he husbanded his men and shells. His army has been called
"one of the most remarkable and admirable military formations ever to have
taken the field."[94] Few armies in history have matched its enthusiasm and
courage. All were volunteers. No one was more confident of the offensive
power of this force than Haig, who "contemplated a complete break-through
like that carried out in May 1915 at Gorlice-Tarnow by the Germans and
Austrians, and then, a wheel and a sweep behind the German front."[95]

Conscious of the civilians' skepticism of a costly attempt at a breakthrough, Robertson masked Haig's true intentions from the War Committee.
As Hankey recorded in the minutes, "Sir W. Robertson assured the Committee that in the suggested movement there was no idea of any attempt to
break through the German lines. It would be only a move to degager [or
relieve] the French."[96]

By the end of May, it was imperative that Britain, irrespective of what the
Italians and Russians could accomplish on their fronts, must attack—and

soon. On May 26, Joffre emotionally informed Haig and Robertson that "the French army would cease to exist"[97] if the British delayed their advance until August.

In the end, it was concern for France, a political reason, that led Lloyd George to accept the offensive. On June 2, his friend Albert Thomas, the French minister of munitions, wrote him:

> Public opinion looks round for the responsibility of the present situation, and becomes restive; it feels nervous when people think of our troops struggling for months round Verdun, after resisting such formidable on-slaughts in the many months before. And what comes into the people's minds is that the English are in a state of inaction, that they have been accumulating enormous forces, but the efficiency of which has not yet been put to the test. I suppose this has been mentioned to you from various sources of information: but not much would have to happen to undermine, as it were, the confidence our country has in British co-operation.[98]

Although Lloyd George still believed that the best policy was "holding the enemy in check during 1916 until the Allies are fully equipped for a great offensive later on," he bowed to the inevitable.[99] In reality, Lloyd George was to *never* believe that conditions were right for a massive and prolonged British offensive in the West. And general headquarters's tactics in 1916 served to reinforce his opposition to the "Westerners'" strategy.

The army leadership was dominated by cavalry officers (five of the nine generals who commanded armies during the war were horse soldiers) and the resulting "cavalry spirit" led to haste and disproportionate losses. Although the British Expeditionary Force now had more guns on their front than the Germans, British artillery tactics were rigid and unimaginative. As the British official history admits: "Too little attention was paid by the General Staff to the advice of the artillery and engineer experts, who, recall-ing the methods of fortress warfare, suggested the concentration of artillery fire on particular sections rather than spreading it nearly evenly."[100] The problems of siege warfare had been largely neglected by an overly optimistic general headquarters. As A. J. P. Taylor has noted: "Nothing had been learnt from previous failures except how to repeat them on a larger scale."[101]

A further weakness of the British offensive—which was no fault of the soldiers—was the artillery's inability to kill the enemy in their dugouts on a broad front with high-explosive shells. The Ministry of Munitions had made astonishing strides in the manufacture of shells under Lloyd George's lead-ership, increasing its production of medium shells sevenfold and heavy shells twelvefold since June 1915. But the munitions industry was not yet capable of producing a large number of high-explosive shells for the most common artillery piece—the eighteen-pounder. Moreover, the next most plentiful artillery piece, the 4.5-inch howitzer, fired a thirty-five-pound shell which contained only four pounds ten ounces of high explosive. This was due to the purpose of the shell (designed to explode on impact producing a cloud of shell fragments) and the necessity of having a heavy casing to prevent the shell from disintegrating within the gun when fired. Out of the

Sir Douglas Haig and General Sir Henry Rawlinson at Fourth Army headquarters on the eve of the Somme offensive.

12,000 tons fired by the howitzers and heavy guns in the preliminary barrage on the Somme, only around 900 tons consisted of high-explosive shells.[102]

In volume and weight the British bombardment which began on June 24 far surpassed any previous British artillery barrage, employing over twelve times the weight of shell per mile of front used at Festubert:

> The weight of shells transported to the British guns was 21,000 tons, excluding propellant (the explosive needed to drive the shell up the barrel at the moment of firing). It had taken the efforts of about fifty thousand gunners (almost the number of Wellington's Army at Waterloo), working for seven days, to load this weight into their pieces and fire it at the enemy—or, more precisely, into the area, 25,000 by 2,000 yards square which the British infantry were to attack. In crude terms, this meant that each 2,500 yards had received a ton of shells; or, if numbers of shells are used for the calculation—and about 1,500,000 had been fired—that each 2,000 square yards had received 30 shells.[103]

Most of the shells in this rain of metal, however, were ineffective shrapnel shells. Many of the Germans, sitting on long wooden benches twenty feet or more below the ground, survived the gigantic shelling.

Between 6:30 and 7:30 A.M. on July 1 the most intense fire of the entire bombardment crashed into the German lines. Then the noise of exploding shells was replaced by the sound of officers' whistles. About 140,000 tommies with their bayonets glistening in the bright sun climbed from their trenches and slowly moved in perfect rows across no-man's-land as if they were on a morning stroll. They could not move faster because each man was weighted down with about sixty-six pounds of equipment. German machine gunners were quickly laying down a murderous fire. It was an unequal contest between man and machine. The horrendous losses—almost 60,000 casualties—made July 1 the blackest day in British military history.

On July 3, Lloyd George, Balfour, and Hankey held a grim discussion of the offensive, which thus far had resulted in little progress. To Hankey, Haig's tactics were "sheer slogging reduced to its crudest form." Lloyd George reminded Hankey of the latter's belief in December 1914 that the German defenses in the West were impregnable and that Britain's great opportunity lay in the East[104]—a position to which he himself had steadfastly clung. Second-guessing, however, was a useless exercise. The cult of the offensive was in the ascendancy and Lloyd George knew that he was about to become secretary of state for war, a position which might link his reputation, in part, to the success or failure of the great offensive underway.

NOTES

1. Bonham-Carter, *Soldier True*, p. 5.

2. "Talk with Maurice Hankey at United Service Club," November 8, 1932, Liddell Hart MSS, 11/1932/43.

3. Haig to Lady Haig, June 22 and 30, 1916, Haig MSS, no. 144. It must be noted that Haig concluded his June 22 letter with this sentence: "Anyhow you must realize that *I try* to do more than 'do my best & trust to God,' because of the reasons I give above." But Haig gives no "reasons" above that would indicate that he did.

4. Esher Diary, June 1, 1916, 2/16.

5. E. K. G. Sixsmith, *Douglas Haig* (1976), pp. 164–71.

6. Haig's minute on "Cavalry Operations 20–26th, 1917," n.d., Haig MSS, no. 119.

7. Haig Diary, October 9, 1918, no. 132.

8. Sir James E. Edmonds, compiler, *Military Operations, France and Belgium, 1918*, 5:235.

9. Ibid., p. 196.

10. Robertson to Kiggell, July 5, 1916, and Rawlinson, July 26, 1916, Robertson MSS, I/35/65 and 100.

11. Esher Diary, September 23, 1916, 2/17.

12. See especially his *To Win a War, 1918: The Year of Victory* (1978) and *Douglas Haig: The Educated Soldier* (1963).

13. Memorandum by Robertson, November 8, 1915, CAB 42/5/6.

14. Brigadier-General John Charteris, *Field-Marshal Haig* (1929), p. 66.

15. Brigadier-General John Charteris, *At G.H.Q.* (1931), p. 11.

16. Robertson to Wigram, March 24, 1915, RA GV Q2522/3/172.

17. See Haig Diary, June 26, 1915, no. 101, and Haig to Wigram, June 27, 1915, RA GV 2521/V/133.

18. Robertson to Stamfordham, n.d., but most probably written in late June or early July 1915, Robertson MSS, I/12/3. Robertson also prepared a paper which suggested that strategy

should be the exclusive property of the C.I.G.S. See his "Notes on the Machinery of the Government for Conducting the War," June 30, 1915, Robertson MSS, I/9/6.

19. Haig to Kiggell, July 1, 1915, Kiggell MSS, II/2.

20. These eight divisions were never sent to Gallipoli.

21. Haig Diary, October 17, 1915, no. 103.

22. Ibid., October 24, 1915, no. 103.

23. Robertson to Murray, October 21, 1915, Robertson MSS, I/15/1. For more on Robertson's unhappiness with Kitchener and Murray, see file I/9 in Robertson MSS.

24. Robertson to Haig, November 15, 1915, Haig MSS, no. 103.

25. Robertson to Haig, November 17, 1915, Haig MSS, no. 103.

26. Haig had followed Robertson to London and had put pressure on Asquith and Bonar Law to make Robertson C.I.G.S.

27. Murray to Robertson, November 28, 1915, Robertson MSS, I/15/6.

28. Robertson to Murray, November 30, 1915, Robertson MSS, I/15/7.

29. Stamfordham to Asquith, December 3, 1915, Asquith MSS, 4.

30. Asquith to Stamfordham, December 6, 1915, RA GV Q838/52. Terraine attempts to pooh-pooh the role of the king in the shakeup of the high command in December. *Haig: Educated Soldier,* p. 165. But George V certainly seems to have believed that "he had done the whole thing." See Hankey Diary, December 14, 1915, 1/1.

31. Robertson to Kitchener, December 5, 1915, Robertson MSS, I/9/40.

32. Robertson to Wigram, December 11, 1915, RA GV Q838/61.

33. Hankey, *Supreme Command,* 2:446.

34. Robertson to Repington, October 31, 1916, Robertson MSS, I/33/73.

35. Hankey to Asquith, May 23, 1916, CAB 42/14/12.

36. Ibid.

37. Robertson to Haig, March 8, 1916, Robertson MSS, I/22/30, and Robertson to Murray, March 8, 1916, Murray-Robertson MSS, Add. 52463.

38. Hankey, *Supreme Command,* 2:471.

39. War Committee, February 22 and 29, 1916, CAB 42/9/3 and 7, and March 21, 1916, CAB 42/11/6. Also see Robertson to Lloyd George, March 16, 1916, Robertson, I/33/5.

40. War Committee, December 23, 1915, CAB 42/6/13.

41. Robertson, "Note for the War Committee by the Chief of the Imperial Staff, with Reference to the General Staff Paper, dated December 16, 1915," December 23, 1916, CAB 42/6/14.

42. War Committee, December 28, 1915, CAB 42/6/14.

43. Memorandum by Balfour, December 27, 1915, CAB 42/7/5.

44. War Committee, January 13, 1916, CAB 42/7/5.

45. Ibid.

46. Haig to Robertson, January 13, 1916, Robertson MSS, I/22/14.

47. Robertson, "Note prepared for the War Committee by the Chief of the Imperial General Staff on the Question of Offensive Operations on the Western Front," January 1, 1916, CAB 42/7/1.

48. Robertson, "Memorandum on the Conduct of the War," November 8, 1915, CAB 42/5/6.

49. War Committee, December 28, 1915, CAB 42/6/14.

50. Cruttwell, *History of the Great War,* p. 260.

51. Robertson to Haig, August 29 and November 1, 1916, Robertson MSS, I/22/72 and 86.

52. See "Note by Balfour," January 25, 1916, CAB 42/7/12, and Hankey Diary, January 21, 1916, 1/1.

53. Entries of January 31 and February 1, 1916, *A Diary by Frances Stevenson,* p. 92.

54. Haig Diary, January 30, 1916, no. 104.

55. Robertson to Haig, January 24, 1916, Robertson MSS, I/22/18.

56. War Committee, February 3, 1916, CAB 42/8/1.

57. Ibid., February 22, 1916, CAB 42/9/3.

58. Winston S. Churchill to Clementine Churchill, January 13, 1916, quoted in Gilbert, *Companion, Part 2, Documents: May 1915–December 1916*, pp. 1368–70.

59. Lloyd George to Hankey, February 23, 1916, Lloyd George MSS, D/17/3/18.

60. Hankey to Lloyd George, February 23, 1916, Lloyd George MSS, D/17/3/19.

61. Hankey to Lloyd George, February 25, 1916, Lloyd George MSS, D/17/3/20.

62. War Committee, March 21, 1916, CAB 42/11/6.

63. Lloyd George's minute on a memorandum on the campaign of 1916, dated February 28, 1916, prepared privately for him by his military secretary in the Ministry of Munitions, Colonel Arthur Lee. Lloyd George MSS, D/2/22.

64. Du Cane to Lloyd George ("Notes on the Statement by the Commander-in-Chief of the French Armies on the Military Situation," March 18, 1916 inclosed) April 1916, Lloyd George MSS, D/1/1/16.

65. Haig to Robertson, April 4, 1916, CAB 42/12/5.

66. War Committee, April 7, 1916, CAB 42/12/5. It is interesting that Kitchener, whom Lloyd George had manipulated to depose as Britain's supreme war lord, agreed with the Welshman's criticisms and continued to argue after the April 7 decision that Britain should hoard her manpower in 1916 in preparation for a great attack in 1917. See Esher Diary, April 17, 1916, 2/15.

67. See David R. Woodward, "Great Britain and President Wilson's Efforts to End World War I in 1916," *The Maryland Historian* 1 (Spring 1970): 45–58, and John Milton Cooper, Jr., "The British Response to the House-Grey Memorandum: New Evidence and New Questions," *Journal of American History* 59 (March 1973): 958–71.

68. See War Committee, February 22, 1916, and "Addendum to the Proceedings of the War Committee on March 21, 1916," CAB 42/9/3 and 42/11/6; also see entry of February 23, 1916, *A Diary by Frances Stevenson*, p. 101.

69. Entry of April 14, 1916, *Diary of Lord Bertie*, 1:337.

70. Memorandum by Grey, January 14, 1916, Grey MSS, F.O. 800/96.

71. Taylor, *English History*, p. 53.

72. Roy Jenkins, *Asquith: Portrait of a Man and an Era* (paperback edn., 1966), p. 392.

73. Entry of April 17, 1916, *A Diary by Frances Stevenson*, p. 106.

74. "Sic" in original; Memorandum by Stamfordham, April 16, 1916, RA GV K951/4.

75. Memorandum by Stamfordham, April 19, 1916, RA GV K951/7.

76. Cruttwell, *History of the Great War*, p. 348.

77. Joffre to Robertson, April 25, 1916, CAB 42/13/2.

78. War Committee, May 3, 1916, CAB 42/13/2.

79. Ibid., May 17, 1916, CAB 42/14/1.

80. "The Policy of the Allies in the Balkans. Memorandum by the War Committee," May 17, 1916, CAB 42/14/1.

81. Anglo-French Conference, June 9, 1916, CAB 28/1/1.C.-8.

82. Hankey Diary, May 22, 1916, 1/1.

83. War Committee, March 21, 1916, CAB 42/11/6.

84. Hankey to Asquith, May 23, 1916, CAB 42/14/12. Hankey's letter also included some minor criticism of the secrecy of the Ministry of Munitions.

85. Hankey Diary, May 24, 1916, 1/1.

86. Ibid. There was no formal meeting of the Army Council with minutes and hence Hankey's diary is the only record of its stand.

87. Hankey Diary, May 24, 1916, 1/1.

88. Taylor, *English History*, p. 59.

89. Haig to Robertson, May 20, 1916, CAB 42/14/10; also see Haig to Robertson, May 29, 1916, Robertson MSS, I/22/41.

90. Robertson to Haig, May 19, 1916, Robertson MSS, I/22/38.

91. Army Council (180), May 22, 1916, W.O. 163/21.

92. War Committee, May 24, 1916, CAB 42/14/10.

93. Ibid., May 30, 1916, CAB 42/14/12.

94. John Keegan, *The Face of Battle* (paperback edn., 1976), p. 215.

95. *Military Operations, France and Belgium, 1916*, 1:254.

96. War Committee, May 30, 1916, CAB 42/14/12.

97. Haig Diary, May 26, 1916, no. 106.

98. Thomas to Lloyd George, June 2, 1916, Lloyd George MSS, D/19/6/29.

99. Lloyd George to Thomas, June 3, 1916, Lloyd George MSS, D/19/6/31, and entry of June 6–8, 1916, *Diaries of C. P. Scott*, pp. 214–16.

100. *Military Operations, France and Belgium, 1918*, 5:605.

101. A. J. P. Taylor, *The First World War: An Illustrated History* (paperback edn., 1972), pp. 133–34.

102. Adams, *Arms and the Wizard*, pp. 172–73, 241–45, and Keegan, *Face of Battle*, pp. 227–37.

103. Keegan, *Face of Battle*, p. 234.

104. Hankey Diary, July 3, 1916, 1/1.

5

Wizard in the War Office

SHORTLY before noon on June 6, Lloyd George left the Ministry of Munitions to attend a meeting of the War Committee at 10 Downing Street. The war continued to go badly. Five days earlier the greatest sea battle of the war, Jutland, had ended in a draw. To the profound disappointment of the nation, the proud Grand Fleet had been unable to win a Trafalgar-like victory over the German High Seas Fleet. As Lloyd George approached the cabinet room, an agitated Bonham Carter informed him that another misfortune had befallen the nation. News had just been received that Kitchener of Khartoum, en route to Russia, had gone down with the *Hampshire* when it struck a mine off the Orkneys.

The stunned ministers at Lloyd George's suggestion decided against adjournment and carried on with their work. As Britain's war leaders discussed across the table topics ranging from the Greek situation to routes for merchant ships, Lloyd George and Robertson had their minds on another question—Kitchener's successor.

Wully feared that Asquith would appoint his nemesis, Lloyd George, whose energetically expressed strategical views and criticisms of the generals' conduct of the war made him anathema to the soldiers. With Kitchener dead and Lloyd George in the War Office, the soldiers' defenses might be breached. As soon as the War Committee concluded its meeting, Robertson cornered Hankey, letting him know that "he was very anxious not to have Lloyd George." Later in the day, he got the ear of Asquith. His first choice for the War Office was the army's friend, Austen Chamberlain, the secretary of state for India.[1]

In the following days, Robertson carried on an urgent campaign to deny the Welshman the War Office. Influential allies were the Army Council, certain newspapers, and the king. George V informed Hankey on June 10 that Chamberlain was also his choice and then "went into a most violent diatribe against Ll. George."[2]

For his part, Lloyd George left the cabinet room convinced that he was the leading candidate for the War Office. He had had one foot in the door during the May crisis in 1915 and more recently, in January, Asquith's supporters had felt him out about replacing Kitchener.[3] As head of the War Office, his voice might be raised in Allied council for his single-front approach to the war. In this way the East might compete with the West for British guns and men. Ignored at home, he might find allies in Paris, Rome, and Petrograd. It would not be the first time that Britain's allies had forced the ministers to go against the advice of the general staff. Witness Salonika.

But initially the War Office had little attraction for him if he had to accept Kitchener's figurehead position. For his criticisms of the generals' conduct of the war to have any impact he had to have the army's respect. At the very least he wanted the power to appoint and sack generals. "The soldiers would crawl before the man who they knew had the ultimate power over them," he told Scott on the afternoon of June 6, "and treat anyone who had not with contempt." Obviously relishing the chance of shaking up the generals, he spoke with Scott, "of the need for a new spirit at the War Office and for rather extensive changes of personnel."[4]

The great unanswered questions were: Would Robertson relinquish any of his vast power, and, equally important, would the prime minister pressure him to do so? Also, Lloyd George was uncertain of Bonar Law's position for the Unionist leader could make a strong claim to the seals of the War Office.

On Sunday, June 11, the two most powerful men in Asquith's coalition government met at Aitken's home at Leatherhead. The atmosphere was distinctly frosty at first. Bonar Law, according to Aitken's account, led off with an enumeration of Lloyd George's faults. The minister of munitions deftly sidestepped this personal attack, emphasizing that the important thing was to prevent "a satellite of Asquith or a weak man agreeable to the soldiers" from taking the vital post. He and Bonar Law were the only ones who could prevent this. He was quite prepared to step aside and support Bonar Law. At the end of a long and difficult discussion, Bonar Law declared that Lloyd George was his choice for the War Office.[5] The common bond between the two men was their agreement that the Kitchener-Robertson compact should be destroyed.[6]

With his mind made up, Bonar Law wasted no time in applying pressure on Asquith. It was Whitsun weekend, and Asquith was resting at his cottage on the Thames near Didcot, the Wharf. On Monday morning, when the Unionist leader descended on Asquith at his country home, the prime minister at first offered him the post. But when Bonar Law resisted, he agreed to appoint the Welshman.[7] When he talked with Lloyd George that evening, however, he began to have second thoughts. There is no full record of their conversation, but it is apparent that Lloyd George and Asquith were far apart on the powers the former would have. Over breakfast the next morning with Scott, Lloyd George continued to insist that he must have "the full ordinary powers of the Secretary of State which had been largely withdrawn from Kitchener—especially the ultimate power of appointment to the higher commands." He also admitted that he had threatened Asquith with resignation if "somebody else were put over his head at the War Office."[8]

Lloyd George, of course, had been threatening resignation more frequently than the change of seasons. Before Kitchener's death he saw no prospect of playing a major role within the government in military policy.

Only in opposition might he effectively attack the generals' conduct of the war and the failure of Asquith and the Liberals to overrule them. He had been restrained from resigning, in part, because he saw no great leader among the Unionists. He once told Miss Stevenson, " 'But who is there who would make a fitting Prime Minister? Bonar Law is limp and lifeless; Balfour can never make up his mind about anything. There *is* no one.' "[9] What worried him now was that if he accepted a figurehead position in the War Office, he would only prop up Asquith's sagging government without effecting any change in the direction of the war.[10]

As Lloyd George edged closer to the War Office, the lobbying of the "soldiers' party," as Aitken called it, kept pace with its mounting alarm. Sir John French visited Asquith and pleaded with him. For the sake of the army the prime minister must himself take the War Office. Lord Derby, a favorite of the army, could be made his second-in-command to run things. This was also the sentiment of the Army Council.[11] The soldiers' friends on Fleet Street had their say, especially the volatile H. A. Gwynne, the editor of the Unionist *Morning Post*. Gwynne, a former war correspondent in the Balkans, South Africa, and China, considered himself the protector of the soldiers against civilian interference, and his paper was little more than the mouthpiece of the War Office. In leading articles, the *Morning Post* suggested that "the War Office would be suited ill indeed to Mr. LLOYD GEORGE's qualities." The dynamic Welshman was portrayed as "an energiser rather than an administrator."[12] On June 19, Gwynne came more to the point: "If Mr. LLOYD GEORGE would only learn that his task is to give the soldiers free play to run the war upon their own lines. . . . if he is to be appointed we implore him to make no rash experiments and not to presume that the business of war may be learnt in a month or a year." On the opposite end of the political spectrum, the liberal *Daily Chronicle* offered similar advice: "There is room for an outstanding man, but he must be a man content to work and shine in his own orbit, without infringing on the orbit of the Chief of the Imperial General Staff."[13]

Lloyd George's bid for the War Office presented Asquith with a real dilemma. If he supported Lloyd George on his terms, the "soldiers' party" would be inflamed and Robertson might resign. With public trust in the army high, this would endanger his government. On the other hand, Asquith recognized that "L.G. will not be pleased if his demands are refused."[14] If the minister of munitions resigned, Bonar Law might follow him. Even if Asquith's government survived this blow, an unlikely event, Lloyd George would be more dangerous without than within the government. To placate his headstrong colleague, Asquith offered him the olive branch of the vice-presidency of the War Committee, which was tantamount to making him the vice-premier.[15] Forcing Robertson to modify his arrangement with Kitchener, however, was out of the question. Gambling that Lloyd George's threat of resignation was a bluff, Asquith delayed, hoping that in the end he could mollify all parties by steering a middle course.

On June 17, Lloyd George drafted a long and artful memorandum. Combining reasonableness with the threat to resign, he asserted that he could not accept the War Office "under the humiliating conditions to which poor

Kitchener had been reduced." He denied any intention of interfering with strategy. On the other hand, he argued that if he, as secretary of state for war, were to persuade the Allies to pull together, he must "possess real power and influence," including the right to remove incompetent generals.[16] This self-serving memorandum was destined to gather dust in the Lloyd George Papers. Instead, a short note was sent. "I have given a good deal of consideration to your kind offer of the War Secretaryship," Lloyd George wrote. "I have come to the conclusion that I shall be rendering a greater service to the country in this emergency by not accepting it. As I told you at our interview I thought that I could be of greater use in another sphere. I am still of that opinion."[17]

There the matter seemed to end. Or did it? Lloyd George's vague letter might be read as a letter of resignation. But as usual he trembled at the brink. Advice was sought from Bonar Law, Rufus D. Isaacs (Lord Reading), Aitken, Edward Russell of the *Liverpool Post,* Sir Arthur Lee, and others.[18] The avenues of actions open to him—and their advantages and disadvantages—were outlined in a letter from Lee, a shrewd Conservative politician and the military secretary to the Ministry of Munitions. Lee encouraged Lloyd George to reject a figurehead position in the War Office, which would involve "yourself in difficulties compared with which the Irish bog would be easy travelling." If allowed to retain his position as minister of munitions, Lloyd George should accept Asquith's offer of the vice-presidency of the War Committee. "You would have been acknowledged by the Cabinet and the country as the only alternative Prime Minister," Lee wrote, and resignation later would have a decisive impact. But "to resign now 'because you could not get the War Office on your own terms' would give your enemies a handle for dangerous misrepresentations and enable them to exploit the sneer: 'what was good enough for Kitchener was not good enough for him.' "[19]

Meanwhile, Asquith was receiving equally Machiavellian advice from Edwin S. Montagu, the Liberal politician. Montagu suggested to the prime minister that it would be advantageous to have the government's leading critic in the War Office during the forthcoming offensive, which was certain to result in heavy casualties. What better way to silence the Welshman?[20]

Asquith's calm and unhurried diplomacy was rewarded. Lloyd George had backed himself into a corner by his maneuvering after Kitchener's death. If he rejected the War Office, resignation was the alternative he had given himself. Speaking his mind about the conduct of the war would be satisfying. But the timing was wrong. He would be branded as unpatriotic if he took on the generals on the eve of Britain's greatest offensive to date. Until the "Westerners" failed, he would find little, if any, support for increasing his role in military policy at the expense of one of the nation's most trusted soldiers—Robertson. After much agonizing, Lloyd George must have decided that boring from within the soldiers' citadel was preferable to an uncertain future of being a critic of war policy in the wilderness. There was always the chance that he could gain acceptance for his ideas in Allied conferences. After further discussion with Asquith, he decided to take the plunge on June 24.[21] As for the Kitchener-Robertson compact, which gave the C.I.G.S. authority never possessed by another British general, the prime minister let Lloyd George attempt to make the best deal he could for himself. With no pressure on him from the prime minister, of course, Robertson was unwilling to budge an inch on any fundamental issue.[22]

On June 26, in response to an uncompromising letter from Wully that reiterated the terms of the Kitchener-Robertson compact, Lloyd George fired a Parthian shot, making clear his unhappiness with Robertson's definition of the role of the secretary of state for war. While accepting Robertson's position as the War Committee's sole adviser on strategy, he insisted that he "be kept informed of everything"—not, as Robertson had written, *"all that he should know."* Demanding that he be involved in every stage of the formulation of military policy, he wrote: "It would be humiliating and intolerable if I were to hear your policy expounded for the first time to the War Committee. . . . Political considerations (I mean international politics) and questions of equipment—both in my sphere—are just as essential to the decisions of war problems as knowledge of military strategy."[23]

Lloyd George scored many debating points in this war of letters, but Robertson clearly won the battle. Meanwhile, Asquith moved to pacify the soldiers (and the palace) by appointing Lord Derby as War Office undersecretary. Sandwiched between Robertson and Derby, even the shifty Lloyd George might be kept at bay.

On July 7, the Welshman formally took the seals of office. "We felt just like children going to a new school,"[24] wrote Stevenson of the move from the Ministry of Munitions to the War Office. To his critics, the new look at the War Office bordered on the atmosphere of a children's playground. The change from the formal and very private Kitchener regime was striking. There was now a steady procession of newsmen, politicians, foreign leaders, and secretaries to and from Lloyd George's cavernous new office.

Lloyd George realized that his every action as head of the War Office was being carefully scrutinized. Yet within eleven days after he took office he suggested strategy to the War Committee that was anathema to Robertson. With the Somme offensive underway, Robertson was even more sensitive than usual about "sideshows." Earlier he had gotten the government to adopt a passive policy in Mesopotamia and Egypt.[25] He had also labored unsuccessfully to reduce or liquidate the "Eastern" venture, which caused him the greatest anxiety—the Eastern Army at Salonika. With this background, one can imagine his consternation when Lloyd George pushed his Balkanite ideas on July 18. The French had been pressing the British to launch an attack against Bulgaria to protect Rumania when that country joined the Entente. The ministers, advised by Robertson, however, had only been willing to accept a limited British role to occupy the Bulgarians in Macedonia while Rumania mobilized.[26] By mid-July, however, it became obvious that the French were contemplating a big offensive. When this was discussed by Britain's war leaders, Lloyd George "pointed out that there was another side to the question, which was whether it would not be an advantage to cut out Bulgaria and clear a road to Roumania. This would have the effect of cutting off the Turks. He thought it was worth considering. It would prevent the supply of ammunition to the Turks, and stop Germany from getting food supplies from the east, and would open up a new road to Russia."[27]

When Robertson immediately challenged this view, Lloyd George made no response. He was conscious that his new position made it extremely difficult for him to disagree with the government's sole adviser on strategy. He possessed not a single ally in the War Committee with the possible exception of Bonar Law, and as secretary of state for war he was expected to work in harmony with the C.I.G.S.

For the rest of July and the month of August there existed surprising harmony between Lloyd George and Wully. Robertson gave him copies of official communications between himself and the commanders in the various theaters, information which had been denied him before he went to the War Office. (The C.I.G.S., however, continued to carry on a secret and unofficial correspondence with his commanders in chief through "R" telegrams and "secret and personal" letters to limit any anti-"Western" views which might undermine the strategic advice he was giving the government.)

Robertson's task during this period was to maintain the government's commitment to the great offensive underway on the Continent. A considerable handicap was that he was as much in the dark about Haig's progress as the civilians. Haig's initial attempt at a breakthrough had been an unmitigated disaster, and he had fallen back on the strategy of wearing down the German army. As fresh assaults were launched, Robertson—who had little more than press communiqués to go on—began to press Haig for some encouraging news to give the civilians. "If you would send me a short letter which I could read to the War Committee I am sure it would be to their general interest, and to *your* interest in particular,"[28] he wrote on July 7. Haig responded with a letter which emphasized the growing demoralization of the German army.[29] Haig's optimism, however, was not enough to allay the restiveness of the civilians about the heavy casualties that lay ahead: and for what—the conquest of a few thousand yards of German trenches? "The Powers that be," Robertson wrote Haig as July came to an end, "are beginning to get a little uneasy in regard to the situation. . . . In general, what is bothering them is the probability that we may soon have to face a bill of 2 to 300,000 casualties with no very great gains additional to the present. It is thought that the primary object—relief of pressure on Verdun—has to some extent been achieved."[30]

Another problem for Robertson was an extremely critical analysis of the Somme offensive by Churchill, which was circulated to the cabinet with an introduction by F. E. Smith on August 1.[31] Hankey suspected that Lloyd George had a hand in this memorandum, but there is no evidence to support his suspicions.[32] Robertson certainly did not include Lloyd George with the critics of the Somme offensive, writing Haig on August 1 that "LG is all right provided I can say I am satisfied, and to enable me to do this it is necessary you should keep me acquainted with your views."[33]

On August 5, Wully read a letter from Haig to the War Committee that stressed the relief of Verdun and the assistance given to Russia's great offensive by tying down German soldiers in the West. There was, on the reverse side of the coin, no hint of victory in the near future, with Haig emphasizing that his attack must "go well into the autumn" and that another great offensive should be launched in 1917.[34] Lloyd George joined with the other members of the War Committee in refuting Churchill's criticisms and Robertson was instructed to send Haig a letter "assuring him that he might count on full support from home."[35]

By simultaneous attacks the Allies were putting immense pressure on the Central Powers. Despite his antipathy to frontal assaults with heavy casualties, Lloyd George approved of Haig's now deliberate and unhurried tactics, for the British army was making enormous inroads on German resources on the Somme, with the Germans foolishly attempting to retake every lost yard of trench. "Everything is going marvellously here," Esher reported to Lloyd George. "We have got the Boches by the throat at last."[36] The Russians under General Brusilov finally had their steamroller moving against the war-weary Austrians. Meanwhile, the Italians applied the pressure on the Isonzo while the tenacious French defense of Verdun took a heavy toll from the attacking Germans.

Lloyd George had feared that the Germans would take advantage of the generals' preoccupation with the West, giving up ground gradually, and winning spectacular victories in the East as they had done in 1915.[37] But, as he told the House of Commons in a survey of the war on August 22, Berlin's response had been to play into Britain's hands, throwing men and guns against the British on the Somme, weakening their attack on Verdun and giving the Russians free reign in the East.[38]

In late August, two events occurred which quickly eroded Lloyd George's always fragile support of the Somme offensive. First, on August 27, after weeks of haggling with the Entente over compensation for belligerency, Rumania declared war on Germany and Austria-Hungary. Two days later, Erich von Falkenhayn, the chief of the general staff and the architect of the costly German assault on Verdun, was demoted. His successor was the hero of Tannenberg—the sixty-nine-year-old Field Marshal Paul von Hindenburg. Lloyd George feared that this change in command might signal a shift to the East in German military power.

On September 2, the day after Bulgaria declared war on Rumania, Lloyd George expressed concern to Major-General Frederick B. Maurice, the director of military operations, that Rumania might go the way of Serbia. Dissatisfied with the response he received, he penned a note to Maurice:

We cannot afford another Serbian tragedy. We were warned early in 1915 that the Germans meant in confederation with the Bulgars to wipe Serbia out. In spite of the fact, when the attack came we had not purchased a single mule to aid the Serbians through Salonika. The result was when our troops landed there, owing to lack of equipment and appropriate transport, they could not go inland and Serbia was crushed. . . .

I therefore once more urge that the General Staff should consider what action we could in conjunction with France and Italy take immediately to relieve the pressure on Roumania if a formidable attack developed against her.[39]

Although Robertson maintains in his memoirs that he has no recollection of such a note, it is certain that Maurice informed him of the Welshman's views for he wrote Haig that "L.G. has got the Servian fit again."[40] Robertson's unyielding position was that the best defense of Rumania was to continue hammering the Germans on the Somme. If strong pressure were maintained, he argued, the Germans could only hope to throw Rumania back on the defensive—not destroy her.[41] Robertson's strategy was ratified by the War Committee on September 12 without any opposition from Lloyd George.[42] The secretary of state for war was away, touring the western front.

Lloyd George's visit to the western front in mid-September was to have important consequences for his future relations with the high command. The Battle of the Somme was essentially an artillery battle; and Lloyd George was concerned that general headquarters was mishandling its most destructive weapon. From various sources he learned that the French on the Somme were making better tactical use of artillery. The British artillery plan "followed conventional and rigid lines, being based upon an estimate of the destructive and protective power of the guns and the capacity of the infantry. Subordinate artillery commanders were allowed little initiative." The French commanders, however, emphasized coordination between the more experienced French gunners and infantry, postponing their attacks until the officers in the trenches were satisfied that the enemy's defenses were smashed. The difference between French and British tactics was written in blood. The British Expeditionary Force lost thousands " 'mopping up' ground which had not been conquered by the artillery," while the French tended to expend metal rather than life.[43]

Lloyd George's view of the war up close reinforced his view that the generals were hidebound and unimaginative. With Haig he motored to General Cavan's headquarters to meet with General Joffre, passing through many squadrons of British cavalry on their way to the front. When Lloyd George inquired about their function, Haig explained that they were being brought forward to exploit the anticipated breakthrough of the intensified British attack in mid-September. Later, in the presence of Haig and Joffre, Lloyd George dared express misgiving about the utility of horse soldiers in trench warfare. His doubts were brushed aside, with Joffre remarking "that he expected the French cavalry to ride through the broken German lines on his front the following morning."[44]

As for the soldiers, the more they saw of Lloyd George the politician, the less they thought of him. He could do nothing right in their eyes; even his table manners were faulted. His tour of the front was just a "joy ride." As Haig wrote his wife, "Breakfast with newspaper men, & posings for the Cinema Shows, pleased him more than anything else. No doubt with the ulterior object of catching votes!"[45] Philip Sassoon, Haig's private secretary, was similarly acid in his comments: "I was sorry we hadn't an elephant for them to ride."[46]

A much more serious criticism of Lloyd George's conduct concerned his private interview with General Ferdinand Foch in which he quizzed the French general about differences in French and British artillery tactics and casualty figures.[47] When Foch told Haig of this interview, the British com-

Albert Thomas looks on as Lloyd George expresses his doubts to Sir Douglas Haig and General Joffre about the use of cavalry in trench warfare.

mander in chief was aghast, commenting in his diary: "Unless I had been told of this conversation personally by Gen Foch, I would not have believed that a British Minister could have been so ungentlemanly as to go to a foreigner and put such questions regarding his own subordinates."[48]

General headquarters's reaction to this incident is very revealing of both its intense rivalry with the French and its hostility to politicians who had their own views on military questions. To be sure, Lloyd George knew that he was running the risk of insulting the generals if they learned of his impolitic talk with Foch. But what was protocol when the lives of thousands of soldiers were at stake? Lloyd George wanted the facts, and he had reason to believe that he would not get them from general headquarters. (Throughout the long Battle of the Somme British artillery tactics underwent no fundamental changes.)[49]

If anything, Lloyd George had reason to complain about the "ungentlemanly" behavior of Haig's supporters who used the press against him. Sassoon immediately wrote Northcliffe about the Foch interview and the powerful press lord went on the offensive.[50] Although Lloyd George had attempted to neutralize Northcliffe on his return from France with talk of "too large casualties in proportion to the results gained," the latter would tolerate no criticism of the generals, implied or otherwise.[51] The *Times*

Lloyd George and Lord Reading watch a bombardment during the Somme offensive.

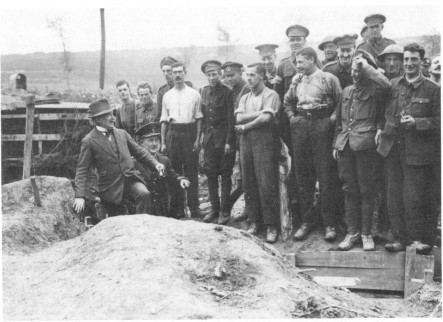

A photographic opportunity: Lloyd George in the trenches.

began to heap praise on the leadership of the British Expeditionary Force and, as a hit at Lloyd George, linked success or failure to the supply of guns and shells provided by the Ministry of Munitions. Gwynne of the *Morning Post* was more blunt, delivering a dark warning to Lloyd George in a leading article: "The Army is perfectly aware of what took place during the recent visit of the WAR MINISTER to France. That particular form of what the French call 'gaffe' must not be repeated; and we may mention that in case of its repetition we shall feel it our duty to publish the facts of the occurrence."[52]

Lloyd George, although infuriated by this press campaign, was all too aware that it was political suicide to be linked with criticism of Haig, who was the embodiment of the army in the public mind. His response, published in the *Morning Post,* was full of praise for the army and its leaders. He also denied that he had gone beyond "his legitimate sphere" on his tour of the front.[53]

Despite the turmoil in the army and press about his talk with Foch, Lloyd George refused to let the matter die, persuading Robertson to agree to the dispatch of Sir John French, who now was commander in chief of the home forces, on a tour of the French front to acquaint himself with French artillery tactics to assist him in the training of troops in Britain.[54] Another obvious motive of Lloyd George's was to collect evidence that would confirm his low opinion of Haig and his subordinates.[55]

During the height of the brouhaha over the Foch interview, Robertson uncharacteristically held his tongue. When word reached the War Office of Lloyd George's talk with the French general, he was eager for a showdown. But Haig, when asked for the facts of the incident, counseled that "the wisest course is to let the matter drop."[56] Robertson took this advice for the moment. "Consumed by dislike and suspicion of Lloyd George,"[57] however, he believed that he soon must put the Welshman in his place. His anger was provoked by more than Lloyd George's implied criticism of Haig and the British red-hatted staff. His worst fears of Lloyd George at the War Office were being realized. The dynamic and irrepressible Welshman was pushing strategy upon the ministers that was independent of the general staff.

In September Robertson's attempt to have British arms play a generally passive role in the East was under attack, with Lloyd George leading the charge. The obscure port of Rabegh on the Red Sea between Medina and Mecca became a focal point of this tug of war. In early June, Sherif Hussein of Mecca, the ruler of Hejaz, led his people in revolt against the Turks. Mecca fell quickly and Medina was beseiged. When Turkish reinforcements were sent south from Syria to Medina, British ministers became concerned that the Turks would continue their advance all the way to Mecca and crush the revolt.

Lloyd George, perhaps taking advantage of Robertson's absence, took the lead on September 1 in advocating military intervention at Rabegh to block the Turkish road to Mecca.[58] Fearing another "side show" in Arabia, Robertson adamantly rejected the idea of sending even a brigade to Rabegh. The usually supine War Committee, however, was reluctant to accept the advice of the general staff. On September 18, Lloyd George suggested that it was a matter of first class importance to help the Sherif if we could. Otherwise our prestige would go. The Chief of the Imperial General Staff could not see how it could be done. He suggested that the Committee should record their view that it was of the highest importance that the Sherif should be supported in every way, and invite the General Staff to say what, if anything[,] could be done. It was important to say whether Sir A. Murray could spare a brigade or not. That was a question for the Staff; the question of the policy of giving assistance to the Sherif was one for the Committee.

The committee readily agreed with Lloyd George that policy must be decided by the civilians and that political considerations justified the proposed military operation. Robertson was instructed, "in consultation with the Admiralty War Staff, to advise as soon as possible what action, if any, he considered could be taken to avert this possibility [Turkish conquest of Mecca]."[59]

As the imperial-minded ministers haggled with the apostle of the "Western" school of thought over intervention in the Hejaz, developments in the Balkans began to pose a greater threat to the generals' "Western" stance. First, there was the increasingly obvious pro-German position of King Constantine's government. As usual Lloyd George favored decisive action over caution when the Balkans were concerned. After Rumania came into the war, he was convinced that all the British and French needed "to do was to give a little push, and Greece would come in."[60] Robertson, supported by the Foreign Office, however, was hostile to any action which would involve Britain more deeply in either Greek politics or the Salonikan venture.

As British policy toward the confused Greek political situation remained in limbo, Lloyd George's impatience grew. Returning to London from his visit to the western front, he got the Greek situation placed on the agenda of the War Committee. Attacking the indecisiveness of his colleagues, he accused them of being "too tender." The British were now the "laughing stock of Europe." The correct policy was to send to Athens a message "by a 14" gun."[61]

The Greek situation was soon eclipsed by a more ominous development in the Balkans. German divisions began to arrive on Rumania's frontier. Lloyd George, realizing that Robertson was certain to block any effort to strengthen Rumania, devised a clever plan to get him out of the way. On September 26, he wrote the prime minister suggesting that Wully should immediately be sent to Russia to confer with the generals there. "The Eastern Generals probably concentrate their minds too exclusively on the East, and I am not sure that the Western Generals are not inclined to commit a similar error by limiting their views too much to the countries where their forces are operating," he noted. Robertson, determined to stand guard in the War Office, was not to be taken in by this stratagem and Lloyd George's proposal was dropped for the time being.[62]

As Lloyd George feared, the German high command was preparing a powerful counterstroke against the thinly equipped and poorly led Rumanian army. Throughout the campaign Rumanian officers were seen "strolling about Bucharest with painted faces, soliciting prostitutes or one another."[63]

One Rumanian general, Robertson reported with disgust to the War Committee, was playing bridge in Bucharest when his army was attacked.[64]

As Robertson expected, pressure immediately began to mount from Britain's allies to beef up the Allied force in the Balkans after Erich von Falkenhayn's Ninth Army began its offensive on September 30, with the Serbian military attaché urgently requesting 100,000 additional soldiers for Salonika. "Of course," Robertson explained to the War Committee, "the despatch of any large forces like that was out of the question." Russia, he emphasized, was the only Allied power in a position to offer assistance.[65]

The general staff's supineness while enemy storm clouds gathered over Rumania was the catalyst for an open breach between the secretary of state for war and the C.I.G.S. on October 9. After listening to Robertson downplay the German threat to Rumania and give his familiar defense of concentrating British forces in the West, Lloyd George launched into a long tirade against what he considered was the general staff's and his civilian colleagues' indifference to developments in the Balkans. If Rumania went the way of Serbia, British prestige "would have absolutely disappeared," he thundered. An Allied conference must be convened at once "to advise some measures which would enable our honour to be saved."[66]

The War Committee was unmoved by Lloyd George's emotional outburst. Even if troops could be spared (and Robertson said none were available), the ministers believed that they would arrive too late. Still, Lloyd George's words embarrassed the War Committee. If Britain sat on her hands while Rumania was destroyed, it would be awkward, if not dishonorable.

At the conclusion of the meeting, Robertson could no longer restrain himself. To his way of thinking, Lloyd George's criticism of the general staff was intolerable. Cornering the Welshman, he let himself go. If the War Committee ignored his advice and sent reinforcements to the Balkans, he thundered, he would "decline to be responsible for its execution."[67] For the next few days the war in Whitehall approached the intensity of the struggle on the Somme.

Robertson, who had more guile than is usually thought, mobilized his supporters against Lloyd George, whom the "soldiers' party" suspected of working with F. E. Smith, Churchill, and Sir John French against the high command. Robertson first took his case to his friend Repington, who immediately passed on Robertson's difficulties with Lloyd George to his volatile employer. Unable to get Lloyd George on the telephone on October 11, Northcliffe invaded the War Office, unleashing his anger on Lloyd George's private secretary J. T. Davies. "You can tell him that I hear he has been interfering with strategy," he said, "and that if he goes on I will break him."[68]

On that same day, Lloyd George received two letters, one from Gwynne admonishing him with the words, "Why on earth can't you let the army alone?" The other letter was from Robertson, accusing him of undermining his authority by meddling in the strategical direction of the war. A copy of his letter, Robertson pointedly noted, was being sent to the prime minister—and to the king, too, he might have added if he dared.[69]

Not unnaturally, Lloyd George suspected collusion among Robertson,

Gwynne, and Northcliffe. And he was right. Robertson was in touch with the editor of the *Morning Post* and he wrote Northcliffe, "The Boche gives me no trouble compared with what I meet in London. So any help you can give me will be of Imperial value."[70] With the recent press attack on him still fresh in his mind, Lloyd George struck back with the strongest letter he had ever composed to Robertson. Exploiting Robertson's indiscretions with Fleet Street, he stressed Northcliffe's visit to the War Office.

> I have found complaints against action taken by the Army Council and myself lodged with the Press—even before they ever reached me. . . . I feel confident that you must agree with me that this state of things is an outrage on all the best traditions of the service, and must tend to impair discipline in all ranks of the army, and I am certain that I shall receive your assistance and that of the Army Council in putting an end to this injurious practice.

As for his alleged "interference" in strategy, Lloyd George noted:

> It ought to be decided whether I have the same right—although I am War Secretary—to express an independent view on the war in the discussions which take place as any other member of the War Council—or whether, as long as I am War Secretary, I must choose between the position of a dummy or a pure advocate of all opinions expressed by my military advisers. . . . You must not ask me to play the part of a mere dummy. I am not in the least suited for the part.[71]

The Army Council did go on record opposing "unauthorized communications from official sources to the Press."[72] But this was an empty victory for Lloyd George. In his battle with Robertson, Lloyd George stood almost alone. Robertson was confident of the backing of the king, much of Fleet Street, and prominent Unionists and Liberals. If necessary, he was even prepared to hand in his resignation. Lloyd George consequently was forced to lay low for the moment, telling Asquith that he was not conspiring with Sir John French, Churchill, and Smith and swearing "that he had implicit confidence in both Haig and Robertson and if either of them were to go he knew no one who could fill their places."[73] Asquith, who saw merit in Lloyd George's criticism of the army's employment of its artillery, rather enjoyed the whole episode for it put Lloyd George on the defensive for a change.[74]

Avoiding an open confrontation with the C.I.G.S., Lloyd George maneuvered in other ways during the following days to help Rumania.[75] The French gave him valuable assistance, with Joffre telling London on October 10 that the Eastern Army, if reinforced with four divisions, two British and two Italian, might succeed in driving Bulgaria from the war with the assistance of the Russians in Dobrudja. When the War Committee discussed Joffre's proposal, Robertson continued to argue that nothing useful could be done in the Balkans. Rumania, he insisted, was not in grave danger; if she "made her dispositions properly she ought to be all right. She was different from Serbia." Lloyd George was generally subdued, prepared to let Joffre's request do his talking for him. In the end, the War Committee, in an attempt to mollify the French and give the appearance of helping Rumania, agreed to send an additional division to Salonika. But to the dismay of Lloyd George, the ministers made it clear that this division could only be employed to fulfill the original role of the Eastern Army: keeping Bulgarian troops tied down in Macedonia.

The Welshman's every move was being carefully observed during this period by Robertson. Robertson feared that Lloyd George, lacking support at home, might attempt to undermine the general staff by working with the French, especially Albert Thomas. On October 11, Robertson reported to the king that Paul Mantoux, the French history professor who served as an interpreter for Thomas at meetings with Lloyd George, had left London for Paris. Since Mantoux was suspected by the War Office of being Lloyd George's secret link with the French government, this probably meant that Paris would soon demand an Anglo-French conference on the Balkans.[77]

Sure enough, an Anglo-French conference was arranged for Boulogne on October 20. When the War Committee discussed the conference, Lloyd George suggested that the British minister of munitions, Montagu, should attend, although munitions was not on the agenda. This was an obvious ploy to assure the attendance of Thomas, the French minister of munitions, an avid Balkanite. Later, when Lloyd George met Thomas at Boulogne, he remarked with tongue in cheek, "Hullo, Thomas, fancy seeing you here!"[78]

At the Boulogne conference, Lloyd George broke ranks with the British delegation, siding with the French, who wanted to strengthen the Eastern Army. Put in an awkward position by the French, who promised to provide their fair share of troops, the British reluctantly agreed to consider the French proposal that Britain provide yet another division. But the British government remained as adamant as ever about extending the original role of the Eastern Army.[79]

Lloyd George, angered that a decision had once again been put off, was given a lift on October 23 by a visit from Thomas, who had been sent to London by Briand to lobby for a major effort in the Balkans. "'Full of beans'" Lloyd George went off to the War Committee the next day "in a most Machiavellian state of mind."[80]

The ministers sat uncomfortably in their chairs. Another Balkan disaster seemed imminent. Rumania, like Serbia before her, might soon be under the Teutonic heel, an event that might have serious political repercussions on the home front. Robertson, however, continued to argue that it was too late to do anything if Rumania collapsed before the spring of 1917.

Lloyd George adroitly exploited the situation. He proclaimed that "the only answer to give the French was that it was too late. If we sent 2 divisions

away from the Somme, it would be the old story of Loos, if there was a failure on the Somme. They would say that if we had only had those 2 divisions, all would have been well. He did not feel disposed to send them two divisions. He thought Roumania would probably make peace before they got there. The Germans would thoroughly frighten the Roumanians by their proximity to Bucharest, they would say that if they would take their oil and their corn, but would pay for it. . . .

The Welshman's gloomy prognostication elicited exactly the response he had expected. Bonar Law and others took exception to his statement. If troops were sent, it might encourage the Rumanians and Russians to fight on. With the political, rather than the military aspects of the situation being stressed, Robertson was put on the defensive. The politicians were his equal in arguing the political effects of a military operation. In the end, the War Committee, over Wully's objections, decided to send an additional division from the western front to the Balkans.[81]

Although Lloyd George clearly relished this triumph over the general staff, he saw no reason to rejoice. As early as June, he had urged the War Committee to improve the offensive potential of the Eastern Army. But the general staff's view had prevailed. Now, once again the British were reacting too late to German initiative in southeastern Europe. Robertson had discounted the German threat to Rumania and argued that the Eastern Army was too weak and disorganized to launch a successful offensive against the Bulgarians. On both counts he was wrong. Not only was Rumania about to be overrun, but the Eastern Army (before most of the reinforcements arrived) captured Monastir in mid-November. Denied reinforcements by the vacillations of the Allies, Sarrail, however, was unable to exploit his victory.[82]

Lloyd George had reached the breaking point by the end of October. Robertson had dictated British military policy throughout 1916, and Lloyd George believed that his strategy had brought Britain closer to defeat than victory. The Germans were in the ascendancy in southeastern Europe and he viewed the Somme offensive as "a bloody and disastrous failure."[83] His frustration over his emasculated and feeble position in the War Office was best summed up by the bitter comment he made to Aitken: "I am the butcher's boy who leads in the animals to be slaughtered—when I have delivered the men my task in the war is over."[84]

In the next few weeks Lloyd George resorted to every ploy in his considerable bag of tricks to overthrow the generals and increase his influence over the direction of the war. Initially he attempted to use his position as secretary of state for war in the councils of the Allies to mobilize the civilians against a repetition of the generals' 1916 strategy.

NOTES

1. Hankey Diary, June 6, 1916, 1/1.
2. Ibid., June 10, 1916, 1/1.
3. Entry of January 31, 1916, *A Diary by Frances Stevenson*, p. 91.
4. Entry of June 6–8, 1916, *Diaries of C. P. Scott*, pp. 216–17.
5. Beaverbrook, *Politicians and the War, 1914–1916*, pp. 207–8.
6. Esher to Robertson, June 21, 1916, Esher MSS, 2/16.
7. Beaverbrook, *Politicians and the War, 1914–1916*, pp. 208–9.
8. Entry of June 13–17, 1916, *Diaries of C. P. Scott*, p. 218.
9. Entry of March 11, 1916, *A Diary by Frances Stevenson*, p. 102.
10. Entry of June 15, 1916, *Lord Riddell's War Diary*, pp. 190–91.

11. Memorandum by Stamfordham, June 17, 1916, and Stamfordham to George V, June 17, 1916, RA GV K951/16–17.

12. *Morning Post,* June 7 and 13, 1916.

13. *Daily Chronicle,* June 17, 1916.

14. Memorandum by Stamfordham, June 17, 1916, RA GV K951/16.

15. See Lee to Lloyd George, June 18, 1916, Lloyd George MSS, D/1/1/21.

16. Memorandum by Lloyd George, June 17, 1916, Lloyd George MSS, D/18/2/19.

17. Lloyd George to Asquith, June 17, 1916, Asquith MSS, 30.

18. Lloyd George, *War Memoirs,* 1:460.

19. Lee to Lloyd George, June 18, 1916, Lloyd George MSS, D/1/1/21.

20. Montagu to Asquith, June 20, 1916, Lloyd George MSS, D/17/16/5.

21. Hankey Diary, June 24, 1916, 1/1.

22. Robertson to Lloyd George, June 24, 1916, Lloyd George MSS, D/18/8/18.

23. Lloyd George to Robertson, June 26, 1916, Robertson MSS, 1/19/3.

24. Entry of July 26, 1916, *A Diary by Frances Stevenson,* p. 109.

25. War Committee, February 29, 1916, CAB 42/9/7.

26. Ibid., July 6, 1916, CAB 42/16/1.

27. Ibid., July 28, 1916, CAB 42/16/8.

28. Robertson to Haig, July 7, 1916, Robertson MSS, 1/22/51.

29. War Committee, July 11, 1916, CAB 42/16/5.

30. Robertson to Haig, July 29, 1916, Haig MSS, no. 107. Haig, incidentally, was greatly provoked by this letter, noting: "Not exactly the letter of a C.I.G.S.! . . . He ought to take responsibility also!"

31. Memorandum by Churchill, August 1, 1916, CAB 37/153/3.

32. Hankey Diary, August 1, 1916, 1/1.

33. Robertson to Haig, August 1, 1916, Robertson MSS, 1/22/62.

34. War Committee, August 5, 1916, CAB 42/17/3.

35. Ibid.

36. Esher to Lloyd George, August 5, 1916, Lloyd George MSS, E/2/11/1. The French protested that Haig was dragging his feet, but Lloyd George told Robertson that the British commander in chief was "playing absolutely the right game." See Robertson to Haig, August 29, 1916, Robertson MSS, 1/22/72.

37. This, incidentally, is what Churchill had warned against in his August 1 memorandum.

38. *H. C. Deb.,* 5th series, vol. 85 (August 22, 1916).

39. Lloyd George to D.M.O., September 4, 1916, Lloyd George MSS, E/1/5/6.

40. Robertson to Haig, September 7, 1916, Haig MSS, no. 108; also see Robertson, *Soldiers and Statesmen,* 2:127, and Repington, *First World War, 1914–1918,* 1:323.

41. Memorandum by Robertson, September 9, 1916, CAB 42/19/6.

42. War Committee, September 12, 1916, CAB 42/19/6.

43. *Military Operations, France and Belgium, 1916,* 2:567, and Captain G. C. Wynne, *If Germany Attacks: The Battle in Depth in the West* (1940), p. 121.

44. Lloyd George, *War Memoirs,* 1:323.

45. Haig to Lady Haig, September 13, 1916, Haig MSS, no. 144.

46. Sassoon to Northcliffe, September 14, 1916, Northcliffe MSS, vol. 8.

47. For Lloyd George's version of this interview, see memorandum by Stamfordham, October 12, 1916, RA GV Q1200/6.

48. Haig Diary, September 17, 1916, no. 107.

49. *Military Operations, France and Belgium, 1916,* 2:566.

50. Sassoon to Northcliffe, September 14, 1916, Northcliffe MSS, vol. 8.

51. Northcliffe to Sassoon, September, 1916, Northcliffe MSS, vol. 8.

52. *Morning Post,* September 28, 1916.

53. Lloyd George to the editor, *Morning Post,* September 29, 1916.

54. Robertson to Haig, October 9, 1916, Robertson MSS, 1/22/80.

55. See Foch's comments to Wilson about French's conversation with him in Wilson Diary, October 17, 1916.

56. Robertson to Haig, September 25, and Haig to Robertson, September 28, 1916, Robertson MSS, 1/22/74 and 76. Haig, who distrusted newsmen as much as politicians, opposed any personal attack on Lloyd George in the press. On the other hand, he was beginning to realize the importance of having the press on his side in the "Westerner"-"Easterner" debate. See Sassoon to Northcliffe, September 29 and October 6, 1916, Northcliffe MSS, vol. 8, and Rawlinson Diary, October 15, 1916, 1/7.

57. Esher to Haig, September 25, 1916, Esher MSS, 2/17.

58. War Committee, September 1, 1916, CAB 42/19/1.

59. Ibid., September 18, 1916, CAB 42/20/3. For the most complete discussion of the Rabegh question, see V. H. Rothwell, *British War Aims and Peace Diplomacy, 1914–1918* (1971), pp. 87–95.

60. War Committee, September 1, 1916, CAB 42/19/1.

61. Ibid., September 18, 1916, CAB 42/20/3.

62. Lloyd George to Asquith, September 26, 1916, and Robertson to Lloyd George, September 27, 1916, Lloyd George MSS, E/2/23/5 and E/1/5/2.

63. Cruttwell, *History of the Great War*, p. 293.

64. War Committee, October 3, 1916, CAB 42/21/1.

65. Ibid.

66. Ibid., October 9, 1916, CAB 42/21/3.

67. Robertson, *Soldiers and Statesmen*, 2:128.

68. Beaverbrook, *Politicians and the War, 1914–1916*, p. 323, and Northcliffe to Sassoon, October 18, 1916, Northcliffe MSS, vol. 8.

69. Gwynne to Lloyd George, October 11, 1916, Lloyd George MSS, E/2/14/1, and Robertson to Lloyd George, October 11, 1916, Robertson MSS, 1/19/7. Gwynne also wrote Asquith imploring him to put Lloyd George in his place. Gwynne to Asquith, October 11, 1916, Gwynne MSS, 14.

70. Robertson to Northcliffe, October 11, 1916, quoted in Reginald Pound and Geoffrey Harmsworth, *Northcliffe* (1959), p. 508, and Gwynne to Rawlinson, October 17, 1916, Rawlinson MSS, 1/8.

71. Lloyd George to Robertson, October 11, 1916, Robertson, 1/19/6.

72. See Army Council (190), October 13, 1916, W.O. 163/21.

73. Memorandum by Stamfordham, October 12, 1916, RA GV Q1200/6.

74. Hankey Diary, October 12, 1916, 1/1.

75. It should be noted that Haig once again played the role of peacemaker, telling a dubious Robertson that Lloyd George, who could do "a great deal of good," should be "humoured." Esher Diary, October 26, 1916, 2/17.

76. War Committee, October 12, 1916, CAB 42/21/6.

77. Robertson to Wigram, October 11, 1916, RA GV Q1200/4, and Hankey Diary, October 16, 1916, 1/1.

78. War Committee, October 18, 1916, CAB 42/22/2, and Hankey Diary, October 19–20, 1916, 1/1.

79. Allied Conference, October 20, 1916, CAB 28/1/I.C.-11, and Hankey Diary, October 19–20, 1916, 1/1.

80. Entry of October 24, 1916, *A Diary by Frances Stevenson*, p. 119.

81. Ibid., and War Committee, October 24, 1916, CAB 42/22/5.

82. Tanenbaum, *General Maurice Sarrail*, pp. 127–28.

83. Hankey Diary, November 1, 1916, 1/1.

84. Beaverbrook, *Politicians and the War, 1914–1916*, p. 320.

6
Lloyd George Attempts to Overthrow the Generals

As the third year of campaigning approached an end, the strain on the nation was great. Whiskey was weaker and dress duller. Houses were in need of paint, fences in need of repair, and roads in need of surfacing. Wounded soldiers in their distinctive blue jackets abounded and telegrams informing parents and wives of the death of loved ones fell like leaves as the Somme offensive continued into the mud and snow of November. Death played no favorites. Asquith lost two nephews and his oldest son, Raymond; Hankey, his brother Donald. Lloyd George, who had two sons in khaki, was luckier. Undersea assault by the German submarine was taking a terrible toll on shipping. Walter Runciman, the president of the Board of Trade, warned the government that "my expert advisers believed that I am far too sanguine in advising the War Committee that the complete breakdown in shipping will come in June, 1917; they are convinced that it will come much sooner than June."[1] Britain's deteriorating financial situation was another matter of grave concern.

Robertson's blunt and sober assessment of the progress of the war added to the penetrating gloom. Germany, he admitted, despite the extensive Allied attacks in 1916, was "fighting with undiminished vigour."[2] This statement was a tacit admission by the general staff that it had underestimated the staying power and resources of Germany. Robertson, in fact, told Lloyd George that Britain would "be well advised not to expect the end at any rate before the Summer of 1918. How long it may go on afterwards I cannot even guess."[3] Robertson's remarkably accurate forecast was a crushing disappointment to the civilians. To be sure, Robertson had never promised that the Somme offensive would defeat Germany. Nor had he underestimated British casualties.[4] But the ministers expected more—whether it had been promised or not—from the high command's "Western" strategy. The major achievement of the offensive, which had gone on long after Verdun had been relieved, was the terrible punishment inflicted upon the German army. But in killing Germans, was the British army itself being bled to death?

Historians still argue over British casualties, a vital question in any assessment of Lloyd George's opposition to the high command's strategy. British as opposed to German losses during the Somme and Passchendaele offensives have attracted the most attention. The student has a startling disparity of figures from which to choose for the official record provides two vastly different sets of figures. In 1922, the War Office published its *Statistics of the Military Effort of the British Empire during the Great War*, which asserted that British losses in the West from 1915 to 1918 were approximately 3 to 2 the corresponding German losses. Only in 1918, when the Germans launched their great attacks against the British, were German losses greater than British losses.[5]

As the conflict between Lloyd George and the generals continued after the war in the publishing houses, German casualties were drastically revised upward and British casualties downward in the British official history by its compiler, Brigadier-General J. E. Edmonds, who argued that the Germans distorted their casualty figures by not including lightly wounded. But it has been convincingly shown that Edmonds's calculations of German casualties bear little, if any, relationship to his evidence.[6] Furthermore, as Liddell Hart has pointed out: "An examination of the figures of dead and wounded throughout the war shows that in the German casualty lists the average ratio was 1 to 2.35 and the British lists 1 to 2.27. That difference in itself shows that the German figures did not exclude the lightly wounded, and thus shatters Edmonds's absurd contention that 33 percent should be added to the German casualty figures for a fair comparison."[7]

That Edmonds was more interested in protecting Haig's reputation through dubious accountancy than in revealing the historical truth is revealed by statements he made to Liddell Hart between the wars.[8] Edmonds freely admitted that he held Haig's tactics in contempt, once remarking, "I have to write of Haig with my tongue in my cheek. One can't tell the truth. He was really above the average—or rather below the average—in stupidity. He could not grasp things at conferences, particularly anything technical."[9] On another occasion he said, "H. had no comprehension of light railways, concrete, or other siege-war matters. He 'shoved the thing along' merely."[10] In sum, "trade-unionism," as Edmonds himself admitted, was his great weakness as a historian.[11]

As the daily parade of ambulances from Charing Cross carrying the wounded from the western front continued, Lloyd George thought that he detected a growing disenchantment with the generals among his colleagues. This, along with his genuine fear that Britain would lose the war unless the civilians asserted themselves over the military, emboldened him. To pressure Asquith, he began talking once again of resignation and of taking his case to the people. He told Hankey on November 1 that he, Albert Thomas, Signor Bissolati, the Italian Socialist leader, and others "would all resign simultaneously & tell their respective fellow countrymen that the war was being run on wrong lines, & that they had better make peace rather than repeat the experiences of 1916."[12]

As always resignation was viewed as a last resort. Before taking this drastic step, Lloyd George hoped to seize the initiative from the generals with a twofold plan. First, he revived his suggestion to send Robertson to Russia to give him a broader outlook. Second, aware that the Allied generals planned to meet in mid-November to plot future strategy,[13] he hoped to arrange a meeting of the Allied ministers to discuss strategy before the generals presented their governments with their usual fait accompli.

On November 3, he launched his campaign to overthrow the generals at a War Committee meeting which, at Hankey's suggestion, did not include "that old dragon Robertson."[14] Free from Wully's fierce scowl, Lloyd George dominated the proceedings as never before. He first read a telegram from the Rumanian statesman Také Jonescu, who implored the British to save his beleaguered state. The secretary of state for war then turned to a minute which he had requested from Robertson on the duration of the war. Robertson's forecast that the war would last at least until 1918, Lloyd George said, was "one of the most serious documents on the war that he had read." He went on to say:

> We were not getting on with the war. We were now at the end of the third campaign of the war. Yet the enemy had recovered the initiative; he had in his occupation more territory than ever before; and he still had some four millions of reserves. At no point had the Allies achieved a definite, clear success. Continuing, Mr. Lloyd George said that the offensive on the Somme had three objects in view:—
> (1.) To relieve Verdun. In this it had succeeded.
> (2.) To break through the German line or capture some important strategic position. In this respect it had failed.
> (3.) To detach troops from the East so as to enable the Russian offensive to succeed, or to protect Roumania. In this respect also it had failed.
> How then, Mr. Lloyd George asked, is the war to be brought to an end? What, he asked, is the plan of the Entente Powers? To be successful in the plan pursued up to the present time it is essential that the anvil should be more damaged than the hammer. . . . the enemy was more careful of his men than we were. The enemy, he pointed out, also had the advantage of being able to give ground, and thus to avoid losses.[15] . . . Mr. Lloyd George then referred to certain other considerations [shipping, food, finances], in regard to which the position of the Allies is difficult. . . . There was also, he pointed out, the possibility that it might become difficult to keep the Entente Powers together. Further it was essential to keep up the spirit of people at home, and this might not be easy where there were no definite victories. The people of this country firmly believed that the Somme offensive means breaking through the German lines, and there would be great disappointment when they discovered that this was not likely to happen.

Lloyd George next reminded the ministers that the public would hold the politicians responsible—not the generals. It was time for the civilian leaders to meet and "take stock of the situation." The "first object of the Conference should be to insist that West should confer with East." To achieve this goal, a military conference should be held in Russia, "which should be attended by the principal generals from the west—preferably General Robertson, Joffre and Castelnau, and Cadorna."

The Welshman's words made an impact on the ministers, although some argued that he was too pessimistic. Significantly, the prime minister was among those who supported the tenor of his remarks. Asquith, who had recently been told by his son Arthur Asquith, who had been invalided from the western front, that the German lines were impenetrable,[16] obviously shared some of Lloyd George's reservations about the generals' conduct of the war. Later, when Hankey, who had not been present, prepared a record of the November 3 meeting from notes and "a full personal explanation" by Lloyd George, Asquith accepted a conclusion with revision that was damning to the high command. Asquith's deletions are in italics and his additions are placed in brackets: "It was generally agreed that the offensive on the Somme, if continued next year, was not likely to lead to decisive results, and that the losses *were would* [might] *making* [make] too heavy a drain on our resources having regard to the results to be anticipated. It was therefore generally agreed that we should *seek for some more promising plan to end the war* [examine whether a decision might not be reached in another theatre]."

The British leaders also accepted Lloyd George's suggestion that a military conference should be held in Russia and that Asquith and Lloyd George should attend a civilian conference in Paris to discuss next year's campaign prior to the generals' meeting at Chantilly. To prevent the military from shortcircuiting this scheme, this decision was neither printed nor circulated.[17]

A "delighted" Lloyd George later dictated a telegram to Hankey to send to Britain's allies. Just as they finished, another draft arrived from Grey which contained the proposal for a military conference in Russia. Alarmed that the generals would block this proposal before it was discussed by the civilians in Paris, Lloyd George removed this section. The two drafts were vetted together, with Hankey taking the final draft to the foreign secretary, who reinserted a vague reference to the proposed conference in the East to show the Russians that they were not being ignored.[18]

On November 7, after Robertson left the cabinet room, the ministers once again discussed the proposed conferences in Paris and Russia. The response had been disappointing. The French, Grey reported, were "lukewarm" and the "Italian reply was tantamount to a refusal." The civilians, however, decided to press on with both conferences.[19]

That afternoon an "intensely indignant" Robertson saw Hankey. The cat was out of the bag—perhaps released by Lloyd George's enemy McKenna. Never one to mince words, Robertson accused Lloyd George of a conspiracy "to get him away & play hanky-panky behind his back."[20] The C.I.G.S. suspected Lloyd George of intriguing with F. E. Smith and Churchill and perhaps even with the French premier, Briand.[21]

The tactful secretary of the War Committee attempted to keep the two volcanoes in the War Office from erupting. Early in the morning on the ninth he wrote a long letter to Robertson explaining the War Committee's reasons for wanting him to go to Russia. In an effort to reassure Wully, he emphasized that the War Committee, although inclined to look East, had not been seduced by Lloyd George's Balkan ideas.[22] Hankey then told Lloyd George over lunch that he must remove Robertson's suspicions of his ulterior motives in suggesting the Russian conference. The Welshman's response was to suggest that he would accompany Robertson to Russia to demonstrate his good intentions. After lunch, Lloyd George turned to what was uppermost on his mind: a draft of a long paper on the war which he had written for the proposed conference in Paris.[23] As Lloyd George read his paper aloud, Hankey must have realized how impossible his role as peacemaker was.

A passionate denunciation of the "Westerners," the paper underscored the Entente failures in Greece, Serbia, and Rumania. Demonstrating that he was as one-sided as Robertson, Lloyd George maintained that the fall of Serbia was the "most irreparable of all Allied failures" in 1915 and that Rumania "may be the turning-point of the campaign" in 1916. A familiar refrain was sounded: "Has anyone mapped out a road to victory? . . . We must have a definite plan. I have heard of only one. People talk of hammering, and of a war of attrition. The success of hammering depends entirely upon whether you are making a greater impression on the barrier or the hammer." If some "victories" were not won soon, he argued, Entente morale would collapse along with its credit.

Lloyd George's brief against the generals was as long on criticism of the "Westerners" as it was short on specific recommendations. His chief point was that "the whole policy of the Allies ought to be coördinated: there ought to be a complete understanding between the East and West."[24] A consistent thread that ran through this document was that Lloyd George had been right in the past, the generals wrong.

Any hope that Hankey had of lowering the temperature in the War Office ended that evening with a letter from Robertson which contained an emotional blast. The rugged North Countryman wrote "that he was out for a row without kid gloves on."[25] It is likely that Robertson, who was threatening resignation, was just as blunt with Asquith, and when it came to a showdown between the secretary of state for war and the C.I.G.S., Asquith, despite his concern about the progress of the war, sided as usual with Robertson.

During the next three days the prime minister undermined Lloyd George's efforts to give Allied strategy a new direction. On the tenth, Asquith told the War Committee that the French had proposed that the Paris conference should take place on the thirteenth. But "this was out of the question," he said, "as it was indispensable to have a Cabinet Meeting on Monday afternoon. The tides at the present time did not serve until mid-day, so that it would be impossible to leave England before mid-day Tuesday."[26] This meant that the conference would now take place on Wednesday, the day the generals conferred at Chantilly.

Asquith's reasons for postponing the Allied meeting were absurd. After all, he could have asked the ministers to meet on Saturday rather than Monday if it were vital to the nation. Their weekend plans were hardly essential. As Hankey noted in his diary, "Runciman was going for a day's shooting, Lord Curzon for a week-end, and Lord Crawford to address his former constituents."[27]

A further disappointment was in store for Lloyd George on Sunday. The

Welshman gave Hankey his paper and dispatched him to the Wharf to persuade the prime minister to include his criticism of the generals' strategy in his speech to the Paris conference. Asquith "flatly declined" to read the original memorandum because it "would outrage Robertson & do no good." He then amended it and turned it back to Hankey. The secretary of the War Committee returned to London and telephoned the bad news to Lloyd George, who decided "to hand" the original paper to the conference himself. The matter did not end there. Perhaps realizing that without the prime minister's support his ideas would have little impact, he agreed the next day, the thirteenth, to allow Asquith to revise the document. Asquith then made extensive revisions, taking "all the sting out of the document."[28]

It seems that Asquith erred badly in underestimating the intensity of Lloyd George's feelings during this period, telling Hankey that "Ll. G. is so erratic & changeable that too much attention must not be paid to him."[29] Lloyd George, however, was not to be put off. It was obvious to him that Robertson could not be humbled as long as Asquith directed the war. On Monday, the thirteenth, he met with Aitken at the War Office. Believing that he had enlisted the support of Carson, who acted virtually as the leader of the Unionists in the Commons because of Bonar Law's support of Asquith, Lloyd George expressed a preference for "a real War Council of three with practically dictatorial powers."[30] Lloyd George's intentions seem clear. Asquith would remain prime minister, but Lloyd George through a small executive council would sidetrack Robertson and give British strategy a new direction. In short, it was Robertson and the military policy he represented—not Asquith—whom Lloyd George hoped to overthrow. Much of Lloyd George's conversation with Aitken dealt with his frustration over Robertson's domination of the War Office. The "smoking pistol" he used then and later to discredit the C.I.G.S. was his September 4 note that he had sent to Maurice warning of Germany's threat to Rumania which the general staff had ignored.

On November 14, Lloyd George, Asquith, Robertson, Maurice, Bonham Carter, and Hankey departed for Paris. Despite the tension between Lloyd George and Robertson, the party was in high spirits. Once, when Asquith's thoughts seemed to dwell on his son Raymond as they passed a war cemetery, Robertson restored the lighthearted mood by exclaiming, " 'there's a fine pair of pants for you, Prime Minister,' pointing to some backyard, where there hung on the clothes line a pair of unmentionables of gigantic proportions and indescribable hue!"[31]

Lloyd George's truncated document, which Asquith continued to revise on the train to Paris, finally saw the light of day on November 15. During the morning Lloyd George and Asquith met with Briand and Admiral La Caze, the acting minister for war, at the Quai d'Orsay before the conference began that afternoon. During this "hole-in-the-corner, informal, unrecorded conversation," as Hankey called it, Asquith took Lloyd George's precious paper from his pocket and "read it, or rather rushed through it, without emphasis or pause." Briand, who had rushed in from a wearing cross examination from Georges Clemenceau at one of the committees of the Chamber of Deputies, was "evidently too ruffled and distracted to take in ideas at such a speed. He asked Mr. Asquith to leave a copy and promised to study it all with great care before the afternoon meeting."[32]

From this dismal beginning the conference went downhill in Lloyd George's view. It is true that the ministers ventilated their hostility toward the generals' control of the war at the first session and approved in principle the proposed Russian conference. But at the second session, despite Lloyd George's lobbying for a Balkan offensive, they docilely considered and approved the generals' plans for 1917 which had been drawn up in General Joffre's writing room at Chantilly. Although the generals gave lip service to knocking Bulgaria out of the war in 1917, their strategy was a repetition of 1915 and 1916. The western front remained the primary theater; if one of the Allies were attacked, the others would launch offensives to relieve the pressure.

An angry and depressed Lloyd George left the conference room. As Haig gleefully noted in his diary, the Welshman had been "crushed."[33] With misgivings, he had taken the War Office some four months earlier, hoping that his idea of treating the war as a single front, giving emphasis to the East as well as to the West, might gain acceptance in Allied councils. But with Asquith unwilling to challenge the general staff, he was and would continue to be impotent.

Later that evening, a despondent Lloyd George told Hankey as they strolled together that he was going to resign. Hankey demurred. As they passed the Vendome Column, Hankey made a proposal that was already on Lloyd George's mind: "You ought to insist on a small War Committee being set up for the day-to-day conduct of the war, with full powers. It must be independent of the Cabinet. It must keep in close touch with the P.M., but the Committee ought to be in continuous session, and the P.M., as Head of the Government, could not manage that. . . . The Chairman must be a man of unimpaired energy and great driving power."[34]

Hankey had been loyal to Asquith, and his view that "a change is urgently necessary"[35] was indicative of the growing concern about Asquith's leadership. After more than eight and a half years in power, the leader of British Liberalism was worn thin. He lacked drive and decisiveness.

Despite his lack of confidence in Asquith, Lloyd George was still prepared to accept his presence in 10 Downing Street. He distrusted the Unionists and saw no William Pitt the Elder among them. Furthermore, the Right generally desired more influence and power for the generals—not less. The Unionists returned his distrust. Percolating within his mind was surely the belief that he was the best man to save Britain. According to his lights, he had been right on Serbia and Rumania; the others, ministers and soldiers alike, had been wrong. But there is abundant evidence that he neither thought that he could become prime minister nor worked to gain the office. His primary concern, if he stayed in the government, was to diminish Wully's authority. Working through an executive committee, he would do Asquith's dirty work for him.

On the day of his talk with Hankey, Lloyd George sent a telegram to

Aitken requesting a meeting with Bonar Law. His course now seemed firmly charted. After many threats of resignation he was determined to either reorganize the machinery of government to give him a dominant position or resign. The time to strike was now because he believed that the impending fall of Rumania would both discredit Robertson and weaken his protector Asquith.[36]

On November 20, Lloyd George met with Carson and Bonar Law for the first time to discuss his plan for an executive committee. The next days were filled with frantic activity. Letters flew back and forth, dinner parties were interrupted, complex negotiations took place in smoke-filled rooms (Bonar Law's incessant pipe smoking guaranteed that) and in the background a press campaign against Asquith escalated.[37]

Meanwhile, the ministers continued their work as usual. On November 21, the War Committee at its regular meeting devoted most of its time to the growing manpower crisis. Later that day, Asquith summoned the ministers once again to the cabinet room. No military advisers were invited. The crisis in the War Office had come to a head. Robertson, convinced that he was being given the "K[itchener] dodge," as he put it, remained dead set against going to Russia. Also, his supporters in the government, especially Curzon and McKenna, were upset over the criticism of the generals at the Paris conference which had been inspired, in part, by Lloyd George.

The conference in Russia, which had now been accepted by all of the powers, dominated the debate. What was the government to do about the intransigence of Robertson? Lloyd George took advantage of the discussion to explain his reasons for wanting Robertson to go to Russia: "In his [Mr. Lloyd George's] view, if the Somme offensive had not succeeded as far as we would have wished, it was due to the fact that there had not been enough pressure exerted simultaneously from the East. The secret of next year's campaign was to prevent the Germans from being able to concentrate one million men on any menaced front. For this reason he would have liked Sir William Robertson to go to the East, and see the front there for himself." But for two reasons, Lloyd George continued, he was no longer pressing Robertson to go to Russia. First, the results of the Chantilly military conference meant that Entente strategy was unlikely to change. Second, the story had been spread by someone that he was trying to get rid of Robertson.[38] When asked whom he had in mind, Lloyd George said that he would tell the prime minister in private. When some ministers protested his secrecy, Lloyd George said, "Very well, then I will tell you. It is the Chancellor of the Exchequer." Although McKenna at first denied this charge, he admitted in the end that "perhaps he had not denied the suggestion that Robertson was being sent because D. wanted to get him out of the way."[39]

There was yet another reason why Lloyd George now wanted to drop the question of Robertson going to Russia. Combining the Unionist leaders to wrest the control of the war from Asquith taxed Lloyd George's ingenuity to the limit. Bonar Law, whose support was crucial, agreed with Lloyd George that the civilians must assert their authority over the military. Carson, however, supported by the Unionist War Committee, which had been organized in January 1916, was the champion of Robertson and Haig. With right wing support necessary, it was not the time to quarrel with Robertson. Hence Lloyd George attempted to woo Carson and his supporters by emphasizing the need for decisive leadership and his commitment to total victory and by soft-pedaling his opposition to the generals' conduct of the war. That he was succeeding was illustrated by a remarkable leading article in the *Morning Post* on November 23. Having earlier raked the Welshman over the coals for his interference with the high command, Gwynne, in a startling reversal, wrote:

> He [Lloyd George] is not a strategist, he is not an administrator; but he is a power which makes for victory; he is a force to which the nation may adhere, which the nation may follow. And we believe also that he now sees the wisdom of working cordially with the Army. He is staunchly supporting Sir William Robertson and Sir Douglas Haig, and is doing all in his power to provide them with the means of victory.

Since Gwynne spoke for the Right, especially Carson, these words were a clear warning to Asquith and his supporters that the Welshman had come to an understanding with the Ulster leader.

On November 25, the triumvirate of Bonar Law, Lloyd George, and Carson and the omnipresent Aitken met at one o'clock at Pembroke Lodge, the home of Bonar Law. A compromise was accepted that resolved their differences. Asquith, was to be asked to accept a "civilian General Staff" of three men with Lloyd George as chairman. Asquith, who was expected to be an infrequent participant, was given the role of a figurehead president. Bonar Law then took a copy of this arrangement to the prime minister, who agreed to consider it.[40]

Paradoxically, as the gulf widened between Lloyd George and Asquith, Robertson, who a few weeks earlier had said that "he would do anything for the Prime Minister,"[41] began to support Lloyd George's efforts to reorganize the government. Wully heartily approved of Lloyd George's energy, decisiveness and extremism on the war, and he shared the Welshman's contempt for the argumentative and vacillating cabinet and War Committee. Fear of an inconclusive peace was also, to an important degree, responsible for his support of Lloyd George.

Earlier, during the first stages of the Somme offensive, there had been concern within the government that Germany might attempt to escape defeat through American mediation; this prompted the British leaders to approach warily possible peace terms on August 10. Lloyd George's sentiments could not have been more "ginger." He attempted to cut short the discussion by bluntly declaring that he "did not think that any terms would be possible for Germany to accept this year." Furthermore, if the United States applied pressure by limiting the supply of cotton (which was essential to the production of munitions), "it would be a declaration of war." When Bonar Law threw his support to Lloyd George, Asquith retreated, suggesting that the committee should "ruminate over the matter."[42]

On August 30, with Lloyd George absent, Asquith returned to the question of peace. The French were now amenable to a discussion of terms, and the prime ministers asked the war leaders to put their thoughts on acceptable peace terms on paper.[43]

As the ministers and military advisers put ink to paper, Lloyd George did not lift a pen. Apparently concerned about both the threat of American intervention and the growing pessimism in the government about Britain's ability to impose its terms on Berlin, he arrogantly bypassed the statesman-like discussion of peace terms going on out of the public limelight. In late September, at the very moment he was under fire by the "soldiers' party" because of the Foch interview, he told an American journalist: "The fight must be to a finish—to a knockout." His famous interview also included a sharp rebuke to President Wilson. "Britain asked no intervention when she was unprepared to fight," he said. "She will tolerate none now that she is prepared until the Prussian military despotism is broken beyond repair."[44] It need not be emphasized that Lloyd George was fully aware of the political advantages of his public commitment to a war *à outrance*.

In November, the discussion of possible peace terms took a new twist. For the first time, a memorandum was circulated to the cabinet that questioned the government's commitment to total victory and suggested a compromise peace.[45] The author of this memorandum was the respected Unionist leader and former foreign secretary, Lord Lansdowne.

Liberal ministers such as McKenna, Grey, and Runciman were not prepared to push for an inconclusive peace. But Lloyd George rightly suspected their genuine commitment to a "knock-out blow." Grey, for example, probably believed that the gloomy military situation along with the dismal financial situation and especially the shipping crisis made a compromise peace the most sensible course of action.[46] In his circumspect reply to Lansdowne, Grey argued that as long as the military advisers remained optimistic about the Allies' ability to "dictate" terms, "peace is premature, and to contemplate it is to betray the interests of this country and of the Allies." But he emphasized that Admiral John R. Jellicoe's view that the German U-boat might force Britain "to conclude peace on unsatisfactory terms" should be placed before the cabinet.[47] Grey perhaps believed that the Admiralty's pessimism, frankly revealed, would do his talking for him.

Lloyd George and Robertson remained poles apart on strategy. But on this issue they were in complete agreement: Germany must be defeated and Britain should dominate the peace settlement. When Robertson was asked to respond to Lansdowne, Lloyd George told him to "speak out quite plainly and not 'be afraid to let yourself go.' "[48]

Robertson clearly let himself go. His memorandum has been called "the most bellicose and offensive document ever inflicted on a British Cabinet,"[49] an opinion with which it is difficult to disagree. After expressing confidence in the Entente's ability to win the war, Robertson heaped abuse upon those who looked favorably upon peace by negotiations: "There are amongst us, as in all communities, a certain number of cranks, cowards, and philosophers, some of whom are afraid of their own skins being hurt, whilst others are capable of proving to those sufficiently weakminded to listen to them that we stand to gain more by losing the war than by winning it. . . . We need pay no attention to those miserable members of society."[50]

Robertson, of course, realized that he was running a risk by supporting Lloyd George's efforts to play a larger role in the war. As he told Robert Donald, the editor of the *Daily Chronicle,* "He was in favour of some arrangement which gave Mr. Lloyd George greater power. He did not mean greater power to interfere with military operations, but greater power in the direction of war policy."[51] Even though Lloyd George goaded Robertson over Salonika,[52] the latter continued to support the Welshman over Asquith. He must have believed that Lloyd George's propensity to meddle in strategy could be controlled. After all, his efforts to change Entente strategy at Paris had been easily deflected.

As Lloyd George probably expected, Asquith banged the door on the proposed executive committee, perhaps composing his letter of rejection almost immediately after Bonar Law had retired. A veteran and extremely skillful politician, Asquith had decided to ride out the political crisis. His high-strung and very political wife did what she could, coming by to pick Lloyd George up at the War Office to take him to the Abbey to hear *Elijah.* Lloyd George, of course, was not to be conciliated. He told Stevenson "that the P.M. is absolutely devoid of all principles except one—that of retaining his position as Prime Minister. He will sacrifice everything except No. 10 Downing St. . . . he is for all the world like a Sultan with his harem of 23, using all his skill and wiles to prevent one of them from eloping."[53]

If anything, Lloyd George believed that his case for demoting the generals and taking the direction of the war from Asquith was becoming stronger by the day. In mid-November Monastir had fallen, proving the general staff wrong in its contention that the Eastern Army was too weak and disorganized to achieve a success against Bulgaria. Meanwhile, the fall of Bucharest seemed certain, with the enemy closing in from the north, the south, and the west.

There was, however, many a slip between the cup and the lip. Lloyd George might be the nation's savior in the press and in the country, but his political support within the government remained weak. The Liberal ministers, with the possible exception of Montagu, stood with Asquith. And the Unionist ministers refused to march with Bonar Law, who himself began to wobble. According to Aitken, the Unionist ministers "saw in the whole plan simply a scheme for the further aggrandisement of Lloyd George, and they were absolutely determined not to proclaim a dictatorship with Lloyd George as dictator."[54] When Aitken, the master manipulator, conveyed this distressing news to him on Friday morning, December 1, Lloyd George teetered on the brink of resignation, no doubt savoring the prospect of speaking his mind publicly. His secretary at the War Office, Lee, had been busily at work preparing a lengthy condemnation of the general staff's Balkan failures for such an event.[55] But in the end Lloyd George decided to play out his confrontation with Asquith a bit longer. Another document, probably drafted by Aitken, was prepared to present to the prime minister.[56] It called for the creation of a small committee of three men, the first lord of the

Admiralty, the secretary of state for war, and a "third minister without portfolio," which would have "full powers, subject to the supreme control of the Prime Minister, to direct all questions connected with the War."[57] Lloyd George then hurried off to see the prime minister.

Shortly after Asquith told Lloyd George that he would consider the proposal they sat together at a regular meeting of the War Committee which did not include the military advisers. The prime minister, who "was rather piano,"[58] was given no respite by his secretary of state for war. The collapse of Rumania weighed heavily on the minds of the ministers. How would this disaster be explained to the country? Lloyd George rejected any statement that Britain had done her best: "We had sent our reinforcements two months too late. He had recommended them to do this the moment that Roumania came in, but he had been told by General Maurice that it was too late for the Allied forces to do what they had since accomplished."[59] His message was clear. Lloyd George—not Robertson and certainly not Asquith, who refused to overrule the general staff—should direct British war policy.

Asquith's reply to Lloyd George's ultimatum arrived later that day. In an attempt to meet his vexatious colleague halfway, he wrote: "I am clearly of opinion that the War Committee should be re-constructed, and its relations to an authority over the Departments be more clearly defined and more effectively asserted." Then came the totally unacceptable qualification. "In my opinion," he noted, "whatever changes are made in the composition and functions of the War Committee, the Prime Minister must be its Chairman. He cannot be relegated to the position of an arbiter in the background or a referee to the Cabinet."[60] To Lloyd George's way of thinking, Robertson might as well chair the executive committee.

Asquith's response prompted Lloyd George to send his famous message to Bonar Law the next day: "I enclose copy P.M.'s letter. The life of the country depends on resolute action by you now."[61]

By this time the political struggle had spilled over onto the front pages of the British press. Supporters of Lloyd George, especially Aitken, were responsible.[62] With the public aware of Lloyd George's ultimatum, the crisis entered a new and much more serious stage.

The Unionist ministers caucused on December 3 and decided that the only way out of the confrontation between Lloyd George and Asquith, which had been exacerbated by the stir in the press, was resignation; not really to raise Lloyd George, but to end the hue and cry over reconstruction. As the Unionist statement stressed: "It is evident that a change must be made and in our opinion the publicity given to the intentions of Mr. Lloyd George makes reconstruction from within no longer possible."[63]

When Bonar Law conveyed these Unionist sentiments to Asquith, the shocked prime minister turned to compromise once again to save his ministry. Lloyd George was summoned for an interview. The Welshman, who was waiting in the War Office, took the news calmly. He lit and smoked a cigar while pondering this crucial meeting with Asquith. The cigar finished, he departed for 10 Downing Street. He may have suspected victory belonged to him. That evening the press was informed that Asquith had consented to a reconstruction of the government.

The next morning Hankey made his way through reporters who blocked the door of the War Office. He found Lloyd George "lying back in an armchair by the fire side looking very tired." His mind was on reorganization and Hankey was asked to "draft some 'rules' for the new War Ctee."[64] If Lloyd George had his way, the new war council would consist of himself, Carson, his old ally over Serbia and compulsion, who would replace Balfour at the Admiralty, and Bonar Law, who had agreed that Lloyd George should be supreme in the War Office, and Arthur Henderson, the Labour leader, to maintain a link with Labour.[65]

Despite his apparent triumph over Asquith, Lloyd George realized that the new arrangement placed him in a precarious and politically dangerous position. Churchill had been quick to point out that:

On him would fall all the brunt of battling with the naval and military Chiefs . . . now restraining the Generals from their costly offensives, now stimulating the Admirals to make a greater and more aggressive contribution to the waging of the war. Acute differences were certain to develop in both directions between the political and the professional views. The appeal in all cases would have been to the Prime Minister who, free from the friction of the discussions of the War Committee, yet fully informed on every point, would have been able to decide with final authority. On the other hand, Mr. Lloyd George, publicly appointed to preside over the Committee actually directing the conduct of the war, would have been held responsible for every misfortune that occurred, and they were bound to be many.[66]

Hankey was alive to another difficulty in the new arrangement. He believed that Lloyd George, who planned to remain secretary of state for war, would quickly have the other members of the executive committee under his spell. This would guarantee "interminable rows with the General Staff, and Ll. G. is nearly certain to shunt Robertson & quite possibly may try & saddle me with the responsibility of giving military advice, a responsibility that in the first place does not pertain to my constitutional position, and in the second place will bring me into serious trouble with the General Staff and its press myrmidons."[67] His talk with Lloyd George on the morning of the fourth confirmed his suspicions. The "Easterner" Hankey was asked to beef up his staff in an apparent attempt to create an alternative source of strategic advice.[68]

Hankey wasted no time in seeking out Robertson and assuring him that he would not allow Lloyd George to use him to bypass the general staff.[69] Robertson was either not worried or was more concerned about Asquith's weak leadership. "'Stick to it,'" he told the Welshman. "'you are all right!'"[70]

It is indeed fortunate for Lloyd George's place in history and Hankey's peace of mind that Asquith had second thoughts. His *volte face* is largely explained by a one-sided description of the crisis that appeared in the *Times* on December 4. Asquith and others naturally enough assumed that its author, Dawson, had been coached by Lloyd George. An injured prime minister informed Lloyd George by letter that he was going back on his deal.

"After full consideration of the matter in all its aspects," he wrote, "I have come decidedly to the conclusion that it is not possible that such a committee could be made workable and effective without the Prime Minister as its chairman."[71]

When this letter arrived at the War Office the next morning, December 5, Lloyd George knew that all hope of compromise with Asquith was gone. His campaign to overthrow the generals which had been launched on November 3 in the War Committee had resulted in an irreparable breach with the prime minister. There could be no turning back now. If Asquith wanted a fight, he would have it. He would resign and the ineptitude of the government and its military advisers would be laid bare, with the collapse of Rumania providing the roll of drums in the background.

In his letter of resignation, Lloyd George wrote not only for the eyes of Asquith, but for posterity. "I have endeavoured repeatedly to warn the Government of the dangers[,] both verbally and in written memoranda and letters, which I crave your leave now to publish if my action is challenged; but I have either failed to secure decisions or I have secured them when it was too late to avert the evils. The latest illustration is our lamentable failure to give timely support to Rumania."[72]

Lloyd George never delivered this attack against the government and the general staff because Asquith, realizing that he did not have the necessary support to continue, resigned. On December 7, Lloyd George kissed the hand of George V. As prime minister, he would now receive the credit for both the successes and failures of British arms. Given the perilous state of the Entente, it was not a comforting thought.

Asquith and his Liberal supporters had been vanquished, but this was not his central objective. Almost by accident he had become prime minister. Bringing the generals to heel and a reorientation of Allied strategy were yet to be accomplished. One thing was certain. The "soldiers' party" was on its guard against any interference with the high command's conduct of the war. Lord Esher accurately mirrored the mood of general headquarters when he wrote in his diary: "Everyone seems to imagine that L.G. as Prime Minister is tantamount to a Sedan or a Tannenburg [*sic*]. . . . This man will think that he has a 'Mandate' to override military and naval opinion."[3] An anxious Haig immediately wrote the king through Wigram:

> I am afraid honestly that he [Lloyd George] may squander our resources on side shows i.e. Salonika.
> On no account should he be allowed to send more units there. I could write to you on this as strongly as I used to do over the Dardanelles adventure. *You* must prevent another such failure.[74]

One reason for Haig's concern was that he feared that his principal objective in 1917—the clearing of the Belgian coast—might be upset by the new government. On November 20, after Robertson had excused himself, the War Committee had discussed the importance of an offensive to destroy the enemy's submarine bases on the Belgian coast, which were a grave threat to British shipping. The Welshman spoke neither for nor against this operation, but some of his colleagues, especially Grey and Asquith, attached the utmost importance to winning control of the Belgian coast. But would Joffre approve of a British offensive that was free from French direction or interference? According to Grey, that was the key question.[75]

On the following day, Asquith instructed Hankey to write the C.I.G.S. "urging an attack on the Belgian ports,"[76] a plan that had long been uppermost in Haig's thinking. Robertson was informed: "There is no operation of war to which the War Committee would attach greater importance than the successful occupation, or at least the deprivation to the enemy, of Ostend, and especially Zeebrugge."[77] Since this letter was not signed by the prime minister, but merely sent to Robertson for his information, it has provoked considerable controversy. Although the War Committee had made no formal decision on the twentieth, with no conclusion being recorded in the minutes, the politicians' encouragement of Haig to embark on the most controversial British offensive of the war—Passchendaele or the Third Battle of Ypres—is a matter of record. On December 1, Robertson wrote Joffre encouraging him to include a great British offensive in Flanders in Allied plans of operation in 1917. Lloyd George contends that Robertson, fearing that the possible breakup of Asquith's government might bring to power an anti-"Westerner," dispatched this letter in an attempt to commit Britain to a Flemish campaign.[78] It is more likely, however, that Robertson, prodded by Asquith and Grey, was trying to break down French resistance.

Whatever the intent of Robertson, Haig, encouraged by Asquith's government in its final days of power, methodically prepared for a gigantic offensive in Flanders during the coming months. His determination to carry out this attack was to be at the center of the civil-military conflict in London during the winter and spring of 1917.

NOTES

1. Memorandum by Runciman, November 9, 1916, CAB 42/23/11.

2. Memorandum by Robertson, October, 1916, CAB 42/22/15.

3. Robertson's minute read to the War Cabinet by Lloyd George, War Committee, November 3, 1916, CAB 42/23/4.

4. Memorandum by Hankey, October 31, 1916, CAB 42/22/14.

5. *Statistics of the Military Effort of the British Empire During the Great War, 1914–1920* (1922), pp. 358–62.

6. M. J. Williams, "Thirty Per Cent: A Study in Casualty Statistics," *Journal of the Royal United Service Institution* 109 (February 1964): 51–55.

7. Captain B. H. Liddell Hart, "The Basic Truths of Passchendaele," *Journal of the Royal United Service Institution* 104 (November 1959): 437.

8. John Terraine, although with some qualification, is too prone to accept Edmonds's figures. In doing so, he has ignored Edmonds's ulterior motives. See his latest discussion of casualty figures in *The Road to Passchendaele: The Flanders Offensive of 1917, A Study in Inevitability* (1977), pp. 343–47.

9. "Talk with J. E. Edmonds," December 8, 1930, Liddell Hart MSS, 11/1930/15.

10. "Talk with J. E. Edmonds," May 6, 1929, Liddell Hart MSS, 11/1929/7.

11. "Talk with J. E. Edmonds," October 27, 1933, Liddell Hart MSS, 11/1933/24.

12. Hankey Diary, November 1, 1916, 1/1.

13. In early October, Thomas had warned Lloyd George about this meeting and had suggested prior consultations by the Allied ministers. Thomas to Lloyd George, October 5, 1916, Lloyd George MSS, E/3/13/4.

14. Hankey Diary, November 3, 1916, 1/1.

15. Actually the Germans had increased their losses on the Somme by refusing to give up ground and by crowding the first trenches with troops. See Wynne, *If Germany Attacks*, pp. 100–132.

16. See Hankey Diary, October 28, 1916, 1/1.

17. War Committee, November 3, 1916, CAB 42/23/4.

18. Hankey, "Note on the above Telegram," November 4, 1916, CAB 42/23/4, and Hankey Diary, November 3, 1916, 1/1.

19. War Committee, November 7, 1916, CAB 42/23/9.

20. Hankey Diary, November 7, 1916, 1/1.

21. Robertson to Haig, November 8, 1916, Haig MSS, no. 109.

22. Hankey to Robertson, November 9, 1916, Hankey MSS, 4/8.

23. Hankey Diary, November 9, 1916, 1/1.

24. Memorandum by Lloyd George, n.d., Lloyd George, *War Memoirs*, 1:545–55.

25. Hankey Diary, November 9, 1916, 1/1.

26. War Committee, November 10, 1916, CAB 42/24/2.

27. Hankey Diary, November 10, 1916, 1/1.

28. Lloyd George, *War Memoirs*, 1:544, and Hankey Diary, November 12, 1916, 1/1.

29. Hankey Diary, November 10, 1916, 1/1.

30. Beaverbrook, *Politicians and the War, 1914–1916*, p. 316.

31. Hankey, *Supreme Command*, 2:559.

32. Ibid., 560, and Lloyd George, *War Memoirs*, 1:556. Lloyd George's memorandum, translated into French, which Asquith read can be found in CAB 28/1/I.C.-12(a), November 15, 1916.

33. Haig Diary, November 16, 1916, no. 109.

34. Lloyd George, *War Memoirs*, 1:574–75.

35. Hankey Diary, November 22, 1916, 1/1.

36. Lloyd George, who earlier had agreed to accompany Robertson to Russia, reversed himself because the approaching collapse of Rumania meant that "he would be required at home." Hankey Diary, November 17, 1916, 1/1.

37. The controversial chain of events which led to Asquith's resignation has been most fully described by Beaverbrook. For discrepancies between Beaverbrook's account of the political crisis in his original draft and the published version, see A. J. P. Taylor, *Beaverbrook* (1972), pp. 101–27. For an illuminating account of the role of the press, see J. M. McEwen, "The Press and the Fall of Asquith," *The Historical Journal* 21 (December 1978): 863–83. See Jenkins, *Asquith: Portrait of a Man and an Era*, pp. 421–63, for Asquith's side of the story.

38. War Committee, November 21, 1916, CAB 42/25/2.

39. Entry of November 21, 1916, *A Diary by Frances Stevenson*, p. 126. Hankey's minutes do not include a full account of this heated discussion. War Committee, November 21, 1916, CAB 42/25/2.

40. Beaverbrook, *Politicians and the War, 1914–1916*, pp. 346–50.

41. Hankey Diary, September 26, 1916, 1/1.

42. War Committee, August 10, 1916, CAB 42/17/5.

43. Ibid., August 30, 1916, CAB 42/18/8.

44. *Daily Telegraph*, September 29, 1916; also see Fry, *The Education of a Statesman*, pp. 232–36.

45. Memorandum by Lansdowne, November 13, 1916, CAB 37/159/32.

46. See Woodward, "Great Britain and President Wilson's Efforts . . ."

47. Memorandum by Grey, November 27, 1916, CAB 37/160/20, and Jellicoe to Asquith, October 30, 1916, Asquith MSS, 1/vol. 17/fol. 129.

48. Robertson, *Soldiers and Statesmen*, 1:280. It is true that Lloyd George, three weeks earlier, had informed Hankey that Britain "had better make peace rather than repeat the experience of 1916." But this was a reflection of his discontent over Robertson's dictatorial control of strategy rather than any sincere desire for a compromise peace. In short, Lloyd George was posturing.

49. Paul Guinn, *British Strategy and Politics, 1914–1918* (1965), p. 175.

50. Memorandum by Robertson, November 24, 1916, CAB 37/160/15.

51. H. A. Taylor, *Robert Donald* (1934), p. 110.

52. Lloyd George to Robertson, November 29, 1916, Lloyd George MSS, E/5/1/2(b).

53. Entry of November 30, 1916, *A Diary by Frances Stevenson*, p. 129.

54. Beaverbrook, *Politicians and the War, 1914–1916*, p. 363.

55. Lee, "Our Salonika-Balkan Policy," December 2, 1916, Lloyd George MSS, E/5/1/3; also see Hankey to Lee, November 24 and 29 and December, 1916, Lloyd George MSS, E/5/15/4–6.

56. Taylor, *Beaverbrook*, pp. 112–13, and Beaverbrook, *Politicians and the War, 1914–1916*, pp. 385–86.

57. "Memo to Prime Minister, December 1st 1916," Lloyd George MSS, E/2/23/9.

58. Hankey Diary, December 1, 1916, 1/1.

59. War Committee, December 1, 1916, CAB 42/26/6.

60. Asquith to Lloyd George, December 1, 1916, Lloyd George MSS, E/2/23/10.

61. Lloyd George to Bonar Law, December 2, 1916, Bonar Law MSS, 117/1/30.

62. Lloyd George has been accused of trafficking with the press, but A. J. P. Taylor argues that he was not responsible for the initial revelations. On the other hand, once the public was aware of his demands, it seems that he did attempt to get his side of the conflict across in the press. See Taylor, *Beaverbrook*, pp. 113–14, and McEwen, "The Press and the Fall of Asquith."

63. "Message to PM from Unionist members of Cabinet, December 3, 1916," Curzon MSS, Eur. F. 112/130. It should be noted that Bonar Law, for reasons that remain obscure, never actually handed this note to the prime minister during his interview.

64. Hankey Diary, December 4, 1916, 1/1.

65. Ibid., November 22, 1916, 1/1.

66. Churchill, *World Crisis*, 3:256.

67. Hankey Diary, December 3, 1916, 1/1.

68. Ibid., December 4, 1916, 1/1.

69. Ibid.

70. Entry of December 5, 1916, *A Diary by Frances Stevenson*, p. 132.

71. Asquith to Lloyd George, December 4, 1916, Lloyd George MSS, E/2/23/14.

72. Lloyd George to Asquith, December 5, 1916, Lloyd George MSS, E/2/23/15.

73. Esher Diary, December 7, 1916, 2/17.

74. Haig to Wigram, December 8, 1916, RA GV Q2521/V/147.

75. War Committee, November 20, 1916, CAB 42/24/13.

76. Hankey Diary, November 21, 1916, 1/1.

77. Lloyd George, *War Memoirs*, 2:1252–53.

78. Ibid., 1250–51.

7
The Nivelle Offensive

LLOYD George's ability to impose his will on the high command depended upon the political support he could muster. In a fight the generals could count on powerful allies. A large segment of Fleet Street, with Northcliffe, Gwynne, and Leo Maxse, the editor of the ultrapatriotic and jingoistic *National Review,* leading the way, was solidly behind Robertson and Haig. In fact, if the recent upheaval in the government had resulted in Lloyd George's resigning and taking his heretical strategical views to the people, the consequences would probably have been disastrous for him. Later, as we will see, when he dropped all restraint and publicly blasted the high command's conduct of the war in an intemperate speech in Paris in November, the violent reaction of the press forced him to beat a hasty retreat.

The political realities made it impossible for Lloyd George to be a supreme war lord like Churchill in World War II, for many Liberals rallied to the fallen Asquith and waited for an opportunity to exploit an open breach between the prime minister and the popular military leaders. With no party behind him, he was vulnerable. As he writes in his memoirs:

> Had there been a united party behind me which, with dependable allies, would have commanded in the House of Commons a majority solid and large enough to carry me through the inevitable vicissitudes of evil as well as good tidings for a period of two years and more, I should have had a freer, a wider and more promising choice. I could then have secured a more homogeneous form of Government and a Government more sympathetic to the War policy in which I believed.[1]

Lloyd George's government by necessity was dominated by his former political enemies—the Unionists. To entice influential Unionists such as Curzon, Robert Cecil, Chamberlain, and Walter Long into his government, he had been forced to promise them that he would retain Haig as commander in chief of the British Expeditionary Force.[2] In another move to placate the supporters of the high command, he had chosen the soldiers' friend Derby as secretary for state of war. The result was that the head of the War Office owed his first allegiance to Robertson and Haig rather than to the prime minister. The composition of his new government also served to increase the influence of Buckingham Palace, for the king's standing with the Unionists, upon whom the survival of his ministry depended, could not be ignored.

Lloyd George's hands, however, were not so tightly bound as it might appear at first glance. The new five-man directorate, the War Cabinet, which ignored the historic cabinet, gave Lloyd George unprecedented power. Its members were not unfavorable to a new direction for Allied strategy if they were carefully handled. Bonar Law had on occasion sided with the Welshman's Balkan views and was unwilling to dance to the general staff's tune. Lord Milner, who after Bonar Law was the essential member of Lloyd George's new team, was not as many assumed an unalloyed "Westerner." His enthusiasm for the empire was increasingly to turn him toward the East. The same was true of Curzon who was vitally concerned with British power and prestige in Asia. The remaining member of the War Cabinet, Arthur Henderson, who was a complete stranger to high strategy and a relative lightweight, could probably be counted upon to support the prime minister against the generals. Another factor which must not be overlooked is that members of the War Cabinet, especially Bonar Law and Milner, desperately wanted Lloyd George to succeed. Consequently, they were prepared to go quite far in supporting him. This was not as true of Unionists such as Cecil, Long, and Chamberlain, who lurked in the background, ready to explode the government if Lloyd George attempted to override the advice of the military.

For Lloyd George, the great unanswered question was: How dependable would the Unionists be in a showdown with the army? They might—through his preternatural ability to persuade—be smartly led onto the field of battle. But would they retreat at a critical moment, leaving him alone and vulnerable? The Welshman's political insecurity goes a long way toward explaining his methods in dealing with Haig and Robertson. At times he boldly confronted them, but more frequently he was cautious, cunning, and at times underhanded, attempting to outflank them rather then meet them head on.

Robertson, as we have seen, had supported Lloyd George over Asquith as the lesser of two evils. Once Lloyd George was installed at 10 Downing Street, he moved to protect his ascendancy in strategy. The sledge hammer and bludgeon were his weapons. On December 8, he composed a letter to the prime minister which was remarkably blunt and tactless even for him. It was nothing less than a strong indictment of Lloyd George himself. Robertson urged Britain's leading "Easterner" to dominate Entente diplomacy and give the Salonikan venture a quick burial. "It is now necessary that some really definite pressures should be taken to put the Salonika matter on a proper footing. If this is done a hideous nightmare will be removed." Wully did not have to mention that the British leader most responsible for this "hideous nightmare" was Lloyd George. The old sores of Rabegh and Rumania were mentioned. "We need to keep our attention on the big things, and not brood and waste brain-power over such petty matters as Rabegh, Persia, etc. It is really pitiable sometimes to see the worried and pessimistic looks of certain people because of some trumpery set-back which matters not at all." The fall of Rumania, to be sure, was a "big splash" for the enemy. But nothing vital has happened." Robertson's familiar theme was: "There is only one way of winning a war, and that is by defeating the chief enemy, and if this principle is kept in view by the War Council a very much smaller expenditure of brain-power will be required to carry on the war."[3] Robertson followed up this insulting letter by giving his standard lecture on "side shows" to the minister at the first meeting of the War Cabinet.[4]

It should come as no surprise that Lloyd George had grave reservations about following the advice of Wully (or "Woolly" as he sometimes referred to him in private). Determined to get a fresh look at the war, he immediately turned to Hankey. Lloyd George's inclination to use the blue-eyed, apple-cheeked secretary as a substitute for the general staff placed the latter in an awkward position. It is a testament to his diplomacy that he usually was on good terms with both sides in this civil-military struggle.

Two days after becoming prime minister, Lloyd George had before him a twenty-nine-page review of the war which he had requested from Hankey. Many of the secretary's ideas could have emanated from the Welshman himself. Unlike the enemy, the Allies had failed to pool their resources. "This is particularly noticeable in the plans concerted at the Chantilly Conference," Hankey wrote. "Each nation is to hammer away on its own Front, regardless of whether it is strategically or tactically the most suitable Front, and whether the winning of the war as a whole can best be achieved there." Lloyd George's brainchild, the upcoming Russian conference, he suggested, offered the Allies an opportunity to pool their resources and treat the war as a common front. He enthusiastically endorsed Britain and France sending heavy guns to support an Italian offensive and a British attack from Egypt against the Turks to capture Jerusalem or Damascus. Hankey also gave support to another of Lloyd George's pet projects: the arming of the Russians if they could put to good use additional weapons.[5]

A sour note sounded by Hankey in his memorandum was his support of another big offensive in France in 1917. Taken in by general headquarters's inflated German casualty figures, Hankey believed that the great battles of 1916 had demonstrated that "the Power which takes the offensive loses less than the Power which takes the defensive. Hence, whether the Italian and Turkish plans are carried out and succeed or not, I would strongly advocate every effort for a gigantic offensive in the West next year."[6]

Lloyd George was "delighted" with the slant of Hankey's memorandum; so much so that Hankey feared that he would be appointed C.I.G.S.[7] As for Hankey's support of a "gigantic" Western offensive, Lloyd George simply ignored this advice. Hankey had admitted in his covering letter that he doubted if the Anglo-French forces had the means to achieve decisive results against the German army. According to Lloyd George's lights, if decisive results were unobtainable in the West, the Allies should look elsewhere for more fruitful theaters. "I decided to explore every possibility before surrendering to a renewal of the horrors of the West,"[8] he writes in his memoirs. In reality, the one-front approach he harped upon amounted to any front but the western front.

Hankey's and Lloyd George's ideas were given a cold douche by Robertson when he was informed of them. If British guns were sent south during the winter and early spring, the Italians might wear them out, he argued. As for an attempt to take Jerusalem during the winter or the dispatch of more troops to Salonika to aid the French, Robertson correctly emphasized the additional strain on British shipping.[9] To his dismay the ministers continued to consider these projects in meetings which he was not invited to attend. "There is a very dangerous tendency becoming apparent," he wrote Haig, "for the War Cabinet to direct military operations."[10]

To get his way, Lloyd George attempted to mobilize Britain's allies against the advice of his general staff. He gained—or so he thought—the support of the Italian commander in chief, General Luigi Cadorna, for a joint Allied effort on the Austro-Italian front. He also courted the Italian minister, Bissolati.[11] He had reason to believe that French ministers such as Thomas and Briand, who had previously shared his pessimism about big attacks in the West, would be his allies. Unknown to him, however, the French government, at least for the moment, had embraced the cult of the offensive in the West.

The attitude of the French government was caused by a change in the leadership of the French army. "Papa" Joffre, France's leading advocate for a war of attrition, was replaced as commander in chief in early December by General Robert George Nivelle, a sixty-year-old artilleryman who had begun the war as a colonel. Dynamic, extraordinarily confident, and distinguished-looking, Nivelle was the Entente's most articulate commander in chief, being fluent in English which he had learned from his British mother.

Nivelle was popular with French politicians because of his personality and several spectacularly successful—though local—attacks at Verdun. His victories, he explained, resulted from his scientific approach to warfare. When he left his forces at Verdun to take command of the French army, he optimistically proclaimed: "The experiment has been conclusive. Our method has been tried out. I can assure you that victory is certain. The enemy will learn this to his cost."[12]

Nivelle rashly predicted that his tactics would end the stalemate in twenty-four or forty-eight hours. Instead of the wearing-down tactics of Joffre, Nivelle bet everything on one throw of the dice—a surprise massive frontal assault. The major difference between this and earlier offensives à outrance was his utilization of artillery, especially the "creeping barrage." Brigadier-General Spears explains:

> The artillery preparation, no longer to be confined to the first line, was to cover the whole depth of the enemy's position. The assault was to be pressed up to and beyond the enemy's last lines of defence, and was to include his heavy artillery position. The infantry, closely supported by the field artillery, was to advance under a continuous barrage preceding the men by seventy metres (approximately seventy-six yards). The waves of the infantry following each other closely were not to allow themselves to be held up by undestroyed hostile defences. They were to pass these, leaving them to be dealt with by small supporting columns.[13]

On December 20, Nivelle, his offensive plans approved by the French government, paid an important visit to Haig, who was initially impressed with the new French commander in chief, whose optimism matched his own. "He is an intelligent man who knows his work," he wrote his wife, "and is of course much better qualified than dear old Joffre to bring this war to a successful end."[14] Haig, however, perceived a grave threat to his own plans in Nivelle's optimism. At the Chantilly conference, Joffre had indicated that the growing exhaustion of the French Army meant that the British must assume the leading role in any great attacks in 1917. This suited Haig perfectly because of his plan to clear the Flanders coast later in the year. In their lengthy meeting, however, Nivelle emphasized that in the coming spring offensive the French expected to play the major role, with the British being given the unglamorous assignment of taking over more line to release French troops for an army of maneuver. The effect might be to blunt the powerful offensive instrument Haig commanded. In short, if the British had to play second fiddle to the French as in the past, Haig's plan of a northern operation in the summer, which Asquith had encouraged him to develop, might be fatally compromised. As Haig later wrote: "I felt therefore that in being asked to modify my plans and take over more line—and further to entrust the Allied cause and the welfare of my own armies, & of this country to General Nivelle's judgment under such conditions, I was confronted with a very serious problem. At the same time I had very good reason for confidence in the ability of my own armies to achieve great success."[15]

The British political leaders first learned of Nivelle's scheme—though not its precise nature—at an Anglo-French conference which began in London on December 26 to examine some worrisome diplomatic and military problems which continued to divide London and Paris. At first the thorny and divisive issue of Salonika held center stage. The French argued that the Eastern Army was threatened on two fronts: the Central Powers on one side and the Greek forces of the pro-German King Constantine from the rear in Thessaly. To save the situation, Sarrail—to the consternation of the British general staff—wanted the British to send two additional divisions from France to the Balkans and support a preemptive strike against the Greeks in Thessaly. With the conference at loggerheads over the Balkans, the French spokesman, Ribot, brought the first session to an end with a discussion of military operations in the West. The French finance minister revealed Nivelle's plan "to break through on a wide front" and then complained about Haig's reluctance to take over more line to enable Nivelle to create his army of maneuver. This question, he emphasized, "was not a question for the General Staffs, it was one for the Governments. He might say quite openly that the Governments, especially the French Government, had hitherto left the conduct of the war too much to the General Staff."[16]

The next day the French continued to press the British government very hard on reinforcing the British forces at Salonika and especially on the question of taking over more French line. Lloyd George assured Ribot of Haig's willingness to cooperate with Nivelle, but the French leader dissented. Haig, he said, "was full of excellent promises, but only promises. He talked of obtaining further troops by lessening the commitments at Salonica; of carrying out the scheme in two or three months' time. But General Lyautey, the new French Minister of War, considered that January 15th must be fixed as the settled date for relieving the French line."[17]

With the Anglo-French military advisers at sixes and sevens, Lloyd George's flexible mind perceived a golden opportunity for his strategic ideas. He was mindful of the need to support the Eastern Army at Salonika. He, of all people, could not afford another great German victory in the Balkans. But the general staff had evidence that Berlin, with the collapse of Rumania, was directing its efforts elsewhere. At any rate, the additional divisions, Robertson maintained, could not arrive until March because of the shortage of transport ships. "By then," Lloyd George argued, "things would be finished at Salonica one way or the other."[18] As for the British taking over more of the front, this would have the advantage of limiting Haig's plan to launch gigantic attacks in 1917. The disadvantage was that, if Nivelle had his way, the "Westerners" would retain their stranglehold on British strategy. Perhaps, however, out of this muddled situation the divided Allied generals might be outmaneuvered and their "Western" plans thwarted. At that very moment, Sir Rennell Rodd, the British ambassador in Rome, was in London at Lloyd George's behest, to convince the War Cabinet that General Cadorna might be persuaded to launch a great attack against the Austrians if he were given guns from the Anglo-French arsenal.[19] And Lloyd George remained much more optimistic about the results of an Allied attack against war-weary Austria-Hungary than against the German army.

On December 28, having gotten the support of the War Cabinet, Lloyd George proposed to the Anglo-French conference that Britain, France, and Italy should immediately meet in Italy to discuss Salonika and the "general question of the whole campaign of 1917 . . . with the object of finding the best method of common action all through."[20] The French, perhaps suspecting a trap, were unenthusiastic. But Lloyd George made it clear to Robertson that he was going to Italy to confer with Rome even if the French refused to accompany him.[21]

Meanwhile, Haig was instructed to cooperate with Nivelle; any differences between the generals would be worked out later by the politicians. As for the Balkans, a decision was delayed on the two divisions until the situation there became clearer.

Lloyd George was never more adroit. His manipulation of the division between Paris and London gave him an opportunity to reverse the decisions of the Chantilly and Paris conferences in November. On December 30, the War Cabinet presented him a carte blanche to "conclude any arrangement" with the Allied leaders at an Allied conference at Rome which the French now reluctantly agreed to attend.[22] This time, Lloyd George believed, there would be no repetition of his humiliation at Paris. As the head of the country which was fast becoming the dominant partner in the anti-German coalition, he would insist that his views be given a fair hearing.

He and Hankey at once set to work drafting a statement on military policy. The finished product, which went through many drafts, emphasized the altered Entente position since the decisions of November. Rumania had been crushed and the Russian front greatly extended and weakened; Berlin, flush with success, might now strike at Russia, the Eastern Army in the

Balkans, or the Italians. What, he asked, "are the plans for the Allies for meeting any of these contingencies?"

> No doubt General Gourko, General Sarrail and General Cadorna has each an admirable plan of his own for meeting the contingency. But what is the plan of the Allies as a whole? The combined offensive against Bulgaria, planned at Chantilly, is no longer practicable and so far as we know the Allies have absolutely no plan, except for each General to continue "punching" on his own Front.[23]

Having prepared the ground carefully, Lloyd George then came to the heart of his paper: a powerful surprise attack in Italy against what he considered the enemy's weak link, Austria-Hungary, to gain Trieste and perhaps the Istria peninsula. "It would have a moral and political effect of the greatest consequence," he argued, "and would be a good counter to the enemy's successes in Roumania."[24]

Lloyd George's plan was neatly conceived. Robertson and Haig, with their narrow preoccupation with the western front, would be placed on the defensive. The general staff's shipping-shortage argument did not apply to the Italian theater. The Italians would surely support a scheme which promised a great addition to their artillery. The French might be won over because the proposed Italian operation might give relief to the Eastern Army as well as Russia. Then there was an important concession made to the "Westerners." He was not asking the generals to abandon their attacks in the West—only delay them until conditions were more favorable. Finally, the political advantages of an Allied victory over the enemy were obvious. The Allies had had little to cheer about since the First Battle of the Marne in 1914.

Lloyd George has been criticized in shocked tones by his critics for ignoring the general staff and clandestinely drawing up war plans for the Rome conference. Indeed, it was an unorthodox, though certainly understandable, procedure for Lloyd George to work through Hankey rather than the head of the general staff. Still, it is quite untrue that Robertson and Haig were in the dark about his strategical ideas. They not only understood his Italian plans but were working mightily to undermine them. The intrigue during the following days in both camps belongs on the pages of a cheap spy novel and does no credit to either the prime minister or the high command.

The wire pulling began in Paris, where Lloyd George and Milner stopped on their way to Rome. After receiving a lecture from Haig about the importance of concentrating all British resources on the western front, Northcliffe paid an unwelcome visit to Lloyd George and lit into him about disregarding the advice of the general staff. If the prime minister did not change his ways, the powerful press lord warned, it would be "impossible to continue to support" his government.[25] In another part of Paris, Lord Esher was coaching Robertson. If the government refused to follow his advice, Esher told Robertson, he should simply refuse to execute the government's orders. In all likelihood, the government lacked the courage to fire him over an issue which involved the civilians overruling the general staff "on a purely military question."[26]

On the train to Rome the jockeying for position continued. In one car Lloyd George buttonholed the French minister of war, Lyautey, while in another car Robertson was telling Sir Henry Wilson that "he thought he had knocked out LG's wonderful proposal to send 300 heavy guns to Italy."[27] As soon as the train pulled into Rome on January 5, a comical race to get the ear of the Italian commander in chief took place. Robertson crossed the finish line first. When Hankey, dispatched by the prime minister, arrived at Cadorna's home, he discovered that Robertson had preceded him. Cadorna, Hankey recorded in his diary, "was not nearly as enthusiastic as he ought to have been; he said of course he could not have too many heavy guns, but he made a number of technical difficulties, and it was clear that he had been got at by Robertson."[28]

Lloyd George was no less active in his lobbying. On the evening of the January 5 he met secretly with Bissolati at the British embassy. The Italian Socialist leader left his meeting with the prime minister "a tremendous partisan of Ll. George's scheme for a concentration on the Italian front." He promised to do all that he could to enlist Cadorna to the cause. Later Bissolati talked to Albert Thomas and in a letter urged the Italian prime minister, Paolo Roselli "to back the project energetically."[29]

The conference had begun in the ornate and spacious salon of the minister of foreign affairs. Since everyone with any influence in Rome attempted to participate, the first session had the appearance of a busy train station on a holiday weekend. Lloyd George and Briand, who were averse to large assemblies, quickly moved the conference to a round table in a small room where only the principal Allied political leaders were admitted. The military leaders, unless they were required for technical questions, were excluded.

After the first formal session on the afternoon of the fifth, Lloyd George suddenly decided to circulate his memorandum to the conference.[30] At 3:30 P.M. on the sixth Lloyd George presented his scheme for Allied support of an Italian offensive. To his dismay, Thomas and Briand, dazzled by Nivelle's promise of a rupture of the German lines, were unenthusiastic, with only the Russian ambassador expressing approval. Cadorna, who had been sitting in an anteroom with Robertson, was then trotted before the ministers. As he spoke, Lloyd George could not believe his ears. Robertson might as well have been addressing the conference. If the guns had to be returned to the western front in time for Nivelle's spring offensive, the Italian general argued, it was not worth accepting them. At these words, a disgusted Lloyd George turned to Hankey and remarked, "The old fellow does not want guns." When Lloyd George suggested that Cadorna might keep his British guns longer if necessary, Thomas expressed surprise. "Mr. Lloyd George, he pointed out, talked as though his resources were unlimited. At one and the same time he talked of sending guns both to Russia and to Italy. How, he asked, could this be done without altering the whole equilibrium of the position on the Western front?"[31] At that point Lloyd George must have realized that his Italian plan was dead for the immediate future.

In the end the prime minister's memorandum was turned over to the general staffs for further study. But the generals were not instructed, as Lloyd George had insisted, to consider the project favorably. Hence it was doomed from the outset. As Robertson informed Buckingham Palace: "Not much will come of it!"[32]

Lloyd George did not emerge empty-handed from the conference. Many of the actions of the ministers furthered Allied cooperation. Russian rearmament was accepted as being essential, an immediate Allied naval and shipping conference was arranged, communications were to be improved between France and Italy (which later saved Italy after Caporetto), and a road was to be constructed from Santi Quaranta on the Adriatic to Monastir to strengthen communications to the Eastern Army. Despite these real gains, Lloyd George viewed the Rome Conference as a dismal failure because his Italian plan had been shelved. Years later, he wrote: "When we came to the main purpose for which the Conference had been summoned—a real and not a sham coördination of strategy—the Conference reached no final decision and the Military Staffs were left in possession of the field."[33]

Lloyd George was infuriated by Robertson's and Haig's efforts to torpedo his efforts to influence Allied strategy before and during the Rome conference. After Wully had outmaneuvered him with Cadorna, the C.I.G.S. had gone so far as to present him with an ultimatum over British reinforcements to Salonika. When Briand made a brilliant plea to the conference for two British divisions, Robertson, following Esher's advice, sent Lloyd George the following note: "I don't know what effect M. Briand's oratory may have upon you in regard to the wretched Salonika business, but it seems only right and fair to you that I should tell you *now* that I could never bring myself to sign an order for the despatch of further British divisions to Salonika."[34] The note contains shades of Lloyd George's humiliating and emasculated position under Robertson in the War Office! The bad taste of this mutinous letter was still in his mouth when he was greeted upon his return to London by a leading article in the *Times*, "THE DECISIVE FRONT." "We must run no risks," Northcliffe's paper warned, "of dissipating our efforts."

A direct and aboveboard solution to Lloyd George's profound differences with Robertson would have been to dismiss him. This was Robertson's position: either the government should rely upon its military adviser or get another whom it trusted. Like Lloyd George, it should be emphasized, Robertson was fully aware that his dismissal might bring down the government. Lloyd George's political insecurity thus dictated that he was saddled with his high-handed C.I.G.S. His only course—unless he capitulated to the generals—was to resort to guerilla tactics rather than open battle. The seeds of Calais were thus planted by Haig's use of the press and Robertson's astonishing arrogance at Rome.

Even though Lloyd George did not have sufficient support to change Britain's military leadership, he did have the backing of his colleagues in the War Cabinet to assert civilian authority over Robertson and Haig in a variety of ways. Briand's famous dictum that "war is much too serious a matter to be left to soldiers and sailors" found considerable support within the War Cabinet. The ministers attempted to make certain that they had access to all information available to the War Office.[35] Also, general headquarters was pointedly instructed to pay more heed to subordinate officers who were closer to the action in tactical questions.[36]

Meanwhile, Haig and Nivelle were experiencing considerable difficulty in reaching an understanding about the British role in the spring offensive. Fearing that Nivelle's plan "means pinning our faith to the success of these operations for clearing the Belgian Coast, and very possibly the abandonment of the Northern operations," Haig wrote the French commander in chief: "If I am not satisfied that this larger plan, as events develop, promises the degree of success necessary to clear the Belgian coast, then I not only cannot continue the battle but I will look to you to fulfill the understanding you have given me verbally to relieve on the defensive front the troops I require for my northern offensive."[37]

With Haig's proposed Flanders operation competing with his own offensive plan, Nivelle attempted to enlist Lloyd George's support when the prime minister passed through Paris on his way home from the Rome conference. Unwilling to confer with Nivelle without Haig being present, Lloyd George invited both Nivelle and Haig to appear before the War Cabinet.

Just before these discussions began in London on January 15, Lloyd George revealed the intensity of his feelings to Haig and Robertson about the manner in which the British high command had conducted the war in 1916. Haig dryly summarized in his diary the tongue lashing he received as follows: "His general conclusions were that the French Army was better all around, and was able to gain success at less cost of life, that much of our loss on the Somme was wasted, and that the country would not stand any more of that sort of thing, that to win, we must attack a soft front, and we could not find that on the Western front."[38]

Within a matter of hours after this tirade, however, Lloyd George seemed to change his mind about the advisibility of a great offensive in the West. General Nivelle's lucid and self-assured presentation of his new tactics was, in part, responsible for this remarkable *volte face*.

Nivelle's appeal to the prime minister is easy to understand. His plan, as it was now fully revealed, seemed diametrically opposite to the plodding, costly, and drawn-out attacks of Haig and Joffre. Here was a general who promised immediate success with an economy of losses. Further, Lloyd George believed that Nivelle had an abundance of imagination and a better grip on modern war with his emphasis on surprise and Lloyd George's favorite weapon—the big gun and high-explosive shell. In a revealing statement to Miss Stevenson, Lloyd George said: "Nivelle has proved himself to be a Man at Verdun; & when you get a Man against one who has not proved himself, why, you back the Man!'"[39] Even if Nivelle failed, his plan seemed to be an improvement over the previous offensive plans agreed upon at the Chantilly conference because Haig was assigned a secondary role in the offensive to draw off the German reserves at Arras before Nivelle's great blow was delivered on the Aisne. British casualties might consequently be smaller than in the original plan.

Lloyd George saw yet another advantage in supporting Nivelle. He believed that it would be immediately apparent if Nivelle's offensive miscarried. As Hankey put it, "Nivelle promised a smashing blow or nothing."[40] If the German lines could not be ruptured, Lloyd George planned to resurrect his Rome strategy. Since Nivelle proposed an early offensive, there would be plenty of time to switch off to Italy. "Modesty," Cadorna now assured him, had prevented him from supporting Lloyd George at Rome. Encouraged by the prime minister, the Italian commander in chief prepared an offensive plan which, it must be noted, included British divisions as well as guns.[41]

After the British ministers jumped on Nivelle's bandwagon at the London conference, Robertson attempted to show them the error of their ways. Although Nivelle promised immediate success, Wully pointed out that the French might get bogged down and "the question of success or failure may hang in the balance for some considerable time." It was not only foolish but dangerous "to give the impression that we are staking everything on the result of one battle or on our ability to win a great strategical victory." Repeatedly he hammered home the point that Nivelle's offensive might jeopardize Haig's plan to clear the Flanders coast.[42]

The general staff's criticism was ignored, in part, because it was considered self-serving. Clearly this view was not without foundation. As Lord Esher noted in his diary:

> Of course their amour propre and ours come into conflict. This is not a negligible factor in our Army. If D.H. is obliged to take over all the line they ask for, it will hamper him to such an extent that *his* plans of attack will probably not be possible.
>
> Kiggell and Tavish Davidson [D.M.O. at general headquarters] are very angry. They say, with truth, that D.H.'s arrangement with Nivelle was an agreement, and that the politicians should not intervene. There will be a good deal of "feeling" in our Army if the whole glory of the Spring offensive is handed over to the French.[43]

Still, it would be grossly unfair to write off the objections of Haig and Robertson to self-interest alone.

Even though Haig agreed to conform to Nivelle's attack plan, Lloyd George did not trust him. His suspicions were raised by Haig's reluctance during the London conference to take over more line and his desire to delay the attack until Italy and Russia were also prepared to apply pressure. From confidential French sources he discovered that Nivelle shared his apprehension of the field marshal.[44]

The War Cabinet took the unusual step of instructing Robertson to order Haig to carry out, "both in the letter and in the spirit, the agreement made with General Nivelle on the 16th January, 1917, in order that the British Expeditionary Force may be able to carry out its share of the operations at the date laid down in the aforesaid agreement. . . . on no account must the French have to wait for us owing to our arrangements not being complete."[45]

Even after the War Cabinet's direct order to Haig, Lloyd George remained convinced that general headquarters would not give its full cooperation to Nivelle. The French continued to pile the pressure on Haig to hasten his offensive preparations, with the British commander in chief responding that he could move no faster because of the condition of French railways. This railway crisis had been long building, with the British offensive in the previous summer being hampered by the deterioration of the French rail transportation system. Robertson once summed up Lloyd George's days in the War Office with this remark: "There is nothing of much interest to record, for he was connected with no measure having any special influence on the course of the war."[46] To the contrary, Lloyd George made at least one important contribution to the war effort: the assignment of one of his favorites in the Ministry of Munitions, Sir Eric Geddes, a former manager of the North Eastern Railway, to the problem of transportation in France and elsewhere. Although Geddes now confirmed Haig's contention that the state of French railways was "seriously handicapping"[47] British offensive preparations for 1917, Lloyd George refused to put aside his suspicions of Haig's ulterior motives.

This matter came to a head on February 13–14. First, Robertson complained at length on February 13 in the War Cabinet about the ministers' interference with British military operations. Referring to the tight restrictions placed upon Haig, he accused the ministers of insisting that the field-marshal was "expected to attack whether he be ready or not." If the government continued to demand "that the state of our preparations must be subordinated to the plans and wishes of the French, notwithstanding the breakdown of the French railway system," the ministers—not Haig—must accept full responsibility for any military disaster.[48] Second, Robertson received an early-morning telegram from Haig on the fourteenth requesting an immediate meeting of himself, Nivelle, and the British and French ministers to resolve the transportation crisis.[49]

Convinced that the high command was using the issue of French railways to undermine the decisions made at the London conference, Lloyd George began to consider ways to bring his generals to heel. The answer might be some form of unity of command, which had first appealed to Lloyd George when he was lobbying for Anglo-French military intervention in the Balkans in 1915. Since the beginning of the year there had been signals from Paris that French political and military leaders favored the creation of a unified command on the western front.[50] The British commander in chief at Salonika, General George F. Milne, had already been placed under Sarrail over Robertson's objections. When Briand had made this suggestion at the Rome conference, Robertson had vehemently argued that the British government "could not possibly put British troops really under a foreign general."[51] Ultimately, the same arrangement that had previously existed between the British commander in chief, Ian Hamilton, and the French commander at Gallipoli had been accepted. Milne reserved the right to appeal over Sarrail's head to his government if there was disagreement. In early February, when Milne had protested Sarrail's movement of a British brigade outside of the area of British operations, the War Cabinet had overruled Derby and Robertson and backed Sarrail.[52] If Milne could be made Sarrail's subordinate in the Balkans, Lloyd George may have reasoned, why could not Haig be placed under Nivelle? Haig's request for another Anglo-French conference opened the door to such an arrangement.

The prime minister was in a especially dangerous mood in mid-February because of an interview that Haig had with some French journalists on February 1. When garbled accounts of this interview appeared in the British press on the fifteenth, it created a sensation. Questions were asked in Parliament, the king was shocked, and the War Cabinet instructed Derby to investigate the circumstances and authenticity of the interview. Haig's boast that the Allies were certain to break the German lines and his discussion of the preparations were not only uncharacteristic of him, they violated the king's regulations.[53] The prime minister's fury, however, was largely explained by another remark attributed to Haig. The field-marshal had complained about the shortage of guns and shells; and Lloyd George, still smarting from the press attacks on him that had followed his interview with Foch, took this as a criticism of his leadership of the Ministry of Munitions.[54]

On the day that Haig's interview appeared in the press, Lloyd George interrupted a discussion between Hankey and Commandant Bertier de Sauvigny, the assistant French military attaché, who was the French high command's link to the British War Office. The Frenchman's account of this meeting, which was forwarded to Nivelle and the French minister for war, Lyautey, made agreeable reading in Paris. Characterizing Nivelle as "the only man who is capable of bringing the operations to a successful conclusion this year," Lloyd George proposed placing the British army at his disposal. Without strong pressure from the French for subordinating Haig to Nivelle, however, he was pessimistic about gaining the necessary political support to achieve this goal.[55] Thus was set in motion the famous conspiracy between certain British politicians and the French against the British high command. Hitherto little has been known about the discussions within the British government that preceded and followed the Calais conference. Material recently made available sheds much new light on this subject.

Robertson had been greatly concerned by Haig's request for another Anglo-French conference to discuss Nivelle's offensive. "So long as Ministers take part in the discussion of plans of operations," he immediately wrote Haig, "we shall always have trouble of the worst kind I am sure. Soldiers understand each other and I have some hope that Nivelle will see you and that the two of you will come to a satisfactory agreement. . . . They [the ministers] have so many axes to grind, whereas if you and Nivelle can come to some sort of a settlement the two Governments will have to agree. Of course if you do not come to a settlement they will have to intervene I suppose."[56] Little did Robertson know that his worst fears about his government's intervention with the high command's conduct of the war were about to be exceeded.

On February 20, after Robertson informed the War Cabinet that Nivelle and Haig had come to an understanding about the timing of the offensive, the ministers decided to hold an Anglo-French conference anyway. Robertson's contention, which has gained wide acceptance, is that the sole purpose of the conference was to discuss the railway crisis.[57] But as the minutes of the War Cabinet reveal, the civilians desired a conference "so that a definite understanding might be reached and an agreement drawn up and signed by the Heads of the two Governments respectively, not only so far as the railways are concerned, *but also in regard to the operations of 1917.*"[58]

Thus it is beyond doubt that Robertson, despite his denials, knew that the Calais conference was being held, in part, to achieve a unity of views between the two governments about Nivelle's offensive. On the other hand, he had no inkling that Lloyd George and other ministers were contemplating a unified command, or put more directly, the placing of Haig under Nivelle.

On the eve of the conference the War Cabinet held an important meeting. Around the table sat only Curzon, Bonar Law, Hankey, Lloyd George, and Balfour, the foreign secretary, who had been asked to attend. Conspicuous by their absence were Derby and Robertson. Robertson, whose hostility to any arrangement that would limit the freedom of the British army was well known, was at work in the War Office because he had been told that it was unnecessary for him to attend. The prime minister was authorized

> to ask General Nivelle and Field-Marshal Sir Douglas Haig to give him a full explanation of their plans for the campaign of 1917; to use his best endeavours to ascertain any point on which there might be a difference of opinion between the two Commanders-in-Chief; in concert with M. Briand to decide any such differences of opinion on their merits; and to aim more especially at the adoption of such measures as might appear best calculated, as the result of the discussion at the Conference, to ensure unity of command both in the preparatory stages of and during the operations.[59]

The brief minutes of this important meeting give no hint of the discussion that took place. In fact, the conclusion quoted above was drafted as an after-thought on the prime ministers' instructions as the British delegation was on its way to Calais.[60] Hankey's entry in his diary does not contribute much, informing us only that the civilians decided "that as between Haig and Nivelle, Ll. G. should support the latter."[61] In the Royal Archives, however, there is a most revealing note of a conversation between Stamfordham and Curzon in which the latter gives the arguments that apparently proved decisive in the ministers' decision to give Nivelle supreme command.

> The War Cabinet were determined to ensure Unity of Command both in the preparatory stages of and during the forthcoming operations. The arguments in favour of Nivelle were—
> 1. The French had practically twice the number of troops in the field that we had.
> 2. We were fighting on French soil to drive the enemy off French soil.
> 3. Independent opinion shows that without question the French Generals and Staffs are immeasurably superior to British Generals and Staffs, not from the point of view of fighting but from that of generalship, and of the knowledge of the science and art of war.
> 4. The War Cabinet did not consider Haig a clever man. Nivelle made a much greater impression on the members of the War Cabinet—of the two in existing circumstances Nivelle was the right man to have supreme command.

Curzon also placed great emphasis on the political considerations involved. The approaching attacks "were to be a supreme effort on the Western Front. . . . Any failure might have a tendency to break up the alliance. The French numbers were becoming depleted. Hence it was of paramount importance that the whole responsibility for the preparation and carrying out of the plans of this supreme effort should be in the hands of the French. We must leave them no loophole through which want of success could be attributed to us."[62]

The War Committee's belief in the superiority of French generalship cannot be left without further comment. How was it possible for the British politicians to believe after the futile and costly French strategy and tactics in 1914 and 1915, which had cost so many British lives, that the British generals were inferior to French generals? The answer can be found in the flexible and imaginative tactics used by the French on the Somme and at Verdun. Because the French limited their objectives and effectively coordinated their artillery with their infantry, the War Cabinet was convinced that French casualties were proportionately smaller than the British.[63]

After Lloyd George met privately with Briand, the Calais conference opened on the twenty-sixth at 3:30 P.M. in a small downstairs room in the Hotel of the Gare Maritime. After a routine discussion of the railway transport question, the Anglo-French political and military leaders paused for tea. The discussions, resumed at 5:30, then took a turn that made Haig and Robertson sit uneasily in their chairs. Transportation was no longer the issue. Nivelle, with the aid of maps, described his plan of attack without any mention of Haig's foot-dragging. Unhappy with these generalities, Lloyd George attempted to coach the French general. Was Nivelle satisfied with the existing arrangement between himself and Haig? "He hoped that he would feel no delicacy or reserve in expressing his full opinion. The situation was far too serious for such reserves. It was far better that he should say it now than that there should be any misunderstanding afterwards." Briand quickly chimed in: "General Nivelle and Field-Marshal Sir Douglas Haig should speak their whole minds and state exactly what they considered was required to ensure complete co-operation and the best possible dispositions for our forces." Given his cue, Nivelle's face turned red. His usual glibness abandoned him and he "beat around the bush." After thanking Haig for his previous cooperation, he finally came to the point: "He did not anticipate any difficulties between the Commanders-in-Chief, who were veritable brothers in arms. He considered, however, that there must be certain rules which should not only guide the relations of the Generals themselves, but should also be binding on their successors if either of them disappeared." The day's session came to an end when Lloyd George and Briand requested Nivelle to put in writing his thoughts on the "rules" that should govern the relationship between the two Allied commanders in chief.[64]

The British delegation then took a stroll before dinner, with Lloyd George and his generals going their separate ways. The distance between them was about to widen in a different and explosive fashion. Returning from his walk, Lloyd George met with Briand, Lyautey, and Nivelle. When Hankey was summoned to this gathering, the prime minister handed him a typed page which had been prepared a week earlier at Nivelle's headquarters. "What do you think of it?"[65] the prime minister wanted to know. The document, "Projet d'Organisation de l'Unité de Commandement sur le Front occidental," represented unity of command with a vengeance. Haig had been reduced to the status of an adjutant-general, with the British commanders receiving their commands directly from French headquarters. Only personnel and discipline remained in Haig's province. The stunned Hankey showed no emotion, but asked for time to study this extraordinary document.

Wully first learned of this proposal as he finished his dinner. His "face went the colour of mahogany, his eyes became perfectly round, his eyebrows slanted outwards like a forest of bayonets held at charge—in fact he showed every sign of having a fit. 'Get 'Aig,' he bellowed to The Monument [Major C. C. Lucas, Robertson's private secretary]."[66]

Haig's and Robertson's rage was certainly justified and is explained by more than their injured pride and their opposition to the laudable concept of a unified command. The British army, which had made astonishing strides in its size and fighting ability, was now arguably the cornerstone of the Entente. On the other hand, the depleted French forces were becoming demoralized; and Haig had been concerned for some time that the French, in an attempt to maintain their ascendancy on the western front, might attempt to incorporate the British forces into their own army. To their consternation and disbelief, the prime minister was a willing accomplice in or even the instigator of such an "amalgam."[67] Rather than accept this humiliating arrangement, Haig and Robertson were prepared to resign.

The two generals were soon knocking on Lloyd George's door. The prime minister, who had worked himself into "an extra-ordinary frame of mind," did not flinch before their fury. When Haig suggested that his "Tommies" would refuse to serve under a Frenchman, Lloyd George fired back: "Well, Field-Marshal, I know the private soldier very well. He speaks very freely to me, and there are people he criticises a good deal more strongly than Gen. Nivelle!"[68] He then played his ace in the hole. The War Cabinet, he informed the shocked and incredulous generals, was behind him.

But could Lloyd George really depend upon the Unionists to support the extreme French proposal which called for the virtual abolition of Haig's position as commander in chief of the British army? It was one thing to place Haig under Nivelle for the forthcoming operation; quite another matter to hand over the British army lock, stock, and barrel to the French. That Lloyd George had gone too far is indicated by Hankey, who told Haig that "Lloyd George had not received full authority from the War Cabinet for acting as he was doing."[69]

After a restless night, Lloyd George was prepared to retreat—but not far. He came to Calais expecting a " 'hard fight,' " but as he told Miss Stevenson before departing for Calais, " 'I mean to have my way.' "[70] His rash acceptance of the French position, however, placed his authority and prestige on the line with the generals over a clearly flawed command arrangement.

Fortunately he was rescued from his predicament by a face-saving compromise which all parties accepted after tense negotiations which shifted from room to room. According to the new formula, Haig's position was to be based on Milne's relationship to Sarrail, which had been established by the Rome conference. And it was made clear that this arrangement would be terminated at the end of Nivelle's offensive. Also Haig retained the freedom to direct operations on his own front. Relieved that the original French proposal had been dropped, Robertson and Haig, with considerable misgiving, signed the new arrangement.

With his generals' signatures on the Calais agreement, Lloyd George thought that he had won a major victory over the high command: Haig, in whom he had no confidence, had had his role considerably diminished in the approaching offensive. In his haste to support Nivelle at Haig's expense, however, Lloyd George had been largely responsible for establishing a faulty system of supreme command. It was unsound, if not dangerous, for Nivelle to command the French army and at the same time exercise executive authority over the British forces. Foch in 1918 and Eisenhower in 1944–45 occupied a position above the national armies involved, and were responsible to the Allied governments equally. With Nivelle responsible only to the French government, national sentiment in Britain was certain to be inflamed. During the following days, the Calais agreement was a ticking bomb threatening to blow apart Lloyd George's fragile ministry.

Returning to London, Lloyd George gained the War Cabinet's acceptance of the Calais agreement by telling the ministers that Haig's relationship to Nivelle had been little changed because the field marshal, on Kitchener's instructions, had subordinated his strategy to the French in the West since taking command. With his signature on the agreement, Robertson at first held his tongue. But, upon leaving the cabinet room, he wrote Haig: "He [Lloyd George] is an awful liar. His story to the War Cabinet gave quite a wrong impression this morning. . . . I cannot believe that a man such as he can for long remain head of any Government."[71]

Across the Channel, Haig's irritation with Nivelle was rising. (Had he known the French general's involvement in the conspiracy against him, one wonders what he would have done.) On the day that the Calais conference broke up, Nivelle sent him a brusque letter demanding to know of his offensive preparations and requesting the appointment of Sir Henry Wilson as head of the newly created British mission at French general headquarters. Nivelle's dictatorial tone and his choice of Wilson made Haig's blood boil, for the lanky Irishman was widely (and incorrectly) considered by the British army to be more favorable to French than British interests. "Briefly it is the type of letter which no gentleman could have drafted, and it also is one which no C in C of this great British Army should receive without protest,"[72] an offended Haig wrote in his diary.

Haig had more than Nivelle on his mind at this juncture. While at Calais, he had received word that the German army was withdrawing many miles behind the existing front to a new defensive position—the Hindenburg Line (or Siegfried Stellung). The vastly improved German defenses and the additional reserve divisions created by the shorter German line altered the strategical picture in the West, and enabled Haig to question the advisability of Nivelle's attack ("a blow in the air"). Asserting that the Germans now had the initiative, he argued that his first concern must be the threat of a German thrust against his forces between Lille and the sea (the Ypres sector) to capture the Channel ports. If he committed his reserves to Nivelle as demanded, he warned his government in a memorandum on March 2, "the safety of the British Armies might be gravely endangered."[73] Haig's fear of a

German attack, though mistaken, was probably genuine; but his position was suspect because if Nivelle's attack had to be abandoned, he would regain full authority over his army, save it, or so he feared, from being broken up and incorporated in the French army, and clear the way for his Flanders operation.

Whatever position he took, Haig could count on Robertson's strong support. After probing the mood of London, Robertson had decided to lead a mutiny against the Calais agreement. The Army Council and Derby were solidly behind him, with the secretary of state for war threatening resignation and complaining to Lloyd George about his exclusion from the crucial February 24 meeting of the War Cabinet.[74] The nationalistic passions aroused by Haig's humiliation were certain to bring many Unionists, especially Cecil, Long, Chamberlain, and Carson, into the War Office's camp.[75] And then there was the support of Buckingham Palace, whose reaction to Haig's warning that Calais might be the first step toward incorporating the British army into the French corps bordered on hysteria. Lloyd George's motives, always suspect to George V, were given the worst possible interpretation. Major Clive Wigram, the king's equerry, told an incredulous Rawlinson that "L.G.'s reason for wishing to do so [placing the British Army under Nivelle] is based on his ultimate intention of breaking up the Monarchy and introducing a republic with himself at the head and that he foresees the loyal adherence of the Army to the Monarch is his chief obstacle—For this reason he desires to weaken it by breaking it up and distributing it amongst the French Armies."[76]

On March 2, Robertson prepared a memorandum for the eyes of the War Cabinet making clear his opposition to Calais. He had only signed the agreement, he argued, because constitutionally the War Cabinet's position left him no other alternative.[77] On that same day he wrote Haig, encouraging him to stand up to Nivelle and assuring him of the Army Council's support. "I am sure you will do all you can to smooth things over; but on the other hand it is bad to lay up certain trouble in the future, and if things seem really to have reached the breaking point it may be best to have it all out now."[78] The next day, with a discussion of his memorandum about to take place in the War Cabinet, he fired off another letter to the field marshal, suggesting that if Haig had any criticism of his new relationship with Nivelle, he should put them before the War Cabinet immediately.[79]

Meanwhile Robertson waged a vigorous campaign to wean the civilians away from the prime minister.

> The rugged old man stumped up and down Ministers' rooms, or glowering at them from under his enormous eyebrows banged the table and repeated again and again that Nivelle was answerable to the French Government alone and that therefore the French and not the British Government was the supreme authority over our army. Was that what was wanted? he growled, baring his teeth in the alarming way he had: well, if so, tell the country.[80]

The C.I.G.S. gained unwitting support from an unexpected quarter—the French. Haig had passed on his memorandum of March 2 to Nivelle and enclosed a covering letter to the French general questioning the details of his offensive. The normally composed Nivelle was now in an anxious and cranky mood; to him Haig's attitude "appeared disobedient and his doubts almost sacrilegious."[81] When Nivelle forwarded Haig's memorandum to his government, it in turn demanded, on March 7, that the British government require Haig to comply with the Calais agreement.[82] Meanwhile, Nivelle wrote Haig insisting that his attack "must not be reduced by a single man, or gun."[83] He also secretly got in touch with Lloyd George and gave his opinion "that the situation cannot improve as long as Sir Douglas Haig remains in command." His choice for Haig's successor was General Sir Robert Gough, the young and dashing commander of the Fifth Army.[84]

As the Calais agreement began to unravel, Lloyd George was faced with a serious dilemma. Convinced that Haig's appreciation of the situation created by the German withdrawal was an attempt to destroy the decisions at Calais, his combative instincts prompted him to fight back. He considered either firing Haig or goading him to resign, although it was certain that Robertson's and Derby's resignation would immediately follow. With the abrupt disappearance of Britain's military leadership, his ministry might disintegrate. On the verge of a momentous decision he turned to the individual whose advice he valued most—Hankey. Working late into the evening of March 7, Hankey prepared a paper that considered the consequences of such a drastic development. In his memorandum, Hankey, who had polled the members of the War Cabinet, pointed out that only Bonar Law, more out of loyalty than conviction, would support the dismissal of Haig. He then wrote:

12. Personally I believe that, if Haig resigned, the Government would very likely be defeated, and that, even if they recalled him, they would be in jeopardy, unless Haig was at once appointed to some other active command. I do not under-rate the very strong case that would be made for the change, but, even so, I believe that the result would be to cause elements to coalesce which would never otherwise do so. The late Prime Minister would, I believe, on this issue rally to him his old followers, and many waverers; they would be joined, from sheer mischief, by the disunited Irish, by the pacifists, and possibly by some Tories. Court and society influence, and all elements within reach of the General Staff would be thrown into the scale against the Government, and, whether the Government were defeated or not they would be very seriously weakened. I have not the remotest idea how an appeal to the country would result, but at the present time an election on such a subject would not strengthen national unity.

13. On the political side, therefore, the arguments appear to me overwhelmingly in favour of Haig's retention. If, however, this is considered impossible, it is of the first importance that he should not resign, but should be recalled, and should, if possible, be given a high military command e.g. at Salonica.[85]

On the morning of March 8, the prime minister paced up and down the cabinet room, hotly arguing with Hankey, who supported the retention of Haig. Lloyd George then attended a meeting of the War Cabinet in which the ministers insisted that another Anglo-French conference was necessary to resolve the differences between Haig and Nivelle.[86] On the following day, incensed by French arrogance, the War Cabinet went a step further. It instructed Lloyd George to demonstrate the War Cabinet's "full confidence" in Haig at the next Anglo-French conference.[87]

Lloyd George now had no choice but to beat a hasty retreat. Without the support of the War Cabinet, he dared not remove Haig. He had to ask himself: Was this the issue to break up his government and go to the country in a general election? The mandate that had brought him to power had been total victory over Germany—not support of the French against the leadership of the British army or interference with the military's conduct of the war. The Dardanelles Commission report, published on the ninth, which by implication blamed the "amateur" strategists for that disaster, would certainly not strengthen his position in any quarrel with the army. Under the circumstances, he would almost certainly go down in defeat. It is ironic that his opponents, fearing that a general election might return him to power with all restraints removed, did not press him so hard as they might have. Buckingham Palace urged Derby and Haig not to resign[88]; and there were no attempts to arouse the volatile and bombastic press.

On the eve of the Anglo-French conference in London, Haig's and Robertson's supporters kept up the pressure. Derby, in a memorandum which the prime minister had requested, pointed out that Balfour, Carson, and members of the War Cabinet, including Bonar Law, convinced of Haig's good intentions, were furious with the French attitude.[89] On the day the conference began, George V in an acrimonious interview took the prime minister to task for being kept in the dark about the Calais arrangement. After all, "as Head of the State and of the Army, he had *his* responsibilities" and he "objected to being kept in ignorance of matters affecting the welfare of the Army." He bluntly informed Lloyd George that the "whole Army" was certain to "strongly resent" being placed "under the command of a foreign General." If this state of affairs "were known in the Country it would be equally condemned." Lloyd George held his ground, asserting that "in the event of any such public expression of feeling, he would go to the country and would explain matters and very soon have the whole Country on his side."[90]

Despite these brave words, the prime minister was in full retreat. In a private meeting with Nivelle and at the conference, he went out of his way to point out that "Field-Marshal Sir Douglas Haig possessed the full confidence of the War Cabinet, and was regarded with admiration in England."[91]

For once Lloyd George was in harmony with Robertson as they worked to take some of the sting out of the Calais agreement. Prodded by Wully, Haig agreed to accept Wilson as the head of the British mission at French general headquarters. But, at the same time, it was made clear to Nivelle that Wilson, who was to report directly to Haig rather than Robertson in London, was not to act as a British chief of staff. In short, the function of his British mission was limited to liaison and was not to be used by Nivelle to increase his control over the British army. Lloyd George also took the lead in removing the threat of an amalgam of the two armies, insisting that the British army should not be "mixed up with the French Army."[92] Meanwhile, at the

War Office, Haig and Nivelle, under Robertson's watchful gaze, succeeded in reaching an agreement on the offensive.

Robertson had reason to be pleased by the results of the Anglo-French conference. To his great relief, he now apparently had Haig and Nivelle working in unison; perhaps now the soldiers might get on with the war without division between the commanders in chief giving the civilians another excuse to interfere in military matters. Also, many of the most objectionable elements in the Calais agreement, especially the tendency by the French to incorporate the British army into their own, had been resolved to the advantage of the British. As for Lloyd George, his continued commitment to Nivelle was disastrous. To be sure, he had succeeded in stilling the intense passions aroused by Calais that threatened his government without abandoning unity of command in the West. But his support of Nivelle had cost him dearly and the damage was ultimately to be greater. His devious methods deepened the high command's distrust of him and he was about to be tarred with Nivelle's failure to rupture the German lines. In his discussion with Hankey on March 8, the latter had urged him to force the French to reconsider their strategy in light of the German withdrawal to the Hindenburg Line. In the new situation, Hankey argued that Haig's plan to attack in Flanders, where the enemy "is bound, either to fight, or to surrender some objective of strategical or political importance,"[93] offered a better chance of success. Lloyd George, however, refused to reopen a discussion of Allied plans at the London conference, and consequently increased his own responsibility for Nivelle's unsuccessful offensive. The War Cabinet, however, on March 14, did agree that Haig should be allowed to prepare for his northern operation if the French failed to break through.[94]

With his reputation intimately linked to Nivelle's success or failure, Lloyd George's anxiety mounted as the time for the French offensive approached. Each day seemed to bring new complications. The German withdrawal to the Hindenburg Line had undercut Nivelle's tactical plan because of the shorter and stouter German defensive position and the additional reserves freed from the trenches. Meanwhile, inexcusable security lapses on the part of the French destroyed any hope of surprising the Germans. Shopkeepers in Paris openly discussed the date of the attack; and German raids on French trenches resulted in the capture of documents which revealed the nature of the approaching offensive.

Just after the Anglo-French conference in London broke up an ill political wind blew toward Nivelle's headquarters from Paris. On March 15, the French minister for war, General Lyautey, was shouted down when he attempted to speak to a night session of the French Chamber. He responded by shouting "at the gesticulating mob three words which the official stenographers did not take down, very military words which described exactly what he thought of his audience."[95] His subsequent resignation resulted in the collapse of Nivelle's political support, with Premier Briand resigning on the nineteenth. The new ministry under the financier Ribot was hostile to Nivelle's strategy because it threatened to deplete further the war-weary French army. The driving force in the government was the brilliant and iconoclastic minister for war, Paul Painlevé, who had boycotted Briand's government because of his opposition to Nivelle's offensive. The cautious and defensive-minded Philippe Pétain was his favorite general.

The new mood in Paris coincided with other events that radically transformed the entire grand-strategic landscape that had existed when the plans for the spring offensives had been made. In Petrograd, revolution swept the streets, with the tsar abdicating on March 15. Although it was by no means certain that Russia would fall out of the war, the situation was clouded with uncertainty. Meanwhile, the United States was being daily pushed closer to a declaration of war by Berlin's reopening of unrestricted U-boat warfare in February. The German submarine campaign was indeed a mixed blessing. It eventually brought America into the war, but at the same time it put immense pressure on the already perilous shipping position of the Allies. Elsewhere, the Italians were showing little fight and were bombarding the British government with pleas for assistance to ward off a combined Austro-German attack which they anticipated. Other than America's inexorable slide toward war, the only encouraging news came from the periphery. On March 11 Baghdad fell to General Sir Stanley Maude. Although of no real strategic value, this success in Mesopotamia had significant political consequences. Britain's bargaining position at any peace conference was strengthened and the allies were given something to boost their war-weary spirits.

Ironically, as the day of the British and French attacks neared, Lloyd George found himself arguing against diverting forces away from the western front. First, in early March, Bissolati showed up in London to lobby for Anglo-French troops and guns being dispatched south of the Alps. Since Bissolati wanted these reinforcements more for *defensive* rather than offensive purposes, it was easy for Lloyd George to say no. He even found himself using the general staff's argument that the approaching Allied offensive in the West would keep the Germans from concentrating on Italy.[96] The Welshman took bitter pleasure in reminding the Italians that their lack of support at Rome had placed him "in the position of appearing to thrust an undesirable gift upon a reluctant recipient."[97] Then, on the very day the British launched their attack in April, Painlevé paid Lloyd George a visit and advocated strategy which bore a strong resemblance to Lloyd George's earlier proposal. The French minister for war "appeared to desire" that four British and four French divisions be sent to Italy.[98] However much Painlevé's strategy may have appealed to Lloyd George, it was too late for him to dismount from the Nivelle horse he was riding. Painlevé was given no encouragement.

Another consideration for Lloyd George was the growing belief in London that Austria-Hungary, after the death of Francis Joseph in late 1916, might be persuaded to make a separate peace. In January, when the War Cabinet had discussed detaching Austria-Hungary, Robertson had stressed the military advantages. It "would eliminate 47 Austro-Hungarian divisions now on the Eastern front, and set free 149 Russian divisions to deal with 78 German divisions now on the Eastern front."[99] The Russian Revolution in March made peace with Vienna even more urgent. At Folkestone on April 11, in an atmosphere of great secrecy, Ribot had shown Lloyd George a letter from

Francis Joseph's successor, Emperor Charles, which suggested a compromise peace, but offered no concessions to Italy.[100] Lloyd George immediately recognized the divisive nature of this document: Italy would feel betrayed. Still, he apparently held the slim hope that Italy might be bought off with concessions in Asia Minor. He also found justification in this peace feeler for his desire to put pressure on Austria on the Italian front if Nivelle's attack miscarried.

As these crosscurrents tugged Lloyd George first this way, then that way, the great spring offensive began. The British led off on April 9 to draw off the German reserves. Haig's first objective was Vimy Ridge, which was north of Arras. Nivelle's attack a week later in miserable weather fell far short of his objectives and belied his last words to his troops: "L'heure venue! Confiance! Courage! Vive la France!" Judged by the standards of previous general French assaults, the results of Nivelle's attack were generally impressive and his losses hardly unusual.[101] A breakthrough, however, proved to be a mirage and the impact on French morale was devastating. Meanwhile, Haig won a brilliant victory initially at Vimy Ridge which surpassed anything achieved by British arms on the Somme in 1916. The attempt to exploit the capture of Vimy Ridge with cavalry, however, was characterized by considerable confusion and little success.

When it became obvious that Nivelle had not broken through, Lloyd George was faced with a great dilemma. The French informed him that they wanted to break off the offensive and wait for the recovery of Russia and for America, which had come into the war on April 6, to send assistance. When Lloyd George sounded out Haig about the military situation, however, the field marshal was horrified at any suggestion that the Allies should stand on the defensive. "But I must say at once," he wrote in his diary, "that it would be the height of folly for the French to stop now just when the Germans had committed the serious fault of retiring, meaning to avoid a battle, but had been forced to fight against their will. . . . If offensive operations are stopped in France, the enemy will be given time to recover from the blows he received on the Somme[,] at Verdun, Arras, and now on the Aisne."[102]

Lloyd George, humbled by Nivelle's failure and Haig's success, was in no position to support the French over his generals, however much their views might parallel his own. The chickens hatched by his support of Nivelle at Calais had come home to roost. An immediate result of Nivelle's failure was a demand by Robertson that the Calais agreement be given a quick burial.[103] With Nivelle in disgrace and the French government wobbling, there could be no argument against restoring the complete independence of the British army.

Freed from the yoke of Calais, Haig was prepared for his army to assume the major burden of defeating the German army. On April 19, Haig wrote Robertson that "the results so far attained this year show that we have already reduced considerably, by previous efforts, the enemy's resisting power. . . . I consider that the prospects of success this year are distinctly good . . . and that it would be unwise, unsound and probably, in the long run, more costly in men and money to cease offensive operations at an early date."[104] Haig, of course, was not just thinking of following up his Vimy

Ridge success; his primary interest was the great blow he wanted to deliver in Flanders later in the year.

But was Haig's strategy the right one with support from Britain's war-weary allies uncertain? It could be argued that the British army, the best and most reliable Allied force in the field, would have to deliver massive blows against the German army to keep the anti-German coalition from crumbling. But was it wise for Britain to take on the Germans almost singlehandedly? As we will see there were no easy answers to the profoundly complex questions facing the British government.

NOTES

1. Lloyd George, *War Memoirs,* 1:620.

2. "Memorandum of Conversation between Mr. Lloyd George and certain Unionist ex-Ministers, December 7, 1916," Curzon MSS, Eur. F. 112/130.

3. Robertson to Lloyd George, December 8, 1916, Robertson MSS, I/19/9. It is possible that Robertson never sent this letter for there is not a copy in the Lloyd George MSS.

4. War Cabinet (1), December 9, 1916, CAB 23/1.

5. The reader should be aware of the revisionist contention that by 1916 Russia was producing an adequate supply of war material. See Norman Stone, *The Eastern Front, 1914–1917* (1975), p. 13.

6. Memorandum by Hankey, December 8, 1916, CAB 42/19/2. This important memorandum never became an officially numbered paper and was later filed curiously and incorrectly with the Cabinet Papers for September 1916.

7. Hankey Diary, December 20, 1916, 1/1.

8. Lloyd George, *War Memoirs,* 1:818.

9. Robertson to Lloyd George, December 12, 1916, Robertson MSS, I/33/12, and memorandum by Robertson, December 29, 1916, W.O. 106/1511.

10. Robertson to Haig, December 24, 1916, Robertson MSS, I/22/97.

11. C. Delmé Radcliffe to Lloyd George, December 15 and 25, Lloyd George MSS, F/56/1/1 and 3.

12. Brigadier-General E. L. Spears, *Prelude to Victory* (1939), p. 32.

13. Ibid., p. 42.

14. Haig to Lady Haig, December 20, 1916, Haig MSS, no. 146.

15. Haig, "Notes on relations with French C in C [Joffre and Nivelle], 1916–1917," n.d., Haig MSS, no. 215 K.

16. Anglo-French Conference, December 26, 1917, CAB 28/2/I.C.-13(a).

17. Ibid., December 27, 1916, CAB 28/2/I.C.-13(b).

18. Ibid.

19. See War Cabinet (20), December 27, 1916, CAB 23/1.

20. Anglo-French Conference, December 28, 1916, CAB 28/2/I.C.-13(d), and War Cabinet (21), December 28, 1916, CAB 23/1.

21. Robertson to Haig, December 28, 1916, Robertson MSS, I/22/100.

22. War Cabinet (23), December 30, 1916, CAB 23/1.

23. Cabinet Paper G 106 of January 1917, CAB 24/3.

24. Ibid.

25. Haig Diary, January 1, 4-6, 1917, no. 110.

26. Esher Diary, January 4, 1917, 2/17.

27. Hankey Diary, January 4, 1917, 1/2, and Wilson Diary, January 4, 1917.

28. Hankey Diary, January 5, 1917, 1/2.

29. Ibid. and E. Capel Cure (a member of the staff of the British embassy in Rome) to Lloyd George, n.d., Lloyd George MSS, F/56/1/16.

30. On the train to Rome, Lloyd George had "decided definitely" against circulating his memorandum. Hankey Diary, January 5, 1917, 1/2.

31. Lloyd George, *War Memoirs,* 1:854, and Allied Conference at Rome, January 5–7, 1917, CAB 28/2/I.C.-15(b).

32. Robertson to Wigram, January 12, 1917, Robertson MSS, I/12/31.

33. Lloyd George, *War Memoirs,* 1:858–59.

34. Robertson to Lloyd George, January 6, 1917, Lloyd George MSS, F/44/3/6.

35. War Cabinet (12 and 92), December 20 and March 9, 1917, CAB 23/1 and 2.

36. Ibid. (50), January 31, 1917, CAB 23/1; also see Lloyd George to Robertson, January 25, 1917, Lloyd George MSS, F/44/3/8.

37. Haig's comments on Nivelle's proposed operation, January 11, 1917, Robertson MSS I/23/2/4, and Haig to Nivelle, January 6, 1917, Haig MSS, no. 110.

38. Haig Diary, January 15, 1917, no. 110.

39. Entry of January 15, 1917, *A Diary by Frances Stevenson,* p. 139.

40. Hankey, *Supreme Command,* 2:629.

41. Rennell Rodd to Lloyd George, January 12 and 15, 1917, Lloyd George MSS, F/56/1/17 and 19.

42. Memorandum by Robertson, January 24, 1917, Robertson MSS, I/21/50/2, and General Staff memorandum, March 20, 1917, W.O. 106/1512.

43. Esher Diary, January 17, 1917, 2/17.

44. Hankey Diary, January 17, 1917, 1/1.

45. War Cabinet (36), January 17, 1917, CAB 23/1.

46. Robertson, *Soldiers and Statesmen,* 1:179.

47. War Cabinet (59), February 9, 1917, CAB 23/1.

48. Ibid. (64), February 13, 1917, CAB 23/1.

49. Haig Diary, February 13, 1917, no. 110.

50. See Esher Diary, January 13 and February 13, 1917, 2/17–18.

51. Robertson to Wigram, January 12, 1917, Robertson MSS, I/12/31.

52. War Cabinet (63), February 12, 1917, CAB 23/1.

53. Stamfordham to Derby, February 15, 1917, Derby MSS, 920 (17).

54. Derby to Lloyd George, February 19, 1917, Lloyd George MSS, F/14/4/20.

55. Spears, *Prelude to Victory,* p. 546.

56. Robertson to Haig, February 14, 1917, Robertson MSS, I/23/7.

57. Robertson, *Soldiers and Statesmen,* 2:205.

58. Author's italics. War Cabinet (75), February 20, 1917, CAB 23/1. Also see Robertson to Haig, February 24, 1917, Haig MSS, no. 110.

59. War Cabinet (79), February 24, 1917, CAB 23/1.

60. Hankey to Stamfordham, March 4, 1917, RA GV Q1079/17.

61. Hankey Diary, February 24, 1917, 1/1.

62. "Memorandum on a conversation between Lord Curzon and Lord Stamfordham on Sunday 4 March 1917," RA GV Q1079/6.

63. It must be emphasized that the contention that French losses were proportionately smaller than the British could not be supported by hard evidence. Later, in December, when Lloyd George instructed Hankey to prepare a comparison of "the British and French ration of wastage to combatant strength," Hankey was unable to collect the necessary figures to contrast French and British casualties. Hankey to Lloyd George, December 24, 1917, Lloyd George MSS, F/23/1/36. Nevertheless, French tactics were apparently superior to those employed by general headquarters. Lieutenant-Colonel Wetzell, the chief of operations sector on the German general staff, noted in December 1917: "The artillery, like the British tactics as a whole, is rigid and stiff *(reichlich starr).*" *Military Operations, France and Belgium, 1918. The German March Offensive and its Preliminaries. Appendices,* appendix 20.

64. Hankey Diary, February 26, 1917, 1/1, and Anglo-French Conference, February 26–27, 1917, CAB 28/2/I.C.-17(a).

65. Hankey Diary, February 26, 1917, 1/1.

66. Spears, *Prelude to Victory,* p. 143.

67. Haig, "Notes on relations with French C in C [Joffre and Nivelle], 1916–1917," n.d., Haig MSS, no. 215 K.

68. Hankey Diary, February 26, 1917, 1/1.

69. Haig Diary, February 26, 1917, no. 110.

70. Entry of February 24, 1917, *A Diary by Frances Stevenson,* p. 146.

71. War Cabinet (82), February 28, 1917, CAB 23/1, and Robertson to Haig, February 28, 1917, Haig MSS, no. 110.

72. Haig Diary, February 28, 1917, no. 110.

73. Cabinet Paper G.T. 114 of March 7, 1917, CAB 24/7.

74. Derby to Lloyd George, March 6, 1917, Lloyd George MSS, F/14/4/24, and Derby to Stamfordham, March 4, 1917, RA GV Q1079/18.

75. See, for example, Walter Long to Curzon, March ?, 1917, Curzon MSS, Eur. F. 112/113.

76. Haig to George V, February 28, 1917, RA GV Q832/130, and Rawlinson Diary, March 12, 1917, 1/7. I am indebted to Professor Trevor Wilson for bringing to my attention the above quote from the Rawlinson Diary.

77. Cabinet Paper G.T. 93 of March 2, 1917, CAB 24/6.

78. Robertson to Haig, March 2, 1917, Robertson MSS, 1/23/9.

79. Robertson to Haig, March 3, 1917, Robertson MSS, 1/23/10.

80. Spears, *Prelude to Victory,* p. 184.

81. C. E. W. Bean, *The Australian Imperial Force in France, 1917,* 4:139.

82. Eric Drummond to Lloyd George (note in French communicated by the French embassy inclosed), March 7, 1917, Lloyd George MSS, F/3/2/14.

83. Nivelle to Haig, March 6, 1917, Spears MSS.

84. The copy of this note, dated March 7, 1917, is not addressed or signed, but it appears clear that it is from Nivelle, who sent it to Bertier de Sauvigny in London, who passed it on to the prime minister. See Lloyd George MSS, F/162/1, and Hankey Diary, March 10, 1917, 1/1.

85. Memorandum by Hankey, March 7, 1917, CAB 63/19.

86. War Cabinet (91), March 8, 1917, CAB 23/2.

87. War Cabinet (92), March 9, 1917, CAB 23/2, and Hankey Diary, March 10, 1917, 1/1. Lloyd George's defensive attitude was demonstrated when he refused to allow the personal statements that he and Robertson made about Calais at this meeting to be circulated, arguing that his statement had not been made in response to Robertson's and that the C.I.G.S.'s written statement differed from his verbal statement. See Hankey Diary, March 20, 1917, 1/1, and Robertson to Hankey, March 17, Hankey to Robertson, March 21, and Robertson to Hankey, March 30, 1917, Spears MSS.

88. See Derby to Stamfordham, March 4, and Stamfordham to Derby, March 5, 1917, RA GV Q1079/18–19; also see Stamfordham to Haig, March 5, 1917, RA GV Q832/134.

89. Derby to Lloyd George, March 10, 1917, Derby MSS, 920 (17).

90. Unsigned memorandum, March 12, 1917, RA GV Q1079/35.

91. Anglo-French Conference, March 12–13, 1917, CAB 28/2/I.C.-18.

92. Ibid.

93. Memorandum by Hankey, March 7, 1917, CAB 63/19.

94. Haig Diary, March 14, 1917, no. 110. Actually Haig's preparations for an offensive were *already* considerably advanced.

95. Spears, *Prelude to Victory,* p. 202.

96. War Cabinet (83), March 1, 1917, CAB 23/2, and entry of March 1, 1917, *Diaries of C. P. Scott,* pp. 265–66.

97. Lloyd George to Rennell Rodd, March 24, 1917, Lloyd George MSS, F/56/1/26.

98. See Lloyd George's account of his conversation with Painlevé in War Cabinet (116), April 10, 1917, CAB 23/2.

99. War Cabinet (37A), January 18, 1917, CAB 23/13.

100. For Lloyd George's penciled copy of this letter, see Lloyd George MSS, F/50/1/3. Also see Lloyd George, *War Memoirs*, 2:1175–1204, Lowe and Dockrill, *Mirage of Power*, 2:256–60, and Harry Hanak, "The Government, the Foreign Office and Austria-Hungary, 1914–1918," *Slavonic and East European Review* 47 (January 1969):161–97.

101. *Military Operations, France and Belgium, 1917*, 1:498.

102. Haig Diary, April 18, 1917, no. 112.

103. Cabinet Paper G.T. 477 of April 17, 1917, CAB 24/10. Also see Smuts's suggestion in Cabinet Paper G.T. 549 of April 13, 1917, CAB 24/11.

104. Haig to Robertson, April 19, 1917, Haig MSS, no. 112.

8

Passchendaele:
The Rack of Choice

LLOYD George's freedom to respond to the fluid political and military situation facing the Allies had been limited by his involvement in Nivelle's offensive. The members of the War Cabinet who had supported Nivelle over Haig—no less than himself—were in a chastened mood. Their authority in military policy had been lowered, Robertson's and Haig's prestige and influence enhanced. One also suspects that Lloyd George's confidence was shaken—at least for the moment. In the past he had been able to keep his distance from the big attacks in the West and make a plausible case for being right about Serbia, Rumania, etc. Now, for the first time, his reputation was entwined with the planning and failure of a great western attack. No matter how deep-rooted his skepticism of Haig's and Robertson's plans, he now shrank from overruling them. His irresolute—at times even noncommittal—stance in the coming months is more readily understood when this is kept in mind.

On April 18, armed with an appreciation of the military and political situation which he had requested from Hankey, he left for the Continent to confer with the Italians and the French. The secretary of the War Cabinet warned him that the war might last until 1918 or longer and that it was essential for the Allies to conserve their resources—especially their manpower—and avoid "economic distress" to "maintain that healthy public opinion which is essential to success." On the other hand, Hankey rejected the Pétain-Painlevé policy of standing on the defensive and waiting for America. "We must do the enemy all the damage we can," Hankey wrote. "This can best be done by fighting a great battle with the object of recovering the Flanders coast, which would be the most effective way of reducing our shipping losses. We must not anticipate quick results. But even a battle of the Somme type, in which we should rely mainly on our unequalled heavy artillery, if prolonged throughout the summer, might produce great results. If the enemy retires he gives us what we want. If he stands, he exposes himself to colossal losses from our heavy artillery. Either way we stand to gain."[1] The perplexing problem facing Lloyd George was: How could another massive attack in the West be reconciled with conserving Britain's staying power?

After a disappointing conference with the Italians at St. Jean de Maurienne on April 19 about the possibility of making a separate peace with Austria-Hungary, Lloyd George met with Ribot, Painlevé, and Nivelle in Paris. Advised by Haig that it would be a disastrous mistake to diminish the pressure on the Germans, the prime minister pressed the French (and got their assurances) to continue their attacks to enable the British to move into the second phase of their offensive, which promised to win control of essential coal mines and enable the Lens-Arras railway to be utilized.

While in Paris Lloyd George sought to defuse his explosive relations with the military with humor. Emerging from one session with the French politicians, he approached Maurice, who had been waiting outside the conference room, and said: " 'It is settled. Two English and two French Divisions are to go to Salonika. They are to be selected from the Western Front, and to go at once.' " The stunned director of military operations on the general staff, who did not realize that the prime minister was pulling his leg, stiffly replied: " 'Very well, Sir, I will let Sir Douglas know.' "[2] It is not recorded that Maurice or "putty nose" laughed when he realized that the prime minister was joking.

It should not be thought that Lloyd George's support of the continuation of the Anglo-French attacks in April indicated any fundamental change in his strategic views. With the French and Russians tottering, it might be disastrous to encourage them not to fight. Furthermore, the next stage of Haig's spring operation seemed promising. "To Lloyd George's mind," Hankey has written, "there was all the difference in the world between a battle fought with definite strategic, tactical or economic objectives and the *guerre d'usure* as typified by the Somme."[3]

The French reaction to Nivelle's setback was very much on the minds of the British ministers during this period. On April 24 at Amiens, Nivelle reiterated to Haig that the French would continue their offensive. But how much longer could Nivelle speak for the French army? The word in London was that his days were numbered and that General Pétain would soon be directing French military operations. If this were true, the French might not be counted on for heavy fighting. Anxiety over French morale was intensified by the tightening noose of the submarine campaign, the worsening manpower crisis, and the continued decline of Russia.

Robertson shared the civilians' concern about French war-weariness and British manpower. Realizing that Nivelle's failure opened the way for Haig's Flanders operation, he wanted to make certain that Haig realized that his future strategy and tactics must be linked to the available supply of men in khaki. On April 20, he wrote Haig: "To my mind no war has ever differed so much from previous wars as does the present one, and it is futile, to put it mildly, hanging on to other theories when facts show them to be wrong. At one time audacity and determination to push on regardless of loss were the predominating factors, but that was before the days of machine guns and other modern armament." Instead of aiming at distant objectives or a breakthrough, Robertson suggested cautious and deliberate tactics to wear down the enemy by "inflicting heavier losses upon him than one suffers oneself."[4]

Haig's mind, however, remained fixed on distant objectives in Flanders, and, with the French discouraged about the prospects of their attack, he wanted to switch off to his northern operation. For the present, however, as he informed Robertson, he wanted the Anglo-French attacks to continue to exhaust German reserves and encourage the Italians and Russians to fulfill their Chantilly obligation of simultaneous offensives.[5] Lloyd George, when informed by Robertson of Haig's desire to continue his attacks a while longer, was dubious but open to persuasion.[6]

On April 30, London was given a clear signal that the Pétain-Painlevé strategy was in the ascendancy in Paris when news arrived that Pétain had been appointed chief of the general staff. Nivelle, relegated to the status of a figurehead commander in chief, would be allowed to linger on for a bit longer.[7] With another inter-Allied conference scheduled in Paris within the next few days, the War Cabinet held a crucial meeting on May 1 to discuss the position that the British delegation should take. Robertson, Sir Henry Wilson, Jellicoe, Derby, and Cecil, who was acting secretary of state for foreign affairs while Balfour led a British mission to the United States, were there to give their expert advice. Another participant who was about to make his first important contribution to British strategy was the South African general and statesman, Jan C. Smuts, who had fought against the British in the Boer War. Smuts, who had arrived in London in March to participate in a conference of dominion prime ministers, had greatly impressed Lloyd George with his broad strategic views and the civilian perspective he brought to military questions. To get a fresh look at the war, Lloyd George had asked Smuts to prepare his assessment of the strategy of the war. Lloyd George may have hoped that a different point of view from that of the general staff would emerge from Smuts's appreciation. If so, he was to be disappointed, for the South African, fresh from a visit with Haig at general headquarters and in frequent contact with Robertson, endorsed the field marshal's plan to secure the Flemish coast.[8]

During the War Cabinet's discussion, Lloyd George gave the French arguments as he saw them for putting a brake on big and costly attacks in the West until the Russian situation "cleared up definitely one way or the other" and American power began to play a role in Europe. He suggested that the French would favor an active defensive strategy in the West, consisting of "repeated surprise attacks designed on a less ambitious scale," while the Allies employed their "surplus strength to clear up the situation elsewhere— in Syria, for example—and to eliminate Turkey, then Bulgaria, and finally, perhaps even Austria from the War." Although Lloyd George did not speak either for or against the French position of limited offensives, it was clear where his sentiments lay. "If Russia collapsed," he maintained, "it would be beyond our power to beat Germany, as the blockade would become to a great extent ineffective, and the whole of the enemies' forces would become available to oppose the Western Allies. We could not contemplate with equanimity the prospect of entering a Peace Conference with the enemy in possession of a large slice of Allied territory before we had completed the conquest of Mesopotamia and Syria." Britain's shrinking manpower weighed heavily on the prime minister's mind; and he warned his colleagues that Britain did not have sufficient men to both maintain its shipping and take on the German army without the undiminished support of the French and Russians.

Those present, however, expressed no sympathy for adopting the Pétain-Painlevé strategy, which Robertson and Smuts "characterised as equivalent to a defensive policy." To do so would allow the Germans to finish off Russia and perhaps Italy. Also, shipping losses might make impossible a great effort later. Smuts's contribution proved to be decisive. He stressed "that to relinquish the offensive in the third year of the War would be fatal, and would be the beginning of the end. It would be impossible to keep up the spirits of the people and pessimism and despair would be rife among the Allies, while the Germans would be correspondingly cheered and would have time to recover their spirits. . . . If we could not break the enemy's front we might break his heart."[9]

When Lloyd George left for Paris for the inter-Allied conference, his duty was clear, for the War Cabinet had instructed him to "press the French to continue the offensive."[10] Lloyd George's heart was not in this assignment, but he had no choice but to support his generals. In Asquith's ministry, it had been easier to be a critic of the high command; now, as prime minister, he would be held directly responsible if he ignored military advice and pushed policies that failed. Clearly he could not afford another Calais. Besides, at this critical moment in the war, it might be dangerous to support any slackening of the Allied effort because an almost irresistible momentum for a compromise peace on the part of Britain's European allies might be the result. French spirits must be boosted. If that proved to be impossible, he would then reopen the discussion of future Allied strategy. On the day before the conference began, he met with Haig and Robertson and told them that he was prepared to support whatever policy they decided upon.[11]

On the morning of May 4, prior to the plenary session of the conference, Robertson chaired a meeting of Haig, Nivelle, and Pétain at the Ministry of War. Later, during the plenary session with the ministers and military advisers present, Robertson presented a short report of this meeting. His statement, as a result of the differing views of Haig, Robertson, and Pétain, was imprecise and open to several interpretations. The ministers were told:

> We are, however, unanimously of opinion that the situation has changed since the plan for the offensive, begun in April, was agreed upon by the two Governments, and that this plan is no longer operative. It is no longer a question of aiming at breaking through the enemy's front and aiming at distant objectives. It is now a question of wearing down and exhausting the enemy's resistance, and if and when this is achieved to exploit it to the fullest extent possible. In order to wear him down we are agreed that it is absolutely necessary to fight with all our available forces, with the object of destroying the enemy's divisions. We are unanimously of opinion that there is no half-way between this course and fighting defensively, which, at this stage of the war, would be tantamount to acknowledging defeat. We are all of opinion that our object can be obtained by relentlessly attacking

with limited objectives, while making the fullest use of our artillery. By this means we hope to gain our ends with the minimum loss possible.

Having unanimously agreed to the above principles, we consider that the methods to be adopted to put them into practice, and the time and place of the various attacks, are matters which must be left to the responsible Generals, and that they should at once be examined and settled by them.[12]

Pétain then expressed support for Robertson's statement. "Very shortly," he said, "the position was to maintain an offensive by limited action with definite objectives, and the British Generals made it clear that the full forces of the French and British Army were to be employed for this end." With the British and French generals in apparent agreement that future attacks, although heavy and prolonged, were to be limited in their objectives with emphasis on expending metal rather than men, Lloyd George supported the "Westerners" in the strongest possible terms. His fighting words were intended to buck up the French and he made it clear that the British commitment to the offensive depended upon the support the French were prepared to give. "We must go on hitting and hitting with all our strength until the German ended, as he always did, by cracking." When Ribot talked of guarding against excessive losses, Lloyd George emphasized that he expected the French to fight vigorously: "We were ready to put the full strength of the British Army into the attack, but it was no good doing so unless the French did the same. Otherwise, the German would bring his best men and guns and all his ammunition against the British Army and then later against the French. Tentative and feeble attacks were really more costly in the end."[13]

Since Haig believed that the Paris agreement sanctioned his Flanders operation, exactly what military policy was Lloyd George supporting? The generals talked of new and restricted tactics to wear down the enemy at the smallest possible cost to the attacking troops. Any grandiose objectives or the policy of breaking through the German lines were expressly denied. But both Lloyd George and Robertson knew that Haig, in the event of Nivelle's failure, wanted to shift his attention to Flanders and the War Cabinet had associated itself with this policy in January and March.[14] Did the generals' agreement, then, really overrule Haig's ambitious plan to conquer the Belgian ports and drive the Germans from Belgium as Lloyd George maintains in his memoirs?[15] No minutes exist of the generals' discussion on the morning of the fourth, but it seems clear that Pétain and Robertson were in general agreement that it had. As Pétain told Repington after the meeting, "Robertson had been gradually won over, and had drafted the agreement on the Western front exactly as Pétain would have drafted it. The offensive was to be continued, but it was not to be à longue portée."[16] On another matter there can be no argument. Lloyd George was adamant that the British could not be expected to go it alone. In this he had the support of Robertson, who admitted "that it would be folly to undertake a big attack unless the French really meant business."[17]

Another subject addressed by the Paris conference was Salonika. Lloyd George, because of the shipping crisis and his growing interest in the conquest of Jerusalem, had been cool toward his brainchild since the beginning of the year. The French, however, obstinately pushed for an ever larger commitment to the Balkans. On the eve of the conference, Lloyd George had decided to give Sarrail one more chance with his imminent offensive to defeat Bulgaria. Influenced by the Italians at St. Jean de Maurienne, he "was of opinion that if the Allies were to succeed in inflicting a defeat of any magnitude on the Bulgarians at Salonica, the latter might not only break away from the Central Powers, but might turn on the Turks."[18] This view was based more on Lloyd George's belief in Bulgarian war-weariness than on the offensive power of the Eastern Army. To impress upon Paris that shipping was the weak link of the Entente, Lloyd George included Jellicoe, whose pessimism about the submarine campaign knew no limits, in the British delegation. (In Paris Jellicoe was to warn the French that the Eastern Army might starve by the end of the year if it were not withdrawn or greatly reduced in size.) If Sarrail failed, Lloyd George was prepared to withdraw all or most of the British forces there and transfer them to Egypt for the conquest of Palestine. The results of the discussion of the Salonikan question were extremely satisfying to Robertson. Lloyd George, following the C.I.G.S.'s advice, insisted that the British would begin the withdrawal of one division and two mounted brigades on June 1. Only if Sarrail knocked Bulgaria flat would this decision be reconsidered.[19]

Haig and Robertson were delighted with the prime minister's role in the Paris conference, with Robertson proclaiming "that he was better pleased with the Conference than with any other that had preceded it."[20] The hateful Calais agreement was now a thing of the past; and Lloyd George now sang the praises of British generalship and gave every appearance of having been converted to the "Western" school of thought.

In Lloyd George's case, however, appearances were often deceiving. Although he had accepted and even used the language of attrition, he still rejected a war of exhaustion and was opposed to a second Somme. His instincts told him at Paris that the French were nearing the end of their rope. After his speech exhorting the French to fight, he had been confronted by Pétain in the corridor. "I suppose you think I can't fight," Pétain remarked. "No General, with your record I would not make that mistake," Lloyd George had retorted, "but I am certain that for some reason or other you won't fight."[21] His suspicions of French intentions seemed confirmed when Esher, with his ear to the ground in Paris, wrote Robertson that the "jelly fish" in the French government could not be counted on to fulfill their commitments at the Paris conference.[22] When Robertson passed this letter on to Lloyd George, the latter immediately instructed Robertson to inform Haig that the British government's support of continued assaults in the West was dependent upon the French living up to the Paris agreement. "He [Lloyd George] is anxious that you should clearly realise this in your discussion with Nivelle," Robertson wrote, "because Cabinet could never agree to our incurring heavy losses with comparatively small gains, which would obviously be the result unless French co-operate wholeheartedly."[23]

If Lloyd George had known the true state of the French army he would have been far more anxious and certainly more resolute in his opposition to the continued hammering of the German lines. French soldiers had been broken in spirit by Nivelle's attack which fell so far short of its promised results. On May 3, the 2d Colonial Infantry Division appeared on parade without packs or rifles as it was about to be sent to the front lines. The men shouted, "We're not marching" and "Down with the War."[24] They were brought under control only after their officers promised that they would not have to go "over the top" and attack. Like a drop of oil on water, the French mutiny spread. The "Internationale" was sung by French soldiers on trains carrying them home on leave. Once soldiers marching through a town on the way to the front started baa-ing like sheep being led to the slaughter. By the end of May many French divisions were unreliable. According to Painlevé only two could be counted on between Paris and Soissons.[25] Astonishingly, the French were able to mask the extent of this mutiny from both the Germans and their allies.

The mutinous state of the Russian army, however, was in clear focus in London. Reports from Russia indicated that what has been called the "greatest mutiny in history"[26] was already well advanced by May. On May 9, the day the Petrograd Soviet advocated an international Socialist peace conference, Lloyd George addressed himself to the consequences of Russia's defection. In an apparent attempt to rally support for peripheral operations, especially in Palestine, the prime minister painted an extremely gloomy picture in the War Cabinet of Allied prospects if Russia made a separate peace:

> In such circumstances the best chance for the Allies would appear to lie in a separate peace with Austria, in which Italy might have to be compelled to acquiesce. If we failed to induce Austria to make a separate peace, he could see no hope of the sort of victory in the War that we desired. In these circumstances, it might be necessary to make a bargain with Germany for evacuating Belgium in return for the restoration of her Colonies, and this was a point to which he drew General Smuts' attention. If it should prove impossible to persuade Austria to make a separate peace, he inclined to the view that it would be a mistaken policy to sacrifice hundreds of thousands of lives in attacks on the Western Front, where even now we were doing little more than hold our own, and he would like the War Cabinet to consider whether, in these circumstances, it would be a better policy to concentrate our efforts on a campaign to break up Turkey. Already we occupied Mesopotamia, Russia occupied Armenia, and we were on the borders of Palestine. To continue the process of releasing subject peoples from Turkish oppression would be to gain considerable advantage.[27]

Britain's response to Russia's apparent collapse was examined from all angles during the next few days in London. A successful diplomatic offensive against Turkey, Bulgaria, or Austria-Hungary to balance the defection of Russia, despite its great attraction, did not seem promising. A conference in the Foreign Office on May 12 attended by Curzon, Cecil, Lord Hardinge, the permanent under-secretary for foreign affairs, Hankey, and Leopold S. Amery, the assistant secretary to the War Cabinet, concluded that there was "no sufficient reason" that any of Germany's allies "should sever themselves from an alliance which has already proved to be so successful."[28] Both Curzon and Amery, however, agreed with Lloyd George that the conquest of Palestine was vital to the security of Egypt and Mesopotamia. As Amery, an imperialistic braintruster who had influence far beyond his position in the government because of his close relationship with Lloyd George, Milner, and Smuts, wrote: "The collapse of Russia has, in fact, made Palestine, of the issues still left undecided by the war, one of the most vital for the whole of the British Empire."[29]

It is significant, however, that these imperial strategists, despite their zeal for the conquest of Palestine, supported Robertson's view that Britain had no choice but to continue to concentrate her military power in the West.[30] "By no other means," Curzon emphasized, "does it appear likely that the complete liberation of Belgium, and the evacuation of France, will, if the war continues as long, be secure. For, if these two objects were made the subject of an offer by Germany at an earlier date, while her military strength and that of her Allies is still unbroken, it could only be at the price of conditions which Great Britain alone would have to pay and which would purchase the safety of our Allies by the acceptance of a grave peril to the future of the British Empire."[31] In short, as long as Britain sought the destruction of German militarism, it was unsound to lessen Britain's military commitment to her Continental allies and concentrate on peripheral operations which were so dear to Lloyd George's heart. Thus Lloyd George's most important source for his "Eastern" strategy—the imperialist-minded members of his government—deferred to the general staff.

For the moment Lloyd George had to be satisfied with strengthening the Egyptian Expeditionary Force. This was achieved through a rare compromise with Wully. By mid-May, after it was obvious that Sarrail had achieved no important success against the Bulgarians, Lloyd George agreed to support in Allied councils the general staff's effort to get British troops away from Salonika. But he had his price. These troops were to be sent to Egypt rather than France.[32] Under the terms of this bargain, Robertson was able to pry two divisions away from Salonika, but four still remained at the end of the year.

As Lloyd George prepared the way for a big push against the Turk in Palestine, Haig moved to implement his great offensive. Whatever criticisms may be directed against Haig's plan, and there are many, it cannot be argued that it did not have clear and important strategical objectives. As we have seen, the clearing of the Belgian coast had long held an attraction for British military thinkers ranging from Hankey to Sir John French to Churchill. With German submarines operating from the Belgium coast being responsible for about one third of the British ships lost to the torpedo,[33] many British civilians saw a special British interest in this military operation. Jellicoe also expressed concern about the Belgian ports being used by German destroyers.[34] Furthermore, enemy aircraft on the way to blast and burn London would have to fly over additional anti-aircraft defenses if the coast were in British hands. Also, if the German lines could be ruptured, the liberation of much of Belgium (Britain's major war aim in Europe) and the control of the enemy's vital communications system with its northern front might follow.

Even if the Germans did not give way, they might suffer terrible losses attempting to hold ground that they could not afford to give up.

Haig's plan to achieve these important strategic goals, as he outlined them to Nivelle, Robertson, and his commanders, ran as follows. He would continue the Arras attack to wear down the enemy. Meanwhile, British forces and material would continue to be massed in the north in Ypres, where the main attack would be launched in stages. First the Messines Ridge would be secured for observation and to protect the right flank of his army. A few weeks later the other shoe would drop—the operation to take the Belgian coast. This attack would proceed one step at a time to secure Passchendaele Ridge, Staden Ridge, Clercken Ridge, etc. To reassure Robertson and the civilians, Haig emphasized that "my arrangements commit me to no undue risks and can be modified to meet any developments in the situation."[35]

Despite the deliberate nature of his tactics, Haig was confident that ultimately the German line would be broken, with his cavalry sweeping across western Belgium, conquering Ostend and Zeebrugge, and mopping up the German forces. Since the British generals Herbert Plumer and H. S. Rawlinson, who were involved in the preparations, were not so optimistic as Haig, he chose a fellow cavalryman, the dashing and aggressive General Herbert Gough who was imbued with the "cavalry spirit," to lead the assault with his Fifth Army.

This grandiose plan was questioned by leading French generals. Pétain, although he refused to criticize Haig's plan to his face, continued to oppose "any operations with such distant objectives" and in a conversation with Sir Henry Wilson he emphasized that "with the amount of assistance he could give," Haig was embarking upon "an impossible task."[36] Ferdinand Foch was more blunt, telling Wilson that "he wanted to know who was the fool who wanted Haig to go on 'a duck's march through the inundations to Ostend & Zeebrugge.'" As Wilson noted in his diary, "He thinks the whole thing futile, fantastic & dangerous, and I confess I agree & always have."[37]

Robertson, who shared Lloyd George's concern that the French might not give Haig adequate support and that the British army might consequently be bled white in its attack, was also leery of Haig's plan of a series of consecutive offensives to gain grandiose strategic objectives. At the Paris conference he and Pétain had stressed limited and wearing-down tactics which ran counter to Haig's ultimate objectives. As Robertson's biographer astutely observes:

> The difficulty lay, of course, in limiting each step *in a continuous offensive*. Messines had been correct for it had been complete in itself. Third Ypres would depend on the success of each component step. What would happen to the battle if one of the components failed? If it was broken off, according to the book, then the campaign would halt without completing its strategic purpose, and a lot of lives and effort would have been expended for nothing. If it was kept going, then Wully feared it might degenerate into a second Somme, a human holocaust that he was concerned as the Prime Minister to avoid.[38]

Another concern of Robertson's was Haig's blind faith in Brigadier-General

J. Charteris, the head of the intelligence section at general headquarters, who fed Haig a steady diet of unrealistic reports about the exhaustion of the German army. Intelligence furnished Robertson by George Macdonogh, the director of military intelligence at the War Office, painted a much truer picture of the condition of the German army. Robertson, moreover, was apparently impressed by Repington's warning about fighting in the Low Countries. "I said [to Robertson] that you can fight in mountains and deserts," Repington writes on May 21, "but no one can fight in mud and when the water is let out against you, and, at the best, you are restricted to the narrow fronts on the higher ground, which are very unfavourable with modern weapons."[39]

On May 18, prompted by Lloyd George and Robertson, Haig put the essential question to Pétain. " 'Did the French intend to play their full part as promised at the Paris Conference? Could I rely on his wholehearted co-operation?' "[40] Pétain's misleading response was entirely reassuring as was the French government's reply to Derby's inquiries.[41]

On June 2, only five days before the British attack on the Messines Ridge was scheduled to begin, Pétain was a bit more candid about the exhaustion of the French army, sending his chief of staff, General Debeney, to Haig's headquarters to inform the British commander in chief that he would be unable to launch his supporting attack as promised on June 10. "The French Army is in a bad state of discipline," Debeney ominously told Haig. On the other hand, Pétain's messenger assured Haig that he could count on the French army fulfilling its role in his Flanders operation in the summer.[42] Whether Haig really believed that he could expect wholehearted French support in the future is open to serious question. Debeney emphasized that the French attacks during the next month were to be essentially assaults by artillery and airplanes (a preview, in fact, of Pétain's tactics for the rest of the year). When Sir Henry Wilson saw the notes of the Haig-Debeney conference, he wrote in his diary: "This endorses and underlines all that I have been saying for the last month or more, and I think, and hope, that it will finally dispose of Haig's insane idea of taking Ostend and Zeebrugge."[43] What is certain is that Haig ignored Robertson's persistent pleas for any scrap of evidence that would indicate that the French were not prepared to do their part.[44] Neither Robertson nor the War Cabinet were informed of Debeney's revelation about the exhaustion of the French army. With Lloyd George (and Robertson) insisting that the full cooperation of the French army was the essential requirement for any great British attack, Haig apparently feared that his Messines Ridge attack and, more importantly, his main Flanders offensive would be vetoed by the civilians if he passed on this vital information to London.

In May and early June the War Office and general headquarters were out of step for the first time since Robertson had become C.I.G.S. Unlike Haig, Robertson did not now believe that the German army could be defeated in 1917 or perhaps even in 1918.[45] Within the War Office Charteris was considered "a dangerous fool because of his ridiculous optimism."[46] With Britain's manpower chips dwindling, Robertson was reluctant to raise the ante. Under the circumstances, Lloyd George's policy of "knocking away the props" found some favor in the War Office. Macdonogh told Wilson that he agreed with "the obvious necessity of cutting out the Turk & Bulgar and believes it could be done."[47] Even the apostle of the "Western" school of thought, Robertson, momentarily looked toward the Italian theater, where Cadorna was winding down the Tenth Battle of the Isonzo. On June 7 he met with Foch at Abbeville and stressed a theory that he had held since becoming C.I.G.S.: diplomacy was not supporting the military by detaching the minor powers. Foch then raised an obvious point. A diplomatic offensive without adequate military support was usually doomed to futility. "He said that the French information from Austria was both recent and good. Austria was very anxious to treat for peace, but would only treat when she was beaten. She was, in fact, asking to be beaten, in order to get out of the war with a good face." Robertson's response to this statement was remarkable: "This information raised the whole question of our military policy. Ought we now to concentrate against Austria?" Foch's answer, it must be noted, was that "theoretically, that sounded very well, but there were many practical difficulties."[48]

Two days later Robertson tentatively raised this point with Haig, who recorded the following in his diary: "He wished me to realise the difficult situation in which the Country would be, if I carried out large and costly attacks without full cooperation by the French. When Autumn came round, Britain would then be without an Army! On the other hand it is possible that Austria would make peace, if harassed enough. Would it not be a good plan, therefore, to support Italy with guns?" Haig, of course, viewed such sentiments as being heretical and attempted to bring Wully back into the bosom of "Western" orthodoxy.[49]

After his meeting with Haig, Robertson suppressed his misgivings about the Flanders operation and loyally supported Haig in the great debate which was about to begin over his offensive. Why was this rugged and strong-willed individual, who feared no man, willing to defer to Haig? The answer can be found in his fear that any disagreement between himself and Haig would be immediately exploited by Lloyd George to undermine the "Westerners" and perhaps even to depose Haig. He had always argued that the soldiers must support each other to keep the civilians from interfering in strategy. This had been Robertson's position, it should be emphasized, long before Lloyd George's underhanded tactics at Calais. In early 1916, he had stressed in a letter to Haig that the success of the British army depended largely upon "the extent we at the top stick together and stand firm."[50] The tragic result of Robertson's deference to Haig was that the government's adviser on grand strategy was reduced to the status of Haig's cipher.

When Robertson returned to London he discovered a fresh challenge to the high command's direction of the war. On June 8, the War Cabinet, prompted it seems by a paper written by Milner, had established the War Policy Committee "to investigate the facts of the Naval, Military, and Political situations, and present a full report to the War Cabinet."[51] The War Policy Committee consisted of the prime minister, Curzon, Milner, and Smuts (who had joined the War Cabinet after turning down the opportunity to replace Murray as commander in chief of the Egyptian Expeditionary

Force). Bonar Law was not an official member but he might as well have been because of his involvement in the committee's deliberations.

The origins of this committee can be found in the growing realization on the part of the ministers that the situation had changed since the Paris conference, when Lloyd George had supported a continuation of the offensive throughout 1917. Given the apparently irreversible decline of the Russian army and the uncertain state of the French army, how much longer should the British go on using up its declining manpower by attacking in the West? On June 6, the War Cabinet had received its first official indication that something was wrong with the French army. Macdonogh had "reported that there was serious trouble practically amounting to mutiny, in a number of French regiments, partly as the result of Socialist propaganda, partly on the ground that native troops had been allowed to fire on strikers in the neighbourhood of Paris. It was hoped that this disaffection would be set right in five or six days."[52] This report (apparently through no fault of Macdonogh's) minimized the French mutiny. Hence, for the moment the collapse of the Russian army continued to provoke the greatest anxiety. On June 7, Milner stressed in a paper that "the defection of Russia" had completely derailed Allied military plans, both in the West and in the East. "On the other hand," he wrote, "the entrance of America into the war has introduced a new factor, of great ultimate promise but small immediate value. What are we going to do to fill up the time before the weight of America can be thrown into the scale?" It would not do "to go on without any plan at all. How do we now stand about Palestine, about the Balkan campaign, about the continuance of the offensive on the Western Front? I don't know that we have made up our minds about any of them. I feel as if we were just drifting, and as if there was some danger that, in view of the preoccupation of a number of grave but nevertheless minor domestic questions, we might continue to drift."[53]

The military was none too encouraging about America's capacity to assist the French and British on the western front in the near future. In May the general staff had warned the civilians that an American army would not "be in the field in any theatre of war for a long time to come."[54] And within the next few days, General I. M. Bridges, who had accompanied Balfour's mission to the United States in April, presented a disquieting report on American preparedness. In what Curzon called the "most depressing statement that the Cabinet had received for a long time," Bridges informed the ministers that Washington might only be able to send between 120,000 and 150,000 men to France by January 1, 1918. Moreover, by the end of 1918, the American Expeditionary Force in Europe might number only half a million men.[55] Waiting for America, then, might be a risky policy. On the other hand, these figures suggested that it was more important than ever to keep Haig from exhausting the British army in attack, for the Americans might not be able to fill his depleted ranks. Furthermore, men must be kept out of the army to build the ships to accelerate the transportation of the Americans across the Atlantic.

Lloyd George was clearly delighted with the shift in the mood of the ministers since early May, when he had been pledged by them to support the offensive in the West. At this time he was excited about news that he had just received from the British embassy in Rome. Cadorna, behind the back of his government, had motored to Rome to meet secretly with a member of the British embassy, E. Capel Cure. The Italian general's clandestine movements were probably explained by his government's lack of enthusiasm for the offensive. Cadorna told Cure that his attack on the Isonzo, which was now stalled, would have resulted in a "vital blow" to the enemy if he had had the guns which he had turned down at the Rome conference. Moreover, he expressed the conviction that he could "go right through" to Trieste on the Austrian front between Carso and the sea if the British provided him with 300 or more guns.[56]

Fearing that the continued drift of the government would leave the initiative with Haig, Lloyd George welcomed the creation of the War Policy Committee, which gave him the chance to ventilate thoroughly his view that Austria and Turkey—not Germany—should be the chief targets of the Allies in 1917. One facet of Lloyd George's personality that has clearly emerged thus far in these pages is his extraordinary patience. Stalled by opposition at home or abroad, he returned again and again to his peripheral strategy.

On the same day the War Cabinet created the War Policy Committee, he launched a campaign to deny Haig his cherished Flanders campaign. A report delivered by Sir Henry Wilson gave him some leverage. Wilson "confessed grave doubts as to whether we could count on the continued resistance of the French army and nation until such time as effective military assistance could be received from the United States of America." Despite this admission, Wilson refused to break ranks with Haig in other respects. He would not confirm "the rumours which had reached the War Cabinet [Macdonogh's report of the sixth] that an incident had occurred in the French army amounting almost to a mutiny." He also emphasized that "Pétain could not hold the French army together through another winter without some real success, whether military or diplomatic." When pressed by the War Cabinet for his personal views on where a great victory might be won, he said "that he could see no reasonable prospect of this in Mesopotamia, or Egypt, or on the Western front, with the possible exception of Flanders, where he understood that Field-Marshal Sir Douglas Haig was hopeful." On the other hand, he admitted that the prospect of Haig's offensive "would be considerably reduced if the French would not develope [sic] an attack on a large scale in concert with the British offensive."[57]

Although Wilson had been guarded, even deceptive, in his remarks, his comments had a considerable impact on the ministers, and it was agreed that his views "strongly reinforced the arguments given by Lord Milner in his Memorandum of June 7 in favour of a fresh stock-taking of the whole war situation." Conveniently overlooking his support of Nivelle, Lloyd George stressed

that up to the present time the Government had been guided in their war policy entirely by the views of their naval and military experts. He himself had always felt some misgivings about this course owing to the fact that in a large number of instances all through the war the advice of the experts proved to be wrong. Recent events had confirmed the view that, like everyone else, they were not infallible. He pointed out that, at the Paris Conference on May 4 & 5 he and Lord Robert Cecil, after prolonged discussion, had supported the naval and military experts without hesitation, although it involved forcing on the French Government an unpalatable decision. Now the position had changed.

Lloyd George then came to the nub of the problem. The French were showing signs of exhaustion, but in the weeks ahead Haig planned a "gigantic operation." The attack underway at the moment—the Messines Ridge assault—was just a preliminary. Yet Robertson, Lloyd George noted, "did not believe that the main British operation could be attended with success unless the French would undertake an offensive on a corresponding scale."[58]

The prime minister allowed no defeatism to creep into his assessment of the military situation. With the strain great in every quarter this was not the time for hand-wringing or loss of faith in eventual victory. The ministers, in fact, were so concerned about preventing a peace atmosphere from developing that two days earlier they had rejected Hankey's practical suggestion that "detailed secretarial arrangements" be made for the "eventual Peace Conference" which might take place "within months or years." The ministers agreed that nothing must be done to "create a peace atmosphere or give the impression that the Government were making preparations for a Peace Conference."[59]

"Personally," Lloyd George noted, "he inclined to the view that General Wilson had probably been too pessimistic [about the exhaustion of the French]. . . . He himself believed, however, that we could achieve both a military and diplomatic success, and he shared General Wilson's view as to the importance of this."[60] Any discussion of strategy, however, had to await the return of Robertson from France. It would soon be obvious to all, if it was not already, that Lloyd George believed only in the possibility of winning a major victory over the Austrians or Turks.

The stage was now set for the greatest and most intense debate of the war between the "Easterners" and "Westerners." In the next weeks the War Policy Committee held sixteen meetings, usually in the morning, but twice at dinner meetings which went on late into the evening, before the committee's report was ready to be laid before the War Cabinet for its approval on July 20.

Lloyd George viewed the question as the most important yet before his government. With the losses on the Somme burned in his memory, he was obsessed with limiting British casualties. If Haig were allowed to take on the German army practically singlehandedly before the Americans arrived on the scene, the British army might be destroyed by the formidable and, to Lloyd George, impassable German defenses. This was consistent with his views on how the war should be waged. Although his Liberal colleagues in Asquith's government thought him an extremist on compulsion, a common denominator of his strategic views was to limit British losses. He had lobbied for guns for Russia to allow the colossus of the East to wear down the Germans, intervention in the Balkans to involve Balkan soldiers in the anti-

The trustee of his nation's manpower inspects the grave of a British soldier.

German coalition, attacks against the Turks, in which British casualties were often relatively light, and Nivelle's offensive, which assigned a secondary role to the British army. Now, if the ministers accepted his plan to attack Austria, assuming that Rome would not reject the dubious honor bestowed upon it, the Italians would do most of the killing and dying.

Unable to divert the generals away from the West during the first months of his premiership, Lloyd George and his colleagues in the War Cabinet had used manpower as a means to force Haig to adopt less wasteful tactics. There is a revealing discussion of the War Cabinet's policy in a memorandum by Hankey, dated April 18, 1917. It must be quoted at some length.

> 41. Man-Power is now the most difficult of the problems which the War Cabinet has to face under the economic head. Their policy has never been very explicitly defined and may in time lead to a difficult parliamentary situation. . . . with the probability of a prolongation of the War, the Government feel it to be more and more dangerous to mortgage the future by reducing our man-power by any drastic steps. . . .
>
> 42. Although is has never been formulated in the War Cabinet Minutes it is understood that the policy of the Government is first, by keeping the War Office short to compel the soldiers to adopt tactics that will reduce the waste of man-power. The French are alleged to have accomplished their successes in 1916 with losses about half those incurred by the British army. Some British Generals are known to be far more careful of human

life than others, and these are not the least successful leaders. The War Cabinet, it is understood, intend to force this fact upon the Higher Command, in order that they in turn may compel subordinate leaders to exercise great care in this matter. Further, they desire the War Office to work out their own salvation by a careful substitution of elderly and partially fit men and coloured men for fit men in all services behind the lines. The Government would also like to see the adoption of a system of reduced numbers of battalions in divisions. Although this would undoubtedly reduce the total *numerical* strength of the army, it would not reduce the *effective* strength in anything like the same proportion for the reason that the *effective* strength is largely dependent on mechanical means, such as guns, machine-guns, trench mortars, and tanks; all these latter are continually increasing, so that the *effective* strength of a division of 9 battalions in 1917 would be incomparably greater than that of a division of 12 battalions in 1914.

43. If this is the policy of the Government it might be as well to place it on record in the War Cabinet Minutes at an early date.[61]

Although the War Cabinet's policy of keeping the army short of men was never formally recorded in the minutes, the government refused to support universal national service or the further combing out of war-related occupations. As Derby lamented in June, "it seems clear that, practically, the Army is now provided with men after all other needs of the Nation have been cared for."[62] The War Cabinet, however, enjoyed no success in attempting to get Haig to reduce British divisions from twelve to nine battalions.[63]

With the burden of fighting the German army shifting to the British after Nivelle's failure, the civilians' approach to the manpower question changed. Preserving Britain's staying power rather than forcing Haig to change his tactics became their primary concern. Haig's growing anger over the government's refusal to supply him with all of the men he demanded is understandable. When Robertson, after conferring with Lloyd George in late May, informed him with some exaggeration that he would receive "only scraps" in future drafts, Haig's frustration boiled over: "For the last two years most of the soldiers have realised that Great Britain must take the necessary steps to win the war by herself, because our French Allies had already shewn that they lacked both the moral qualities & the means for gaining the victory. It is thus sad to see the British Govt. failing at the XIIth hour!"[64] Haig's belief that Britain was "at the XIIth hour" was at the heart of general headquarters's differences with the War Cabinet over manpower. Haig thought that he might defeat Germany in 1917; the civilians did not. Hence, Lloyd George and others were determined to maintain Britain's ability to fight on. Men were needed to plow, build ships, and turn out munitions as well as man the trenches on the western front. Furthermore, the government was worried about the impact of further compulsion on the mood of Labour. Maintaining home morale might mean the difference between victory or defeat as the war continued into 1918 or even 1919.

The War Policy Committee meetings need not be described in exhaustive detail because the reader is already well acquainted with most of the arguments of the "Easterners" and the "Westerners." The battle lines were drawn at its first meeting on June 11. Robertson argued that Britain had no choice but to continue the offensive in the West and noted that the British army was confident that it could "beat the Germans by themselves."[65] The prime minister countered with his view that the Italian front offered the British greater opportunities than the formidable German defenses in the West. He read a private letter from Sir Rennell Rodd, the British ambassador in Rome, which described a secret interview that Cadorna had with a member of the British embassy. The Italian commander in chief had asked for more guns from the British and had expressed the conviction "that the Italian front provided the enemy's most vulnerable point on the Western Front."[66] Robertson immediately demurred. If the Italians had to have more guns, let them come from the guns allotted to the Palestine expedition rather than from Haig's army.

Just before the committee adjourned for the day, Lloyd George begged the military and civilian leaders to consider his strategy with an open mind:

In his view the great defect of the War had been that we have always hit the enemy at his strongest instead of his weakest side. If we had concentrated against Austria earlier in the War we might have knocked her out and isolated Germany. In his opinion, our strategy must be considered again without any preconceived ideas. This was the only chance of rescuing ourselves from a tight place. The news from Russia was very discouraging and Colonel Spiers [the way Sir Edmund Spears, the head of the British Military Mission in Paris, spelled his name in 1917], an officer of great knowledge of the French, actually talked of the possibility of a Revolution in France. On the other hand, he could see no serious indication of cracking in Germany. The Germans were stronger on the Western Front that ever in men, and guns, and leadership.[67]

On the following day, after Robertson had withdrawn from the committee, the British leaders heard evidence from General Delmé Radcliffe, who was the British military representative attached to the Italian army. Radcliffe was generally optimistic about the results of giving Cadorna the 300 British heavy guns he desired. In opposition to Robertson, he said that the guns could be sent secretly. Once the guns were in place, if Russia's collapse did not lead to a considerable strengthening of Austria's defenses, he thought that Trieste could be in Italian hands by the "beginning of September."[68]

As always Lloyd George's great weakness was his amateur standing. To be sure, he had had his Italian scheme buttressed by the professional advice of General Radcliffe and General Cadorna. But was this enough justification to overrule the head of the general staff and the commander in chief of the British Expeditionary Force? The totality and complexity of modern war had given the soldiers unprecedented authority in Britain.

No one understood Lloyd George's Achilles' heel better than Robertson. On June 13, he wrote Haig: "Argue that your plan is the best plan—as it is—that no other would even be *safe* let alone decisive, and then leave them to reject your advice and mine. They dare not do that." If necessary, Robertson was apparently prepared to refuse to issue orders to transfer men and guns to the Italian front. "They will never go while I am C.I.G.S.,"[69] he assured Haig. In sum, the generals, like Lloyd George, had closed their minds as the War Policy Committee considered Britain's next move in the war.

On June 19, Haig appeared before the War Policy Committee to begin a dramatic week of debate of his plan. He spread on a table before the ministers a raised map which he had brought with him. As he explained his step-by-step approach of consecutive offensives, he "made a dramatic use of both his hands to demonstrate how he proposed to sweep up the enemy—first the right hand brushing along the surface irresistibly, and then came the left, his outer finger ultimately touching the German frontier with the nail across."[70] As Haig stood over his map, his self-assurance filled the room. Even Lloyd George—who earlier had warned the committee about Haig's optimistic nature—admitted that his plan was a "splendid conception." But in his next breath Lloyd George wanted to know if Haig's plan was "practicable at the present time." The prime minister and the committee put a series of tough questions to the field marshal. Did the Allies really have a clear superiority on the western front when the decline of the French army was taken into account? Could the French really occupy the Germans? Or would Haig have to take on most of the German army singlehandedly? What about the growing manpower crisis in Britain and the possibility that the British army might be exhausted in the attack?

Haig's response was to emphasize both the necessity of fighting the Germans hard in 1917 and the growing exhaustion of their army. If the country could not furnish him with enough guns and men to carry through his operation, he assured the committee that he could cut his losses by limiting his attacks to gaining only his first objective.

At the end of the meeting Lloyd George made a passionate appeal to his generals not to squander British manpower in an attack which was premature and could not achieve its ultimate objectives.

> The Prime Minister asked General Robertson and Sir Douglas Haig to realize our own difficulties in regard to manpower. We were now reduced to the point where we had to scrape up men where we could. Every time we scraped . . . there was trouble in the House of Commons or a strike. . . . He did not want to fail, and did not want to go in for it unless he was sure that it could be carried through. The alternative was to face a tremendous row in the country in regard to men. . . . The United States of America had not yet developed their resources, and by the end of the year would not have more than 150,000 to 160,000 men in France. The burden on us, therefore, was very great, and it was very important not to break the country. Yesterday the Committee had been considering the shipping situation, and there again the demand for men was more insistent every day. He wanted the country to be able to last. He did not want to have to face a Peace Conference some day with our country weakened while America was still overwhelmingly strong, and Russia had perhaps revived her strength. He wanted to reserve our strength till next year.[71]

The meeting adjourned, Lloyd George rushed off to the wedding of his daughter Olwen. It was a mark of his obsession with future military plans that, right up to the moment he accompanied Olwen to the altar, he talked with Hankey about Haig's plan—much to his wife's annoyance, it should be noted.[72]

On June 20 and June 21 the divergent views of the prime minister and his generals came to a head. At noon on the twentieth the War Office and the Admiralty joined hands in an attempt to demolish Lloyd George's Italian dreams. Robertson, after grumbling about his exclusion from "most of the recent meetings of the 'Cabinet Committee on War Policy,'" read a paper which argued against sending guns to Cadorna. The old, but nonetheless valid, argument of the advantage of interior over exterior lines was stressed. Haig followed with similar sentiments. Before reading his paper, he made this significant statement in light of future developments. "He was fully in agreement with the Committee," he noted, "that we ought not to push in attacks that had not a reasonable chance of success, and that we ought to proceed step by step. He himself had no intention of entering into a tremendous offensive involving heavy losses. His plan was aggressive without committing us too far." Thus Haig continued to encourage the notion that his attack, which proceeded by stages, could be stopped at any time if the cost seemed to outweigh the gain.

Jellicoe, who had been abruptly summoned to the War Policy Committee, then weighed in with his oft-expressed and exaggerated view that Britain's survival depended upon clearing the Belgian coast. If the Germans were not dislodged in 1917, they never would be because "he felt it to be improbable that we could go on with the war next year for lack of shipping." This prompted a disbelieving Lloyd George to remark sarcastically that, if Jellicoe were correct in his alarming forecast, "we should have far more important decisions to consider than our plans of operations for this year, namely the best method of making tracks for peace."[73]

Hankey, incidentally, believed that Jellicoe and the high command were in collusion and that the first sea lord's statements before the War Policy Committee were "rigged."[74] Robertson and Jellicoe may indeed have been in collusion. But Jellicoe's pessimism was as old as it was notorious.

At the tenth meeting of the War Policy Committee, Lloyd George made his most powerful effort to stop the Flanders offensive. What strikes this writer is that Lloyd George, despite the support he enjoyed from key members of the War Cabinet, in effect surrendered to the generals before he made his statement.

> His view was that the responsibility for advising in regard to military operations must remain with the military advisers. Speaking for himself, and he had little doubt that his colleagues agreed with him in this, he considered it would be too great a responsibility for the War Policy Committee to take the strategy of the War out of the hands of their military advisers. . . . If after hearing my views, and after taking time to consider them they still adhered to their previous opinion, the responsibility for their advice must rest with them.

One is left with the unhappy conclusion that Lloyd George was unfairly attempting to place the responsibility for any failure squarely on the soldiers.

Robertson, whom Lloyd George sensed had misgivings about Haig's plans, bore the brunt of his attack. The C.I.G.S. was accused of changing the position he had taken at the Paris conference of not risking a great attack unless the French could be counted upon to contribute their whole strength and of opposing an offensive which aimed at distant objectives.

The prime minister's pessimism matched Haig's optimism. If the attack failed, as he thought likely, "it would lower the *moral* of the people, weaken the Army, and, above all, undermine confidence in the military advisers on which the Government acted." He urged the high command to consider the alternatives: Pétain tactics in the West and the dispatch of guns to Italy to enable the Italians to deliver a great blow with the political objective of detaching Austria. The latter suggestion offered many advantages in Lloyd George's view: "The umbilical cord of the Central Alliance would be cut and no more ammunition could reach Bulgaria and Turkey, and both would have to make terms." The capture of Trieste (which could be reached after a relatively short advance) would be a sufficient reward to persuade the Italians to come to terms with Vienna; Russia would be given relief and might stay in the war; even if the Germans sent reinforcements to Italy, "you would be fighting them and wearing them out. But this could be taking place at the expense of the Italians and not of our men. . . . It would be the first time that the Italian resources of man-power had been properly utilised to pull their full weight in the War."[75] In short, according to Lloyd George, nowhere in 1917 could such great gains be achieved by such a short advance and with such a small British investment.

The great flaw in Lloyd George's strategy was his acceptance of the widely held (and probably erroneous) view that Austria was desperate to accept a separate peace in 1917 without being soundly defeated.[76] As Robertson took pains to point out, the capture of Trieste, in all likelihood, would not be the resounding blow that drove Vienna to her knees. But Lloyd George's view of Austrian weakness was certainly no wider of the mark than Haig's conviction that the German army was nearly finished.

Lloyd George's brief against the "Westerners" infuriated Robertson. "I was made to feel like a witness for the defence under cross-examination," he later wrote in his memoirs, "the Prime Minister appeared in the dual capacity of counsel for the prosecution and judge."[77]

Haig and Robertson prepared papers defending their "Western" stance and rejecting Lloyd George's alternatives. In a brief two-page note, Haig asserted that his review of the evidence made him more confident than ever that the German army was near the breaking point: "The German Army has already lost much of that *moral* force without which physical power, even in it's [sic] most terrible form is but an idle show. In fact, the optimistic views I hold and the advice I have given are justified by the present condition of our opponent's troops."[78]

Robertson attempted to defend himself against Lloyd George's charge that he had altered his position since Paris.

> I do not now, and I did not at Paris, advise aiming at distant objectives, coute que coute, but at wearing the enemy down. . . . It is admitted by the

War Cabinet that we must continue to be active somewhere on the Western Front, and I consider now, as I did at Paris, that Sir Douglas Haig's
plan does this in a direction which, if the enemy weakens, can be exploited
to very great advantage, while at the same time it permits of our modifying
our operations if the situation demands. The ultimate objective is undoubtedly the Northern Coast, but I certainly do not advocate spending
our last man and last round of ammunition in an attempt to reach that
Coast if the opposition which we encounter shows that the attempt will
entail disproportionate loss.

As for the French role in the offensive, he noted: "It seems to me that we
must give the French the opportunity to fight. If they do not fight we must
act accordingly, and the plan will permit of this. In any case, French defection is not a good reason for sending British troops to another theatre, for
Germany may counter us by heavily attacking the French. . . ."
The Calais fiasco and the Italians' apparent lack of offensive spirit were
used as a club to smash Lloyd George's Italian strategy. Robertson wrote:

I know very little of Cadorna's qualifications. He has not shewn any
marked ability in the war as yet, and for the British Government to entrust
the fate of the war to him seems a very serious step. It is agreed that the
War Cabinet is now about to take, perhaps, the greatest decision of the
war, and I feel it my duty to quote what I said to them when the British
Armies were placed under the command of General Nivelle:—"It causes
me very grave anxiety as to our final success in the war. The next battle
may well govern the final issue, and we have placed our troops under a
Commander, a foreign officer, who has yet to prove his fitness for so great
a command." I feel this anxiety more at the present stage than in February
last.

In my opinion there is no chance whatever of gaining a great success on
the Isonzo unless we send a considerable number of divisions as well as a
large amount of artillery. It is notorious that the Italians are miserably
afraid of the Germans. They themselves have confessed as much.[79]

Although Robertson did his best to support Haig, his paper served to
underline some loose thinking in Haig's battle plan. To mollify Robertson
and the more cautious ministers, Haig talked of an offensive to exhaust the
Germans without disproportionate losses to his own army. At the same time,
however, he thought big, aiming at distant objectives and the destruction of
the German army. These grandiose objectives might make impossible a
policy of attrition which worked (as the War Cabinet insisted) to the advantage of the British army, especially if the weather turned nasty in Flanders.
Heavy rain might make the battlefield a vast sea of mud which would bog
down and exhaust the infantry and considerably reduce the effectiveness of
British artillery.
Robertson's somewhat tentative remarks about Haig's offensive, in contrast to the field marshal's sanguine view, gave the Welshman a chance to
divide the high command. On June 25, he said: "Field-Marshal Sir Douglas
Haig's Memorandum was quite clear on this point [success of operation]. He
wished to know whether Sir William Robertson shared this feeling." After

beating around the bush, Robertson was pressed by the ministers to stand beside Haig. He said that he accepted Haig's position as reflected in the following quote: "If our resources are concentrated in France to the fullest possible extent, the British armies are capable, and can be relied on to effect great results this summer, results which will make final victory more assured, and may even bring it within reach this year."[80]

This meeting concluded with no positions altered. After eleven meetings, the War Policy Committee had failed to reach a decision. Lloyd George had prodded the generals to reconsider their plan, but their minds remained as closed as his. As for Lloyd George's colleagues on the committee, Milner and Bonar Law remained skeptical in varying degrees, with Smuts and to a lesser extent Curzon supporting Robertson and Haig. As long as Lloyd George and his colleagues were unwilling to override their military advisers, Haig had the upper hand. As Hankey noted in his diary, "Lloyd George felt that he could not press his amateur opinions and over-rule them, so he gave in, and Haig was authorized to continue his preparations."[81] Thus, although the field marshal returned to France without the ironclad commitment that he wanted from the civilians, the implementation of his plan was now almost inevitable. Only a clear French admission that they could not give the British attack significant support could prevent the offensive.

While in London, Haig, alarmed by Jellicoe's defeatism, had attempted to shake up the Admiralty. Confidence in the leadership of the Admiralty had been low for some time. In April the civilians had been stunned by the loss of 373 Allied and neutral ships, most of them by undersea assault. By mid-May Britain had only a nine weeks' supply of wheat. Although it was obvious that new methods were needed to protect Allied shipping, Lloyd George had moved cautiously, in part, because he was locked in a struggle with the generals over his support of Nivelle. Taking on the admirals and their formidable civilian head, Carson, at the same time had no appeal for him. Prodded by Hankey, however, he patiently prepared a case against the Admiralty. Concern that the admirals might lose the war unless changes were made strengthened his hand. On April 25, the War Cabinet authorized him to visit the Admiralty to "investigate all the means at present used in anti-submarine warfare."[82]

On April 30 Lloyd George made his much-publicized foray from Downing Street to the Admiralty. Max Aitken even has him occupying the first lord's chair, a colorful but apocryphal account.[83] Lloyd George, according to Hankey, actually had a pleasant lunch with Jellicoe and flirted with one of his little girls.[84] The truth is that Lloyd George's visit was anticlimactic. The Admiralty, albeit grudgingly, had already decided to adopt the convoy system three days earlier.[85] This innovation exceeded all expectations in time, but many anxious months lay ahead. Lloyd George perhaps deserves criticism for his belated action and his inflated claims for instigating the convoy system which saved Britain from economic strangulation. Still, he showed considerable courage and audacity in his determination to overrule if necessary the professionals on a strictly technical question, the first such occasion that he was prepared to do so.

Lloyd George, however, was not as bold in giving the Admiralty new leadership. He feared Carson and the support that Jellicoe enjoyed in Parliament and in the press. It has been suggested that the prime minister used Haig in his conflict with Jellicoe and Carson in June. "Encouraged by Lloyd George," Aitken has written, "Haig became at once the Prime Minister's battering ram against the gates of Carson's stronghold at the Admiralty."[86] To the contrary, unpublished entries in Haig's diary reveal that Haig pushed Lloyd George rather than the reverse. On June 20, Haig dropped in on Eric Geddes, who had recently become controller of the navy. After Geddes had gone on at some length about the "feeble" and "vacillating" leadership of Jellicoe, Haig agreed to arrange a meeting with the prime minister to enable Geddes "to put the whole position of affairs before him." Four days later Haig's efforts to reform the Admiralty took an astonishing turn. Over lunch Geddes suggested that Robertson should be appointed head of the board of Admiralty and Haig immediately agreed.[87]

Haig's motives may have been purely patriotic for Robertson's toughness and organizational ability were legendary. But Haig may have felt that it was time for Robertson to leave the general staff. No soldier could have supported Haig more forcefully or successfully than Robertson, but Haig's confidence in him had been undermined by the latter's skepticism about his campaign in Flanders and his inability to pry more men in khaki out of the government.

On June 26, Lloyd George, Geddes, and Haig breakfasted at 10 Downing Street. (Milner later was asked to join the group.) One can well imagine Lloyd George's surprise and delight at Geddes's and Haig's suggestion that Robertson should replace Carson at the Admiralty.[88] He had long hoped to destroy the Robertson-Haig monolith in strategy; and now, wonder of wonders, Haig was offering him an opportunity to end Robertson's strategical dictatorship with minimal political fall-out.

Unhappily, it was all too good to be true. When Haig informed Wully of the suggestion that he head the Admiralty, he not surprisingly vetoed the idea. Lloyd George then turned to other means to shake up the Admiralty. In July he finally succeeded in replacing Carson with Geddes. In a face-saving move, suggested by Milner and seconded by Bonar Law, Carson was "promoted" to the War Cabinet. Carson, however, made it clear that Lloyd George could not have Jellicoe's head as part of this bargain. The first sea lord's dismissal thus was delayed until the end of the year.

We now shift our attention back to the British government's consideration of Haig's offensive. In early July the signals from France continued to be ambiguous. After a visit with the French military leaders, Robertson reported to the War Policy Committee that Foch "was all for making the French do their utmost, and had shown himself a strong supporter of the policy agreed to at the Paris Conference of 4 and 5 May." On the other hand, Robertson admitted that Pétain was reluctant "to talk much of the forthcoming operations. His conversation was mainly of diplomacy and the desirability of getting Turkey and Bulgaria out of the War." Another report on French morale was furnished by Wilson, who was hurriedly called to the committee by telephone. Quizzed by the prime minister, Wilson "said that the French undoubtedly meant to fight, and would try to do so, but he did not think they would make a great attack."[89]

British speculation that the French would not fight, however, was worthless as long as the French continued to maintain that they would support the British offensive. Lloyd George hoped to get a clearer picture of French intentions at another conference in Paris. But the French kept putting him off. On July 6, the ministers discussed the position they should take in any conference with the French. The prime minister opposed pressuring the French to participate in an attack about which he had profound doubts. If the committee insisted, he said, he would support its position. But Lloyd George wanted two of his colleagues (he must have been thinking of Curzon and Smuts) to press the French, because "he did not believe in the plan, and they would put it with greater force."

For the first time the committee discussed an attack on Turkey as an alternative to Haig's operation in the event that the French did not "attack decisively," with Smuts arguing that Britain had a much greater opportunity to separate Turkey than Austria from Berlin with a military-political offensive.[90]

As the French continued to deceive London about their intentions, it became apparent that Haig could not be put off any longer. On July 16, the War Policy Committee met over dinner at 10 Downing Street. Although the ministers had by now discussed launching offensives all round the Mediterranean—from the Balkans to Alexandretta to the Italian front—they kept coming back to Flanders. As Robertson had predicted, the civilians, faced with a united front of their military advisers, dared not overrule the technicians of warfare. With great foreboding, the committee acquiesced. This decision to allow Haig to go forward was formally ratified by the War Policy Committee on the morning of July 18. Hankey then prepared a report for the full War Cabinet, which approved the plan on the twentieth in a "rough and tumble meeting."[91]

The ministers' capitulation was made easier by a delusion that Haig had fostered: the offensive, which went forward in stages, could be stopped at any time if it proved too costly. If the battle degenerated into a second Somme, the War Cabinet was prepared to accept Lloyd George's scheme of concentrating on Austria-Hungary. The War Cabinet's intentions were made clear to Haig when it gave him permission on July 20 to attack.[92]

Lloyd George viewed the approaching battle as one would a water spigot. It could be turned off as quickly as it was turned on. A serious flaw in his thinking was that the civilians, having accepted the domination of the military in the military sphere, were in a weak position to claim the authority to assess the success or failure of Haig's efforts. Robertson and Haig had promised no immediate breakthrough as Nivelle had. Instead, Robertson had cautiously stressed wearing the enemy down. As long as Haig claimed that Germans were being killed in equal or greater numbers than the British, he could always claim a measure of success. It would be weeks, if not months, after the first British soldiers left their trenches before it would be known if Haig's ambitious objectives were obtainable. Unless Haig gave up on his attack, an extremely unlikely event given his unrivaled optimism, Lloyd George and his colleagues would be running the risk of stopping the battle prematurely and the generals could accuse the civilians of saving the German army from destruction and leaving Allied ships open to attack from the Belgian coast.

After the War Cabinet's decision, Robertson informed Haig of the prime minister's obvious desire to halt the attack soon after it was launched. He wrote:

> The fact is that the Prime Minister is still very averse from your offensive and talks as though he is hoping to switch off to Italy within a day or two after you begin. I told him that unless there were great miscalculations on your part, and unless the first stage proved to be more or less a disastrous failure—which I certainly did not expect it would be—I did not think it would be possible to pronounce a verdict on the success of your operation for several weeks.[93]

Haig was infuriated by the conditions placed on his offensive and by Robertson's suggestion that the War Cabinet might "pronounce a verdict" on the success or failure of his attack after a few weeks. In a strong letter to Robertson, he made clear his opinion that the "Commander on the spot" alone should decide whether or not to push on with the offensive.[94] Having gained their approval, Haig, of course, had every right to expect the support of the ministers. As the trustees of British manpower, however, the ministers had a right—even an obligation—to restrain Haig if the cost of his attack began to outweigh the advantages. Haig's optimism and bulldog determination made him a poor judge of the effectiveness of his assaults.

Robertson, who shared some of Lloyd George's skepticism about Haig's plan, bore the brunt of the field-marshal's anger. When Wully paid Haig a visit on July 22, he was bluntly told "to be firmer and play the man, and, if need be resign, should Lloyd George persist in ordering troops to Italy, against the advice of the General Staff."[95]

Stung by Haig's harsh words, Robertson did what he could to mollify him. On July 24, he pointedly inquired of the ministers if he could inform Haig that "he may depend upon their whole-hearted support" and if the government would first obtain Haig's "views before coming to any decision as to cessation of the operations."[96] Lloyd George relented on both points but it remained obvious to all of the participants in the great debate that the civilians had little enthusiasm for the Flanders offensive.

On July 31, the most powerful fighting force ever put in the field by the British Empire began its attack along a fifteen-mile front. *The heavy firing near here at 4.15 woke me up,* Haig recorded in his diary. "The whole ground was shaking with the terrific bombardment." Of greater significance, his last entry on that day mentioned the start of the torrents of rain which soon turned the churned-up battlefield into a treacherous sea of mud: "Heavy rain fell this afternoon and aeroplane observation was impossible. The going also became very bad and the ground was much cut up."[97] The rain continued, and Haig noted the next day: "A terrible day of rain. The ground is like a bog in this low lying country!"[98]

The tottering of the anti-German coalition placed Britain in a profoundly complex predicament and restricted her freedom of action. There were no easy answers in the immensely complicated strategic chessboard. On only one point was there agreement between the civilians and the military: German militarism must be destroyed to secure the British Empire and a satisfactory peace on the Continent. There remained considerable disagreement about the means to this end. The majority of the War Cabinet did not believe in Haig's plans. But were Lloyd George's paper schemes any better? That was the alternative with which the ministers were faced if they vetoed the Flanders offensive. In sum, there were obviously great risks in either the high command's or Lloyd George's approach to winning the war.

The military was able to make a strong case for hitting the Germans hard in the West in 1917. It could be argued that France's and Russia's decline made the British army more of a captive of the western front than ever at this juncture. But the French high command would have been satisfied with limited British attacks and the taking over of more of the French line. Haig deserves criticism for his willingness to accept Somme-like losses at this perilous stage of the war when he had been repeatedly warned by Robertson and the government that Britain was running short of men. With French support for his attack suspect, he was even more at fault in his unrealistic thesis that the British army could smash the German army in 1917. This error was compounded by his refusal to break off his attack in October and November, when it was obvious to almost everyone but himself that he could not achieve his objectives. For his part, Robertson was wrong to keep his doubts about the offensive from the civilians. The one-sided presentation of the military clearly stacked the deck in favor of the effort to clear the Flemish coast.

On the reverse side of the coin, Lloyd George's role in the Passchendaele decision does him no credit. His policy of holding down British losses until the Americans arrived in force by limiting the costly bludgeoning in the West and by attacks on Berlin's allies, especially Austria, to drive them out of the war may have been the best strategy under the circumstances. But his premises were as weak as Haig's.

As the nation's supreme leader, Lloyd George cannot escape responsibility for the mud and blood of the Flanders offensive. His courage did not match his strong convictions. Despite his weakened position in military policy after Calais and the united front of the government's military advisers which limited his freedom of action, he could have followed his instincts and overruled the military. Instead, he avoided this awesome responsibility. After scoring many debating points and putting the generals on the spot, he caved in, accepting the generals' plans while at the same time attempting to undermine them with his desire to attack Austria via Italy.

His political insecurity was always uppermost on his mind. He could have carried most of the War Cabinet with him. But what about Parliament and the country? Although he had cleverly neutralized the powerful Northcliffe in May by persuading him to head a British war mission to the United States, the generals had many equally vocal supporters in the press. His refusal to support his generals might spark a national debate about his war leadership.

"There would have been a great outcry in Parliament and the Government would have been upset," Hankey has written, "long before decisive victory would have been achieved on the Italian Front. It was a case where a possibly second-best plan in which the Army's trusted leaders believed more than did the statesmen, was preferable to what may, intrinsically, have been a better plan, but which must have upset national unity. The decision was unavoidable."[99]

How ironic it is that in the final analysis Lloyd George was paralyzed by the very power he sought to control the military. It is perhaps fair to speculate what the Welshman's position in June and July would have been if Asquith had still held the reins of power. Lloyd George would almost certainly have roundly condemned the prime minister for not standing up to Haig and Robertson and vetoing the offensive. He would have been contemptuous of the argument that the civilians could not overrule the generals on strategic questions when the life and limb of tens of thousands of soldiers from Britain and the empire were at stake. It is significant that no decision of the war was to cause him more regret. As he admits in his memoirs, "it is one of the bitter ironies of war that I, who have been ruthlessly assailed in books, in the Press and in speeches for 'interfering with the soldiers' should carry with me as my most painful regret the memory that on this issue I did *not* justify that charge."[100]

It will probably always be argued whether the decision to launch the Passchendaele offensive was a case of Greek tragedy, or the tragedy of necessity, where one laments, "What a pity it had to be this way," or of Christian tragedy, the tragedy of possibility, where one says, "What a pity it was this way when it might have been otherwise."

NOTES

1. Memorandum by Hankey, April 18, 1917, CAB 63/20.
2. Esher Diary, April 20, 1917, 2/19.
3. Hankey, *Supreme Command*, 2:625–26.
4. Robertson to Haig, April 20, 1917, Robertson MSS, I/23/21.
5. Haig to Robertson, April 29 and 30, 1917, Robertson MSS, I/23/25, and I/14/78.
6. Robertson to Haig, April 30, 1917, Haig MSS, no. 112.
7. Cabinet Paper G.T. 594 of April 30, 1917, CAB 24/11.
8. At this juncture, Smuts used his considerable prestige to support the professionals against the amateurs and their "interference" in strategy. When he sent his appreciation of the situation to Robertson, he noted: "I hope what I have said may be of some help to you so far as the War Cabinet is concerned." Unhappy with France's previous domination of strategy in the West, Smuts found Haig's plan appealing because it was free of French interference and served special British interests. However, unlike Haig, he did not believe a breakthrough possible and he regretted "that the British forces have been so entirely absorbed" by the battle for France. But with Britain's allies wavering, he believed that Britain must keep the pressure on the German army and avoid gambles in the outlying theaters. He hoped that the pounding of German defenses might destroy the will of the enemy. Alas, as Smuts admitted, "victory in this kind of warfare is the costliest possible to the victor." See Smuts to Robertson, April 29, 1917,

Robertson MSS, I/21/64, Cabinet Paper G.T. 597 of April 29, 1917, CAB 24/11, and Rawlinson Diary, April 8, 1917, 1/7.

9. War Cabinet (128A), May 1, 1917, CAB 23/13.

10. Ibid.

11. Haig Diary, May 3, 1917, no. 113.

12. Cabinet Paper G.T. 657 of May 5, 1917, CAB 24/12.

13. Anglo-French Conference, May 4–5, 1917, CAB 28/2/I.C.-21.

14. At both Anglo-French conferences in London to discuss Nivelle's plans, Haig had made clear his intention to Nivelle and the British ministers that he planned to return to his Flanders operation if the French failed to achieve their objectives. More recently, on May 1, he sent a memorandum to the War Cabinet suggesting that his northern operation be implemented. There is, however, no record of the War Cabinet discussing his memorandum. See Terraine, *Road to Passchendaele*, pp. 1–84, Hankey's memorandum prepared for the prime minister, "The Development of the Military Plans of the Allies in the Principal Theatres of War During 1917," Cabinet Paper G.T. 1925 of September 1, 1917, CAB 24/25, and memorandum by Haig, May 1, 1917, Derby MSS, 920 (17).

15. Lloyd George, *War Memoirs*, 1:927.

16. Repington, *First World War, 1914–1918*, 1:559.

17. Cabinet Committee on War Policy (10), June 21, 1917, CAB 27/6.

18. War Cabinet (124), April 23, 1917, CAB 23/1.

19. Cabinet Papers, G.T. 606 of May 1, and G.T. 657 of May 5, 1917, CAB 24/12.

20. Repington, *First World War, 1914–1918*, 1:560.

21. Lloyd George, *War Memoirs*, 2:1258.

22. Robertson to Lloyd George (Esher to Robertson, May 11, 1917, inclosed), May 13, 1917, Lloyd George MSS, F/44/3/12.

23. Robertson to Haig, May 14, 1917, Haig MSS, no. 113.

24. Richard M. Watt, *Dare Call It Treason* (1963), p. 182.

25. Paul Painlevé, *Comment J'ai Nommé Foch et Pétain* (1923), pp. 129–50.

26. William Henry Chamberlin, *The Russian Revolution*, vol. 1: *1917–1918, From the Overthrow of the Czar to the Assumption of Power by the Bolsheviks* (paperback edn., 1965), p. 239.

27. War Cabinet (135A), May 9, 1917, CAB 23/13.

28. Cabinet Paper G.T. 703 of May 12, 1917, CAB 24/13.

29. Cabinet Paper G.T. 831 of May 20, 1917, CAB 24/14.

30. See Robertson's appreciation of the situation in Cabinet Paper G.T. 678 of May 9, 1917, CAB 24/12.

31. Cabinet Paper G.T. 703 of May 12, 1917, CAB 24/13. Curzon had earlier warned the subcommittee of the Imperial War Cabinet on territorial desiderata in the terms of peace that if Britain's allies failed to achieve their war objectives, "they might press us to give up our oversea conquests in order to help them out of their difficulties." Subcommittee of Imperial War Cabinet (4), April 23, 1917, CAB 21/77.

32. Robertson, *Soldiers and Statesmen*, 2:143. Also see War Cabinet (134), May 8, 1917, CAB 23/2.

33. Captain S. W. Roskill, "The U-Boat Campaign of 1917 and Third Ypres," *Journal of the Royal United Service Institution* 104 (November 1959): 440–42. Roskill makes the telling point that if the ports had been taken, the subs would have moved elsewhere and continued their undersea assault. Furthermore, there were other, less costly ways of shutting down these submarine bases.

34. See Cabinet Paper G.T. 497 of April 18, 1917, CAB 24/10. Fears over surface warships using the Belgian ports proved to be unfounded.

35. See Haig Diary, May 7, 1917, and Haig to Nivelle, May 5, 1917, Haig MSS, no. 113; also see Haig to Robertson, May 16, 1917, W.P. 1, CAB 27/7.

36. Wilson to Haig, May 20, 1917, Haig MSS, no. 113.

37. Wilson Diary, June 2, 1917.

38. Bonham-Carter, *Soldier True*, p. 251.

39. Repington, *First World War, 1914–1918*, 1:571.

40. Haig Diary, May 18, 1917, no. 113.

41. War Cabinet (144), May 23, 1917, CAB 23/2.

42. Haig Diary, June 2, 1917, no. 114.

43. Wilson Diary, June 4, 1917.

44. See Robertson to Haig, April 28, 1917, Robertson MSS, I/23/23, and Robertson to Haig, May 17, 1917, Haig MSS, no. 113. For a defense of Haig's actions, see Terraine, *Haig: Educated Soldier*, pp. 296–305.

45. Repington, *First World War, 1914–1918*, 1:571.

46. Wilson Diary, June 8, 1917.

47. Ibid.

48. "Conference held at Abbeville on the 7th June, 1917, between General Foch and General Sir William Robertson," W.O. 106/1513.

49. Haig Diary, June 9–10, no. 114.

50. Robertson to Haig, March 8, 1916, Robertson MSS, I/22/30. When Robertson told the ministers of his conference with Foch at Abbeville, he gave no indication that he had seen merit in assisting the Italians. He only indicated that the Italians might soon launch an attack. Cabinet Committee on War Policy (1), June 11, 1917, CAB 27/6.

51. War Cabinet (159), June 8, 1917, CAB 23/3.

52. War Cabinet (156), June 6, 1917, CAB 23/3.

53. "Note by Milner," June 7, 1917, War Cabinet (159A), June 8, 1917, CAB 23/16.

54. See Cabinet Paper G.T. 744 of May 17, 1917, CAB 24/13.

55. Repington, *First World War, 1914–1918*, 1:581, and memorandum by General Bridges, June 14, 1917, W.P. 5, CAB 27/7.

56. Rennell Rodd to Lloyd George (notes of Cure's conversation with Cadorna, June 2, 1917, inclosed), June 5, 1917, Lloyd George MSS, F/56/1/41.

57. Wilson's statement is a poor reflection of his character. He knew that Foch and Pétain opposed Haig's strategy but did not say so. Opposed himself to Haig's "insane" plan, he favored detaching Bulgaria and Turkey. Wilson Diary, June 8, 1917.

58. War Cabinet (159A), June 8, 1917, CAB 23/16.

59. Ibid. (156), June 6, 1917, CAB 23/3. Also see Cabinet Paper G.T. 938 of June 5, 1917, CAB 24/15.

60. War Cabinet (159A), June 8, 1917, CAB 23/16.

61. Memorandum by Hankey, April 18, 1917, CAB 63/20.

62. Cabinet Paper G.T. 965 of June 7, 1917, CAB 24/15.

63. If divisional pioneer battalions are included, the reduction would be from 13 to 10 battalions.

64. Robertson to Haig, May 26, 1917, Haig MSS, no. 113, and Haig to Robertson, May 28, 1917, Robertson MSS, I/23/28.

65. There is conflicting testimony on this point. Robertson, as noted here, talked of Britain winning "the war by herself." Moreover, in his statement before the Cabinet Committee on War Policy on June 19, Haig seemed to indicate that he would be satisfied if the French, rather than launching vigorous infantry attacks, restricted their activities largely to a prolonged artillery barrage which would mystify the enemy and force him to keep reserves in the French sector. Terraine, however, points to Haig's memorandum of June 12, which indicated that he expected help from the French and perhaps even from the Russians. See Terraine, *Road to Passchendaele*, pp. 131–35.

66. See Rennell Rodd to Lloyd George (notes of Cure's conversation with Cadorna, June 2, 1917, inclosed), June 5, 1917, Lloyd George MSS, F/56/1/41.

67. Cabinet Committee on War Policy (1), June 11, 1917, CAB 27/6.

68. A significant portent for the future was the mention at this meeting of the necessity of creating "a permanent Board of Allied Strategy" to enable the Allies to execute effectively campaigns away from France and Flanders. Cabinet Committee on War Policy (2), June 12, 1917, CAB 27/6.

69. Robertson to Haig, June 13, 1917, Haig MSS, no. 114.

70. Lloyd George, *War Memoirs*, 2:1277.

71. Cabinet Committee on War Policy (7), June 19, 1917, CAB 27/6.

72. Hankey Diary, June 30, 1917, 1/3.

73. Cabinet Committee on War Policy (9), June 20, 1917, CAB 27/6.

74. "Talk with Sir Maurice Hankey at U.S. Club," November 8, 1932, Liddell Hart MSS, 11/1932/43.

75. Cabinet Committee on War Policy (10), June 21, 1917, CAB 27/6.

76. Lowe and Dockrill, *Mirage of Power*, 2:260. The general staff could find little evidence that Austro-Hungarian troops were suffering from a " 'loss of moral.' " See Cabinet Paper G.T. 1319 of July 7, 1917, CAB 24/19.

77. Robertson, *Soldiers and Statesmen*, 2:242, n.2.

78. Note by Haig, June 22, 1917, W.P. 18, CAB 27/7.

79. Memorandum by Robertson, June 23, 1917, W.P. 19, CAB 27/7.

80. Cabinet Committee on War Policy (11), June 25, 1917, CAB 27/6.

81. Hankey Diary, June 30, 1917, 1/3.

82. War Cabinet (126), April 25, 1917, CAB 23/2.

83. Lord Beaverbrook, *Men and Power, 1917–1918* (1956), p. 155.

84. Hankey Diary, April 30, 1917, 1/1.

85. Steven Roskill, *Hankey Man of Secrets*, vol. 1: *1877–1918* (1970), pp. 379–85 and Arthur J. Marder, *From the Dreadnought to Scapa Flow*, vol. 4: *1917, Year of Crisis* (1969), pp. 152–65.

86. *Men and Power, 1917–1918*, p. 164.

87. Haig Diary, June 20 and 24, no. 114.

88. Haig's diary entry does not make clear who made this suggestion, but it clearly originated with Geddes and Haig. Haig Diary, June 26, 1917, no. 114. The Cabinet Committee on War Policy, with no members of the military present, discussed the Admiralty situation on June 27. Unfortunately no notes were taken. See Cabinet Committee on War Policy (12), June 27, 1917, CAB 27/6.

89. Cabinet Committee on War Policy (13), July 3, 1917, CAB 27/6. Three days later in a memorandum Wilson was more direct, writing: "The French themselves will win no real success, I doubt even if they will put in another serious attack, this year." Wilson, however, had changed his tune since early June, now arguing that Haig's offensive was necessary to keep the French in the war. See Cabinet Paper G.T. 1313 of July 6, 1917, CAB 24/19, Haig Diary, June 28, 1917, no. 114, and Wilson Diary, June 27, 1917.

90. Cabinet Committee on War Policy (15), July 6, 1917, CAB 27/6.

91. Robertson to Haig, July 21, 1917, Robertson MSS, I/23/40.

92. War Cabinet (191A), July 20, 1917, CAB 23/13.

93. Robertson to Haig, July 21, 1917, Haig MSS, no. 115.

94. Haig to Robertson, July 21, 1917, Haig MSS, no. 115.

95. Haig Diary, July 22, 1917, no. 115.

96. Cabinet Paper G.T. 1532 of July 25, 1917, CAB 24/21.

97. Haig Diary, July 31, 1917, no. 115.

98. Ibid., August 1, 1917, no. 115.

99. Hankey, *Supreme Command*, 2:702. Given the lack of spirit in the Italian army and government, of course, there might never have been a "decisive victory" on the Italian front.

100. Lloyd George, *War Memoirs*, 2:1304.

9

Strain

A valid criticism of Lloyd George's leadership during this period is that, having accepted Haig's Flanders offensive, he immediately attempted to undermine it. To be sure, as Haig's massive assaults made little headway, especially in October and November, it can be argued that Lloyd George was not so resolute as he should have been in trying to prevent Haig from wearing down the largest British army ever put in the field in a single theater before or since. Still, with the government promising its "whole-hearted support," Haig deserved a fair chance.

In the following pages we will examine the inventive Welshman's complicated and at times mysterious maneuvers to restrain Haig. The tactics he considered—and Britain has known few greater political tacticians—ranged from switching off to another theater to a compromise peace with Germany at Russia's expense to the resurrection of a unified command. The immovable and granite-willed C.I.G.S., who served as a buffer between general headquarters and the prime minister, bore the brunt of Lloyd George's machinations. The unending haggling over strategy obviously took its toll on both men.

Because of the strain on British shipping, an offensive against the Turks was held in abeyance for the moment by the British government.[1] But the War Cabinet favored assisting General Cadorna in the autumn if Haig failed and, to implement this policy, accepted Wully's request that he be allowed to make all arrangements with Foch and Cadorna in his "own way" at the Allied conference in Paris in late July. "I promise the Cabinet that this method of procedure shall not interfere with the execution of the plan if and when it is adopted,"[2] Robertson wrote on July 19. The C.I.G.S., however, had no intention of allowing either Foch or Cadorna to choose Italy over Flanders in 1917. With Britain assuming the major burden of fighting the German army, he was going to insist on the support of Haig's offensive. The Russian offensive underway in mid-July made his task easier at first. With the Russian army active, it seemed important for the Italians to apply the pressure in their theater as soon as possible; hence, the War Cabinet agreed that it was "undesirable" for Wully to make "*definite* arrangements with

Cadorna" at once for assisting him because he might be encouraged to delay his attack on the Isonzo scheduled for mid-August.[3]

The course of the last Russian offensive of the war, however, quickly gave Lloyd George reason to question his high command's strategy. Instead of reviving the Russian army, it proved to be its death rattle. Austro-German counterattacks drove the Russians back in panic along a 140-mile front and many heavy guns were captured. Anti-war demonstrations broke out in Petrograd, and the peasant soldiers, in Lenin's phrase, began to vote for peace with their legs. Working at cross purposes, the prime minister and Robertson crossed the Channel to attend the Allied conference in Paris.

On July 23, Lloyd George dined with Thomas and attempted to convert him to his Italian scheme. He also believed that he had Painlevé in his pocket.[4] Meanwhile, Robertson met with Foch and Cadorna on July 24. Russia's collapse was not allowed to intrude upon plans already made. In Lloyd George's purple prose, Robertson "flourished the Chantilly agreement in their faces and held them to their bond, which was just as binding but more comprehensive than that of Shylock, for it included the spilling of blood."[5] In actual fact, both Foch and Cadorna realized the dangers of flip-flopping from one war plan to another. Such infirmity of purpose was debilitating to the Allied cause, and Foch and Cadorna agreed with Robertson that any change in Allied plans was "for the moment impossible."[6] Only after the present operations were over could a joint effort against Austria on the Italian front be considered.

The Allied conference began on July 26 with a depressing report by Foch on the consequences of Russia's leaving the war. Lloyd George immediately pounced on the suggestion that the Allies might eventually be forced to fall back on the defensive. Calling this a "counsel of despair," he urged the Allies to adopt military plans to knock Turkey and Austria out of the war.

> What was the use of our holding our own? Germany was in possession of Belgium, North France, Serbia, and mistress of a great part of the Ottoman Empire. Merely to hold on was, therefore, he claimed, to face a disastrous peace.
> To get Turkey out of the war was important, but to get Austria was infinitely more so. . . . Short of this he could see nothing but the prospect of going blindly to disaster.

Lloyd George's words were coolly received. Foch questioned the ability of the Allies to achieve "decisive" results against Turkey and Austria; and Thomas pointed out "that the British and French troops were about to commence a very heavy offensive, and he questioned the possibility, particularly in view of the general weariness in France, of sustaining a further action in co-operation with the Italians in September."[7]

Having failed to rally Britain's allies to his peripheral strategy, Lloyd George walked out of the conference in an angry and frustrated mood. He began "talking wildly of resigning and 'telling the country the truth.' "[8] Turning down an invitation from Haig to witness the launching of his attack, he hurried back to London.

Robertson's mood matched that of Lloyd George's. Furious with the

An unhappy Sir William Robertson and his alter ego Major-General Sir Frederick Maurice at the Paris inter-Allied conference in July 1917 where Lloyd George has dropped "his usual bomb" on grand strategy.

prime minister for "his usual bomb" at the Allied conference, he wrote Kiggell, "This was the *worst* conference I ever attended."[9] To keep the wavering civilians on course, he put pen to paper to poke holes in Lloyd George's thesis that Russia's likely defection made it imperative to win a victory on the periphery. To the contrary, he argued, if Russia left the alliance, making it possible for Berlin and Vienna to transfer troops from the East to the West and allowing the Turks to concentate all of their resources against the British, it was necessary to bring to bear more, not less, of Britain's military power in France.[10] Wully also took pains to remind the members of the War Cabinet that they had pledged their "whole-hearted support" to Haig.[11] Why, he wanted to know, were the civilians constantly snapping at Haig's heels when he was involved in the greatest battle ever fought by the British army?

Robertson was especially on edge because of a division in the generals' camp that appeared in early August. Foch, who had supported Robertson's "Western" stance at Paris, now talked about the futility of continuing to hammer away on the western front in 1918 if Russia fell out of the war. Foch, in fact, could hardly have been more Lloyd Georgian about the conduct of the war after the present campaigns were over. He spoke of concentrating on Germany's allies[12] and of the need to create a central body—an Allied general staff—to formulate and coordinate Allied military operations. When

the Allies resumed their discussions at a conference at London on August 7–
8, Lloyd George sought to take advantage of the Foch-Robertson split. He
even discussed with Painlevé the idea of making Foch supreme commander,
but such a move was obviously premature and he dared not revive the fierce
passions of Calais. Hence he had to be satisfied with laying the groundwork.
"Had we really worked as one Government and one General Staff," he told
the Allied conference, "it was his belief that we should already have won the
war." The prime minister also lectured the ministers about leaving the initiative with the generals—"the responsible Ministers should decide the Allies'
policy, whether they should try to detach any of the enemy Powers, and so
on, and then when the policy was decided the soldiers must conform their
strategy to it."[13]

Lloyd George had hoped to delay Cadorna's attack, which was scheduled
to start in about a week, until mid-September. By that time it might be
possible to shift the ten divisions and 400 guns to Italy that Cadorna said
were necessary for a decisive victory over Austria. In this, however, he got
no support from Foch. On August 7, Foch and Robertson at a military
conference reaffirmed the decision made two weeks earlier at Paris, with
Foch agreeing "that it was now too late to attempt to change the military
plans for 1917." Furthermore, both generals "agreed that it is not possible to
send any further batteries of artillery from the Western Front to the Italian
Front to be ready for action in September of this year. These batteries would
necessarily have to be withdrawn from the troops in action."[14]

Although Robertson succeeded in protecting Haig's flanks at the London
conference, he saw alarming cracks appearing in the defenses of the "Westerners." "Unfortunately," he wrote Haig, "Lloyd George has got the French
with him as well as the Italians. Foch is hopeless. . . . He seems to have
made up his mind that it is hopeless looking for good results on the West
Front. This will make my task much harder." Foch's suggestion of an Allied
staff in Paris set alarm bells ringing in his head: "As the French keep rubbing
in that it is necessary to have a Central Staff at Paris I can see Lloyd George
in the future wanting to agree to some such organization so as to put the
matter in French hands and to take it out of mine. However we shall see all
about this."[15]

Haig, like Robertson, was adamantly opposed to raising Foch's authority
for he had no faith in the Frenchman's generalship ("the old man is done") or
his strategy ("utterly stupid"). Moreover, "the idea of organising an Allied
Staff in Paris is quite unsound, even if a really good French Staff Officer
were in existence."[16] Although sympathetic with Robertson's difficulties
with the civilians, Haig kept his distance. He had more important things on
his mind—his battle with the German army.

Haig's initial thrust, hampered by buckets of rain, had achieved little.
Nonetheless, acutely conscious of the doubting Thomases in the War
Cabinet, Robertson and Haig put as optimistic a face as possible on the
results of the first days' fighting, with Robertson emphasizing in the War
Cabinet that French troops were cooperating and the offensive was "pro-
gressing successfully."[17] Haig's progress report to the War Cabinet was
practically ebullient in spite of strong German counterattacks which retook

some of the ground gained in the initial assault. Haig contended that "the total of his casualties exceeds ours very considerably and not improbably by as much as 100%." Viewing the initial stage of his offensive, which proceeded by bounds, as a tactical laboratory for future attacks, Haig was certain of ultimate success. "They [results of the battle] entirely confirm our ability to overcome the enemy's artillery even under the most unfavourable conditions, and to assemble our troops for assault and launch the assault even under the enemy's direct observation. They confirm further that the British Armies can be relied on to drive the enemy from any position by the combined efforts of the infantry, artillery and aeroplanes and to do so without undue loss."[18]

The reader may have noted that tanks were not mentioned in Haig's report. Prior to the British attack, the tank corps headquarters had sent a memorandum to general headquarters warning that if the extensive drainage system in Flanders was destroyed by bombardment, the terrain would quickly become a veritable swampland; and indeed the tank had been neutralized by the mud. In choosing Flanders, of course, Haig had been influenced by many factors, political, strategical and so forth, but the fact remains that he saw the tank "in its present state of development" as a "minor factor" in his choice of a battlefield.[19]

Haig's report to the War Cabinet also proves that he and his subordinates had almost no understanding of the German army's new elastic defensive system which thinned the defenders in the first trenches. Captain G. C. Wynne, the British authority on tactics in the West who played the major role in compiling the Passchendaele volume in the official history, explains:[20]

> The enormous expenditure of ammunition and loss of two weeks of valuable time of the preliminary bombardment was not only lavished upon a position the Germans already regarded as a derelict extension of no-man's land, but it churned up a great stretch of country that was to exhaust the assaulting battalions even to cross. The main objectives given to the assault troops were those front-line regiments which the Germans from the outset regarded as sacrificed, but which the compulsory halts in the advance enabled to rally and to cause heavy losses before they were captured or slaughtered. These delays also gave ample time for the counter-attack divisions to make full preparations.[21]

The mud and water of Flanders, rather than faulty tactics, however, were more responsible for stymieing Haig's assault in August. The horrendous conditions facing the British army in the Flanders quagmire have best been described by Gough, who led the attack with his Fifth Army.

> Many pens have tried to describe the ghastly expanse of mud which covered this water-logged country, but few have been able to paint a picture sufficiently intense. Imagine a fertile countryside, dotted every few hundred yards with peasant farms and an occasional hamlet; water everywhere, for only an intricate system of small drainage canals relieved the land from the ever-present danger of flooding; a clay soil which the

slightest dampness turned into a clinging mud, and which after rain resembled a huge bog. Then imagine this same countryside battered, beaten, and torn by a torrent of shell and explosive—a torrent which had lasted without intermission for nearly three years. And then, following this merciless scouring, this same earth was blasted by a storm of steel such as no land in the world had yet witnessed—the soil shaken and reshaken, fields tossed into new and fantastic shapes, roads blotted out from the landscape, houses and hamlets pounded into dust so thoroughly that no man could point to where they had stood, and the intensive and essential drainage system utterly and irretrievably destroyed. This alone presents a battleground of tremendous difficulty. But then came the incessant rain. The broken earth became a fluid clay; the little brooks and tiny canals became formidable obstacles, and every shell-hole a dismal pond; hills and valleys alike were but waves and troughs of a gigantic sea of mud. Still the guns churned the treacherous slime. Every day conditions grew worse. What had once been difficult now became impossible. The surplus water poured into the trenches as its natural outlet, and they became impossible for troops; nor was it possible to walk over the open field—men staggered wearily over duckboard tracks. Wounded men falling headlong into the shell holes were in danger of drowning. Mules slipped from the tracks and were often drowned in the giant shell holes alongside. Guns sank till they became useless; rifles caked and would not fire; even food was tainted with the inevitable mud. No battle in history was ever fought under such conditions as that of Passchendaele.[22]

It is sometimes suggested that Haig was ignorant of the horrors of the Passchendaele battlefield but his description of the conditions was not that different from Gough's. "In many places the men could only get forward by assisting each other out of the breast-high mud and water in the shell holes,"[23] he reported to the War Cabinet through Robertson on August 21. Yet he continued to push in his attacks "when his guns could neither subdue the enemy's artillery nor screen their own infantry, and when the infantry could not retain its freshness."[24] His primary motivation, it would appear, was his fear that, if he halted his attack, he would give the civilians the excuse they needed to cancel his operations and switch off to another theater. This, in the end, was the great tragedy of the suspicion and hostility that characterized general headquarters's relations with the War Cabinet and vice versa.

Although Lloyd George believed that his lack of faith in Haig's offensive had been fully justified by its lack of success, he was uncertain of his support within the War Cabinet and he feared the political consequences of overruling Haig and Robertson. In mid-August, Hankey found him "obviously puzzled, as his predecessor was, as to how far the Government is justified in interfering with a military operation."[25]

Having failed to seize the initiative from his generals in formulating military plans for 1917, he was looking ahead to 1918. Although the London conference had instructed the Italian, French, and British general staffs to prepare plans to strike at Germany's allies,[26] he knew that this decision was meaningless as long as Robertson remained supreme in the realm of strategy. To undermine the general staff, he sought to exploit the jealousies between the "ins" and "outs" of the British army. His allies were Sir John French, who was obsessed with hatred for Haig and Robertson, and the ambitious Sir Henry Wilson, of whom it was once maliciously said by an army colleague that he became sexually aroused in the company of politicians. Wilson, who has flitted across these pages, was about to become a central figure in Lloyd George's conflict with Haig and Robertson. In early July, the lanky Irishman had resigned as Head of the British mission at French headquarters and returned to Britain to cultivate both the flowers in his garden and the nation's political leaders who held him in high regard because of his amusing, easy manner and apparently well-informed views on the military situation. An unemployed Wilson—with good reason—was viewed as a positive danger by Haig and Robertson. "His danger is that of any loose gun in a ship," was the way Esher put it.[27]

As the high command feared, Wilson was soon involved in talks with Lloyd George concerning the direction of the war. On August 17, he visited with French, who told him of Lloyd George's scheme to create a committee of three generals, including himself and Wilson, to examine proposals put forward by the general staff. Wilson demurred, proposing instead the creation of an Allied body to develop plans for the 1918 campaign, which would "leave R.[obertson] in but to put him under a superior direction."[28]

Wilson later informed Derby of the general nature of his conversation with French about a form of unity of command. Not surprisingly, just before he departed with French on August 23 for a meeting with Lloyd George, who was resting at Sir George Riddell's home near Hurstpierpoint in Sussex, he received an anxious visit from Robertson, who wanted to know if he were still a "Westerner," and if so, requesting his support because he was carrying a " 'heavy load.' " Wilson insisted that he had not broken ranks with the army, and indeed he viewed the western front as the primary theater for the British army, but in opposition to Haig and Robertson, he saw merit in the "side shows," especially if they were conducted during the "mud months" of the winter, when military operations in the West were stalled.[29]

Later that day Wilson explained his plan "of three PM's & 3 soldiers to be over all C.I.G.S. & to draw up plans for the whole theatre from Nieuport to Baghdad" to an interested Lloyd George. After delivering a blistering attack on Robertson, Lloyd George explained the dilemma with which he was faced. "He said he was not in a position nor had he the knowledge to bring out alternative plans & to insist on their adoption as it would always be said that he was over-ruling the soldiers. That it was because of his profound disquiet that he had thought of forming a commt. of Johnnie & me & another but he now quite agreed with me that that would not work & that my plan was infinitely better."[30]

During the following days, Wilson, who was Lloyd George's choice to be the British military representative on any Allied war council, attempted (on the prime minister's instructions) to win the support of Milner, Bonar Law, and Carson for his scheme.[31] Although none of the ministers consulted offered opposition to Wilson's proposal, it was pushed into the background by some startling news from the Italian theater.

Lloyd George had given Wilson the impression that he planned to stop

Haig's offensive within the next ten days, and on August 26 a telegram from the British ambassador in Rome gave him the necessary pretext. Rodd reported that Cadorna's Eleventh Battle of the Isonzo was beginning to offer the prospect of "a complete smashing of the Austrian Army."[32] This news, which proved to be exaggerated, when put beside recent information that Austria might be on the verge of abandoning its alliance with Germany,[33] appeared to offer conclusive proof that Lloyd George had been right all along. In a "ferment of excitement," he wrote Wully suggesting that Italy's allies give her support to turn "the Austrian retreat into a rout."[34] Although he dared not tell Robertson, the prime minister was thinking of the dispatch of 300 guns and British divisions which would almost certainly bring Haig's attack to an end.[35]

Robertson, who saw Lloyd George's proposal as the thin edge of the wedge in shutting down Haig's offensive, was not deceived. Like the prime minister, he was desperately tired and out of sorts because of the continuous battling over strategy. In his view, the prime minister was "a real bad 'un" and "an under-bred swine." With the exception of Smuts, the other key members of the War Cabinet were no better; Milner was "a tired dyspeptic old man," Curzon, "a gas-bag," and "Bonar Law equals Bonar law."[36]

On August 28, with Lloyd George still in Sussex, Wully launched into a bitter tirade in the War Cabinet. After a distorted description of the formulation of Allied military plans in 1917, he made the incredible statement that "the general staff, therefore, had no hand in not adopting the Italian plan. It was ruled out by the action of the War Cabinet." Ignoring the conditions carefully placed on the Flanders operations by the ministers, he attacked them for wanting to change plans every week or so. "No plan is of any good," he thundered, "unless carried out with confidence and resolution." He went on to warn that the wavering of the prime minister and his colleagues was bound to have a serious impact on the morale of the British army in France. Twisting facts to bolster his argument, Robertson insisted that no immediate aid could be given Cadorna because "it was impossible to transfer large numbers of guns to that Front in less than a month."[37]

Robertson and Lloyd George began a face-to-face confrontation at Riddell's home the following day. To soften Robertson, apple pudding, his favorite dish, was placed before him at lunch. In the end Robertson acquiesced in the dispatch of a telegram to the British ambassador in Rome which offered substantial British support to Cadorna, although it would involve "breaking off the offensive in Flanders," if the Italian commander in chief would guarantee a decisive defeat of the Austrian army.[38] Robertson's belief that no such assurance would be forthcoming from Cadorna—not the two generous helpings of apple pudding he consumed at lunch—probably explains his willingness to agree to this telegram.[39]

The amicable conclusion of Robertson's meeting with the prime minister did not conclude the row over guns for Italy. General Delmé Radcliffe and Foch joined in the clamor for sending artillery to Cadorna, who was expected to continue his attacks into October. Since Albert Thomas had been at Riddell's home in Sussex with Lloyd George, the War Office was convinced that Foch's request "was a put up job" between Thomas and Lloyd

George. Robertson dug in his heels, now claiming that he had not agreed with the telegram to Rome and was in no way associated with it.[40]

With Foch and Haig on their way to London, Lloyd George returned to Whitehall from Sussex. But his heart was no longer in the battle. The Italian offensive which had burned so brightly for a few days now smoldered with the Italian army stalled in rugged country. On the other hand, Haig remained confident that he could attain his objectives, and the Admiralty submitted memoranda emphasizing the crucial importance of taking the Flemish ports.[41] Furthermore, Lloyd George found no inclination on the part of his colleagues in the War Cabinet to overrule the high command. Even Milner, who had been in favor of Lloyd George's Italian project, supported Haig. Once the government had decided upon an offensive, he argued, the commander in charge of it should be given a free hand. If Haig's forces were weakened to support the Italians, "he would feel that he had not been treated quite fairly and that is a fatal frame of mind for a commander actually engaged in difficult operations."[42]

On the morning of September 4, Foch and Haig attempted to resolve their differences without success. Foch wanted to take all of the guns he planned to send south of the Alps from the French First Army on Haig's left which was participating in the Flanders offensive. Haig and Robertson dissented, with Haig arguing that the removal of some 100 guns on his front would be detrimental to his attack and Robertson reminding the French that Haig had a right to expect the same cooperation from them that he had earlier given Nivelle.[43]

Later that day the War Cabinet took up the matter. Carefully avoiding any criticism of his generals' strategy, Lloyd George stressed the political considerations involved in the Italian request for assistance. If the British refused to cooperate with Foch, the Italians might be angered and the anti-German coalition damaged, he limply observed.[44] The mood of the War Cabinet, however, was to support Haig over Foch; and during the Anglo-French conference that immediately followed, Lloyd George stood with his generals, arguing against denuding the British front of 100 guns because it "would unduly weaken the great attack which was in progress."[45] Eventually a compromise was worked out, with 100 French guns (50 from the French First Army) being added to Cadorna's artillery. This was a small price indeed for the British high command to pay for the continuation of the Flanders offensive. Whereupon Cadorna shocked Lloyd George with the news that he planned no further major offensive for the rest of the year.

The guns for Italy episode was the closest Lloyd George ever came to stopping Haig's attack. But when it came to a showdown, he pulled back. In Hankey's words, "L. G. had been very truculent about the idea of overruling the soldiers, but, when he came to the point, he funked it." Yet it is fortunate that Lloyd George's instincts told him that it was not "the moment for a row with the soldiers."[46] If he had overruled Haig and Robertson and ordered them to send 300 or more guns and perhaps some British divisions to Cadorna, Robertson would probably have resigned, precipitating a political crisis. Cadorna's stunning *volte face* would then have cut the ground out from under the prime minister. Coming on the heels of his association with Nivelle's failure a few months earlier this interference with the military could well have destroyed his premiership.

Routed by his generals once again, Lloyd George gave every appearance of being on the verge of a breakdown. Hankey found him "restless and neurotic, unstable & rather infirm in purpose, neuralgic & irritable, exacting and difficult to please."[47] A human dynamo, he had maintained an incredible pace since become prime minister, pushing himself and his colleagues to the limit. By August 22, when he took a month's leave from the War Cabinet, broken only by a return to London for the debate over guns for Italy, the War Cabinet had been in almost continuous session, with 222 meetings in less than 260 days. There were other meetings as well, the Imperial War Cabinet, the War Policy Committee and many inter-Allied conferences. Involved with almost every nut and bolt of Britain's warmaking machinery, he entertained a stream of visitors both inside and outside of the government. Particular attention was paid to the press lords and to key members of his government. Almost every morning he made the short journey down the corridor to Bonar Law's residence at 11 Downing Street. There, through a haze of pipe smoke, he played his ideas off the chancellor of the exchequer.

His mastery and domination of the War Cabinet in many areas was truly remarkable. But his influence in military policy, where he dared not act unilaterally, remained limited. The War Office was immune to his magical ways; and the ministers were opposed to overruling the military authorities. Unable to escape the Flanders quagmire, he was overwhelmed with a sense of impotence.

On September 5, he retreated to Criccieth, his Welsh home. There, suffering from nervous exhaustion, his condition worsened. On September 13, he wrote Miss Stevenson: "Since I left you I have had a really bad time. . . . I *must* stay down as long as I can be spared. Otherwise P.[ussy] will soon have to find another Tom Cat. I am asking Hankey down for a weekend."[48] When Hankey arrived, he discovered the prime minister "rather despondent at the failure of the year's campaigning and disgusted at the narrowness of the General Staff, and the inability of his colleagues to see eye to eye with him and their fear of over-ruling the General Staff."[49]

Unable to get on in the Italian theater, Lloyd George's mind was now fixed on Turkey. Earlier, on August 10, he had gotten the War Cabinet to send instructions to the new commander of the Egyptian Expeditionary Force, "Bull" Allenby, "to strike the Turk as hard as possible during the coming Autumn and Winter."[50] Although Robertson was "dead against" any attempt to conquer Palestine, he did not oppose this decision, because he believed that he could limit Allenby's assault to a hard knock on the Gaza-Beersheba line. In secret correspondence with Allenby, a fellow student at the Staff College two decades earlier, he made his intentions clear.[51]

Determined to have his way on a great offensive against Turkey, Lloyd George discussed ways of getting the general staff to bend to the will of the War Cabinet without provoking a political crisis. Hankey suggested reviving the War Policy Committee "to bring Robertson to heel without a row."

Given the prime minister's desire to "abandon all activity on the western front and to concentrate our efforts against Turkey," this was naive advice to say the least.[52]

On September 17, Milner arrived to participate in these discussions. He agreed that "the western front affords no opportunity for achieving complete success and that it is necessary to devote our main efforts against Turkey."[53] Milner's support of Lloyd George's strategy, however, was of little value because he believed, as he told Riddell, "that the soldiers stand well with public, who do not know the facts and have short memories, and that a quarrel with the soldiers would therefore involve an attack which would dishearten our people and hearten the enemy." Milner wanted "to carry the soldiers with the Cabinet."[54] Lloyd George knew better. Bonar Law had just reported that he believed that Wully had "no hope of anything coming of Haig's offensive,"[55] but Lloyd George was convinced that the C.I.G.S. would never break ranks with the field marshal. The only way to break the general staff's stranglehold on strategy was either to divide Robertson's power or replace him; either move might destroy his government. It is no wonder that Hankey noted in his diary after Milner's departure: "Lloyd George's neuralgia, I regret to say, is not much better."[56]

On September 22, sensational news reached Criccieth that raised the prime minister's sagging spirits. On September 19 the Foreign Office had received a telegram, dated September 18, from Sir A. Hardinge, the British ambassador in Spain, which included the following bombshell: "Minister of State says he has heard through a Spanish diplomatic representative that German Government would be glad to make a communication to ourselves relative to peace."[57] Accompanying the news of this German peace feeler via Spain was a missive from Balfour which urged the prime minister to immediately include all of Britain's allies in this indirect peace approach.[58]

Lloyd George hesitated to accept Balfour's advice. His agile mind quickly perceived that a peace which satisfied the French on Alsace-Lorraine and the British on Belgium could only be made by sacrificing Russia to German demands in the East.[59] At the bottom of Lloyd George's willingness to sacrifice an ally to get a favorable peace was his obsession with Passchendaele. As he had told Riddell three weeks earlier: "Unless the war is conducted on different lines we are certain to lose it, and that unless a change is made it would be better to make the best peace possible."[60] Haig's and Robertson's domination of military policy thus had momentarily weakened the resolve of the author of the "knock-out blow" for total victory. Seeing a way to prevent more bloodshed in Flanders, Lloyd George's spirits were lifted; that night he and Hankey sang "The Bay of Biscay" in a duet.

The next day he hurried back to London to discover another peace feeler, via the French, which if genuine, seemed too attractive not to consider seriously. A meeting in Switzerland had been proposed through intermediaries between former Premier Briand and Baron Oskar von der Lancken, the former head of the chancery at the German embassy in Paris and now a high official in the German occupation government in Belgium. Briand had informed his government of this approach and the British in turn had been apprized of these developments.[61]

On September 24, the ministers without their military advisers held a secret session in which the minutes were not circulated. Balfour compared the German peace kites via Spain and France, throwing his support to the Spanish approach because it was official even though there had been no mention of terms. On the other hand, the informal approach through Briand, which included the restoration of Belgium and Serbia, territorial concessions to Italy and colonial concessions to Britain, and the cession of Alsace-Lorraine to France, was "so favourable" that Balfour saw "sinister" motives behind it. If not a trap to divide the alliance, it was certainly a clear invitation to abandon Russia. The foreign secretary's recommendation was at once to involve Britain's allies in the official German offer through Spain.

Lloyd George balked at Balfour's advice. Before bringing in all of Britain's allies, especially Russia, he wanted to explore the Briand-Lancken channel as well. With the mutinous Russian army inactive and with Socialist and anti-war sentiment prevailing in Petrograd, he was prepared to consider sacrificing Russia for a good peace. If Russia abandoned her allies, as seemed likely, could Britain achieve her war objectives? "If we came to the conclusion that the Soviet was going to destroy our prospects of success," he went on, "then Russia ought to pay the penalty."[62]

Lloyd George was walking through a mine field and he knew it. Walls in London were placarded with clenched fists, symbolizing a "knock-out blow" against the German army, and the majority of the British people were still solidly behind the war. Still, the heavy losses in 1917 suffered by Haig's army (by the end of the year British casualties would approach 760,000)[63] made the government fearful of the growth of defeatist or anti-war sentiment. As Robertson once wrote Haig, "There are gradually accumulating in the country a great many wounded and crippled men who are not of a very cheery disposition; there are others who are mere wasters and without patriotism; and finally, there are the various Labour Unions etc. On the whole there is a fairly formidable body of discontented or half-hearted people."[64] What was now a trickle might become a flood under the right circumstances. Witness the growing war-weariness of Britain's Continental allies. Already cracks in British Labour's support for the war were beginning to develop.[65] The small Independent Labour party had been aggressively pushing a peace by negotiation and its anti-war stance was mirrored by the Union of Democratic Control, which had been created by Liberal elements in 1914 to influence foreign policy. In August the government had been confronted with a proposed conference of the Second International at Stockholm. If held, it might become a rally by the European Left for a compromise peace that was not in Britain's interests. Henderson, the Labour representative in the War Cabinet, had been forced to resign because he refused to oppose the Stockholm conference. The emerging debate about Britain's war aims placed Lloyd George in a precarious position. If it became known that the prime minister was favorable to a compromise peace, forces might be unleashed that could not be controlled. Britain's smoothly-running engine of war might break down if the prime minister was caught, as he once expressed it to C. P. Scott, between "the extravagance of the Jingo and the cantankerousness of the pacifist."[66]

During the discussion of the German peace moves, Lloyd George found support—tentative though it might be—for a peace short of total victory. But the two members of the War Cabinet, whose support was crucial, Milner and Bonar Law, were for fighting on. Milner was unequivocal in his opposition; and Bonar Law favored continuing the struggle if there were "reasonable grounds" for expecting victory. Without the support of Milner and Bonar Law, Lloyd George retreated a step. He said that he agreed with those who wanted to continue the war, "but only provided that the Chief of the Imperial General Staff would advise that we could smash Germany, with Russia out of the war and the blockade gone. Germany would be able to supply herself in course of time with wheat, copper, tungsten and other metals."[67]

In the end Lloyd George won his point, with the War Cabinet deciding to leave Britain's allies in the dark about Germany's apparent willingness to negotiate while Lloyd George further explored the matter with the new French Premier Painlevé, who had replaced Ribot on September 13. Lloyd George then immediately left London on an all-night trip to France. The next morning over breakfast on a train at Boulogne he conferred with Foch and Painlevé. From the premier, he learned that the French government considered the approach to Briand bona fide. But, at the same time, there was considerable uncertainty about Berlin's terms. They might be far less generous than originally thought. A disturbing fact that emerged from these discussions was that the French had once again postponed their offensive to assist Haig.[68] The situation was fraught with danger. The Italians had stopped all offensive action for the rest of the year; now the French had apparently decided to do likewise; and, of course, the Russians appeared finished.

With Robertson, Lloyd George then drove to Haig's general headquarters near St. Omer to get the field marshal's view of the German peace feelers and to determine the progress of his recent attacks which had begun on September 20. General Herbert Plumer, rather than Gough, now had the principal role in the offensive. On a narrow front, supported by a thousand-yard-deep artillery barrage, Plumer's forces advanced in clouds of dust rather than rain, making real, though limited progress. Buoyed by Plumer's success, general headquarters was in high spirits. As Britain's war leaders talked, messages flowed in from the front; and the progress of the offensive was shown on a large map. One by one the German positions were taken. Haig's remarks reflected his supreme confidence in his army, with the following exchange taking place:

> *Field Marshal Haig* said that we could not desert Russia.
> *The Prime Minister* said that the British people would not fight in order to win for Russia, what she herself was unwilling to fight for.
> *Field Marshal Haig* said that the right course for us was to go on hammering now, and to make the French fight without delay. He believed that the Germans were in a bad way.
> *The Prime Minister* said they were not in such a bad way as not to be able to fight. There was no question of making a peace offer to Germany, but only whether we should receive one.

General Robertson stated the Prime Minister's point in the following manner. Russia is practically finished for the purposes of the war—a view he held himself. The Italians are not fighting, and the French are not fighting. How, then, does the war look? We cannot singlehanded defeat the German army.

Field Marshal Haig said that the Germans were now very worn out and had some very poor material in the fighting line. We could punish them severely if only the French would go on fighting on the Aisne.[69]

The conference finished, Lloyd George went off to view German prisoners captured during the day. In a cage he observed "nerve shattered, tired, unshaved, and dirty men." Even though these prisoners "sprang to attention as though under review by the Kaiser," he was obviously impressed by their beaten appearance.[70] Only later did he discover that someone (certainly not Haig) at general headquarters had instructed the Fifth Army corps headquarters to remove all "able-bodied prisoners" from the cage.[71]

Returning to London that evening, Lloyd George to his alarm discovered that Asquith had delivered a speech at Leeds in which he had made the German evacuation of Russia a condition of peace. The actions of the former prime minister had been carefully observed. Previously he had been quietly sitting on the Opposition Front Bench, brooding but loyally supporting the government. In mid-September, however, he had paid Haig a visit at the front and Lloyd George, it seems, feared that his Leeds speech, coupled with his visit to general headquarters, indicated that Asquith was considering a comeback in an alliance with the soldiers.[72] What Lloyd George did not know was that the Foreign Office had encouraged Asquith to make his Leeds speech. Sir Eric Drummond, Asquith's former private secretary and Balfour's present one, had told the Liberal leader of Lloyd George's interest in the sacrifice of Russia in return for generous German terms to the British and French. It is perhaps reasonable to assume that Drummond was acting with Balfour's approval for the foreign secretary was greatly alarmed at the prime minister's trend of thinking. At any rate, it is known that Balfour conspired with Paul Cambon, the French ambassador in London, to undermine any peace negotiations with Berlin.[73]

On September 27, the ministers resumed their secret discussion of the German peace feelers. The prime minister reminded his colleagues of the very precarious military situation. He then emphasized that

> it was very unwise to make any unconditional declaration, such as Mr. Asquith had just made in his speech for the War Aims Committee at Leeds, to the effect that we should not make peace until the Germans were prepared to surrender the territory they had occupied in Russia, which he had treated in precisely the same manner as the occupied territory in France. When we came to consider peace terms, reference must be had to the question of whether Russia was taking her share in the fighting.

In the discussion that followed, Lloyd George discovered that there was almost no support for a compromise peace that would save the lives of tens of thousands British soldiers. Only Carson, who had joined the War Cabinet in July, gave him tentative support. Smuts was noncommittal. George N.

Barnes (who had replaced Henderson), Curzon, Milner, and Balfour spoke in opposition. Bonar Law was not present. The opponents of a compromise peace had little faith in Haig's efforts to defeat the German army, but they were still opposed to a peace that left German militarism unchecked on the Continent and overseas. Balfour defended Asquith's speech at Leeds and warned that the danger of Russia's going out of the war "would be enormously increased if it got about that we are prepared to make peace at her expense." He also "attached great importance to the deprivation to Germany of any Colonies" unless it could be guaranteed "that she would not break the peace, of which at present there appeared to be no prospect." Curzon and Milner were alarmed by the prospect of Germany's domination of Russia.[74]

During the next few days Lloyd George abandoned for the time being any consideration of a compromise peace. On October 4, the *Morning Post,* speaking for the Right, issued a clear warning in a leading article, "PEACE OR VICTORY?"

> The business of our statesmen and of the nation is to see that the blood of our soldiers is not wasted nor their courage betrayed. . . . If our politicians were now to make a peace with an undefeated enemy, it would make our captains sick, and our dead would turn in their serried graves.

On the same day Balfour informed Washington for the first time of the German peace approach. Two days later he called the Allied representatives to the Foreign Office to prepare a joint note to Berlin in response to the German peace feeler via Spain.[75] Meanwhile, Lancken was left cooling his heels in Switzerland because the French government prevented Briand from conferring with him.

Berlin made no official response to the Allied note, but it was soon apparent that the Germans were not in a conciliatory mood and had only hoped to divide their opponents.[76] On October 9, the German secretary of state, Richard von Kühlmann, informed the Reichstag that Germany would "never" make any concessions in regard to Alsace-Lorraine. At the same time, Chancellor Georg Michaelis reiterated his position that Germany's aims were as follows: "We must continue to persevere until the German Empire on the continent and overseas establishes its position."[77]

With no chance of ending the war through negotiation, Lloyd George became more obsessed than ever with launching a gigantic military effort against Turkey. Although Turkey's defeat would not win the war, it would raise the spirits of the Allied people, strengthen Britain's negotiating position in the event of a stalemate, and offer security to Britain's Asian position (especially in Persia). The prime minister envisaged a three-pronged winter assault, with the Turks being squeezed from Palestine, Mesopotamia, and an amphibious attack at Ayas Bay (Alexandretta). Encouraged by Foch's support of future attacks against Germany's allies in August, he believed that the French might be persuaded to provide up to eight divisions for an attack on the Syrian coast, an area where French political interests were strong.

The great technical problem with which he was faced was the shortage of shipping. On September 24, he revived the War Policy Committee to discuss transporting British and French divisions to the Turkish theater. The naval experts admitted that a considerable increase in transport in the Mediterranean was possible if sacrifices were made in other areas. But they argued that the simultaneous landing of eight divisions at Alexandretta was "impossible." On the other hand, divisions could be delivered there in stages. The only decision that emerged from the rambling and inconclusive discussion was the dispatch of two British divisions from France to Egypt to act as a reserve for use in either Mesopotamia (where there was concern that the Germans might threaten Persia) or Palestine. Since there was no intention of taking those troops from Haig until his current operations were over, Robertson at first accepted this decision.[78]

On the following day at Boulogne, Lloyd George raised the question of landing eight French divisions at Alexandretta with Foch. Foch agreed that it was not necessary that these divisions be disembarked simultaneously. With Russia silent in the Caucasus and uncertain of Britain's ability to get on in Mesopotamia and Palestine, however, he argued that a winter attack was "impossible." "The operation could only be envisaged for a distant future, for example, possibly for the summer of 1918, if circumstances were favourable." When pressed by Lloyd George, Foch did agree to study a plan to attack Alexandretta to exploit a British success in Palestine, but he emphasized "that his present intentions were only eventual and potential, and depended on what actually happened in the operations in Palestine and Mesopotamia."[79] In sum, victory almost had to be assured before the French would participate.

Although disappointed with Foch's attitude which was virtually a veto of French participation, Lloyd George remained determined to launch a great attack against the Turks during the Winter. Robertson, more than the technical question of shipping, stood in the way. Russia's demise was much on Wully's mind, and with Germany able to draw on reinforcements from the East, he saw little hope of a decisive victory in the West. Consequently, in his heart, he found it increasingly difficult to oppose diplomatic-military operations against Turkey. On September 27, he sent Haig a revealing letter.

> My views are known to you. They have always been "defensive" in all theatres but the West. But the difficulty is to *prove* the wisdom of this now that Russia is out. I confess I stick to it more because I see nothing better, and because my instinct prompts me to stick to it, than to any convincing arguments by which I can support it.[80]

Despite his doubts, as we will see, Robertson stuck to his "Western" guns. In fact, to thwart Lloyd George's plans, he was about to rig the advice the government received from the Egyptian Expeditionary Force.

On October 3, with Robertson absent, the War Policy Committee discussed a campaign in Palestine. Because of Foch's attitude, Lloyd George now thought of a local success, rather than an overwhelming military victory, to force the Turks into peace negotiations. To entice them to the peace table, he was prepared, to the dismay of the imperialists Curzon and Milner, to make Syria, Palestine and Mesopotamia into protectorates, "similar to that prevailing in Egypt, under the suzerainty of the Sultan of Turkey." He also was in favor of helping the Turks get rid of the capitulations and repudiate their German debts.

When Curzon, whose first choice for an "Eastern" offensive was Mesopotamia, argued for delaying the British attack in Palestine until next year, Lloyd George stressed Macdonogh's view that Turkish reserves were exhausted and then gave a very distorted account of his recent interview with Foch at Boulogne. "General Foch's view was that General Maude could get to Mosul, but that he could not defeat the Turks; that General Allenby should advance as far as possible, and that, when those two Turkish forces were fully engaged, we should land at Ayas Bay with a view to cutting the Turkish communications. General Foch ridiculed the idea that it would be necessary to have eight Divisions in transports at the same time." What Lloyd George failed to reveal, of course, was Foch's belief that the winter attack which he desired was "impossible."[81]

On October 5, when Robertson was brought into these discussions, there was a blowup. With Hankey sick with a cold no minutes were taken of the meeting of the War Policy Committee, but it appears that Robertson and Lloyd George quarreled about the earlier decision of the committee to send two divisions to Egypt as a reserve for Palestine or Mesopotamia. The War Cabinet had never ratified this decision, and Wully, not wanting to incur Haig's wrath or to commit these divisions to Allenby's operations which might make it difficult to return them to the West in the spring, now opposed their dispatch. Lloyd George responded by taking the C.I.G.S. to task for past military blunders.[82] Following this angry exchange, Robertson sent two telegrams to Allenby. One was official, requesting his requirements to inflict a defeat on the Turkish Army facing him. The other was a secret personal "R" telegram which read as follows:

> You will understand that my 42625 of today does not originate with me because apart from the strategy I do not believe that the policy if successfully executed would have the anticipated result. However you are concerned only with planning your reply and in it you should take no chances because of the many uncertain factors. You should also remember that transport, supply, water, time and space are imperfectly realized here and therefore they may need emphasising. I find it impossible to convincingly prove the great differences between the needs and facilities of Turkish and British troops in these and similar matters.[83]

Allenby got the not so subtle hint and set to work preparing one of the most absurd appreciations ever presented to a British government.

Meanwhile, the battle continued between Lloyd George and Robertson over reinforcing Allenby. If Robertson went along with sending the Egyptian Expeditionary Force reinforcements from France to insure Allenby's success, Lloyd George told him, he would take Haig's side on the issue of taking over more of the French line, an explosive question that was coming more and more to the front. "Alternately," Robertson informed Haig, "I *know* he will *not* fight them if I refuse—as I shall—to agree to this plan."[84] On October 8, Robertson had Major-General Sir Arthur Lynden-Bell, who had been Murray's chief of staff in Egyptian Expeditionary Force, in tow when he attended a meeting of the War Policy Committee. Bell argued that Allenby, even if reinforced, could do little. By the summer the limit of Allenby's advance, according to Bell, was the Jaffa-Jerusalem line, and then "this was only a hope."[85] Robertson then prepared a memorandum which argued that "once the decisive theatre has been selected it must be regarded as such, and all other theatres must be ruthlessly treated as secondary and made to do the best they can with what is given them." Uncertain of Turkey's desire for peace, he viewed the proposed military operation as a "gamble, and a gamble at this stage of the war would be even more dangerous than usual." Even if Allenby got to the Jerusalem-Jaffa line, "the military effect would be of no value to us" and more troops would be required to hold this forward position.[86]

With Robertson absent, the War Policy Committee on October 9 discussed the professional military advice that it was receiving. Why, Lloyd George and Milner wondered, were the generals always as pessimistic about "Eastern" ventures as they were optimistic about their assaults against German machine guns and barbed wire in the West? "If Sir Douglas Haig," Milner asserted, "had approached his problem in the same spirit, he could have made an even stronger case against doing no more." Lloyd George's conclusion was that the British commanders in chief in the outlying theaters dared not buck Robertson. "Military officers were dependent for their future promotion upon their superiors, and could not express independent views without jeopardising their future," he said. "Politicians always had their public to appeal to."

Lloyd George's frustration with the biased military advice was so great that he wanted the government to impose strategy on the soldiers. Even though Smuts was the only member of the committee with a military background, he "suggested that a decision should be taken that the Turk was to be defeated in Palestine, and that the General Staff should be informed of this."[87] When it became obvious that his colleagues hesitated to take such a drastic step, the prime minister resurrected his idea of establishing a committee of soldiers to examine the general staff's strategy. At Boulogne on September 25, he had secretly discussed for the second time with Painlevé the placing of Foch in charge of the Allied armies. To blunt criticism of this arrangement in the British press, Parliament and the army, he and Painlevé agreed to achieve this goal in two stages. First, an Inter-Allied War Council with a permanent general staff, with Sir Henry Wilson as the British military representative, would be established. Then, after British public opinion had been prepared, Foch might be appointed supreme commander.[88] Painlevé, who had promised to cross the Channel, when necessary, to assist the prime minister in overcoming the resistance of the British military authorities, was at that very moment about to depart for London with a large French party which included Foch. But, with the French and Italian governments on the verge of collapse ("absolutely *rotten*" was the way Lloyd George expressed it to Wilson),[89] Lloyd George hesitated to implement this plan now. The rigged committee of Wilson and French he planned could give him immediate help, while an Inter-Allied War Council might take weeks to establish. Furthermore, with Haig and Robertson expressing adamant opposition to any central military authority,[90] the political repercussions might be less.

"If a patient was very ill no one would limit themselves to taking the advice of the family doctor," he told the committee. "They would call in a second opinion. He suggested that this might be advisable in this case also."[91] More was at stake than a Turkish offensive: Lloyd George was determined to force his generals into a defensive posture in the West while Britain concentrated her military power on the periphery.

With Russia in chaos and with the "Westerners" unable to show any dramatic successes in the West, Haig and Robertson were on the spot. Haig's offensive, which had made progress during the good weather of September, was now mired in mud and water once again. Yet, in conditions that made the achievement of his grand strategic objectives impossible, the field marshal was determined to continue his attacks. The grave risk that he was prepared to take was that he would not grind down his own forces in the process. Although the manpower situation was serious, the British army could have been kept up to strength for the critical battles of 1918 if he had halted his attacks in early October when the rains returned. At this time, General C. F. Nevil Macready, the adjutant general to the forces, told Rawlinson that he was "fairly satisfied with the man power" and would be able to keep the British army "up to strength if we do not lose more than another 50,000 men before the offensive stops for the year."[92] Haig, it must be recalled, had been warned repeatedly by Lloyd George and Robertson that he must not exhaust his army; his misleading response had been that he would conform his strategy to the manpower available.

When criticized by Churchill after the war, Haig attempted to justify his actions by claiming that Pétain constantly pressed him to continue his attacks to keep the pressure off his war-weary forces.[93] This is nonsense. Haig kept meticulous records and there is no mention in his diary or anywhere else of Pétain ever making such a request. To the contrary, when Pétain talked with Haig at Amiens on October 18, the Frenchman's suggestion to counter any movement of German divisions from East to West was for the field marshal to take over more of the French line rather than continue his offensive, which would delay any extension of the British front. Haig was convinced that the Germans posed no real threat to the French, for the German divisions were "not fit to take the offensive." Moreover, he did not think it possible for the Germans to transfer divisions from the eastern front in time to strike at the French in 1917.[94] Haig's true motives are revealed in a paper to Robertson, dated October 8, which was circulated to the War Cabinet. This paper shows that Haig, given a misleading picture of German strength by Charteris, remained convinced that there was a chance that he could gain decisive results in 1917. If not in 1917, he was certain that his forces in Flanders (if kept up to strength!) would destroy the enemy in 1918 even if Russia made peace.[95] Haig's paper claimed that since April he had defeated seventy-seven German divisions, some of them more than once. The War Office, which surely knew better than to accept the optimistic arithmetic of Charteris, went along with these inflated estimates, arguing in mid-October that Haig had exhausted forty-eight German divisions since the beginning of the Third Battle of Ypres. Maurice even told the War Cabinet that up to October 5 British casualties were about 100,000 fewer than German (148,470 to 255,000).[96] To be sure, Haig's stubborn assaults in Ypres had done considerable damage to the German army, with Ludendorff admitting: "Our wastage had been so high as to cause grave misgivings, and had exceeded all expectations."[97] Despite Ludendorff's testimony, however, there is no reason to believe that the British army had inflicted more lasting damage upon the enemy than it had suffered itself. Furthermore, with many divisions to call upon in the eastern theater, the German army was hardly at the breaking point.

On October 10, with its military advisers absent, the War Cabinet discussed future military policy, including French participation in an attack on Turkey. Haig's paper on October 8 held center stage.

> The view was freely expressed that Field Marshal Haig's memorandum of October 8, O.A.D. 652, did not provide a convincing argument that we could inflict a decisive military defeat on Germany on the West front next year, even if Russia was still able to retain the same number of German troops on the Eastern front as at present, and that if Russia collapsed and the German forces on the Western front became equal, and perhaps, greatly superior, to the Allies, both in men and guns, there was no reasonable probability of a decisive victory.

After the ministers discussed the possibility that Turkey's defeat might release men and guns for action in the West, Lloyd George sprang his trap on the general staff. Stressing the "grave decision" before the War Cabinet, he proposed convening a war council (which included Wilson and French) similar to the one that Asquith had held immediately after Britain came into the war. His ulterior motive, of course, was to diminish the authority of the general staff by giving the ministers different military views from which to choose. As the arbiter among Robertson, Wilson, and French, the War Cabinet would have the upper hand. The War Cabinet went along, agreeing to include French and Wilson in the deliberation of future strategy.[98]

Robertson was naturally insulted and enraged when he learned of Lloyd George's coup, which violated his arrangement with Kitchener and the previous government that made him the sole military adviser to the government. His first reaction was to resign. If he went, many Unionists threatened to follow him through the door. Curzon told Hankey that he, Cecil, Balfour, Derby, and Carson would also probably resign.[99]

Lloyd George's actions might be interpreted as an invitation to Wully to resign. Keeping his government together, however, was more important to the prime minister than Robertson's scalp. Consequently, he attempted to handle the C.I.G.S., "who was as sulky as a bear with a sore head,"[100] with kid gloves at the next meeting of the War Cabinet. He asserted that the War Cabinet's decision to convene a war council "was not due in the slightest degree to any lack of confidence in anyone, more especially the Chief of the Imperial General Staff, in whom they had the utmost confidence." At this meeting, French and Wilson, who were in attendance, were asked to examine the grand strategic landscape and submit proposals for future military policy.[101]

Lloyd George's soothing words may have satisfied Robertson's civilian supporters, but they did not mollify him. "The fact is it is a *very* weak-kneed craven-hearted Cabinet," he wrote Haig, "and L.G. hypnotises them and is allowed to run riot. We shall see what we shall see."[102] As Wully girded his loins for another round with the prime minister, Lloyd George continued to apply the pressure.

Over the weekend, October 13–14, at Chequers, which had just been donated to the nation by Arthur Lee as a place of relaxation for its prime ministers, Lloyd George discussed the creation of an inter-Allied council with a permanent general staff with Foch and Henri Franklin-Bouillon, the voluble and excitable minister of propaganda in Painlevé's cabinet, who was known as "boiling Franklin." Balfour, Smuts and Hankey were also present. The French had arrived in London expecting Lloyd George to urge the creation of an Inter-Allied War Council, which they no doubt hoped would serve as a means of getting Haig to take over more of the French line. Although "boiling Franklin" wanted to establish an inter-Allied staff within the week, Lloyd George held his hand, explaining that immediate action "was quite impossible, as he had not yet even consulted his colleagues on the subject." He only wanted to "ascertain how the French Government would regard the proposal, if made formally."[103]

On Monday, October 15, Lloyd George argued at length with Hankey about future military policy. For the first time he fully revealed his belief that the war could not be won until 1919. He was prepared to admit that the continuation of Haig's attacks in Flanders might force Germany to surrender in 1919. But Britain would no longer have a "first-class" army and the winning blows would be struck by the Americans, whose influence and prestige would overshadow the British. Despite his interest in a compromise peace with Germany two weeks earlier, Lloyd George now "contemplated an overwhelming military defeat, which would absolutely compel the enemy to submit." But, he argued, "this would not possibly be achieved in 1918 by any method." Consequently, he wanted to occupy the Germans in the West in 1918 with "Pétain's tactics" while detaching her allies with "combined military and diplomatic efforts." Then, with the assistance of the Americans, the German army would be smashed in 1919. Significantly, Lloyd George told Hankey that "rather than forego his policy he would hand over the reins of office to some other who would carry it through." The secretary of the War Cabinet, on the prime minister's instructions, immediately acquainted Balfour, Milner, and Curzon with Lloyd George's strategic views. But he only told Balfour of the prime minister's declared willingness to relinquish office if necessary to see his ideas accepted.[104]

The tension between the "soldiers' party" and Lloyd George was now so intense that the government seemed tottering on the brink of destruction. The Welshman's use of Wilson and French against the Robertson-Haig combination and his flirtation with unity of command were like waving a match in a gas-filled room. Robertson was aware of his potential to bring the government down if he desired. But he was under intense pressure from the King, Derby, Haig, and others to remain at his post.[105] Furthermore, his usually sound political instincts told him that the prime minister could not count on the support of a unified War Cabinet.[106] The moment of truth would surely come if Wilson and French, in opposition to the general staff, urged and a majority of the War Cabinet accepted the strengthening of Allenby's forces.

French and Wilson at once began to prepare their papers, with the latter working at Wellington's table at Horse Guards. Lloyd George's Palestinian venture was doomed from the outset because of the Admiralty's support of the general staff and Allenby's preposterous estimate of his requirements for a decisive victory over the Turks. General Liman von Sanders, a German officer with an intimate knowledge of Turkish affairs, prepared the following assessment of the conditions of the Turkish army in late 1917: "Through a series of errors the numerical strength of the combatant troops of the Turkish Army and their fighting efficiency has sunk to a level so low that it cannot be overlooked." By December 1917 there had been no fewer than 300,000 desertions.[107] Although von Sanders was not familiar with the strength of the Turkish forces in Palestine, Allenby was; and he informed Robertson that "the Turks are deserting freely, and their morale is reported to be poor."[108] Yet when he submitted his requirements to reach the Jaffa-Jerusalem line, he asked for thirteen additional divisions, which was almost three times the general staff's estimate, arguing that it might be possible for the enemy to concentrate twenty divisions (including two German divisions which were thought to be en route to Aleppo) against him.[109] As a matter of fact, the German Asiatic Corps that arrived in Palestine consisted of only three battalions of infantry and the rifle strength of the Turks on *all* of their active fronts was only 110,000 by the end of 1917![110] More ammunition was given the "Westerners" by Jellicoe, who stressed the shipping crisis and asserted that the "proposed large troop movement in the Mediterranean would be fraught with the most serious danger to our trade in home waters."[111]

Although French and Wilson found considerable merit in Lloyd George's plan to knock Turkey out of the war, they had no choice but to veto a major operation in that theater because of the appreciations put before them. If plans and preparations had been made earlier, a decisive victory might have been possible. But now, they both agreed, it was too late.

In other areas, the opinions of French and Wilson were music to Lloyd George's ears. French was highly critical of the high command's conduct of the war, devoting twenty of his twenty-six pages to an attack on Haig's and especially Robertson's leadership. The general staff, he argued, had previously been little more than Haig's cipher and had failed to give the government "independent" advice. He asserted correctly that German casualties in the Third Battle of Ypres had been exaggerated by the military authorities and opposed the high command's plan to continue the Flanders offensive in 1918. The "Westerners" talked of "gambles" by the "Easterners," but it was French's view that "the idea of staking the remainder of our resources on one desperate blow after another on the Western front has become much more of a 'gamble' than anything else we have undertaken in the war."

Wilson's paper was less strident in tone, but the high command still received its lumps at his hand. "It is no use throwing 'decisive numbers at the decisive time at the decisive place' at my head if the decisive numbers do not exist, if the decisive hour has not struck or if the decisive place is ill-chosen," he wrote. Both generals also expressed unbounded enthusiasm for the establishment of a supreme war council.[112]

Derby, the generals' staunch defender, Hankey, and Milner were almost certain that Wilson's and French's critical remarks would precipitate Robertson's resignation. As many held their breath, expecting the worst, events on the battlefield pushed this crisis into the background and dramatically strengthened Lloyd George's hand. On October 24, the Central Powers sprang their annual surprise on the Allies. This time their target was Italy. Supported by a barrage of artillery and poison-gas shells, an Austro-German force attacked at Tolmino on the eastern tip of the Italian Isonza. By nightfall panicky Italian soldiers were streaming to the rear. In a classic example of British understatement, General Delmé Radcliffe reported to London: "The real cause of the trouble was the determination of a portion of the troops to leave the field. . . . On the left flank of 2nd Army [which was composed of twenty-seven divisions] it was not a question of troops fighting moderately well, but of their fighting at all. There is still much to be explained in the main but it appears that Germans marched from Tolmino to Caporetto without any resistance whatever."[113]

Lloyd George acted decisively when the magnitude of the Caporetto disaster become clear to him. This stunning defeat in a theater that he had struggled to reinforce gave him new determination. The yoke of Calais was lifted from his shoulders. Now he had Robertson and Haig on the defensive.

After learning that the French were prepared to send assistance to Cadorna on the twenty-seventh, the prime minister ordered a reluctant Robertson to do likewise.[114] His instructions were dictated in an unusual location—the golf clubhouse at Walton Heath. With Italy still on his mind, Lloyd George then went out and played "appallingly badly."[115] Later that day, he and Hankey discussed the situation.

[They] recalled with satisfaction the Memo. we had prepared for the Rome Conference last January, insisting on [a] *defensive,* if not an offensive plan for allied cooperation on the Italian front, which had eventually resulted in arrangements for allied reinforcements being made. Ll. G. of course is furious. The Germans have struck at the weak link, just as he himself wanted to do on the very same spot;—a plan which the General Staff rejected with contempt. Meanwhile Haig's plan has completely failed, as Ll. G. always said it would.[116]

On October 29, with Robertson hurrying to Italy, Lloyd George repeated much of the same sentiments to the War Cabinet. "In a towering rage," he "was most sarcastic and abusive and tried to attribute the whole of the Italian trouble" to the general staff. Derby, after telling Balfour and Curzon that he was going to resign, stormed out of the cabinet room.[117] Threats of resignation, however, could no longer deter Lloyd George. Believing that he now had the right issue with which to take on the high command, he told

Hankey after the meeting that "he would not go on unless he obtained control of the war. He meant to take advantage of the present position to achieve this."[118]

With Robertson conveniently out of the way, Lloyd George moved rapidly to get the ministers behind his concept of a unified command which would, of course, serve to undermine the C.I.G.S.'s strategical dictatorship. On October 30, he told the War Cabinet that previous Allied conferences "were not really Conferences. They were only meetings of people with preconceived ideas who desired to find a formula which would reconcile them. In fact, Conferences were really a 'tailoring' operation at which different plans were stitched together." It was high time to create an inter-Allied general staff with advisory powers. "Its functions would not be to give orders. No Government could concede the right to issue orders, but their duties would be to examine the military situation of the Allies and of ourselves as a whole." For obvious reasons, Lloyd George insisted that the proposed Allied general staff must be independent of the national general staffs. Otherwise, he argued, "each representative would simply fight for the views of his own General Staff."[119]

Lloyd George then cleverly got Maurice to draft a constitution for an inter-Allied supreme war council with a permanent general staff. In Robertson's absence, Maurice had little choice and his actions served to commit the general staff to the arrangement.[120] Article 4 of this draft, which Lloyd George read to the War Cabinet on November 1, would divide Robertson's authority if it were accepted. It read as follows:

4. The military representatives of each nation will similarly receive from the Chief of the Imperial General Staff of his country proposals for future plans of operations, and the military representatives in consultation will then be charged with presenting to the Supreme Council a co-ordinate statement of those plans, together with proposals for the combined action of the Allies. *Should the plans received from the Chiefs of General Staffs not be, in the opinion of the military representatives, the best for ensuring such combined action it will be within their functions to suggest other proposals.*

Derby attempted to protect Robertson by pointing out "that the document had been drawn up at a very short notice, and that in the circumstances it would not represent considered military opinion. It was a basis for discussion only."[121] Derby's words made no impression for Lloyd George was now moving with a strong current. The Caporetto debacle undermined the general staff, and the French political and military leaders, cultivated by Lloyd George, appeared eager for a unified command. To make certain that the French stood with him, Lloyd George made it clear to Painlevé that any extension of the British front was dependent upon the creation of an inter-Allied war council.[122] On November 2, the War Cabinet accepted "in principle" an inter-Allied war council with Lloyd George's protégé Henry Wilson as the British military representative on the permanent Allied general staff.[123] A unified command was now almost a reality. It was the beginning of the end for Robertson.

Lloyd George, ever mindful of his precarious political position, had resorted to intrigue and fancy footwork rather than direct action in his attempts to control the high command. The scrupulous course of action would have been to give Haig a direct order to stop the Flanders offensive. Years later, in a conversation with Liddell Hart, he admitted, " 'Could I have stopped Passchendaele?' he thought of giving the order—'And Haig would have obeyed it; he would not have resigned. But they would have said I had spoilt the chance of a decisive success and of saving us from danger from the submarines.' Haig was sure he could reach Roulers, and so free Ostend."[124]

Yet the fact remains that long after it was obvious to Robertson, Lloyd George, and many of the ministers that Haig's grandiose strategic objectives were unobtainable in 1917, Lloyd George allowed the costly attack to continue. Hankey's view was that Lloyd George gave Haig free rein in October "knowing that the bad weather was preventing a big success" to discredit the "Westerners" and wrest control of the strategy for 1918–1919 from them.[125] If Hankey is correct, this is indeed a harsh indictment of the prime minister.

Another direct course of action would have been to strengthen his political position through a general election, which the War Cabinet had considered and rejected after Henderson's resignation over the Stockholm conference

Passchendaele: the mud of Flanders in October 1917.

affair. The advantage of an election from the War Cabinet's point of view would be that "the direct authority of the whole country might be behind the government in their future conduct of the war."[126] On the other hand, was it prudent to allow a national debate on the progress of the war? The military situation was far less promising than the public had been led to believe by the tightly censored press. The ministers feared that elements favoring a compromise peace might have their voices raised.[127] An additional concern for Lloyd George, if he called an election in response to Henderson's resignation, was that he might be placed in the awkward position of having to defend Haig and Robertson against attacks on Britain's military policy. After all, he was ultimately responsible for the successes and failures of the British army. In the spring and summer of 1917 he wanted all criticism of the high command to be confined to the cabinet room. After Churchill delivered very skillful attacks (which mirrored Lloyd George's own views) on British military policy in Parliament, he had braved violent Unionist opposition and appointed him minister of munitions in July to silence him. And, of course, there was always the chance that Lloyd George, who believed that he alone could bring the country through its great crisis, might be defeated and his placed taken by someone completely subservient to the military.

Dominant in the inner councils of the government, he was uncertain of his support in the country throughout 1917, especially if he were forced to fight an election over his "amateur" strategic views. Kenneth O. Morgan has astutely observed, "In the wider political arena, on the periphery, his standing was far more uncertain. At each level of political support, Lloyd George, so dominant elsewhere, was the most precarious of premiers. His downfall seemed imminent from week to week. Only extraordinary feats of political equilibrism appeared to keep his ministry in being."[128] In 1917 Labour's mood was uncertain; the Irish were angry; most of the Liberals were loyal to Asquith; and his Unionist backing depended upon his ability to retain the support of men such as Curzon, Balfour, Cecil, Long, Chamberlain, and Carson.

Still it is possible that Lloyd George underestimated his political strength. Asquith, who was under the circumstances the leader of the Opposition, suffered from a fatal weakness. "An Opposition in wartime might have been expected to claim that it could run the war better than the existing Government. This claim was so grotesque in view of what had gone before that Asquith never dared to make it,"[129] A. J. P. Taylor had acidly written. Also, many Unionists, despite their misgivings at times, saw no alternative to Lloyd George's dynamic leadership. Balfour spoke for them in a letter to his nephew, Cecil, who was a strong supporter of the generals:

> After all you must not expect perfection. You see Lloyd George's faults, and they are not difficult to see. But do you think he can be improved upon out of our existing material? Is there any one of his colleagues in the present War Cabinet you would like to see in his place? Do you believe there is in the House of Commons any genius on the Back Benches fit for the place? Do you think there is somewhere in the undistinguished mass of the general public, some unknown genius to whom, if we

could but find him, we might entrust the most difficult, and the most important, task with which British statesmanship has ever been confronted?[130]

NOTES

1. See Report of the Cabinet Committee on War Policy, August 10, 1917, CAB 27/6.

2. Robertson, "War Policy on West Front," July 19, 1917, W.P. 43, CAB 27/7.

3. War Cabinet (191A), July 20, 1917, CAB 23/13.

4. Hankey Diary, July 23, 1917, 1/3.

5. War Memoirs, 2:1380.

6. Cabinet Paper G.T. 1529 of July 24, 1917, CAB 24/41.

7. Allied Conference, July 26, 1917, CAB 28/2/I.C.-24(a).

8. Hankey Diary, July 26, 1917, 1/3.

9. Robertson to Kiggell, July 27, 1917, Kiggell MSS, IV/7, and Robertson to Haig, August 9, 1917, Haig MSS, no. 116.

10. Cabinet Paper G.T. 1549 of July 29, 1917, CAB 24/21.

11. Robertson to Milner, August 7, 1917, Milner, dep. 45.

12. See, for example, Wilson Diary, August 7, 1917.

13. See Allied Conference, August 7–8, 1917, CAB 28/2/I.C.-25, and Painlevé, *Comment J'ai Nommé Foch et Pétain*, p. 241.

14. See War Cabinet (200A), July 31, 1917, CAB 23/13, and Cabinet Paper G.T. 1641 of August 7, 1917, CAB 24/22.

15. Robertson to Haig, August 9, 1917, Haig MSS, no. 116.

16. Haig to Robertson, August 13, 1917, Haig MSS, no. 116.

17. War Cabinet (200), July 31, 1917, CAB 23/3.

18. Cabinet Paper G.T. 1621 of August 4, 1917, CAB 24/22.

19. Haig to E. H. Tennyson d'Eyncourt, August 27, 1917, Lloyd George MSS, F/44/3/20.

20. Wynne, however, refused to have his name associated with this volume because of Edmonds's editing which whitewashed general headquarters' mistakes.

21. Captain G.C. Wynne, "The Development of the German Defensive Battle in 1917, and its Influence on British Defence Tactics, Part I," *The Army Quarterly* 34 (April 1937): 23.

22. General Sir Hubert Gough, *The Fifth Army* (1931), pp. 214–15.

23. Cabinet Paper G.T. 1814 of August 21, 1917, CAB 24/24.

24. *The Australian Imperial Force in France, 1917*, 4:945.

25. Hankey Diary, August 15, 1917, 1/3. To neutralize the king, Lloyd George told him that if Haig's attack failed, it would "be his duty to appeal to the King, (whom he regards with himself as a Joint Trustee of the Nation), and demand some change of plan, such as that proposed in his Memorandum [Lloyd George's paper presented to the Cabinet Committee on War Policy in June]." Account of Lord Stamfordham's interview with Lloyd George, August 14, 1917, RA GV K1185/4.

26. Allied Conference, August 8, 1917, CAB 28/2/I.C.-25(e).

27. Esher to Haig, June 25, 1917, Haig MSS, no. 214 f.

28. Wilson Diary, August 17, 1917.

29. Ibid., August 22–24, 1917.

30. Ibid., August 23, 1917.

31. Ibid., 24–25 and 27, 1917.

32. Decypher of telegrams from Rennell Rodd, August 26, 1917, Lloyd George MSS, F/56/1/47.

33. See Hankey Diary, August 14, 1917, 1/3. On August 11, Lloyd George had sent Henry

Norman, a member of the Inventions Panel in the Ministry of Munitions, to Paris to talk with Painlevé about secret Austro-French negotiations in Switzerland. These discussions gave the impression that the Austrian emperor had "a profound desire . . . to have peace at the earliest possible moment." Further, Emperor Charles seemed "willing to go to almost any lengths [for peace], even if these involve a rupture with Germany." On August 14, the War Cabinet discussed these negotiations with no notes being taken. See Norman, "Memorandum for Prime Minister concerning certain conversations in Switzerland," August 15, 1917, Lloyd George MSS, F/160/1/13.

34. Hankey Diary, August 26, 1917, 1/3, and Lloyd George to Robertson, August 26, 1917, Lloyd George MSS, F/44/3/19.

35. Entry of August 27–28, 1917, *Lord Riddell's War Diary*, p. 267, and Note on Lord Stamfordham's interview with Lloyd George, August 14, 1917, RA GV K1185.

36. Robertson to Kiggell, August 9, 1917, Kiggell MSS, IV/9, and Robertson to Haig, August 9, 1917, Haig MSS, no. 116.

37. War Cabinet (225A), August 28, 1917, CAB 23/13. As a matter of fact, Robertson had never bothered to ascertain how long (about two weeks) it would take to transfer the guns. See Maurice to Kiggell, August 29, 1917, Kiggell MSS, V/119.

38. Cypher telegram to Rennell Rodd, August 29, 1917, Lloyd George MSS, F/56/1/48.

39. Hankey Diary, August 29, 1917, 1/3.

40. Cabinet Paper G.T. 1918 of August 31, 1917, CAB 24/25, Robertson to Maurice, August 31, 1917, Robertson MSS, I/25/4, and Cecil to Balfour, September 4, 1917, Balfour MSS, add. 49738.

41. Cabinet Paper G.T. 1928 of September 3, 1917, CAB 24/25.

42. Milner to Bonar Law, September 10, 1917, Milner, dep. 354.

43. Cabinet Paper G.T. 1931 of September 4, 1917, CAB 24/25.

44. War Cabinet (227C), September 4, 1917, CAB 23/13.

45. Anglo-French Conference, September 4, 1917, CAB 28/2/I.C.-26.

46. Hankey Diary, September 4, 1917, 1/3.

47. Ibid., September 5, 1917, 1/3.

48. Lloyd George to Miss Stevenson, September 13, 1917, quoted in Taylor, *My Darling Pussy*, p. 21.

49. Hankey Diary, September 14, 1917, 1/3.

50. See War Cabinet (210A), August 10, 1917, CAB 23/13.

51. See Robertson's correspondence with Munro and Allenby, August 1, 1917, and Allenby to Robertson, August 26, 1917, Robertson MSS, 1/32/65–66 and 70.

52. Hankey Diary, September 16, 1917, 1/3.

53. Ibid., September 18, 1917, 1/3.

54. Entry of September 22, 1917, *Lord Riddell's War Diary*, p. 275.

55. Bonar Law to Lloyd George, August 18, 1917, Lloyd George MSS, F/30/2/25.

56. Hankey Diary, September 21, 1917, 1/3.

57. Cabinet Paper G.T. 2143 of September 18, 1917, CAB 24/27.

58. Balfour, "Peace Negotiations," September 20, 1917, CAB 1/25.

59. Hankey Diary, September 22, 1917, 1/3.

60. Entry of August 27–28, 1917, *Lord Riddell's War Diary*, p. 267.

61. (Unsigned), "Notes on conversation with M. Briand," October 29, 1917, Lloyd George MSS, F/160/1/8.

62. War Cabinet (238A), September 24, 1917, CAB 23/16.

63. *Statistics of the Military Effort of the British Empire During the Great War 1914–1920*, p. 361. If Dominion losses are included, the figure was over 820,000. War Cabinet (300), December 17, 17917, M.P.C. 19, CAB 27/14.

64. Robertson to Haig, September 15, 1917, Robertson MSS, I/23/51.

65. See Marvin Swartz, *The Union of Democratic Control in British Politics during the First*

World War (1971), pp. 147–69, and Chris Wrigley, *David Lloyd George and the British Labour Movement: Peace and War* (1976), pp. 177–231.

66. Lloyd George to C. P. Scott, January 15, 1918, Lloyd George MSS, F/45/2/10.

67. War Cabinet (238A), September 24, 1917, CAB 23/13.

68. Lloyd George, *War Memoirs*, 2:1242, Hankey Diary, September 25, 1917, 1/3, and War Cabinet (239A), September 27, 1917, CAB 23/13.

69. See Hankey's notes of this conference, September 26, 1916, in CAB 1/25/16.

70. Hankey Diary, September 26, 1917, 1/3, and the prime minister's remarks in War Cabinet (240), September 27, 1917, CAB 23/4.

71. Lloyd George, *War Memoirs*, 2:1316.

72. Entries of September 21 and October 20, 1917, *Lord Riddell's War Diary*, pp. 274–75 and 285.

73. Balfour to Lloyd George, September 24, 1917, Lloyd George MSS, F/3/2/30, and Rothwell, *British War Aims and Peace Diplomacy*, pp. 106–7.

74. War Cabinet (239A), September 27, 1917, CAB 23/13. Walter S. Long, the secretary of state for the colonies, and a staunch defender of the high command, was quick to remind the War Cabinet that the interests of the dominions must not be ignored in any peace discussions with Germany. Cabinet Paper G.T. 2172 of September 29, 1917, CAB 24/27.

75. Hankey Diary, October 6, 1917, 1/3, Foreign Office to Sir William Wiseman, October 4, 1917, F.O. 800/201, and Balfour to Paris, Washington, Tokyo, Rome, Petrograd, the Hague, Berne, Madrid, Copenhagen, Stockholm, and Christiania, sent October 8, received October 9, 1917, F.O. 115/2264.

76. For German motives, see Fritz Fischer, *Germany's Aims in the First World War* (paperback edn., 1967).

77. *Times* (London), October 11, 1917.

78. Cabinet Committee on War Policy (17), September 24, 1917, CAB 27/6, and Robertson to Haig, September 24, 1917, Robertson MSS, 1/23/53.

79. Anglo-French Conference, September 25, 1917, CAB 28/2/I.C.-27(a).

80. Robertson to Haig, September 27, 1917, Robertson MSS, 1/23/54.

81. Cabinet Committee on War Policy (18), October 3, 1917, CAB 27/6.

82. Hankey Diary, October 6, 1917, 1/3.

83. Robertson to Allenby, October 5, 1917, Robertson MSS, 1/14/95.

84. Robertson to Haig, October 6, 1917, Haig MSS, no. 118.

85. Cabinet Committee on War Policy (20), October 8, 1917, CAB 27/6.

86. Cabinet Paper G.T. 2242 of October 9, 1917, CAB 24/28.

87. Cabinet Committee on War Policy (21), October 9 (misdated October 11), 1917, CAB 27/6.

88. Painlevé, *Comment J'ai Nommé Foch et Pétain*, pp. 244–46.

89. Wilson Dairy, October 5, 1917.

90. See Cabinet Papers G.T. 2243 of October 8, and 2242 of October 9, 1917, CAB 24/28.

91. Cabinet Committee on War Policy (21), October 9 (misdated October 11), 1917, CAB 27/6.

92. Rawlinson Diary, October 2, 1917, 1/9.

93. Major-General Sir John Davidson, *Haig: Master of the Field* (1953), p. 115, and Charteris, *Field-Marshal Haig*, pp. 280–82.

94. Haig Diary, October 18, 1917, no. 118, and Cabinet Paper G.T. 2243 of October 8, 1917, CAB 24/28.

95. Cabinet Paper G.T. 2243 of October 8, 1917, CAB 24/28.

96. War Cabinet (251), October 17, 1917, CAB 23/4.

97. General Erich von Ludendorff, *Ludendorff's Own Story: August 1914–November 1918*, 2 vols. (1919), 2:92.

98. War Cabinet (247A), October 20, 1917, CAB 23/13.

99. Hankey Diary, October 10, 1917, 1/3.

100. Ibid., October 11, 1917, 1/1.

101. War Cabinet (247B), October 11, 1917, CAB 23/13.

102. Robertson to Haig, October 11, 1917, Robertson MSS, I/23/58.

103. "Secretary's Notes of a Conversation at Chequers Court on Sunday, October 14, 1917," CAB 28/2/I.C.-28. Earlier Lloyd George had attempted to win President Wilson over to an inter-Allied council and staff. See Lloyd George to President Wilson, September 3, 1917, Lloyd George MSS, F/60/1/1, and Hankey Diary, August 28, 30 and September 3, 1917, 1/3.

104. *Supreme Command*, 2:705–6, and Hankey Diary, October 15, 1917, 1/3. Of the three ministers whom Hankey spoke to, Milner was apparently the most congenial to Lloyd George's strategic views. On October 17, he wrote Curzon expressing his opposition to "the policy of Hammer, Hammer, Hammer on the Western Front." Milner to Curzon, October 17, 1917, Curzon MSS, Eur. F 112/113. Five days after Lloyd George talked with Hankey he gave the following definition of military victory to Scott: "I asked what he meant by military victory," Scott writes. "Would the forcing back of the Germans to the line of the Meuse and evacuation of a great part of Belgium be victory? He said, Yes, it would, but there was no prospect of that next year." Entry of October 20, 1917, *Diaries of C. P. Scott*, p. 308.

105. See, for example, Haig to Robertson, October 11, 1917, Robertson MSS, I/23/57, and Haig Diary, October 11, 1917, no. 118.

106. Robertson to Haig, October 12, 1917, Robertson MSS, I/23/59.

107. Sanders, "Condition of the Turkish Army today," December 13, 1917, quoted in Liman von Sanders, *Five Years in Turkey* (1927), pp. 189–97.

108. Allenby to Robertson, October 19, 1917, Robertson MSS, I/32/73/1.

109. Allenby to Robertson, October 9, 1917, W.P. 52, CAB 27/8.

110. Captain Cyril Falls and Lieutenant-General Sir G. MacMunn, *Military Operations, Egypt and Palestine. From June 1917 to the End of the War*, vol. 2, part I, p. 27, and Cabinet Committee on Man-Power (1), December 10, 1917, CAB 27/14.

111. Jellicoe, "Reinforcement of the Army in Palestine," October 13, 1917, CAB 27/8, and Cabinet Paper G.T. 2250 of October 9, 1917, CAB 24/28.

112. French, "The Present State of the War, the Future Prospects, and Future Action to be Taken," October 20, 1917, W.P. 60, and Wilson, "The Present State of the War, The Future Prospects, and Future Action to be Taken," October 20, 1917, W.P. 61, CAB 27/8.

113. Cabinet Paper G.T. 2438 of October 27, 1917, CAB 24/30.

114. Robertson to Lloyd George and Lloyd George to Robertson, October 27, 1917, Lloyd George MSS, F/44/3/27–28.

115. Hankey Diary, October 27, 1917, 1/3.

116. Ibid.

117. See Derby to Haig, October 29, 1917 (not sent), Derby MSS, 920 (17), and War Cabinet (259), October 29, 1917, CAB 23/4.

118. Hankey Diary, October 29, 1917, 1/3.

119. War Cabinet (259A), October 30, 1917, CAB 23/13.

120. Hankey Diary, October 31, 1917, 1/3.

121. Author's italics. War Cabinet (262), November 1, 1917, CAB 23/4. Also see Derby to Lloyd George, October 31, 1917, Lloyd George MSS, F/14/4/75.

122. See Lloyd George to Painlevé, October 30, 1917, War Cabinet (259A), October 30, 1917, CAB 23/13.

123. War Cabinet (263), November 2, 1917, CAB 23/4. At one time it appears the ministers were prepared to allow Robertson to become the British permanent military representative if he relinquished his position as C.I.G.S. See Maurice to Delmé Radcliffe, November 31, 1917, Robertson MSS, I/14/96/1.

124. "Talk with Lloyd George at Criccieth," September 24, 1932, Liddell Hart MSS, 11/1932/42c.

125. Hankey Diary, October 21, 1917, 1/3.
126. War Cabinet (212), August 11, 1917, CAB 23/3.
127. Ibid.
128. Kenneth O. Morgan, *Lloyd George*. Introduction by A. J. P. Taylor (1974), pp. 113–14.
129. A. J. P. Taylor, *Essays in British History* (paperback edn., 1976), p. 245.
130. Balfour to Cecil, September 12, 1917, Balfour MSS, Add. 49738.

10

The Supreme War Council and British Military Plans for 1918

WITH the backing of the War Cabinet, Lloyd George left London on November 3 on one of his most crucial missions of the war. The task facing him was formidable and the stakes were high. If he failed, he knew that Haig and Robertson wanted to continue the Flanders offensive next year, which might break the spirit of the British Expeditionary Force. Lloyd George marched under the banner of "supreme command," but his real purpose was to take the war away from the "Westerners," who had been in control since late 1915. He would use the artichoke method, stripping away one leaf of the general staff's authority at a time. With his man Wilson as a member of the Allied general staff, he hoped to have two sets of military opinion from which to select. Never again would he occupy the impossible position he had found himself in during the Passchendaele debate. Then it had been his amateur strategy against the monolithic military bloc, with Haig, Robertson, and Jellicoe all speaking with one voice.

In addition to Wilson, he counted as his chief allies Milner, Smuts, and the zealous imperialist spokesman and military-affairs busybody Leopold Amery. During the following months these men were to play the key role in attempting to impose a strategy on the army that had the immediate objective of advancing imperial interests rather than the defeat of the German army, which they did not think possible in 1918. Nothing less than the redeployment of part of the British army outside of France was contemplated. As Milner put it to Wilson, "We are now threatened by Pétain's latest proposal [extension of British line], with the *stereotyping* of our worse source of weakness, *the permanent* immobilisation of seven-eighths of our strength and our interest in part of France, gaining no additional control, having nothing up our sleeve for a blow elsewhere."[1] The creation of the Supreme War Council, even if dominated by Britain, however, would not in itself give British strategy flexibility. "To secure the necessary power and influence, it is essential, first of all," Amery argued:

that those representatives [on S.W.C.] should be liberated from a rigid strategy which regards only one small section of the Allied front as a serious theatre of war and treats all the rest of the front as of no real consequence. Such a strategy leaves our representatives in any Allied Conference without freedom of choice and therefore without influence. Our whole position relative to the French would be altered if, even for the sake of argument alone, we discussed the possibility of moving 20 of our divisions elsewhere, and made them realise that those divisions are really ours to use as we like.[2]

Amery's memorandum, pretentiously entitled "The Turning Point of the War," was given to Maurice by Lloyd George on the train to Paris. Maurice countered with the familiar argument of the German advantage of interior lines.[3] Amery, Milner, Lloyd George, and others, however, no longer bought this argument because they believed that the deterioration of German rails and engines had limited German mobility.[4] In addition to the limitations placed on British freedom by coalition warfare, a fatal weakness of this attempt to give British arms flexibility was that Germany, by taking the initiative in 1918, might dictate to Britain where she must concentrate her military power.

The only member of the War Cabinet to accompany Lloyd George was Smuts, whom Lloyd George had chosen, in part, to bring him more solidly into the anti-"Western" camp. In Paris, Lloyd George took advantage of a meeting with General Pershing, the commander in chief of the American Expeditionary Force, to lobby for unity of command. Then he was quickly on to Italy. Originally the Italians had suggested Nervi rather than Rapallo for the crucial inter-Allied conference, which Hankey thought perfect "for the comic papers in the present state of Italian "nerves!"[4]

At Rapallo an angry and defensive Robertson was waiting. He had been at Cadorna's headquarters when Maurice secretly cabled him of Lloyd George's intentions and he correctly saw in the proposed arrangement an attempt to diminish his authority. With his enemy Wilson on the Allied general staff, he might be responsible for executing military plans with which he disagreed and had played no role in formulating. The permanent military representatives, he later wrote, "were in the happy position of the man who can say, 'Heads I win, tails you lose.' "[5] Convinced that Derby had let the army down in his absence, he believed that he could "make it more or less all right" when the prime minister came up against him.[6] Hankey, however, took the rebellious Wully aside and bluntly told him that it was futile to resist because the War Cabinet had given Lloyd George a free hand to create the Supreme War Council.

On November 7, in the New Casino Hotel, the Allied ministers discussed a draft of the proposed inter-Allied war council which had been accepted by Smuts and Franklin-Bouillon the previous evening. Painlevé, in his high, piping voice, made the awkward suggestion that Foch, the chief of the French general staff, should become the French permanent military representative on the Allied general staff. If this were done, Robertson would clearly be the logical British permanent military representative as well as C.I.G.S. Lloyd George, however, succeeded in forcing Foch to relinquish his position in the French ministry of war. The first formal meeting of the Supreme War Council that afternoon represented a considerable triumph for the prime minister. Completely outmaneuvered, Robertson's rage was something to behold. When the Allied representatives first broached the subject of unity of command in the West, he rose from his seat and walked out, stopping to tell Hankey, "I wash my hands of this business."[7]

Lloyd George was quick to exploit the shattered defenses of the military in other ways. In opposition to Haig, who argued that the best way to assist the Italians was to continue his Flanders operations, the prime minister ordered two more British divisions to leave for Italy; ultimately, 200,000 Anglo-French troops were sent south to assist the shell-shocked Italians, with the front stabilizing along the Piave river.

Other dramatic events in early November served to erode the authority of the British high command. Allenby, without any reinforcements from France, broke through the Turkish defenses on the Gaza-Beersheba line, prying open the gate to the Holy City. On the same day, November 7, that Allenby finished his successful battle, the Bolsheviks completed their overthrow of the feeble provisional government by storming the Winter Palace. With Russia in Bolshevik hands, Haig's desire to launch yet another big attack in the West before the Americans arrived in force seemed madness.

Meanwhile, Haig finally called a halt to the last and bloodiest phase of his offensive with the capture of the village of Passchendaele, which had been reduced to a heap of rubble. Haig's optimism had had a boomerang effect. None of the grand strategic objectives which he had carefully outlined to the civilians to gain their support had been obtained. A few miles of enemy territory had been captured, but in the process the British army had been badly battered, losing perhaps three men for every two of the enemy.[8] The last day of the battle, November 10, was representative of Haig's rigid and costly tactics, with 3,000 men being killed and 7,000 wounded.

The ministers' loss of faith in Haig, however, was not shared by the general public because the press had touted every British advance as a "victory" over the enemy. Furthermore, many newspapers continued to argue that the war must be left in the hands of the professional soldier. The *Morning Post* and the *National Review* were especially outspoken in this respect, and Lloyd George believed that the papers of Gwynne and Leo Maxse were kept abreast of his differences with Robertson by the C.I.G.S. himself. During the secret debate over guns for Italy, Maxse praised Robertson and warned against "gambling" on the part of the civilians. The "supreme direction of the war," he blustered, must "remain in the hands of the soldiers, and in theirs alone."[9] Leading articles by Gwynne, like the "The Amateur and the Soldiers" and "Political Strategy," also hammered away at civilian meddling in strategy in September and October.[10] Believing that these editorial opinions were inspired by the general staff, Lloyd George attempted to take advantage of the Italian setback to swing the press in his direction; he and his private secretary, William Sutherland, attempted to work up a press campaign against the general staff's strategy and for his concept of a supreme war council in late October and early November.[11] "If politicians and civilians are to have nothing to say about the conduct of the war," Scott's *Manchester Guardian* proclaimed on November 1, "then the nation is being wagged from its least intelligent end, and that surely is not conducive to success." As for the German coup in Italy, the *Evening Standard,* asserted on October 30, "We believe that there were men in English statesmanship who saw all this, who had a true perception of the moral as well as the material things at stake, and who were for sending all possible help to Cadorna. But despite the overwhelming case in favour of such a plan it did not meet with military support." The *Daily Chronicle* called for an inter-Allied war council, and the *Observer* chimed in with "SEE IT WHOLE."[12] The *Morning Post's* sentiment, "TALK LESS TRASH!,"[13] was generally drowned out in the din raised in the London press for a single-front approach to the war. Even papers such as the *Star* and *Daily News,* which previously had given unbending support to the military, approved of a central organization to direct Allied military efforts.[14] It appeared that Lloyd George might be right when he had admonished Gwynne for his support of the generals against the civilians before he left for Rapallo. "I too have an army—the people,"[15] he blustered. To silence Haig and Robertson, he criticized them to their face for using the press against him. Never mind that it was, in Hankey's words, "a case of the pot calling the kettle black."[16]

Buoyed by the apparent success of his press campaign, Lloyd George attempted to deliver a knock-out blow to the British high command at a luncheon in the old banquet hall of the French Ministry of War attended by deputies and senators at which Painlevé announced the creation of the Supreme War Council. It was clearly not an impulsive act; an earlier speech drafted by Smuts was torn up and Lloyd George and Hankey spent hours on the one that he delivered. The result was a speech that he had been bursting at the seams to give since his failure to redirect Allied strategy during the last days of Asquith's ministry.

In what quickly became his most controversial speech of his wartime premiership, Lloyd George reopened old wounds, especially the defeat of Serbia and Rumania. His central theme was that previous inter-Allied conferences had resulted in "a collection of completely independent schemes pieced together. Stitching is not strategy. So it came to pass that when these plans were worked out in the terrible realities of war, the stitches came out and disintegration was complete." As each Allied general pursued his own offensive plan, the Germans with their centralized direction of the war won victory after victory by striking at the vulnerable points in the Allied defenses. To be sure, the Allies had had their victories. But, as Lloyd George noted in an especially sharp jab at the "Westerners": "When I look at the appalling casualty lists, I sometimes wish it had not been necessary to win so many."

In an obvious comparison between the results of Haig's Flanders operation and the Austro-German breakthrough at Caporetto, he said:

> When we advance a kilometre into the enemy's lines, snatch a small shattered village [Passchendaele] out of his cruel grip, capture a few hundreds of his soldiers, we shout with unfeigned joy. And rightly so, for it is

the symbol of our superiority over a boastful foe and a sure guarantee that in the end we can and shall win.

But what if we had advanced 50 kilometres beyond his lines and made 200,000 of his soldiers prisoners and taken 2,500 of his guns, with enormous quantities of ammunition and stores? What print would we have for our headlines.

Significantly Lloyd George told his countrymen what he had been saying in private. "Personally I had made up my mind that, unless some change were effected, I could no longer remain responsible for a war direction doomed to disaster for lack of unity."[17]

Before making his speech, Lloyd George had sent Smuts back to London to create a favorable press; and the *Daily Telegraph, Evening Standard, Observer, Daily Chronicle,*and *Manchester Guardian* continued their support of his actions. But his blast against the generals at Paris proved to be a serious political error because the Supreme War Council was now linked (quite correctly) to his conflict with the high command over the higher strategy of the war. There was even concern that Haig and Robertson might be eased out. On the day before Lloyd George delivered his Paris speech a political correspondent in the *Sunday Times* had started tongues wagging with his suggestion that the formation of the Supreme War Council was the prelude to new leadership on the western front and in the general staff.

Thus Lloyd George found himself in the midst of a political crisis which was largely of his own making when his train pulled in at Charing Cross on the afternoon of November 13. The *Times* and the *Daily Mail,* desperately afraid that the "Old Gang" might be returned to power if Lloyd George faltered, were both somewhat circumspect in their comments. The Supreme War Council was supported in principle, but Lloyd George was warned that he must not use it to meddle in strategy. Other papers were unrestrained in their opposition. The *Daily News* accused Lloyd George of attempting to make himself a "military dictator"; the *Nation* wrote of "THE IMPOSSIBILITY OF MR. GEORGE"; The *Star* cried "HANDS OFF THE BRITISH ARMY!"; and the *Spectator* argued that the "risks run by having at the head of affairs a man capable of such levity, such irresponsbility, such recklessness, such injustice, are beyond endurance."[18] The *Globe, Morning Post,* and *Westminster Gazette* joined in the chorus of opposition.

Indignation over Lloyd George's challenge of the generals' previous conduct of the war in his Paris speech boiled up in Parliament. Nothing else was being discussed in the lobby. When Asquith rose on the thirteenth to ask Bonar Law if the prime minister were prepared to make a statement regarding "the very serious matters touched on in his recent speech in Paris," cheering erupted on both sides of the chamber. The debate quickly centered on the role and authority of the permanent military representatives. Would they usurp the functions and powers of the general staffs of the Allies?

Robertson, who had preceded the prime minister to London, had been busy. He believed that he had made a serious mistake in not forcing a governmental crisis over Lloyd George's use of Wilson and French.[19] Now, faced with the Italian debacle and the Allied decision at Rapallo, he was fighting an uphill battle to protect his position. But, encouraged by Haig, he was determined to resist the "new Soviet."[20] He voiced his opposition to Asquith, Colonel House, Woodrow Wilson's alter ego and special diplomatic agent, General Tasker H. Bliss, the American chief of staff and soon to be appointed permanent military representative on the Allied general staff, and the generals' favorite military correspondent, Repington.[21] He also sounded the tocsin in the War Office, receiving the support of Derby and the Army Council.

If the Army Council had its way, Wilson would be gagged. On November 12, the Army Council decided to inform the War Cabinet that it "presumed that the technical advice given by the British Military Representative will be given on behalf of the Army Council, and that he will be subject to the authority of, and receive his instructions from, the Army Council."[22]

Lloyd George's response to the rising criticism was to read the terms of the Rapallo agreement among France, Italy, and Britain to the House of Commons on November 14. Whatever his long-range plans, he was protected for the present from the emotional charge of handing the British army over to foreigners because from the very first he had made it clear that the Supreme War Council was to be an advisory body with executive authority firmly in the hands of the respective national governments. The sticky point in the new machinery was the relationship between Robertson and Wilson. The Rapallo agreement gave the Supreme War Council the power to review the campaign plans prepared by the national general staffs and change them if necessary. Did this, then, pit the British military representative against the C.I.G.S.? Rather than unity of control, would not this create duality of military counsel? The next day the *Globe* warned: "THE GENESIS OF AN UNWORKABLE SCHEME. THE DISESTABLISHMENT OF THE GENERAL STAFF." And Robertson wrote Derby: "All military advice to the Supreme Council should remain in the hands of the responsible military advisers of the respective governments. Dual advice can only lead to delay, friction, weakening of responsibility and lack of confidence amongst the troops."[23] In his anxiety to control Haig and Robertson, Lloyd George, as he had at Calais, found himself defending a faulty system of unifying Allied military policy.

During the next few days the tug of war between Lloyd George and the War Office over the control of "Ugly" Wilson intensified. Faced with his gravest political crisis to date, Lloyd George at first could not make up his mind whether to stand firm or retreat. At first the War Cabinet stood firm, informing the Army Council on November 16 that even though Wilson was clearly "subject to the authority of the Army Council. . . . it should be understood that the British Permanent Military Representative will have unfettered discretion as to the advice he offers."[24] On November 18, however, he received a letter from Curzon that warned him that Chamberlain, who had just returned from a visit with Haig, and many other Conservatives could not support the government unless they were given reassuring answers in Parliament on the charge that Lloyd George was attempting to divide Robertson's powers.[25] This disturbing news, along with steady pressure from Derby, forced Lloyd George to give ground on the question of the powers and responsibilities of Wilson, a matter which the Rapallo agreement had almost nothing concrete to say. To pin Lloyd George down, Derby prepared a record of Lloyd George's comments in their conversation of the seventeenth and returned it to him on the eighteenth. After Lloyd George made a few deletions and additions, it read as follows:

(1). All proposals to be discussed at a Supreme General Council will be initiated by the respective Governments, and will not be put before the Supreme Council until, in our case, the War Cabinet has had it in front of them, and heard the opinion of the C.I.G.S. on the proposal.

(2). The Allied Staff shall have no power of initiation of independent proposals unless ordered to do so by the Supreme Council themselves, and any such proposals they may wish to make follow the same procedure as in (1).

(3). The C.I.G.S. will accompany you to any meetings of the Supreme Council whenever a decision has to be arrived at on military matters.

(4). The Allied General Staff will give their advice as a whole, and not as individuals.[26]

Lloyd George initialed every point in this document, but he did not return it to Derby. Instead, he wrote him on the twenty-sixth, noting that he was in "substantial agreement" with the points in his letter and that he was willing for Robertson, who would remain the "official" adviser to the War Cabinet, to accompany him to all Supreme War Council meetings. On the other hand, he resisted a precise definition of Wilson's role which would make him an extension of the War Office. "It would be a mistake to lay too much emphasis on details at the beginning,"[27] he wrote. Four days earlier, in fact, Wilson had told the prime minister that he would send his "reports to him & not to anyone else."[28]

What had happened between November 18 and 26 was that Lloyd George had scored a great personal triumph over his critics. On November 19, Lloyd George made one of his rare appearances in Parliament for a full-dress debate with Asquith, who, in support of the generals, was making his first serious attack on Lloyd George's leadership. In a packed and excited House, the Welsh Wizard was in splendid form. Starting slowly, he built toward a rhetorical climax with passion and gesticulations. Even so critical an observer as Repington had to admit that "the whole House rose to him and rocked with joy."[29]

Lloyd George's speech, however, was little related to his previous actions or the chief criticisms of the Rapallo arrangement. Denying any previous interference with the general staff's strategy, he praised the generals, emphasized his support of the army, and claimed that he had only attempted to wake up the nation with his Paris speech. His motive in pushing the Supreme War Council was the "co-ordination" of Allied plans, not the diminishing of Robertson's authority or the creation of a generalissimo.[30] What had happened, one might ask, to the Lloyd George who had delivered the blistering attack in Paris against the "Westerners"?

Both Robertson and Lloyd George were generally satisfied with the outcome of the row over the Supreme War Council. To Lloyd George's great relief, he had avoided a division in the House and escaped careful scrutiny of Wilson's and Robertson's relationship. On the other hand, Robertson had reason to be satisfied. Although Lloyd George had indicated in his Paris speech that he wanted the Supreme War Council to have real power, he had been forced, as Robertson wrote Haig, "to say that it would have practically no power at all."[31] Given the right to attend the Supreme War Council, Wully hoped to be able to "keep things on right lines."[32] The troublesome issue that lay ahead was Wilson's position as co-adviser to the Supreme War Council. With the backing of the prime minister, would he stay in his place? Or would he allow himself to be used against the general staff?

In the conflict over strategy, the high command appeared to have the upper hand immediately after Lloyd George's success in Parliament because of developments on the western front. Both Robertson and Haig continued to resist a defensive strategy in 1918, and their advice received what appeared to be a resounding vote of confidence on November 20. At twilight the ground shook at Cambrai as 1,000 guns opened up. Then, without a sustained artillery barrage, a force of approximately 380 tanks, supported by a swarm of aircraft overhead, rolled over the vast thicket of German barbed wire, completely catching the enemy off balance. With relatively few casualties, the British pushed the Germans back from three to four miles on a six-mile front, and the formidable Hindenburg Line was pierced. Unfortunately, this great tank offensive, which had been originally planned as a gigantic raid, was inadequately supported. According to the historian's prejudices, the necessary reserves had been either ordered to Italy by Lloyd George or used up in the last and futile phase of Haig's Flanders offensive. The cavalry force, which Haig had stubbornly maintained in his rear to exploit a breakthrough, was useless. The two cavalry divisions brought up to gallop through the broken lines refused to go forward. Although their commander in chief did not realize that horse soldiers did not belong on the same battlefield with trenches and machine guns, the cavalry officers, who were in no mood for Light Brigade heroics, did. Haig's comment was, "They must be blind."[33]

At first euphoria reigned in the corridors of the War Office. Indeed, the attack had been designed, in part, to restore the prestige of the British army. The War Office encouraged the ringing of church bells and the displaying of flags to celebrate the most spectacular advance of the war for Haig's army. In one day the British had advanced almost as far as they had in 100 days of heavy fighting in Flanders where tanks were ineffective.

The news from Cambrai could not have come at a better time for the embattled Robertson. He immediately moved without success to halt the flow of British troops to Italy and emphasized that the Third Army's success had been partly due to the concentration of German reserves at Ypres.[34] He also gave support to Haig's view that the enemy was in a bad way. When the War Cabinet held a preliminary discussion of future military policy, he argued that "the position of the Germans was worse than we were sometimes inclined to think. . . . On the whole, it was dificult to explain the cessation of the offensive against Roumania and the failure to exploit the Italian *débâcle* except on the ground of inactivity. . . . [he] thought that Germany's military power was probably a good deal less and the condition of the Austrian armies a good deal worse than we had thought to be the case."[35] Robertson had just advised the War Cabinet that Haig should continue his attacks next year to keep the initiative in the hands of the Allies. Otherwise the enemy would attack "at a time and place of his own choosing—that is, in circumstances in which the chances of victory are in his favour."[36] Lloyd George, of course, took a dim view of this advice. Given the existing balance of forces in the West, he believed it suicidal for either side to launch massive attacks in 1918. After all, the Allies, often enjoying a 5 to 3 superiority in rifles, had been stymied since 1914. If the German high command were prepared to throw their last reserves against Allied breastworks bristling with machine guns, so much the better. Significantly, Haig himself believed that the Germans would be foolish to launch an all-out attack in 1918. On December 16, he told Charteris "that the correct strategy for them [the Germans] is to play a waiting game and not commit themselves to a big attack."[37]

Lloyd George's best hope of restraining Haig and Robertson was the new Supreme War Council and in late November he journeyed to Versailles to establish this new body on a firm footing. He was alarmed to discover that France's new premier, the fierce-tempered Clemenceau, was out to torpedo the arrangement at Rapallo by making Foch chief of staff as well as permanent military representative. "This would mean Robertson and Haig," an unhappy Wilson recorded in his diary, "and we should be where we have been all along."[38] Lloyd George met this challenge head on by threatening to return to London immediately if Foch held both positions. Clemenceau then agreed to send General Maxime Weygand to Versailles as the French permanent military representative, with Foch moving to the French ministry of war as chief of staff. This compromise, however, violated Lloyd George's principle that the permanent military representatives should be independent of the national general staffs. Weygand was certain to be Foch's mouthpiece. "He is my doormat," Foch once commented, "I use him to wipe my boots on."[39] Wilson, in fact, was now the only permanent military representative expected to be truly independent of his general staff. General Bliss, the American permanent military representative, had just stepped down as chief of staff because he had reached the age limit; and Cadorna, the Italian permanent military representative was for all practical purposes an extension of the Italian general staff. It did not take Wilson long to realize his weak position. "I have come to the following conclusions: That Clemenceau intends to direct the whole war by using Foch to work with Robertson, and then by sending Weygand here to impose his (Clemenceau's) will on Versailles by Foch through Weygand."[40]

Despite Clemenceau's lukewarm attitude toward the Supreme War Council, Lloyd George achieved his major objective: permanent military representatives were instructed to examine the military situation as a whole and make recommendations about the operations to be undertaken in 1918.[41] Before these instructions were issued, Lloyd George emphasized that the war had become one of exhaustion and might be decided by endurance rather than a military decision. In short, conserving Allied manpower might be the key to success.

While Lloyd George lobbied for a defensive posture at Versailles, events at Cambrai decided the issue. The British had found it hard going after their initial thrust, attempting to hold on to a dangerous salient with soldiers who had fought without rest since the twentieth. On November 30, the Germans penetrated the British southern flank and the Third Army was sent reeling back. In only two days the Germans recaptured much of the territory they had lost and only the spirited stand of the Guards Division prevented a greater disaster. With the termination of the Battle of Cambrai on December 3, "the British and the Germans resembled two tired boxers, neither of whom was capable of doing the other any serious harm."[42] Haig collected his army commanders and told them that, in all likelihood, the British army would assume a defensive position during the next few months. On December 13, the permanent military representatives, in their first joint note, recommended that a "co-ordinated system of defence from the North Sea to the Adriatic must be adopted by the Allies."[43] And on December 19, Robertson assured the War Cabinet that "it was fully realised by Sir Douglas Haig that we must act on the defence for some time to come, and he had no offensive plans in mind at present."[44]

The end of the 1917 campaign found the British army in a bad way. In mid-December it was described thusly:

> The British Armies in France have been engaged practically continuously since last April in exhausting offensive operations involving considerable wastage and great fatigue. Every division has been engaged in battle several times and while on defensive fronts, necessarily thinly held during the operations, they have also had heavy work. The Artillery personnel particularly has been engaged almost continuously in operations demanding their utmost efforts night and day during the above period.
>
> The whole Army is therefore at present much exhausted and much reduced in strength. Many divisions in the line urgently require relief, while the great majority of those for the first time being in reserve are neither sufficiently rested to relieve them nor really fit to be thrown into a fight to meet an emergency. . . . of the divisions at present in reserve behind the British front, only those belonging to the Australian and Canadian Corps are fit for duty in front line. . . .[45]

The accuracy of this description would appear to be beyond dispute, for the author was none other than Haig himself. In this same document, Haig commented on the state of disrepair of British defenses. Constantly on the attack, the British had neither the men nor the time to look after their fortifications. Although not touched upon directly by Haig, the nerve of his forces was beginning to falter. Cases of drunkenness, desertion, and psychological disorders were increasing. Men home from the front frequently spoke with great bitterness about "the waste of life during the continued hammerings against the Ypres Ridge."[46]

When Parliament heard an exaggerated account of the successful German counterattack at Cambrai from one of its members, there was a reaction bordering on panic. The War Cabinet was hardly less disturbed as it gradually learned of the magnitude of the setback. Haig was on the spot as never before. When the War Cabinet met on the fifth, pointed questions were put to the military authorities. Why the delay in forwarding the news of the German breakthrough on the thirtieth? "If we had inflicted a corresponding reverse on the enemy," one minister harrumphed, "the news of our success would have been communicated within a few hours." The fact that Maurice had given a full and accurate account of the disaster on the third to the War Cabinet did not convince Lloyd George and other ministers that general headquarters had been frank in its first reports of the German attack. Also, how had the Third Army been caught so completely by surprise when the British had air superiority? Furthermore, how was such a vigorous German offensive, their first in the West since Verdun, possible? After all, the military authorities had consistently emphasized the "weakness and deterioration" of the enemy.[47]

With the stench of failure in everyone's nostrils, Lloyd George considered shaking up the high command. With some justification, he believed that Haig had misused the British army and that the country could no longer afford his leadership. Moreover, he was furious with the army's machinations during the establishment of the Supreme War Council. (No matter that many of the criticisms of the actual machinery were legitimate.) On December 1, he vented his rage to Esher. Speaking with "great bitterness and vehemence," he complained "of the 'intrigues' of the Army" against the civil authorities. "His means of information are varied and go deep into the camp of his opponents," Esher wrote Haig. "Of this there was ample proof from what he said to me."[48]

Lloyd George's case against Robertson seemed even stronger. After the permanent military representatives had been instructed by the Allied ministers to examine and report on the military situation, the army council had renewed its efforts to tie Wilson completely to the War Office. On December 7, Wilson had been instructed to forward all proposals he planned to make at the Supreme War Council to the Army Council for its review.[49] A far more serious matter was Robertson's unscrupulous efforts to thwart Lloyd George's Palestinian scheme. On December 11, without any of the reinforcements that he had requested, Allenby made a triumphant entry into Jerusalem. On the previous day, Lloyd George had discovered to his amazement that the Turks now had a rifle strength of 21,000 in Palestine. On the other hand, the British had 95,812 rifles and 14,249 sabres in Egypt and Palestine.[50] Yet, he was quick to remember, Allenby had requested thirteen more divisions and a total force of almost half a million men to take Jerusalem.[51] Robertson's guerrilla action against the Supreme War Council was bad enough. But his "cooking" of the advice received by the War Cabinet was clearly intolerable. No modern prime minister would or should tolerate such conduct.

On the afternoon of December 11, Lloyd George approached Derby about the removal of Haig and Robertson from their posts. Cambrai and Allenby's capture of the Holy City were used as a noose to hang them. Stopping short of sacking his generals, the prime minister suggested to Derby that Haig be given the Joffre treatment by appointing him generalissimo of all British forces. Robertson would be cast aside by giving him an equally high-sounding but unimportant assignment. Derby, however, refused to abandon Haig and Robertson. If they were pushed aside, he hinted that he would resign.[52] This would almost certainly precipitate the political crisis which Lloyd George hoped to avoid through his face-saving maneuver. Unable to gain the support of Derby, Lloyd George had to be satisfied for the moment with the secretary of state for war's willingness to pressure Haig to dismiss his most important subordinates; Charteris, his myopic chief of intelligence, being the primary target. In this Derby had the wholehearted support of Robertson, who suggested to Haig that he also dismiss Lieutenant-General R. C. Maxwell, a move that he had urged Haig to make as early as August. Eventually, Derby included Kiggell, Haig's chief of staff, whom he considered a "tired man," in this purge.[53] Lloyd George is sometimes given credit for these dismissals, but the War Office, it would appear, was just as interested, if not more so, in surrounding Haig with new men. One advantage might be to still the criticism of the army that was surfacing in the press after Cambrai.

On November 12, in the opening stages of the political crisis over the Supreme War Council, Northcliffe had returned from his mission to America to be greeted by a letter from Repington. "Welcome home! You have returned to find an Allied Staff created at Paris contrary to the desires of our leading soldiers at home and abroad, and contrary to the public interest."[54] The arrival of the Great Beast alarmed Lloyd George, and he immediately attempted to neutralize him by offering him the head of an air ministry when it was created. Northcliffe, however, publicly rejected the offer, arguing that it might gag him. His independence retained, Northcliffe, however, did not use his influence to support the army against the prime minister. The Cambrai failure was apparently decisive in his shift of allegiances. On December 12, the *Times* demanded an inquiry into the failure of the Third Army and "the prompt removal of every blunderer." At the same time Sassoon was bluntly informed by Northcliffe, "There is the memory of a dead man or the knowledge of a missing or wounded man in every house. Outside the War Office I doubt whether the Higher Command has any supporters whatever."[55] As important as Northcliffe's support was to Lloyd George, it should not be exaggerated. In fact, with some calling Northcliffe's papers the "Georgecliffe Press," his support at times proved to be a serious liability.

The climate of mutual suspicion and distrust between the government and the army, which had never been worse, was an important element in the crucial discussions about manpower which began in earnest in December. Throughout 1917, the army had been unable to persuade the government to extract all of the men it demanded from civil life and had been forced to comb out category "A" men (men fit for combat) from the home forces and administrative units in France. This had not been accomplished without sparks flying between the War Office and general headquarters. Robertson was angered by the implication that he was keeping soldiers at home that Haig might use; furthermore, he could not understand Kiggell's reluctance to make better use of all the men available in France. On August 17, he suggested to Haig that he "immediately" take steps to "scrape up" combat soldiers behind his front (some 41,000 were found from the administrative units). He also pointedly informed Haig that everything possible was being done to send him men from the home service divisions.[56]

On the day the Cambrai fighting died down, the Army Council, instructed by the prime minister to review the manpower situation which had been exacerbated by the gigantic losses suffered by the British army in 1917, prepared a memorandum which emphasized the dire necessity of immediately replacing Haig's losses and providing for his wastage in 1918. If this were not done, the Army Council warned, "the war may well be lost" because "of the probable release of enemy forces on the Russian front."[57]

Since the high command had just ignored Russia's collapse and advocated a continuation of the offensive, many ministers tended to believe that the Army Council was crying wolf. In the War Cabinet, with Lloyd George absent, it was

> pointed out that the War Office view of the military situation in France, as submitted to the War Cabinet, had undergone a complete change during the last three weeks. Three weeks ago, so far from there being any question of the German breaking through our lines, there had been most optimistic reports regarding the deterioration in the German *moral* and the superiority of the British over their opponents, in numbers as in everything else.[58]

In response to the War Office's plea for more men, the War Cabinet decided to create a Manpower Committee, the fourth such committee on manpower since July 1915, composed of Lloyd George, who served as chairman, Curzon, Barnes, Carson, and Smuts. Much has been made about the fact that no member of this committee had military experience (unless General Smuts is counted) and its alleged failure to call upon the general staff for advice.[59] But this charge is a distortion propagated by Robertson and his apologists. Macready, Macdonogh, Maurice, and other military authorities (though not Robertson) were, in fact, called before this committee to give evidence.

That the War Office's evidence was viewed with considerable skepticism, however, is beyond doubt. In truth, the War Office's figures and statements were, in Hankey's words, "utterly unreliable, as their facts are twisted to support their argument."[60] One is reminded of Disraeli's comment, "there are lies, damned lies, and statistics." A few examples are illuminating. In early January, Haig's dispatch of December 25, 1917, was published in the *London Gazette,* with the field marshal making the incredible claim that he had defeated 131 German divisions with "less than half that number of British divisions" in 1917. "What a lie!" was Wilson's retort.[61] Furthermore, Macdonogh, who held Charteris's optimistic arithmetic in contempt, backed his ridiculous estimate of approximately 1,000,000 German casualties on the British front in 1917.[62] With general headquarters and the War Office claiming in effect that one British division was equal to two German divisions, how could the British Expeditionary Force claim to be in peril in 1918?

Besides the quibbling over numbers, there was a deeper and more profound difference between the civil and military authorities: the civilians emphasized maintaining Britain's economic strength and the military authorities focused their attention almost exclusively on the maintenance of Britain's military strength. This question of priorities, faced by every government engaged in total war, was well stated by Hankey in a note for the new committee. He noted that the ministers

> face a situation which differs in two very important particulars from that which has confronted previous Cabinet Committees on the same subject. These are, first: the economic crisis instead of being a danger to be guarded against, is actually present: and, second: that the seriousness of the military man-power crisis is not merely that we shall not smash the enemy if the men are not forthcoming, but that the enemy may smash us.
>
> The problem that confronts the Committee, therefore, is to avert a military catastrophe without plunging us into an economic catastrophe equally fatal to the cause of the Allies.[63]

At the heart of this conflict was the War Cabinet's conviction that victory was not possible in 1918. Consequently, Britain should limit her losses in 1918 by maintaining an active defense while American troops flowed across the Atlantic, giving the Allies the necessary military muscle to defeat the German army in 1919 or 1920. In the interim, food must be grown, ships built to transport American divisions across the Atlantic, and poison-gas shells, tanks, and airplanes produced as an alternative to human-wave attacks to break the stalemate. Furthermore, British finances depended upon maintaining the export industries. Economic collapse might release a tidal wave of defeatism across the country.

To conserve British manpower, the ministers were interested in adopting French tactics, which employed artillerymen in equal or greater numbers than infantry. Anthoine's six divisions in the Flanders offensive had suffered only 8,525 casualties and impressive local successes had been gained at Verdun and La Malmaison with small loss. Also, the French did not conduct constant raids of enemy trenches in quiet sectors, a common practice on the British front. Many ministers believed that the difference in British and French tactics was reflected in the anticipated wastage for the two armies in 1918, French wastage being considerably below that predicted for the British army (over 1,000,000). On December 10, Lloyd George, stunned by this huge figure, ordered Hankey to write Clemenceau, requesting information on the apparently "cheap" methods of Pétain.[64] A French staff officer, Colonel Duffieux, duly arrived in London a week later. On the morning of December 18, the civilians, without their military advisers, quizzed the Frenchman about Pétain's tactics. Colonel Duffieux wasted no time in emphasizing that any comparison of the limited French attacks at Verdun and La Malmaison with Haig's all-out assaults was like comparing apples with oranges. The French attacks had only nibbled at the Germans and could not "bring about a decision." Moreover, he warned in an appreciation, any forecasts for losses in 1918 were inexact and would depend upon "the intensity of the German effort."[65]

This last point was also emphasized by the British military authorities. On January 7, the Army Council warned:

> There is nothing in the experience of this war or in any other to support the argument that a defensive policy necessarily entails fewer losses than an offensive policy. . . . If he [the enemy] forces the fighting—as he is almost certain to do—the Entente must also fight, and there are no grounds whatever for supposing that, in that event, our wastage this year will be less than in the past three years.[66]

How true! From the start of the German offensive on March 21 to April 15 the British army suffered 221,000 casualties.

But would the Germans gamble their last reserve divisions in an all-out effort to win the war in 1918? During the deliberations of the Manpower Committee, the Allies, according to the War Office, had a superiority of 18½ divisions in the West. The civilians were fully aware of the danger of just counting heads[67]; German divisions were obviously superior, for example, to Portuguese divisions. But, with more and more American divisions becoming available by the last half of 1918 to balance German reinforcements from the East, they had good reason to believe that the Allies could hold their own in 1918 in the West.

Incredibly, the ground was cut from under the War Office by the man who could claim to speak with the greatest authority about the British position in the West—Haig. On January 7, Bonar Law put the direct question to the British commander in chief: " 'If you were a German Commander, would you think there was a sufficient chance of a smashing offensive to justify incurring the losses which would be entailed?' " After expressing confidence in his troops holding the line if he were furnished the drafts he needed, Haig shocked Robertson and Derby with his answer. He said that a policy of limited attacks "seemed to him to be the more probable course for the enemy to adopt, because an offensive on a large scale made with the object of piercing the front and reaching Calais or Paris for instance, would be very costly. . . . If he attacked and failed his position would become critical in view of the increasing forces of the Allies in August."[68]

A shaken Robertson told Haig after they left the cabinet room that his statement would be taken by the civilians as an assurance that the Germans would not deliver a great attack in the West in 1918. Consequently, it would now be impossible for him to secure the drafts necessary to maintain his Army.[69] Haig immediately attempted to correct this impression in a written statement to the War Cabinet, but the damage had been done. After all, how much attention could be paid to a man who appeared to change his opinions from hour to hour?

After grappling with often conflicting figures supplied by the general staff, adjutant general's department, and Ministry of National Service, the Manpower Committee set the nation's priorities, with the army virtually coming in last. The adjutant general maintained that approximately 600,000 category "A" men must be withdrawn from civil life by November 1918 to maintain the British armies overseas at their present establishments.[70] Yet the Manpower Committee allocated only 100,000. The navy, air force, shipbuilding, food production, and even timber-felling were given a higher priority than the field forces. The War Office was understandably shocked. But it must be pointed out that the demand for 600,000 category "A" men was an impossible one. When the massive German attacks in 1918 forced the government into the most draconian combing out of men from the vital occupations, only 372,330 category "A" men could be found for the army from January to November 1918.[71]

At the same time, it must be admitted that the government was taking a calculated risk (which was both political and military) by not providing more recruits for the army. Lloyd George quite rightly emphasized the importance of maintaining Britain's staying power, but this was not his only, or even primary, motive in refusing to meet the demands of the army for men. On December 1, he told Esher: "Now he [Haig] wrote of fresh offensives, and asked for men. He would get neither. He had eaten his cake, in spite of warnings. Pétain had economised his."[72] In short, Lloyd George was once again using manpower to force Haig to change his methods. In addition to preventing him from launching big and costly attacks, Lloyd George was determined to force Haig to reduce his cavalry force and the number of battalions in each British division from 12 to 9 (or 13 to 10 if pioneer battalions are counted), something the government had attempted to force on Haig since early 1917 without success.[73] In modern warfare more emphasis was placed on artillery and machine guns than on infantry shock tactics, and the French and Germans had already reduced the number of battalions in their divisions to 9 without altering their effectiveness. An additional advantage from the War Cabinet's point of view was that this reduction in battalions might allow a strategical reserve to be created to deal with any surprise German move.[74] Haig argued, without success, that his divisions should be reduced in number to bring his 12-battalion divisions up to strength. He may have been primarily concerned with the disruption caused by the reduction of battalions in his divisions, but he may have had a political motive. The disappearance of some of his divisions would focus public attention on the government's failure to provide him with the recruits he demanded.

Lloyd George's position exposed him to the deadly charge of letting the army down if anything went wrong. Having shaken Asquith's government to its very foundations on the issue of compulsion, he, of all people, recognized the potency of this accusation and was extraordinarily sensitive about his vulnerability. No matter that if the 250,000 category "A" men immediately requested had been drafted in December, they could not have been trained and sent to Haig before the German onslaught.

Lloyd George's position on recruiting must be carefully separated from one of the most enduring myths of the war: that Lloyd George starved Haig's army by holding back many of the 449,000 category "A" men in the home forces who were available for drafts overseas. This is an emotion-laden charge because the German army came perilously close to victory in 1918. "It is obvious," Edmonds has written, "that the British Armies in France could have been brought up to full establishment before 21st March without unduly weakening the forces elsewhere had the Government so willed."[75] Churchill, who was not privy to the discussions of the Manpower

Committee, echoes this most serious imputation.[76] Often repeated, this version has become part of the folklore of the war. For this reason, it is important to quote almost verbatim a discussion that took place in the Manpower Committee on December 15:

(5) THE PRIME MINISTER stated that it was most desirable that as many men as could be spared from the Home Defence should be sent to France to relieve the men who had been fighting from the duty of manning the trenches on the fronts that were not actually heavily-engaged battle fronts. . . . He understood that, including one Division in Ireland, there were 8 mobile Divisions at home who could be drawn upon for this purpose. They could also be employed in France in preparing the new defensive lines behind our front.

GENERAL MACREADY stated that there was great difficulty in carrying out this proposal, owing to the reluctance of the Military Authorities in France in accepting these lower-category men. He had ordered 15,000 to be got ready to proceed overseas, and 8,000 had actually gone, but he gathered that Sir Douglas Haig could not find employment for more than 11,000.

GENERAL SHAW [Chief of General Staff, Home Forces] explained to the Committee the organisation of the Home Service Divisions. More than half the Infantry in these Divisions consisted of graduated Battalions, i.e., Battalions containing boys of 18, who were drafted overseas as they became 19. In the Home Service Divisions referred to there were only 31,000 fully-trained "B" men [men fit for service abroad but not for general service]. He added that the function of Field-Marshal Lord French was not to lay down how many men were to be allocated for the purpose of Home Defence by the War Office. The question of cutting down the Home Army was one for the War Office to decide, in consultation with the Admiralty.

(6) Attention was drawn to the large number of troops retained in Ireland.

GENERAL SHAW stated that there were nearly 80,000 men in khaki in Ireland, according to the latest return, but there was in Ireland only one mobile Division, namely the 65th. This Division, on November 29, contained 16,100 men, of whom 7,800 were Category "A", including "A.4", boys of 18 and 6,000 "B."

THE PRIME MINISTER suggested that equal value, from the point of view of maintaining order and suppressing a disturbance, might be got out of a very much weaker Cavalry Division as can be got out of the existing Infantry retained in Ireland, and he threw out the suggestion that if the relief of any considerable number of troops in Ireland could be arranged, they might be replaced by one Cavalry Division from France.[77]

Far from holding men back in the home forces, Lloyd George pressured the military authorities to draw on these forces to assist Haig, a recommendation which was also made by the Manpower Committee. (The War Office's utilization of men in khaki is a subject that certainly deserves further study.) Edmonds actually contends that Haig's "fighting strength" decreased from January to March 1918.[78] Yet elsewhere the official history notes that Haig received 174,379 men when 32,384 Dominion forces and 7,359 labor and nonfighting troops are included, an increase of some 15 percent in his fighting strength.[79] Part of this confusion over figures no doubt derives from Haig's refusal to include men in the tank corps, machine-gun corps, and Royal Air Force in his "fighting strength."

The general reserve was held back in Britain prior to March 21 on the authority of the War Office. Proof of this is the testimony of C. J. L. Allanson, a lieutenant-colonel on the general staff in 1918. This is what Allanson told Liddell Hart:

> It was even more unfair to blame L.G. for holding back the reserves in 1918. For this was on the advice of the War Office, that the general reserve of 120,000 men was kept at home instead of in France. The advice they formulated was governed by the assurance given in a note from Haig, that in face of the German offensive he would be able to hold his 3-line front in France for 18 days with the forces he had. On that basis the General Staff recommended keeping the general reserve in England, giving three main reasons for that recommendation: i) that it would be better concealed there from the enemy's intelligence—as experience showed that the enemy found it difficult to discover anything that was happening in England whereas he was able to locate units when they arrived in France— and that it would be quite possible to move the reinforcements across the Channel within the 18 days limit. ii) that it would better conserve the morale of the nation suffering from the effect of Passchendaele—the public, i.e. the families of the troops, had come to feel that men sent to France were as good as dead, so that to keep as many as possible in England might make all the difference in the way that the country weathered the winter. iii) that these men would be spending their money at home instead of in a foreign country, thus helping the economic situation.
>
> Allanson saw the note when it came back from the Prime Minister and it bore a comment from him to the effect that he could add a further reason, "I don't trust Haig with men."[80]

It is, of course, true that the War Cabinet's enthusiasm for military operations on the periphery, especially in Palestine, limited the number of men that Haig could draw upon from other fronts to bolster his defenses. After the German offensive began on March 21, approximately 100,000 men and some artillery were eventually sent from Italy, the Balkans, Palestine, and Egypt to the western front.[81] The 52d and 74th divisions (and some battalions taken from other divisions) came from the Egyptian Expeditionary Force to which the politicians had, in opposition to the general staff, assigned an offensive role in 1918.

The manpower question, which was to play an ever-increasing role in the strategic considerations of the civilians, was in a sense the litmus test of the government's commitment to the British army's playing the dominant role in the defeat of the German army. Humanitarian considerations and the belief that the German lines could not be broken under existing circumstances had strengthened Lloyd George's opposition to blood-draining assaults aimed at decisive results. Although he would not have put it this bluntly, he based his hopes for an overwhelming military victory on the shedding of American rather than British blood. But America had been slow to mobilize for war, and many British military authorities believed that the American Expeditionary Force might not be a powerful offensive instrument until 1920. Could Britain's remaining Continental allies hold on for that long? The events of 1917 offered little encouragement. Russia had gone out of the war, signing an armistice with the Central Powers in mid-December; the Italians had almost collapsed; and the French were war-weary.

The grim military situation forced the prime minister to consider a redefinition of his "knock-out blow"; even a compromise peace was not rejected outright. Conversations with Scott during the last half of December, in all likelihood, reveal his true sentiments. On December 19, Lloyd George told Scott that an unsuccessful German bid for victory in 1918 *"might be regarded as amounting to military victory."* After being touched deeply by a graphic account of the horrors faced by British soldiers on the western front by Philip Gibbs, a war correspondent for the *Daily Chronicle,* he told Scott, "I warn you that I am in a very pacifist temper."[82]

These private sentiments were in sharp contrast to his public statements. London was rocking from the shock waves of the publication of Lord Lansdowne's letter in the *Daily Telegraph* which urged the Allies to liberalize their war aims and seek an end to the war through negotiation. In his response to Lansdowne, the prime minister had proclaimed that there was no "half-way house between victory and defeat." Further, negotiations with an unhumbled Berlin would represent "a betrayal of the great trust with which my colleagues and I have been charged."[83] Betrayal of his mandate for victory or no, Lloyd George was not about to close his eyes to an opportunity to end the slaughter on terms that Great Britain might accept. He observed with growing interest the peace discussions going on between the enemy and the Bolsheviks at the Polish fortress town of Brest-Litovsk. In late December, Count Ottokar Czernin, the spokesman for the Central Powers, in response to the Bolshevik appeal for a statement of peace terms, had appeared to open the door to general peace discussions based on the Bolshevik formula of no annexations or indemnities.

On December 28, the War Cabinet discussed Czernin's conciliatory peace offer to the Bolsheviks. Unfortunately this discussion is lost to history because on Lloyd George's orders Hankey's busy pen was stilled. From Balfour's correspondence with Cecil, however, we know that the ministers "agreed that Czernin's speech could not be treated as non-existent, and that a statement would have to be made about it as soon as Parliament met."[84] There was apparently no discussion of the specifics of the British response. Clearly what was left unsaid was that a peace that satisfied Allied interests in the West could only be bought with the sacrifice of Russian territory.

Before formulating a response to Germany, the War Cabinet asked Robertson for his professional view of Britain's future military prospects. A beleaguered Wully took advantage of this opportunity to restate his case for standing on the defensive on the periphery and bringing to bear more of Britain's military power in the West. As for eventual victory, well, that depended on the government's finding sufficient men for the army. "So far as the British Army is concerned it will, undoubtedly, become weaker month by month and not stronger, unless more men are provided than those foreshadowed in the recent draft Report of the Cabinet Committee," he warned. Robertson's message to the civilians was clear. If they decided to continue the war, ignoring the general staff in the process, they would bear full responsibility for any future defeats.[85]

We now know that Germany was not interested in general peace negotiations as the war entered its fifth year.[86] Berlin sought only a separate peace with Russia at Brest-Litovsk. The French and British were to be dealt with on the battlefield to ensure German hegemony in Europe. Lloyd George feared as much. "At the moment, Germany was in the hour of triumph," he told his colleagues, "and this was the atmosphere of the German people. In these conditions, no German Government could concede all that we were bound to insist on." He also expressed doubt that Czernin's statement was a "*bona fide* peace offer." On the other hand there is evidence to suggest that Lloyd George wanted to give Berlin a reasonable way out of the war, if not now, later. As he told the War Cabinet, he wanted Britain to go "to the extreme limit of concession" to demonstrate "to our own people and to our Allies, as well as to the peoples of Austria, Turkey, and even Germany, that our object was not to destroy the enemy nations."[87] There was always the chance that Germany would silence her guns if she were allowed to retain part of her conquests in Russia.

On January 3, Lloyd George cautiously approached the question of Britain's commitment to Russia.

> One point which he proposed to add, if the War Cabinet agreed, was that if the Russian democracy had not taken the responsibility of entering into negotiations with the enemy by themselves, we would have stood by them, as we intended to stand by the French democracy.[88]

On the following day he came more to the point. In opposition to the Foreign Office's position, he said:

> it was necessary to give warning to the Bolsheviks that we did not any longer consider ourselves bound to fight on in Russian interests, so that there would be no misunderstanding on the subject in the future; also, *that he wished to give a hint to the enemy in the same direction.*[89]

Lloyd George's subsequent war aims speech on January 5 before a trades union congress in Caxton Hall included the following statement:

> The present rulers of Russia are now engaged, without any reference to the countries whom Russia brought into the War, in separate negotiations, with their common enemy. . . . if the present rulers of Russia take action which is independent of their Allies we have no means of intervening to arrest the catastrophe which is assuredly befalling their country. Russia can only be saved by her own people.[90]

Lloyd George's famous January 5 speech did not call for the destruction of Germany or Austria-Hungary. Turkey was to retain its capital and the "rich and renowned lands of Asia Minor and Thrace." Nor did his speech demand the destruction of the German navy or a war indemnity. (There was, however, mention of reparation for Belgium.) There was no mention of British annexation of Germany's overseas possessions. Instead, the German colonies should be "held at the disposal of a Conference whose decision must have primary regard to the wishes and interests of the native inhabitants."[91]

Without any territorial ambitions in Europe, the British leaders found it both easier and safer than her Continental allies to soften their war objectives. If a peace were made on the basis of Lloyd George's January 5 statement, the empire would emerge from the war stronger than ever. Mesopotamia, Arabia, Syria, and Palestine would be liberated from Turkish rule and were almost certain to fall under French or British influence. Under the cloak of self-determination, Germany's captured colonies were not to be returned.

The Welshman's mercurial nature makes the historian tread warily when making an assessment of his intentions. It is true that there were strong domestic pressures on the government from radicals and trade unions to liberalize war aims. And the anti-imperialist pressures from Woodrow Wilson and Lenin could not be ignored. But it would seem that answering the critics of Allied war aims was clearly not the only purpose of Lloyd George's January 5 speech. A trades unionist meeting had only been chosen as his audience because Parliament was not in session. Giving Britain the possible option of a negotiated peace with Germany or a separate peace with her allies, if not uppermost in his mind, was one purpose of his speech.[92] British war aims had also been brought into line with his peripheral strategy which strengthened Britain's imperial position.

The reaction to Lloyd George's speech was mixed. Woodrow Wilson was naturally delighted. Clemenceau publicly endorsed Lloyd George's views but privately he believed "that Germany can and should be beaten flat."[93] On January 18, Lloyd George in a public speech apparently attempted to elicit a response from Berlin: "There has been no response from any man in any position in Germany that indicates a desire on the part of the ruling powers in that land to approach the problem in a spirit of equity."[94] When Berlin finally replied on January 24 its words were disappointing. Chancellor Georg Hertling in the Central Committee of the Reichstag emphatically rejected the British peace move and Wilson's Fourteen Points address, which followed three days later.

Never far from Lloyd George's mind during this period was a British military operation to remove Turkey from the war. After the fall of Jerusalem, he was anxious for Allenby to push on and complete the conquest of Palestine by advancing 100 miles to Dan (a biblical reference to a place that no longer existed). He also contemplated the conquest of the distant railway junction at Aleppo, which would cut Turkish communications with Mesopotamia. Even if this failed to knock Turkey out of the war, Lloyd George believed that it would free ships and men for other theaters. One can imagine his anger when he discovered that Robertson, at the very moment that Jerusalem fell, ordered howitzers removed from Egypt without consulting the War Cabinet.[95]

In retrospect the unhappy consequences of the conflict between the general staff and Lloyd George in 1917 over the Turkish campaign was the adoption of a policy of half-measures. Because of Lloyd George's insistence, Jerusalem was taken but this was of no strategical value whatever its moral and political importance. Because of the general staff's obstruction, Allenby was kept on a leash and prevented from attempting to win a quick and overwhelming victory that would have enabled Britain to recall some of her considerable military resources from the East by early 1918 to meet the growing German threat in the West. By December, of course, it was getting rather late in the day. If the Germans tried for victory as early as March, it was too late to defeat Turkey during the winter and reinforce Haig with troops from the East.

Robertson, with his gaze fixed on the German buildup in the West, raised many objections to any further advance by Allenby. Just to reach Dan, he argued, Allenby would have to be furnished about 90,000 drafts to make good his losses and deficiencies. To reach Aleppo, he would need an additional eight or ten more divisions. As for eliminating Turkey from the war, Robertson argued that it was "militarily impossible, unless and until a strong military force is first constituted in the Caucasus."[96] As usual Allenby played along with Robertson, claiming that he would require sixteen or eighteen divisions in addition to his mounted corps to advance in Aleppo.[97] With a fraction of that force Allenby later annihilated the Turkish forces facing him. Attacking in September he advanced 350 miles in thirty-eight days, capturing 75,000 prisoners with only 5,000 casualties.

Seeing only sinister motives in Robertson's and Allenby's advice, Lloyd George and the War Cabinet considered ways of bypassing the general staff. Political considerations as usual played an important role in shaping their strategical views. The collapse of Russia had given Berlin a northern route to India by way of the Black Sea, the Caucasus, and the Caspian. Turkey also was now free to extend her influence in Persia, the Caucasus, and Turkestan. Amery, who considered Robertson's pessimistic appreciations "farcical," linked the Turkish campaign to this emerging Turko-German threat to the British Empire in the East.[98] There was a glimmer of hope in London and Paris in late 1917 and early 1918 that the eastern front might be revitalized and a barrier erected to thwart the expansionist designs of Germany and Turkey by persuading Japan to intervene in Russia to give support to the anti-Bolshevik movement which had sprung up in southern Russia.[99] The destruction of Turkey, Amery argued, might be a more realistic way of assisting the anti-Bolshevik elements above the Black Sea.

> The control of South Russia is in fact for the Germans the only condition on which they can put Turkey on its legs again, check our advance, and carry out their scheme for linking up the Turks of Asia Minor with the Turkish population of the Eastern Caucasus, North-Western Persia, and Turkestan in a Pan-Turanian combination which would be a most serious threat to our whole position in the East . . . . And, indeed, there is always the hope that if we can eliminate Turkey quickly, and get into direct touch with South Russia through the Dardanelles, we can keep our friends in Russia going permanently and turn the tables upon the Germans in that part of the world.[100]

"Ugly" Wilson (fourth from left in front row) and the British section of the Supreme War Council at Versailles in January 1918.

The attention paid to Amery's appreciations is a good example of the propensity of Lloyd George and his colleagues to look to the British section at Versailles for advice (and support) rather than the general staff. Amery's official status at Versailles was that of political secretary, but his position was more exalted than that. In his own words, he was the "personal representative of Lloyd George and Milner, and liaison officer with the War Cabinet."[101] Despite the War Office's frantic attempts to control Wilson, he was, in Milner's words, "going strong, & as full of ideas as an egg is full of meat."[102] Taking his instructions directly from the prime minister (usually via Amery), he examined a wide range of military problems, including German intentions in 1918. An interesting, though hardly fruitful, war game was played by his staff, with the British officers responsible for divining German plans wearing their hats backwards to give them the appearance of being German staff officers.[103]

Furious with Robertson's attempt to thwart a campaign against the Turks, Lloyd George, supported by the War Cabinet, considered taking advantage of Parliament's recess in late December and appointing Wilson C.I.G.S. When Wilson was abruptly called to London, he objected to being put in

Robertson's shoes. Instead, he suggested that more power be given to Versailles to reduce Robertson "from the position of a master to that of a servant."[104]

If anything, Wilson's hurried trip to London made Lloyd George more anxious than ever to have him at his side. The two men talked for hours about future British military policy, with Wilson telling the prime minister what he wanted to hear. He was not given a "Western" lecture or badgered about drafts. Instead, the articulate Irishman, who agreed with his defensive policy in the West, mesmerized him with talk of his war game at Versailles. Lloyd George's suggestion that Germany would concentrate on expanding her influence in the East in 1918 rather than attack in the West was not greeted with grunts of dismay as would have been the case with Wully. To the contrary, Wilson treated him as an equal in the formulation of military policy and thought his contributions "valuable."[105]

To make certain that collusion between Allenby and the general staff would not undermine a great British campaign against Turkey, which Lloyd George confidently expected Wilson to shepherd through the permanent military representatives at Versailles, the prime minister and Amery pondered placing Smuts, who would report direct to the War Cabinet instead of to the War Office, in charge of all naval and military operations against Turkey. "With Wilson at Versailles & the East delegated to Smuts," Amery wrote Lloyd George, "I don't think the old gang can give too much trouble— if they do you can deal with them."[106]

Smuts, who had a high opinion of his own generalship, readily agreed to this scheme and on January 15, he and Amery left London for Versailles. Smuts was Wilson's second important guest from London within the week for Robertson had earlier paid him a visit to lobby against a campaign against Turkey. Wilson was taken aback and cool toward the appointment of Smuts as commander-in-chief and high commissioner to Palestine, Mesopotamia, Armenia, the Caucasus, and the eastern Mediterranean. "Whew! Whew! Whew!" he wrote in his diary. But his enthusiasm for eastern operations seemed to match Lloyd George's. "The Boches," he told Smuts, "could not get a decision agst. us, that we could not get one agst. him in the West & thereupon we ought to try to knock out the Turk."[107]

During the next few days, the British staff was instrumental in getting the permanent military representatives to accept, on January 21, the following suggestion in their proposals for the 1918 campaign (Joint Note 12):

> To inflict such a crushing series of defeats upon the Turkish Armies as would lead to the final collapse of Turkey and her elimination from the war would not only have the most far-reaching results upon the general military situation, but might also if not too long deferred, be in time to enable the Allies to get into direct touch with, and give effective help to, such elements of resistance to German domination as may still exist in Roumania and Southern Russia.[108]

The force of this suggestion, however, was weakened by the condition insisted upon by the French that no British forces in the West would be withdrawn to assist the offensive against Turkey.

Robertson naturally protested this decision, arguing that Allenby did not believe that he had sufficient forces to achieve the objectives assigned to him by Versailles. Who was in the best position to advise the War Cabinet, Robertson wanted to know, Versailles or Allenby and the British War Office?[109] Demonstrating its contempt for the general staff, the War Cabinet's response was to send Smuts to Egypt.[110] As the War Cabinet's "deputy on mission," he was expected to impose the War Cabinet's will on the Egyptian Expeditionary Force.

As the meeting of the Supreme War Council approached to consider the campaign plans for 1918, Lloyd George contemplated drastic action to put British strategy and tactics in different hands. One cannot help shaking one's head in wonderment at the prime minister's ingenuity and audacity as he intensified his efforts against the army leadership. To ease the protector of Robertson and Haig out of the War Office, Lloyd George proposed to Derby that he go to Paris as the British ambassador.[111] As the genial aristocrat pondered and then rejected this offer, Lloyd George considered sending Robertson halfway around the world to India as commander in chief of the British forces there.[112] What better fate for the apostle of the "Western" school of thought than exile in the East. As for Haig, Lloyd George hoped to replace him if a better soldier could be found.[113] On January 18, he turned to Smuts at lunch and said, "I wish you would go out to the Western front & go right round in order to find out who are the rising men, & to see the new defences they are making to meet the forthcoming German offensive." If a replacement for Haig could not be discovered, Lloyd George wanted to send Hankey to general headquarters as chief of staff to watch over him.[114]

At noon on the twenty-first, with rumors rife in journalistic circles and the lobbies of Parliament that Haig's demise was imminent,[115] Smuts and Hankey left London for the western front. Their next five days were to be filled with danger and tension as they surveyed the leadership of the British Expeditionary Force and inspected its defenses. Wearing steel helmets and gas masks, they climbed in and out of trenches in the battle zones of the First, Fourth, and Fifth Armies as dogfights took place overhead and an occasional German shell came their way. Every step of the way they talked with officers of the British army, who treated them with remarkable civility, given the suspicious nature of their tour.

On the evening of the twenty-first they had dinner with Haig at general headquarters. To his surprise, Hankey discovered much "peace talk" in the nerve center of the British army. Haig, who, it would appear, was shaken by the refusal of his government to furnish him with the men he demanded and the intense French pressure on him to extend his line, told Smuts and Hankey that

> so far the British Empire had got most out of this war, certainly a good deal more than even Germany, and he doubted whether we would gain more by continuing the war for another twelve months. At the end of that period we would be much more exhausted and our industrial and financial recovery would be more difficult, and America would get a great pull over us. There were besides the dangers from the collapse of Italy or France or

both. . . . He doubted whether America would be a really serious factor even in 1919 from her present rate of progress.[116]

Although Haig had two or three offensive plans up his sleeve, he displayed none of his old enthusiasm. Hankey wrote Lloyd George on the twenty-second: "No-one now talks of the offensive, nor thinks that anything can be done in that line. The Americans they believe will not be of much use for the offensive before 1920." Lloyd George was surely pleased to learn from Hankey in this same letter that "most people here feel doubtful whether the Germans will really attack in force, but everyone is preparing to meet the attack if it comes."[117]

As Lloyd George plotted against the army leadership, the general staff prepared a counterattack. Its willing tool was Repington, who was widely considered the nations's most authoritative military correspondent. When his employer Northcliffe, in Repington's view, "tied himself to L.G.'s chariot wheels,"[118] he began negotiations with Gwynne in early December to join his paper. On the eve of the public announcement that he was transferring his pen to the War Office's organ, the *Morning Post,* he wrote Gwynne on January 19 that the general staff was urging him "to begin by exposing the man-power muddle . . . . to do through you about the men and what I did through the Times about the shells."[119] Repington encountered no difficulty in acquiring the evidence he needed because the general staff gave him the adjutant general's top-secret tables on manpower.[120] As Repington busied himself writing an article that was certain, as he put it, to "raise cain," Northcliffe raised some of his own. On January 21, Lovat Fraser of the *Daily Mail,* which called itself "The Soldiers' Friend," under the heading "Things Hidden," lashed out at "the ridiculous 'theory of attrition' " and accused the general staff of squandering Britain's manpower by pursuing "the strategy of the Stone Age" in the West. Since this press attack occurred on the very day that Hankey and Smuts departed for general headquarters to seek a successor for Haig, one can be forgiven the suspicion that the prime minister was behind it all. Quite the reverse, however, seems to have been the case. The last thing Lloyd George wanted was any suggestion that he was at the beck and call of Northcliffe, who inspired hatred in many quarters because of his often clumsy and megalomanical attempts to manipulate public opinion. The army rallied to Haig; during his tour of the front Smuts discovered that Lovat Fraser's virulent assault was "greatly pre-occupying the minds of nearly all the officers whom I met."[121] There was outrage in Parliament and the Unionist War Committee on January 24 passed a resolution supporting Haig and Robertson and demanding that the government condemn the press campaign being waged in Northcliffe's papers against the generals. Even before this reaction, Lloyd George had urged Northcliffe to cease his attacks. "I could have taken him out and shot him," the Welshman told Lord Stamfordham, who quickly perceived that the prime minister's anger was provoked, not from any disagreement with the criticisms, but because he now dared not shake up the army's leadership.[122] Another restraint on Lloyd George was that, alas, Smuts and Hankey were unable to uncover another Marlborough or Wellington. The only capable replacement for Haig they could find, it seems, was General Claud Jacob, who commanded the II Corps.[123] His elevation from relative obscurity was hardly worth the political price that Lloyd George would have to pay, especially after Northcliffe butted in.

On January 24, Repington exploded his bomb in a piece addressed to the British public that accused the War Cabinet of "procrastination" and "cowardice" in tackling the manpower question.[124] By providing the army with only 100,000 category "A" recruits in 1918, he charged in his first article for the *Morning Post,* Lloyd George and his colleagues were betraying the army. "The one question," he wrote, "which concerns most deeply every man, woman, and child in the United Kingdom is whether Sir Douglas Haig's armies will not be sufficiently reinforced to enable them to compete with the enemy on fair terms, and my opinion is that they will not be."

Lloyd George was indignant when he picked up his copy of the *Morning Post*. Where but from the War Office could Repington have gotten his facts and figures? Only three days earlier he had taken Robertson and Derby to task for the sudden and startling increase in German strength reported in the most recent summary of military intelligence, charging the military authorities with an attempt to "create panic" and attempting to show that the War Office was playing a conjuring trick with some of its estimates.[125] Now he correctly suspected that the general staff was taking its case to the public through Repington. In high dudgeon he wrote Derby:

> As you are aware, the General Staff have altered their figures of enemy numbers from time to time, and a most serious change in their view on this subject has been effected within the last two or three days. But clearly Colonel Repington has been supplied with the very latest General Staff intelligence as to enemy numbers and also as to our reserves, but he publishes these figures without any of the qualifications contained in the Staff report. This is a gross breach of Army Regulations, and if someone in the General Staff Department continues to supply secret intelligence to the press with whatever object I must, after submitting the facts to His Majesty, take the House of Commons into my confidence and take stern action.[126]

When Derby was slow in replying, Lloyd George wrote with ever more heat. "If an ordinary soldier had been the offender he would have been shot without any compunction; and you will forgive me for saying that I think it is the duty of the Secretary of State to search out the culprit ruthlessly and deal with him."[127] When Derby finally responded on the twenty-ninth, he attempted to exonerate any member of the general staff of complicity with Repington, arguing that Clemenceau and other French authorities, with whom Repington kept in close touch, were a more likely source for his information.[128]

Repington's article did not create as great a stir in the press as might be thought, but it served as a prelude to another of his press attacks which threatened to bring down Lloyd George's government. His subject this time concerned the granting of executive authority over a proposed Allied general reserve to an executive war board at Versailles chaired by Foch.

NOTES

1. Milner to Wilson, November 3, 1917, Milner MSS, dep. 354.

2. Amery, "The Turning Point of the War," October 31, 1917, and Maurice, "An Answer to the 'Turning Point of the War,'" November 11, 1917, Milner MSS, dep. 354.

3. See Amery to Smuts, October 15, 1917, Smuts MSS, 680, and Milner to Wilson, November 3, 1917, Milner MSS, dep. 354.

4. Hankey Diary, November 4, 1917, 1/4.

5. Robertson, *Soldiers and Statesmen*, 1:216.

6. Robertson to Haig, November 4, 1917, Haig MSS, no. 119.

7. Allied Conference, November 7, 1917, CAB/2/I.C.-30(c), and Lloyd George, *War Memoirs*, 2:1441.

8. These are Liddell Hart's calculations. Although Liddell Hart, an apostle of the indirect approach to warfare, is hardly without bias in his treatment of World War I, his estimates seem more fair-minded than the "cooked" estimates of casualties propagated by Edmonds. See "The Basic Truths of Passchendaele," p. 438.

9. Maxse, "Sir William Robertson," *National Review* 70 (September 1917), pp. 41–52.

10. *Morning Post,* September 5 and October 23, 1917. For Lloyd George's reaction to Gwynne's leading articles, see Wilson Diary, October 5 and 16, 1917. Articles by the "Old Soldier" in the *Morning Post* were thought by some to be the work of Robertson. In conversation with Rawlinson, Gwynne would neither deny nor admit that the "Old Soldier," who obviously was as inside figure, was Robertson. There is some evidence to suggest that Esher may have been the author of these "Western" pieces. See Rawlinson Diary, November 17, 1917, 1/9, and Gwynne to Esher, July 4 and 19, 1917, Esher MSS, 5/52.

11. For proof that Sutherland was Lloyd George's chief contact with the London press, see F. Guest to Lloyd George, February 26, 1918, Lloyd George MSS, F/21/2/13.

12. *Daily Chronicle,* November 1–2, 1917, and *Observer,* November 4, 1917.

13. *Morning Post,* November 6, 1917.

14. *Star,* November 5, 1917, and *Daily News,* November 6, 1917.

15. Entry of November 6, 1917, *A Diary by Frances Stevenson,* p. 165.

16. Wilson Diary, October 31, 1917, Haig Diary, November 4, 1917, no. 119, and Hankey Diary, November 4, 1917, 1/4.

17. *Times* (London), November 13, 1917.

18. *Daily News,* November 14, 1917, *Nation,* November 17, 1917, *Star,* November 15, 1917, and *Spectator,* November 17, 1917.

19. Esher Diary, November 10, 1917, 2/20.

20. Haig to Robertson and Robertson to Haig, November 12 and 15, 1917, Robertson MSS, 1/23/65–66.

21. Hankey Diary, November 15, 1917, 1/4, and Repington, *First World War, 1914–1918,* 2:131.

22. Army Council (236), November 12, 1917, W.O. 163/22.

23. Robertson to Derby, November 15, 1917, Robertson MSS, 1/20/11.

24. War Cabinet (276), November 16, 1917, CAB 23/4.

25. Curzon to Lloyd George, November 18, 1917, Lloyd George MSS, F/11/8/18.

26. Derby to Lloyd George, November 18, 1917, Lloyd George MSS, F/14/4/77; how rattled Lloyd George and his supporters were at this moment is indicated by a letter Amery wrote the prime minister which made the astonishing claim that the Supreme War Council's "object is to make things easier for our strategists, to give Robertson & Haig more, and not less free play." Amery to Lloyd George, November 18, 1917, Lloyd George MSS, F/2/1/6.

27. Lloyd George to Derby, November 26, 1917, Lloyd George MSS, F/14/4/80.

28. Wilson Diary, November 22, 1917.

29. Repington, *First World War, 1914–1918,* 2:138.

30. *H. C. Deb.*, 5th series, vol. 99 (November 19, 1917).

31. Robertson to Haig, November 22, 1917, Robertson MSS, I/23/67.

32. Robertson to Milne, November 23, 1917, Robertson MSS, I/34/36.

33. Haig's minutes on a memorandum, "Cavalry Operations November 20–26th, 1917," prepared for his eyes only. Haig MSS, no. 119.

34. See War Cabinet (279–80 and 282), November 21–22 and 26, 1917, CAB 23/4.

35. Ibid. (281), November 23, 1917, CAB 23/4.

36. Robertson, "Future Military Policy," November 19, 1917, Robertson MSS, I/17/5.

37. Charteris, *At G.H.Q.*, p. 273.

38. Wilson Diary, November 27, 1917.

39. "Talk with Edmonds," September 23, 1929, Liddell Hart MSS, 11/1929/15.

40. Wilson Diary, December 3, 1917.

41. Supreme War Council, December 1, 1917, CAB 28/3/I.C.–36.

42. *Military Operations, France and Belgium, 1917*, 3:305.

43. "Joint Note 1," December 13, 1917, W.P. 69, CAB 27/8.

44. War Cabinet (302), December 19, 1917, CAB 23/4.

45. Haig, "Memorandum on the Question of an extension of the British front," December 15, 1917, M.P.C. 21, CAB 27/14.

46. See the comment by Auckland Geddes, the Ministry for National Service, and General Macready's concurrence with these sentiments. Cabinet Committee on Man-Power (2), December 11, 1917, CAB 27/14.

47. Minister quoted is not identified in minutes. War Cabinet (292), December 5, 1917, CAB 23/4.

48. Esher Diary, December 1, 1917, Esher MSS, 2/20, and Esher to Haig, December 2, 1917, Haig MSS, no. 214f.

49. Army Council (240), December 5, 1917, W.O. 163/23, and R. H. Brade to Wilson, December 7, 1918, Lloyd George MSS, F/23/1/31. In his diary, Wilson notes that he immediately wrote Hankey about Brade's letter, but he did not send in a formal protest until December 15, 1917. See Wilson Diary, December 9, 1917, and Wilson to Lloyd George. (Brade's letter inclosed), December 15, 1917, Lloyd George MSS, F/23/1/31.

50. Cabinet Committee on Man-Power (1), December 10, 1917, CAB 27/14, and General Staff, "Estimated Strength of opposing forces," December 8, 1917, M.P.C. 5, CAB 27/14, and War Cabinet (296), December 12, 1917, CAB 23/4.

51. Allenby virtually had to apologize to Robertson for his success. In opposition to the advice that Robertson had given the War Cabinet, he asserted that he could more easily defend the Jerusalem-Jaffa line than his old Gaza-Beersheba position. Allenby to Robertson, December 7, 1917, Robertson MSS, I/14/109.

52. Derby to Lloyd George, December 11, 1917, Lloyd George MSS, F/14/4/83.

53. See Derby to Lloyd George (Derby to Haig, December 12, 1917, inclosed), December 13, 1917, Lloyd George MSS, F/14/4/85, Haig Diary, December 15, 1917, and January 1, 1918, nos. 120 and 123, and Robertson to Haig, August 24, 1917, Haig MSS, no. 116. Another casualty among Britain's war lords, which was unrelated to Cambrai, was Jellicoe, who was dismissed on December 24.

54. Repington to Northcliffe, November 12, 1917, Northcliffe MSS, vol. 101.

55. Northcliffe to Sassoon, December 13, 1917, Northcliffe MSS, vol. 8.

56. Robertson to Haig, August 17, 1917, Robertson MSS, I/23/45.

57. Memorandum by Derby, December 3, 1917, Army Council (239), December 3, 1917, W.O. 163/22. One suggestion by the Ministry of National Service, which the Army Council resisted, was to lower the age for service in France from nineteen years to eighteen years and six months. See "Memorandum by the Army Council on the Memorandum of National Services on the Problem of the Maintenance of the Armed Forces," November 28, 1917, Robertson MSS, I/11/13.

58. War Cabinet (293), December 6, 1917, CAB 23/4.

59. See, for example, John Terraine, *Impacts of War, 1914 and 1918* (1970), p. 138, and Robertson, *Soldiers and Statesmen*, 1:317.

60. Hankey Diary, December 6, 1917, 1/3.

61. Lieutenant-Colonel J. H. Boraston, ed., *Sir Douglas Haig's Despatches: December 1915–April 1918* (1919), pp. 133–35, and Wilson Diary, January 9, 1918. Haig probably believed these figures because as late as January 7, he believed that "the best defence would be to continue our offensive in Flanders." Haig Diary, January 7, 1918, no. 123.

62. General Staff, "Estimates of German casualties on the British front and on other fronts in 1917," December 11, 1917, M.P.C. 10, CAB 27/14. Apparently the figure was closer to 500,000. See *Statistics of the Military Effort of the British Empire During the Great War, 1914–1920*, p. 361.

63. Hankey, "Note by the Secretary," December 8, 1917, M.P.C. 2, CAB 27/14.

64. Cabinet Committee on Man-Power (1), December 10, 1917, CAB 27/14.

65. Anglo-French Conference, December 18, 1917, M.P.C. 23, CAB 27/14, and "Note on attacks with a limited objective by the French General Staff," December 16, 1917, M.P.C. 24, CAB 27/14. When this Anglo-French conference turned to French defensive preparations in its afternoon session, Robertson and Macready were included.

66. Cabinet Paper G.T. 3265 of January 7, 1918, CAB 24/38.

67. See Draft Report of Cabinet Committee on Man-Power, March 1, 1918, CAB 27/14.

68. War Cabinet (316A), January 7, 1917, CAB 23/13.

69. Robertson, *Soldiers and Statesmen*, 1:320–22.

70. Macready, "Summary of the requirements of the Army in men in order to maintain fighting efficiency of the Expeditionary Forces," December 10, 1917, M.P.C. 4, CAB 27/14.

71. *Statistics of the Military Effort of the British Empire During the Great War, 1914–1920*, pp. 371–74.

72. Esher Diary, December 1, 1917, 2/20.

73. See Draft Report of Cabinet Committee on Man-Power, March 1, 1918, CAB 27/14.

74. When this was being advocated in late 1917 the British government hoped that American battalions might be brigaded with British troops to restore British divisions to their original strength. Discussions among the French, British, and Americans leading to this, however, went nowhere. See Robertson, *Soldiers and Statesmen*, 1:326–31 and Hankey *Supreme Command*, 2:744–46.

75. *Military Operations, France and Belgium, 1918*, 1:52, n. 1.

76. Churchill, *World Crisis*, 4:91–102, and Churchill to Lloyd George, January 19, 1918, Lloyd George MSS, F/8/2/3.

77. Cabinet Committee on Man-Power (4), December 15, 1917, CAB 27/14.

78. *Military Operations, France and Belgium, 1918. Appendices*, Appendix 7, and War Cabinet (316), January 7, 1918, CAB 23/5.

79. *Military Operations, France and Belgium, 1918*, 1:52, n. 1, and B. H. Liddell Hart, *Through the Fog of War* (1938), p. 273. These reinforcements, however, still fell some 160,000 men short of what Haig originally demanded.

80. The government after March 21 discovered 106,000 men (nine-tenths infantry) available for immediate dispatch to France. When 88,000 men home on leave and 18,000 trained men available as drafts up to April 20 were added, some 212,000 men were found to send to France by April 20. "Talk with Colonel C. Allanson," August 19, 1937, Liddell Hart MSS, 11/1937/69, and War Cabinet (372), March 25, 1918, CAB 23/5. Another consideration for the general staff was that the Admiralty did not reject the possibility that the German navy might transport an invasion force of 160,000 men to the British Isles. See Robertson's memorandum, "Troops required for Home Defence." Cabinet Paper G.T. 3212 of January 3, 1918, CAB 24/38.

81. Hankey, *Supreme Command*, 2:803.

82. Entries of December 16–19 and 28, 1917, *Diaries of C. P. Scott*, pp. 322 and 324.

83. *Times* (London), December 15, 1917.

84. War Cabinet (307A), December 28, 1917, CAB 23/13, and Balfour to Cecil, December 28, 1917, Balfour MSS, Add. 49738.

85. Cabinet Paper G.T. 3145 of December 29, 1917, and G.T. 3191 of January 3, 1918, CAB 24/37.

86. Fischer, *Germany's Aims in First World War,* pp. 475–509, and John W. Wheeler-Bennett, *Brest-Litovsk: The Forgotten Peace, March 1918* (1938), pp. 99–148.

87. War Cabinet (312–13), January 3, 1918, CAB 23/5.

88. Ibid. (312), January 3, 1918, CAB 23/5.

89. Author's italics. War Cabinet (314), January 4, 1918, CAB 23/5.

90. Lloyd George, *War Memoirs,* 2:1514.

91. Ibid., 2:1510–17.

92. David R. Woodward, "The Origins and Intent of David Lloyd George's January 5 War Aims Speech," *The Historian* 34 (November 1971): 22–39. Confirmation that this was Lloyd George's intention can be found in Hankey Diary, December 29, 1917, 1/3.

93. Esher to Hankey, January 13, 1918, Lloyd George MSS, F/23/2/9.

94. *Times* (London), January 19, 1918.

95. Lloyd George to Robertson, December 11, 1917, Lloyd George MSS, F/44/3/38, Lloyd George to Robertson, December 14, 1917, Robertson MSS, I/19/13, and War Cabinet (296–97), December 12–13, 1917, CAB 23/4.

96. Cabinet Paper G.T. 3112 of December 26, 1917, and G.T. 3191 of January 3, 1918, CAB 24/37.

97. Allenby to Robertson, December 20, 1917, Appendix IV, in Cabinet Paper G.T. 3112 of December 26, 1917, CAB 24/37.

98. Amery to Lloyd George, December 30, 1917, Lloyd George MSS, F/2/1/10, and Amery, "Note on Sir W. Robertson's Memorandum of 26th December," December 30, 1917, CAB 25/41.

99. David R. Woodward, "British Intervention in Russia During the First World War," *Military Affairs* 41 (December 1977): 171–75, and "The British Government and Japanese Intervention in Russia During World War I," *Journal of Modern History* 46 (December 1974): 663–85.

100. Amery to Lloyd George, December 29, 1917, Lloyd George MSS, F/2/1/9, and Amery, "The Military and Strategical Position in the Turkish Theatre and South Russia as a Whole," January 4, 1918, CAB 25/68, and Amery, "The Turkish and South Russian Problem," January 4, 1918, CAB 25/43.

101. L. S. Amery, *My Political Life,* vol. 2: *War and Peace,* 1914–1929 (1953), p. 129.

102 . Milner to Lloyd George, December 23, 1917, Lloyd George MSS, F/38/2/27.

103. Initially Wilson resisted being pinned down about German intentions. When he finally submitted a report at the prime minister's urgings, he was wide of the mark, arguing that the best time for any German attack would be after May 1 and incorrectly predicting the point of the German assault. See Hankey to Lloyd George (Wilson to Hankey, December 27, 1917, inclosed), December 29, 1917, Lloyd George MSS, F/23/1/37, and *Military Operations, France and Belgium, 1918,* 1:78.

104. Wilson Diary, December 30, 1917.

105. Ibid.

106. Amery to Lloyd George, January 12, 1918, Lloyd George MSS, F/2/1/11.

107. Wilson Diary, January 16, 1917.

108. Wilson to Lloyd George ("Joint Note 12" inclosed), January 20, 1918, Lloyd George MSS, F/4/7/9, and Duncannon to J. T. Davies, January 21, 1918, Lloyd George MSS, F/47/7/10.

109. Robertson to War Office, January 25, 1918, CAB 25/68.

110. War Cabinet (332), January 28, 1918, CAB 23/5. Robertson, however, continued to fight

a rearguard action to limit Allenby's military operations. See Robertson to Allenby, February 2, 1918, Robertson MSS, 1/32/80. Allenby responded on February 23, after Robertson had been forced out as C.I.G.S.: "Smuts had a clear policy of action formed in his mind; and we merely discussed the method of carrying it out. I won't go into questions of Imperial Strategy; but, from a local standpoint, the plan appears possible." Allenby to Robertson, February 23, 1918, Robertson MSS, 1/21/86.

111. Derby to Lloyd George, January 18, 1918, Lloyd George MSS, F/14/5/2.

112. Hankey Diary, January 19, 1918, 1/3.

113. "Talk with Lloyd George at Criccieth," September 24, 1932, Liddell Hart MSS, 11/1932/42c.

114. Hankey Diary, January 18, 1918, 1/3.

115. Milner to Lloyd George, January 18, 1918, Lloyd George MSS, F/38/3/4.

116. Smuts to Lloyd George, January 21, 1918, Lloyd George MSS, F/45/9/9, and Hankey Diary, January 21, 1918, 1/4. Earlier Haig had told Repington: "We should either make war or make peace." Repington, *First World War, 1914–1918*, 2:174.

117. Hankey to Lloyd George, January 22, 1918, Lloyd George MSS, F/23/2/11.

118. Repington, *First World War, 1914–1918*, 2:149.

119. Ibid., p. 191, and Repington to Gwynne, January 19, 1918, Gwynne MSS, 21.

120. Repington to Gwynne, January 20, 1918, Gwynne MSS, 21. Roskill erroneously suggests that Amery was the source of Repington's information. Roskill, *1877–1918*, p. 480.

121. Cabinet Paper G.T. 3469 of January 27, 1918, CAB 24/40.

122. Stamfordham, "Record of a conversation with the Prime Minister," January 22, 1918, RA GV F1259/4.

123. "Talk with Lloyd George at Criccieth," September 2, 1932, Liddell Hart MSS, 11/1932/42c.

124. Repington had assured Gwynne that either Maurice or Macdonogh would get this article past the censor, but the editor of the *Morning Post* simply ignored the Official Press Bureau. See Repington to Gwynne, January 20, 1918, Gwynne MSS, 21. For British censorship during the war, see Edward Cook, *The Press in War-Time with Some Account of the Official Press Bureau* (1920).

125. War Cabinet (326), January 21, 1918, CAB 23/5. One result of the new War Office tables was to place in jeopardy the Manpower Committee's calculations which had been based on earlier statistics supplied by the military authorities. To place the blame where he believed it belonged, Hankey suggested to Lloyd George that the committee's manpower conclusions be adopted at once "and, if any alteration is required in the Report or conclusions it ought to be clear that the responsiblity rests with the Department who furnished incomplete figures and not with the Committee." Hankey to Lloyd George, January 24, 1918, Lloyd George MSS, F/23/2/12. The War Office's new estimates were, in fact, placed in brackets after the original figures or in footnotes in the final manpower report.

126. Lloyd George to Derby, January 24, 1918, Lloyd George MSS, F/14/5/4.

127. Lloyd George to Derby, January 28, 1918, Lloyd George MSS, F/14/5/5.

128. Derby to Lloyd George, January 29, 1918, Lloyd George MSS, F/14/5/6.

11

Command of the Allied General Reserve and the Fall of Robertson

THE Supreme War Council had not met since early December and a whole host of military questions begged for an urgent settlement. The permanent military representatives at Versailles continued to issue joint notes, but until the Allied leaders met and acted upon them, they were only suggestions. Meanwhile, Robertson strenuously worked behind the scenes to effect a common military policy among himself, Pétain, Haig, Foch, and Pershing. If he succeeded, he would be able to keep Versailles in its place. "The Versailles people are doubtless doing their best," he wrote Haig, "but they cannot well help being a probable source of mischief unless we responsible people have made up our minds on all points *beforehand* and are in accord with the French."[1]

Differences between the French and British and even within the French high command, however, made any common policy for the Allied generals impossible. When a military conference was held at Compiègne on January 24, Pétain and Foch at once fell out over the latter's enthusiasm for spirited counterattacks in 1918. Uncharacteristically, the offensive-minded Haig sided with the cautious Pètain. Foch's stance, he believed, was "admirable in theory, but not practicable because we have not the necessary forces."[2] Other divisive issues were the escalating French demands that Haig give relief to the French army by extending his line and the creation and command of a strategic Allied general reserve. These two questions were related because, if Haig had to reduce his reserves by spreading his forces further, enabling the Germans to achieve a considerable superiority in troops by concentrating on a point along his defenses, his best hope of receiving immediate aid would be through calling upon an Allied general reserve under an independent command freed from national considerations.

It will be recalled that at the Boulogne conference in September 1917, Lloyd George accepted the principle of giving relief to the exhausted *poilus* by taking over more of the French line. One result of the extension of Haig's line, as he well knew, would be to limit the British army's ability to launch massive assaults. The War Cabinet then turned the specific arrangements over to Pétain and a thoroughly disgruntled Haig. When Haig talked with Pétain at Amiens in mid-October, he argued that he could give more effective relief to the French by continuing his Flanders attack to draw off and destroy German reserves.[3] Pétain, casting worried glances at Russia's headlong decline, however, feared for the safety of his forces which held over three times the front occupied by the British. To meet the threat of German divisions arriving on his sector from the East, he wanted a shorter line to build up his reserves; and he insisted that the British take over a six-division front extending to the forest of St. Gobain (Barisis). The best that Haig was prepared to do was take over a four-division front. But the final phase of the Third Battle of Ypres, the dispatch of British divisions to Italy, and the fierce fighting around Cambrai prevented this agreement from being implemented and left the British army exhausted and depleted in strength. Some French military leaders, instead of being grateful to Haig for keeping pressure on Germany, were furious with him. Foch criticized "the waste of life & effort at Passchendaele & at Cambrai." Such "individual efforts," he complained to Wilson, "were fatal & upset the general plan, as for example our taking over French line which now we appeared incapable of doing."[4]

Despite the weakened condition of the British army, Clemenceau not only kept up the pressure on the British government, he threatened resignation if the British did not occupy French trenches as far as Berry-au-Bac, some thirty-seven miles beyond Barisis. His demand sprang, in part, from his desire to tie the British down in the West and force the British civilians to furnish Haig with more men.[5] With Haig now assuming a defensive posture, Lloyd George was reluctant to support the expanded French demands. Prodded by Wilson, who believed that French desires should be met to some extent, Clemenceau then agreed to turn the whole question over to the permanent military representatives and abide by their decision.[6] On December 18, Lloyd George and his colleagues in the War Cabinet accepted Clemenceau's position, obviously hoping that their experiment in unifying Allied military policy might resolve this emotional question which was driving a wedge between Paris and London.[7]

On January 10, to the chagrin of Haig and Robertson, the permanent military representatives attempted to split the difference, suggesting in joint note 10 that the British take over the French line to a point east of the Laon-Soissons road, some fourteen miles beyond Barisis. The British high command raised immediate and violent objections. Wully put it very plainly to the War Cabinet: "It is now for the War Cabinet to decide between the Military Representatives, who have no responsibility for the security of the front, and the Field Marshal Commanding-in-Chief, who is responsible for the front and for safe-guarding his communications with England." Haig was even more blunt, telling Hankey that if the War Cabinet supported extending his line beyond Barisis, it "would have to find a new Commander-in-Chief!"[8]

Although Lloyd George's brainchild, the Supreme War Council, was being challenged by his generals, he was not prepared to make an issue of it. If anything, he was inclined to support the army against Versailles. If Haig became responsible for yet another fourteen miles, he would clearly be unable to contribute to an Allied general reserve, which Lloyd George hoped would strengthen Allied defenses and perhaps even enable the Allies to have a more flexible strategy to counter German moves in either the East or the West.

Much has been written about the extension of the British line, but the origins of a strategic reserve, which quickly became entangled with the question of a generalissimo, remains shrouded in mystery. Initially Lloyd George, Milner, and other British political leaders thought only of a British mobile reserve to free some of their troops from the trenches of the West. On November 3, Milner had written Lloyd George:

> The more I think of it, the more dangerous appears to me the idea of tying ourselves up more than ever in France. The soldiers will like it because it keeps their army together, but it means that for the whole of 1918 our Army will be condemned to a merely defensive role, while our more distant expeditions will also be smitten with the paralysis, if not with failure . . . .
>
> The great point is that if, next year at any rate, we cannot make that force strong enough to break through, it is waste to keep it stronger than is necessary for a lively defensive. The force we could afford to withdraw from France *should be the mobile force of the alliance*[,] the strategic reserve, wh. we have never had & without wh. we can never win. It, or some of it, is wanted now in Italy, but that does not mean we should immobilise it permanently in Italy. It goes there for a temporary purpose—to give Italy time to recover, not for ever & a day to hold a slice of Italian frontier.[9]

With the initiative shifting to the Germans as they transferred division after division from Russia to the West, however, the British civilians were forced to consider an Allied (as opposed to British) strategic reserve to throw against the Germans wherever they chose to attack in 1918. Lloyd George's new Supreme War Council might indeed lead to a more coordinated Allied strategy as he claimed. But its machinery, aimed more at reducing Robertson's influence than anything else, was clearly defective, and he had admitted in Parliament that it was essentially powerless. In mid-December, the prime minister apparently attempted to test the political waters with an inspired leading article in the Astor-owned *Observer* which called for giving more power to Versailles as a substitute for a generalissimo and the creation of a strategic reserve.[10]

Almost from the first, Clemenceau preferred a generalissimo to the Supreme War Council. On December 11, the former French minister of war, Alexandre Millerand, after consulting with his premier, told Esher that the Supreme War Council as constituted was "a fifth wheel to a coach, and a further complication." The only solution was for Versailles to act as a general staff to a generalissimo.[11] On December 23, Clemenceau himself lobbied for the creation of an Anglo-French strategic reserve "under a single direction," which seemed to imply a supreme commander, when he met with Milner in Paris to coordinate Anglo-French support of anti-Bolshevik elements in southern Russia.[12]

The French military and political leaders, who thought only in terms of a

Frenchman as supreme commander, were alive to Lloyd George's political difficulties in the aftermath of Calais in placing the British army under a foreigner. Too much pressure in this direction was almost certain to be counterproductive. Surprisingly, the French position on unity of command was supported by Robertson's right-hand man on the general staff, General Maurice. Unlike Haig, Maurice entertained no doubts about German intentions in 1918. Fearful of the consequences of a great German blow against either the French or the British, with no Allied machinery to effect immediate unity of action, Maurice took the lead in exploring the creation of a generalissimo, working through General G. Sidney Clive, the head of the British mission to French general headquarters. Robertson, who may have seen this scheme as a way of destroying Wilson's position, and Pétain immediately gave their support to this plan, but Haig, convinced that he and the French commander in chief could work in unison in any crisis, was adamantly opposed. A fatal flaw in Haig's position, in Clive's prophetic words, was that almost inevitably "mutual support" would "rank after self-preservation" when the moment of truth arrived.[13]

As Maurice and Clive conducted their exploratory talks, Henry Wilson was moving in another direction. Desirous of increasing his authority at the expense of Robertson, he raised the question of an Allied general reserve with Wully on January 9. Masking his true intentions, he told the C.I.G.S. that a certain number of divisions should be taken from Haig and Pétain and placed under either the control of Versailles *or* Robertson and Foch. Later, however, when Wilson talked with Clemenceau, he made no mention of giving Robertson any control over the strategic reserve. When the premier noted that in reality the strategic reserve was to be " 'under Wilson,' " the Irishman readily admitted that this was his intention.[14]

Apparently informed by Robertson of his conversation with Wilson, Maurice breakfasted with the prime minister on January 10. After emphasizing that Versailles, with only advisory power, would never be able to coordinate Allied military operations in battle, he suggested that Joffre be made generalissimo "with Robertson as his Chief of Staff & Italian & American staff officers under them."[15] Although Joffre was the architect of the costly Anglo-French attacks in the first years of the war, Lloyd George was immediately taken with his suggestion. After altering Maurice's proposal in one major respect—Wilson, not Wully, was to be Joffre's chief of staff—he turned to Wilson for his reaction. The Irishman responded with a Machiavellian counterproposal:

> No, believe me a Generalissimo is impossible, nor is such an appointment rendered more practicable by giving him a foreigner as Chief of the Staff. In my opinion the real solution of all our difficulties lies in the further development of the Versailles [idea] which the P.M. set up . . . . I suggest that a Central Reserve be placed *under* Versailles . . . . I believe by this means we shall gain most of the advantages of a Generalissimo and suffer few of the disadvantages.[16]

Wilson and Haig thus combined against an arrangement which promised to save the Allies from many of their difficulties when the great German offensive began. Joffre, although a poor tactician, had proven to be extraordinarily cool in a crisis and was capable of quick, difficult decisions.

With a generalissimo being pushed further into the background, the War Cabinet on January 23 gave Lloyd George and Milner full authority to decide "the disposition and command of the General Reserve on the Allied Western front" during the forthcoming Supreme War Council.[17] Two days later the permanent military representatives approved joint note 14, which urged the creation of an Allied maneuver force for the French and Italian fronts. Not a word, however, was said about its command. That an attempt to give Versailles executive authority over this proposed Allied general reserve was certain to spark an explosion from Robertson with political echoes in London was very much on Lloyd George's mind as he left for the meeting of the Supreme War Council in late January with Milner. Robertson, intensely suspicious of Wilson, immediately made clear his opposition to an Allied reserve independent of his or Foch's authority when consulted by the prime minister. "The advice I submit to you is," he wrote the Welshman, "therefore, that the High Command, as far as executive work is concerned (and this is what matters most during active operations), must necessarily be exercised by the Chiefs of the General Staff . . . . Recognise and settle this point and the question of reserves will then settle itself."[18] With Wilson and Robertson at each other's throats, Lloyd George saw no way to avoid a blowup. "He found it very difficult to know what to do about Robertson & me; though he said he knew what he wanted,"[19] Wilson noted in his diary.

The four-day meeting of the Supreme War Council got off to a rocky start on January 30. Confusion rather than coordination appeared to be the result of Lloyd George's attempt to devise a common approach to Allied war policy, with three sets of military advisers—the permanent military representatives, the chiefs of general staff and commanders in chief—stepping on each other's toes. "They all gave different advice," Hankey wrote his wife, "and the meeting got into a worse state of chaos than I have ever known in all my wide experience."[20] What Hankey perhaps did not realize was that this divided military counsel gave the master manipulator Lloyd George room to maneuver.

A crucial question before the Allied military and political leaders was the security of their forces in the West. Although skeptical of the War Office's arithmetic, the prime minister could not ignore the intelligence reports of the continued flow of German divisions westward. As a substitute to the general staff's intelligence furnished to the War Cabinet, Lloyd George turned to Wilson, who informed him on the eve of the meeting of the Supreme War Council that Germany now had between 168 and 185 divisions in the West and might eventually have 215.[21] If this were correct, the Allied superiority in rifle strength was rapidly disappearing.

When Haig and Pétain were called upon by the Supreme War Council to give evidence, they painted an absolutely desperate picture of the future manpower situation in an apparent attempt to frighten Lloyd George away from his "Eastern" schemes and toward increasing the flow of recruits to the British army. In the event of hard fighting, Haig claimed that he would be down to thirty-five divisions by November even if the Americans accepted amalgamation. Pétain's forecast of his losses was just as gloomy. As for the Americans, Pétain argued that, unless they accepted amalgamation, they "would be of no use to the Allies in 1918, except, perhaps, along some quiet section of the front."[22] Lloyd George, Milner, Hankey, and Wilson listened in disbelief. After all, Haig had just told Wilson that he did not fear a German attack.[23] Hankey mirrored their skepticism when he wrote in his diary: "Haig and Pétain made asses of themselves by absurd, panicky statements in regard to their man-power."[24]

On the following day Foch put Lloyd George on the defensive when he delivered a bitter tirade against the British for not providing their fair share of men. Lloyd George responded heatedly to this charge, emphasizing the heavy casualties suffered by the British army and the essential services in shipping, coal, etc., that Britain was providing her allies. He then appealed to Clemenceau to stop Foch's intervention in what was solely the business of the British government. Foch was silenced but tempers were hardly cooled because Clemenceau then linked Lloyd George's Turkish plans with the declining manpower of the British and French. How, he wanted to know, could Lloyd George support a "side show" when Paris itself was menaced? Lloyd George's response was to argue that "the Allies were in the West taking risks considerably less than had been taken by the Germans on the same front during the war." Did Clemenceau seriously propose that Jerusalem, Baghdad, and Salonika be abandoned? After all, Haig only hoped to get two divisions transferred to his forces if the Palestinian campaign was canceled.[25]

In Hankey's (and no doubt Lloyd George's) view the "Tiger" had been gotten to by the soldiers who wanted to "concentrate everything in the West."[26] Robertson was clearly delighted as he watched the "Tiger" sink his claws into the prime minister. A stronger attack against Lloyd George's strategy could not have been delivered by Leo Maxse, he gleefully wrote Derby. "The P.M. was very badly mauled and I never saw him look more knocked out."[27]

To win French approval for his Turkish campaign, Lloyd George promised that not a single British soldier would be diverted from France to Palestine. Furthermore, any action in Palestine would be delayed for two months to enable the situation in the West to come into clear focus. But the Supreme War Council's tentative support was not gained before Wully had said his piece. When Clemenceau turned to him for his opinion, he emphasized that a defensive posture should be adopted in all secondary theaters. Mincing no words, he said that the permanent military representatives' recommendation was not "a practical plan, and that to attempt it would be very dangerous and detrimental to our prospects of winning the war."[28] Lloyd George was furious with Robertson and let him know it after the meeting. But he had what he wanted—the Supreme War Council's stamp of approval for an offensive against Turkey.

Another question of even more explosive potential remained to be settled: the general reserve and its command. On February 1, Robertson and Foch teamed up to suggest that the general reserve should be controlled by the chiefs of staff from the British and French war offices and special representatives from the United States, Italy, and Belgium. Lloyd George, assisted by Wilson, who busily passed him notes, resisted this proposal. Robertson, the Prime Minister artfully suggested, was too busy with his work in London to direct the general reserve in an emergency.[29] When the ministers adjourned for the day the question of the command of the general reserve remained unresolved.

Fearing that Wilson was about to further undermine him by gaining executive powers, Robertson immediately wrote the prime minister:

> No British officer in France who is not a Member of the Army Council and in direct touch with that body can have the necessary information as to the state of the troops, the supply, munition, and medical situation and other questions essential to the effective control of military operations. On these questions I feel that both the Secretary of State for War and the Army Council should be consulted, as they affect vitally the principles of command and administration of our troops in the field.
>
> 4. There are also constitutional questions to be considered. . . . I do not quite see how a British Commander-in-Chief can be made, constitutionally, to obey the orders of an Allied body, or indeed of anyone except the Army Council and the Secretary of State for War—a Minister of the Crown. If the C.I.G.S. were made a Member of the Versailles body, as is proposed in the case of General Foch, this difficulty could be more easily surmounted perhaps.[30]

Lloyd George, of course, remained adamantly opposed to giving Haig's ally, Robertson, any control over the general reserve. But he did not know exactly what to propose as an alternative. Clemenceau had never really liked Versailles and the acceptance of a true generalissimo over the opposition of Haig might bring down his government. Wilson, whose opposition to a generalissimo had begun to waver, especially if his friend Foch were chosen, rescued the prime minister from his predicament. According to his formula, the permanent military representatives would constitute an executive war board to direct the general reserve, with Foch, who would replace Weygand, serving as the chairman of this body.[31] During breakfast with Wilson, Hankey and Milner on the morning of the second, Lloyd George seized upon this compromise, though one suspects that he did not like giving Foch increased influence over Allied strategy. After all, Foch had just violently attacked him over manpower and had been the most offensive-minded general during the discussions of the campaign of 1918. But Lloyd George now had little choice. The alternative seemed to be enhancing Robertson's and emasculating Wilson's position by accepting the C.I.G.S.'s proposal that he be allowed to sit on the Executive War Board. Furthermore, the creation of an executive war board chaired by Foch (with the reserves under his control he would act virtually as the Allied commander in chief in the West) was a giant step toward creating the supreme commander which Lloyd George had long argued was essential to the efficient conduct of the war.

After meeting privately with Clemenceau and Orlando, Lloyd George brought tears to the eyes of the Allied statesmen with his explanation and defense of Wilson's scheme. Robertson and Haig wanted to cry but for different reasons. Haig at once raised difficulties about the manner in which he would receive his orders for the reserves behind his front. How could a foreign general under the British constitution command British soldiers? The proper channel for his orders was through the C.I.G.S. When Haig persisted in this argument, Lloyd George silenced him by informing the council that he was acting with the full authority of the War Cabinet. When the meeting broke up, a shattered Robertson, who had remained silent during the discussion of the Executive War Board, remained "sitting alone in his place, motionless, his head resting on his hand, glaring silently in front of him."[32]

Because of Lloyd George's willingness to elevate Foch, the thorny issue of the extension of the British line was more easily resolved. Haig, strongly supported by Lloyd George, argued against the acceptance of joint note 10. The upshot of this discussion was that the principle of this joint note was accepted, but the timing of the British takeover of more of the French line was to be worked out by Pétain and Haig. This suited Haig because Pétain assured him in private that he had no intention to " 'taquiner' (worry) me over this."[33] Subsequently this matter became a dead issue and not one additional yard of trench beyond Barisis had been taken over by the British when the German offensive began.

The outcome of the Supreme War Council's deliberations represented a considerable triumph for Lloyd George. His defensive policy in the West had been ratified, with Foch's policy of counteroffensives being toned down.[34] As for the creation and command of the general reserve and an offensive to annihilate Turkey, the British high command had been out-maneuvered.

Although Robertson had been floored at Versailles, Lloyd George knew that he was not down for the count of ten. After the prime minister's attempts to diminish the authority of the high command at Calais and Rapallo, the C.I.G.S. had returned to London to provoke ferment and unrest. He was sure to do so again and the prime minister had to be apprehensive about the outcome, especially if Haig and Derby linked arms with Wully. With the army leadership united against him, the protective shield of the Supreme War Council might not be enough to protect him from the charge of "interference" with the army. The War Office and its supporters might also beat the drum of nationalism against the Executive War Board. Repington's menacing presence in Paris during the meeting of the Supreme War Council had not gone unnoticed. "You must be prepared for a raging, tearing press attack on your decisions over here beginning at once," Amery warned him. The success of any press campaign, Amery went on to write, would depend on the cooperation it received from the War Office. To muzzle the soldiers, Amery suggested that the War Office immediately be given new leadership. Lloyd George took this suggestion to heart, telling Hankey on the way back to London that he wanted to make his ally Milner secretary of state for war.[35]

Meanwhile, Robertson attempted to keep Derby firmly in his corner. To put steel in his backbone, Wully finished a letter to him on the train to London which accused Lloyd George of creating a French generalissimo and of removing Wilson from the War Office's control. "I do not know how or by whom powers are to be delegated to an officer, not on the Army

Council and not directly under you, to issue orders to a Commander-in-Chief of about two million men. . . . Are you prepared to be Wilson's Minister and yet have no control over him?" To make certain that Derby got the message, Robertson added in a postscript: "The Army, the Army Council, the C.I.G.S. and Cs in Chief, will look to you, their Minister, to see that they are not placed in an impossible, unfair, and unpractical position." Once in London, Wully also turned to his old ally, the king, warning him about the "Versailles Soviet."[36]

On February 4, the battle over the command of the general reserve began when Derby entered the cabinet room in a combative mood. He had had his fill of the Welshman's cunning, informing the prime minister in a memorandum: "I might as well have been a dummy for all the advice I have been asked for. . . . It is absolutely impossible for anybody in my position to accept such a situation. I am perfectly certain the Country would not accept it." When Lloyd George brought up the creation of the Executive War Board, Derby withheld his support. Lloyd George shot back that the War Cabinet, with Derby present, had given him full authority to settle the question of the command of the general reserve and the matter had been decided "unanimously by the Allied representatives" at Versailles. He consequently expected the Army Council to implement this Allied decision in good faith. To prevent a national debate over the issue, the War Cabinet then informed the press bureau that no reference to "the formation or command of a General Inter-Allied Reserve" should be allowed past the censor.[37]

Encouraged by Derby and Robertson, the Army Council refused to be buffaloed. The Executive War Board as constituted, it charged, put Haig in "an impossible position" because he had been placed under two authorities, Foch and the Army Council. Furthermore, the arrangement was unconstitutional because it ignored the prerogatives of the Army Council, the governing board of the army.[38]

With Derby and the Army Council backing Robertson, Haig's position was crucial for Lloyd George. At the Supreme War Council meeting, after asking how he was to receive his orders, the field marshal had lapsed into dignified silence. Immediately after the Supreme War Council adjourned, Esher found him "quite undisturbed by the Versailles Resolutions."[39] What explains the different reactions of Haig and Robertson? Haig, of course, disliked strife between the civil and military authorities and at times had served as peacemaker. But this alone does not explain his position. Having made it clear to his government that he had no divisions of his own to spare, he thought that the general reserve might result in the transfer of British divisions from Italy, Salonika, and elsewhere to the West. He also believed that the new Versailles machinery was "so big & clumsy" that it could not interfere with his command any time soon. Finally—and this speaks volumes about his enigmatic personality—he was not overly concerned about Robertson's declining authority because—astonishingly—he felt betrayed by Wully, who had almost been beaten black and blue fighting Haig's battles. Why should he rush to Wully's support, he seemed to suggest to his wife, when the C.I.G.S. had "not resolutely adhered to the policy of 'concentration on the Western front.' He had *said* that this is his policy, but has allowed all kinds of resources to be diverted to distant theatres at the bidding of his political masters."[40]

To jar Haig out of his complacency, both Robertson and Derby wrote him on the seventh. "If it is really so that you agree with the principles," Derby wrote:

> provided the question of the conveyance of orders is settled, then I should be justified in remaining in Office, because it would then be only a question of Robertson opposing a scheme to which you had given your assent. If, on the other hand, you are in agreement with Robertson, and Robertson is got rid of because he won't agree to it, naturally, I should have to go too.

Robertson's letter dealt with the manner in which he wanted his feud with Wilson and the prime minister settled. "The solution is, put me on the Versailles Ctee., then all is well, I think."[41]

Pressure from Derby and Robertson made it clear to Haig that he would be unable to avoid becoming involved in the escalating conflict between the civil and military authorities. With Derby requesting his presence in London, he cabled the secretary of state for war that he would arrive in London on the ninth in midafternoon and indicated that he would support Robertson's position: "I consider general reservoir desirable but do not concur in system set up for commanding it."[42] Haig's assistance, if it were forthcoming, could not come a moment too soon because Lloyd George seemed bent on replacing Wully because of his opposition to the Supreme War Council's decision on the command of the general reserve.

The next few days were arguably the most trying period of Lloyd George's wartime ministry. To enable the reader to make his way through the involved negotiations with their many twists and turns as Lloyd George frantically tried to save his government from disintegration, it is necessary to give a day-by-day account.

FEBRUARY 8 (FRIDAY)

This day began with the publication of an intriguing telegram from Repington in Paris, dated February 5, in the *Morning Post*. "The decisions of the recent Inter-Allied War Council regarding the control of British troops in the field are reported to be of such a strange character that Parliament should demand the fullest details and a Parliament Committee should examine them at once and take the opinions of our General Staff and our commanders in the field concerning the new arrangements." With memories of Repington's revelations about manpower based upon general staff figures fresh on their minds, Lloyd George and his allies can be forgiven for their belief that either Robertson or Maurice was the source of Repington's information. The evidence, however, suggests that Clemenceau, with whom Repington enjoyed the best of relations, was his informant. When the War Office's publicist forwarded Gwynne news of the formation and command of the general reserve, he emphasized that he had not been in contact with any member of the British delegation. Clearly he had no reason to keep anything from a fellow conspirator.[43]

At noon Lloyd George summoned Milner, who had returned from France the previous day, to Downing Street. From this point on Milner became a central figure in the chain of events which led to Robertson's fall.[44] As we will see, he even took a much firmer line than the prime minister and attempted to force his often unsteady hand. Milner was informed that Robertson was to be replaced by Plumer and sent to the northern command at York. Within hours, however, Lloyd George had changed his mind and the political calm of London had been shattered by a provocative headline in an evening paper, the *Globe*. "WHAT HAPPENED AT VERSAILLES? DISQUIETING RUMOURS FROM PARIS REGARDING THE HIGHER COMMAND. DEMAND FOR HOUSE OF COMMONS INTERVENTION." Repington's telegram in the *Morning Post* was reprinted and a ringing call to arms of the "soldiers' party" was issued:

> The veil of mystery with which His Majesty's Ministers have sought to involve the proceedings of the Supreme War Council at Versailles was lifted this morning by a disquieting telegram from the Military Correspondent of the "Morning Post" who is in Paris, and evidently knows the facts that have been so jealously withheld from the House of Commons.
>
> It may be hoped that, as Mr. Asquith was responsible for entrusting the Higher Command to Sir Douglas Haig . . . and Sir William Robertson . . . who both to a peculiar degree enjoy the confidence of the British Army and the British nation—he will not stand by and allow this arrangement to be broken up to gratify the whim of any individuals, however important.
>
> It may also be hoped that the House of Commons, which claims to be the seat of power, will refuse to allow itself to be elbowed out of its proper functions, and that at least we may be allowed to know what is going on behind the scenes, as no arrangement can make for military efficiency that precipitates a crisis in our Higher Command on the eve of a new campaign.

At half past six Milner returned to Downing Street to confer with the prime minister and Derby. Perhaps to blunt public criticism, Lloyd George now thought of making Haig C.I.G.S. and replacing him at general headquarters with Plumer. Lloyd George's wobbling annoyed Milner, who believed that the *Globe's* blistering attack made it imperative for the government to take a firm stand against the War Office and its supporters. Robertson—and Haig, too, if he refused to honor the decision of the Supreme War Council on the general reserve—must be sacked. "I think the sooner we make a move the better," he wrote the prime minister. "This kind of thing cannot be allowed to go on."[45]

But it could and it did! Milner's direct ways were not Lloyd George's ways. With the "soldiers' party" in full battle cry, Lloyd George wanted to make certain that Robertson's position would appear in the worst possible light. At all costs he hoped to avoid taking on Robertson, Derby, and Haig all at once; and he was filled with anxiety about the field marshal's imminent arrival in London.

FEBRUARY 9 (SATURDAY)

Lloyd George, Milner, and Derby resumed their discussions over break-fast. The C.I.G.S.'s relationship with Wilson and the Executive War Board, as the Army Council emphasized, remained the primary stumbling block to the implementation of the Supreme War Council's decisions. Lloyd George agreed to draft a proposal carefully delineating their relationship. On the assumption that Robertson would no longer be C.I.G.S., Lloyd George was prepared to go quite far in satisfying Derby and the Army Council. In his first draft, Wilson was closely tied to the War Office, serving as the C.I.G.S.'s deputy and a member of the Army Council. The major concession that he demanded in return was that the new C.I.G.S. would have pre-Robertson powers, with the Kitchener-Robertson compact being revoked. At half past twelve Lloyd George showed this first draft, which Derby had already per-used, to Milner, who was horrified at the virtual destruction of Wilson's independent position. At this point Lloyd George produced "a totally new proposal," which called for Robertson and Wilson to switch positions.[46] The prime minister's wild gyrations seemed remarkable even for someone with his mercurial personality. Until this moment there had been no suggestion by anyone of making Wilson C.I.G.S. Moreover, the prime minister had appeared absolutely determined to remove Robertson from any position of influence.

The fact that Lloyd George prepared two drafts of the C.I.G.S.'s relation-ship to Versailles has confused two authorities who have written detailed accounts of this crisis. Randolph Churchill has expressed doubt that Lloyd George was ever prepared to make the British permanent military repre-sentative a deputy of the C.I.G.S., and A. M. Gollin, a biographer of Milner, has written: "No historian can hope to plumb this mystery. . . . Was the Prime Minister presenting one group of his colleagues with one document and another faction with a completely different paper?"[47] There is no mys-tery. Lloyd George, as we have seen, only considered making Wilson a deputy of the C.I.G.S. if Robertson were replaced. Then, just a few hours away from his meeting with Haig, he came up with the brilliant ploy of sending Robertson to Versailles and replacing him with Wilson. If Wully accepted this arrangement, Lloyd George and Wilson would direct British military policy and pay him no heed. Also, as Lloyd George told Milner, this arrangement "was much the easiest scheme to carry without serious opposi-tion, as it offered a good position to Robertson." On the other hand, if Wully refused this offer, "he would put himself in the wrong and nobody would have any sympathy with him." Milner was skeptical, but the prime minister had closed his mind to further argument. On Lloyd George's instructions, Milner then telephoned Wilson to depart immediately for London. "What is this?" was the Irishman's puzzled reaction.[48]

Everything now seemed to hinge on whether or not Haig would accept the proposal to have Robertson and Wilson exchange positions. Greeted by Derby at Victoria Station on his arrival, Haig was driven to Downing Street by a roundabout way to give the secretary of state for war time to explain the government's decision to get rid of Robertson. To get around any constitutional difficulties, Wilson was to be made the deputy of whomever became the head of the general staff. Derby, of course, was in the dark about the prime minister's ingenious counterproposal which the Welshman had just divulged to Milner. When Haig sat with the prime minister, he echoed Robertson's position that the C.I.G.S. should sit on the Executive War Board. The wily Welshman then sprang his trap on the unsuspecting Haig and Derby. The field marshal allowed how the army would be "shocked" at Wilson's appointment, and he and Derby agreed that Robertson would be humiliated if he were made Wilson's deputy. But when Lloyd George agreed to make the British permanent military representative "absolutely free and unfettered in the advice he gives" all opposition to sending Robertson to Versailles collapsed. Derby desperately sought a compromise that might satisfy all parties; and Haig, unable to see through Lloyd George's cunning strategy, naively believed that if Robertson were at Versailles he could block any diversion of British military power to the East.[49]

FEBRUARY 10 (SUNDAY)

Sunday was a calm day before the storm broke. Robertson, informed by someone (perhaps Maurice) that the ground had been cut out from under him by Haig and Derby, rushed back to London from Eastbourne, where he had been since the seventh recuperating from a severe attack of bronchitis. Meanwhile, Milner attempted to explain to Wilson the events that had led to Lloyd George's decision to make him C.I.G.S. That the government's previous emphasis on the British permanent military representative's being independent of the War Office was only a smokescreen to hide the destruction of Robertson's position was revealed beyond question by the following comment in Wilson's diary: "If, however, Robertson refuses Versailles, then Milner and I agreed that we would put in someone junior to me & let me have a directing voice in Versailles if I was C.I.G.S."[50]

That evening Lloyd George telephoned Milner from Walton Heath. The king had gone along with Robertson and Wilson switching places and everything seemed settled, he assured Milner. Shortly after this call, however, Milner had reason to believe that the prime minister was overly sanguine. An agitated Major-General William T. Furse, the master general of ordnance and a member of the Army Council, paid him a visit. The only correct solution to the crisis over the command of the general reserve, he angrily argued, was to put the C.I.G.S. (whoever he might be) on the Executive War Board. Otherwise, there would be a duplication of functions. "A regular storm," Milner wrote in his diary before retiring for the night, is "clearly in the offing."[51]

FEBRUARY 11 (MONDAY)

Robertson informed Derby in no uncertain terms that he was not buying the February 9 formula worked out by Derby, Haig, and Lloyd George.[52]

Whatever Robertson might contend, he was not primarily interested in the mechanics of the command of the general reserve. He was desperately trying to keep the control of British strategy out of the hands of Lloyd George and Wilson. Meanwhile, the soldiers and their supporters launched a counterattack. In defiance of the censors, the *Morning Post* published on its front page an inflammatory article by Repington which reported both the plan to smash Turkey and the creation of a general reserve under Versailles. The prime minister, Repington roared, was "teaching soldiers how and where to make war." His conclusion was that Lloyd George must be removed from office.

> My opinion is that by starving our Armies in the field, by advocating adventures contrary to the advice of his legitimate military advisers, and by approving a decision which deprives our Commander in France of his full command, Mr. Lloyd George has clearly and finally proved his incapacity to govern England in a great war. This is the situation which Parliament must clear up in such a manner it thinks best.

The Army Council met during the morning and its military members agreed that all constitutional problems had now been overcome. But they continued to back Robertson's position that the C.I.G.S. should be the British representative to the Executive War Board. If the government did not accept this formula some of the military members, especially Furse and Major-General Robert Whigham, the deputy C.I.G.S., seemed prepared to hand in their resignations.[53]

Repington's indiscretions, more than the Army Council's stance, created consternation in the War Cabinet. "I know nothing comparable to this betrayal in the whole of our history," Lloyd George later wrote in his memoirs.[54] Lloyd George exaggerates. What Repington revealed was far more helpful to the "soldiers' party" than to the Central Powers. When the War Cabinet discussed what action it should take against the *Morning Post,* the director of military intelligence, General George Macdonogh, stressed that, if he were called as a witness, "he would find it very difficult to state on oath in a court of law that information had been given which was likely to be of any great use to the enemy." Nonetheless, after two meetings on the subject, the War Cabinet decided to shut down the paper, only to have Lloyd George suspend this decision later that evening after a meeting with the home secretary.[55]

Lloyd George was not the only one who began to waver. Derby had started the day prepared to honor his agreement with Lloyd George. If Robertson refused to go along, he told Wilson, he "was OUT & he (Derby) would not defend him in the House of Lords tomorrow."[56] Robertson's implacable opposition and the support he received within the War Office, however, weakened the resolve of the portly aristocrat from Lancashire, who had never been known for his steadiness when push came to shove.

Fearing that Lloyd George was contemplating a strategic retreat as he had done so often in the past when faced with a showdown with Robertson, Milner kept up the pressure. "I hope the paper you drew up & showed to me on Saturday afternoon still holds *good* except in so far as it makes the Versailles man a *D*. C.I.G.S. & member of the Army Council, wh. is unnecessary & had better be abandoned," he wrote.

But if there is any question of Robertson having something more than the Versailles job, as defined in that paper, & retaining some over-riding or even concurrent authority at the War Office, then I am sure we are heading for disaster. . . . We are on absolutely strong ground, &, if there is to be a fight, wh. I don't feel sure of, we can win. But let us at least make sure that at the end of the fight we are free men & not still saddled with our Old Man of the Sea![57]

Ironically, one of the strongest supporters of the February 9 agreement was Haig, who visited Robertson in his office and berated him for his refusal to go to Versailles. "It was his *duty* to go to Versailles or anywhere else if the Government wished it."[58] Later Haig visited with the king and told him to encourage Robertson to accept his new position. Then Haig departed from Charing Cross for the peace and quiet of the western front while the battle in Whitehall raged on in his absence.

FEBRUARY 12 (TUESDAY)

Unable to get Wully to budge an inch, Derby told the War Cabinet that he had come to the conclusion "that it would be a great national misfortune" if Robertson were forced out over the issue of the command of the general reserve. Hence, although he favored revoking the Kitchener-Robertson compact, he wanted to retain Wully as C.I.G.S. In addition to Derby, those in attendance this day were Barnes, Bonar Law, Curzon, Lloyd George, Milner, and Balfour. With the exception of Derby, Milner, and the prime minister, none had been involved directly in the negotiations between Lloyd George and the soldiers. With the national clamor inspired by Repington as a backdrop, some of the ministers eagerly grasped Derby's suggestion as a way to end the crisis. Powerful Unionists such as Cecil, Long, and Chamberlain had previously supported the army and there was the real danger that Asquith and his followers might exploit the situation. Curzon, Bonar Law, and Balfour thus supported Derby's solution. Milner, supported by Barnes, spoke long and vehemently against backing away from an arrangement which the prime minister, Derby, and Haig had accepted. Who ruled Britain, he wanted to know, Robertson or the government? Feeling the effects of a severe cold, Lloyd George was not at his best. He delivered a "tremendous tirade" against Robertson's arrogance, but with the War Cabinet divided, he "appeared unable to screw up his courage" to sack him. "He wanted more time to think it over in all its aspects," Milner noted, "so we parted without coming to a decision."[59]

Lloyd George was not about to risk his government until he discovered the impact that the *Morning Post*'s revelations had had on Parliament. Shortly after the War Cabinet adjourned, the Welshman, flanked by Bonar Law and Barnes, looked across the aisle at Asquith on the Opposition

Bench. He was ill at ease because the Liberal leader had refused to give notice of the question he planned to raise. After heaping extravagant praise upon Robertson and Haig, the former prime minister began to hammer away at Lloyd George's interference with military policy. Did Lloyd George plan to remove Robertson or Haig? Was it true that these great generals had had their influence on military policy reduced? There was a world of difference between "coordination" and "subordination." Demonstrating that he had been well briefed on Robertson's position, Asquith asserted that "the Commander-in-Chief ought to get his orders from the Chief of Staff and the Chief of Staff only."

When Lloyd George rose to respond, he spoke with caution and deliberation, refusing to explain fully the Supreme War Council's decision on the creation and command of the general reserve. To do so, he said with passion, would be "treason beyond description." This ploy was hardly fair, and an aggrieved Asquith shot out of his seat. Before he could utter a word, the House erupted in prolonged applause and cheers which grew in intensity and volume. "Loud, angry rolls," was the way the *Daily Mail* put it. And its motivation seemed clear. "It was a violent personal demonstration against the Prime Minister," the *Daily Telegraph* informed its readers.[60]

Lloyd George hastened to apologize for insinuating that Asquith was giving assistance to the enemy with his probing questions, but the House was in no mood to be mollified. The remainder of his speech was delivered before an unfriendly audience. When asked if Haig and Robertson had approved the Versailles decision, he equated silence in open council with approval. "Certainly; they were present there, and all those representatives approved." The prime minister clearly hoped to avoid being tarred with overruling the military authorities. But he was less than truthful in doing so. Twice, as we have seen, Robertson in correspondence with the prime minister had made his opposition clear to the way the Executive War Board had been constituted. After the tongue-lashing he had received from the prime minister because of his outspoken opposition to a campaign against Turkey, it was grossly unfair to emphasize that he had remained silent when the Allied leaders created the Executive War Board.

Lloyd George concluded the debate with a challenge to his critics. "If the House of Commons and the country are not satisfied with the conduct of the War, and if they think there is any Government which can conduct it better, then it is their business, in God's name, to put that other Government in!"[61]

Despite these fighting words, Lloyd George can hardly have been unaffected by the hostile reception his speech had received. More was involved than the government's relations with its military advisers. Many politicians had reached the breaking point with governmental secrecy and the use of the press to sway public opinion. The press lords, with their ready access to the government, were supplanting Parliament. To be sure, the War Office was in constant touch with its supporters on Fleet Street, but Lloyd George was widely considered the greater sinner, and the recent attacks on the leaders of the army in the *Daily Mail* by Lovat Fraser were thought to be the prime minister's handiwork. Northcliffe's brother Rothermere had become a member of the government in late 1917, and on the previous day the *Times* had announced that Lord Beaverbrook, who owned the *Daily Express,* had been appointed minister in charge of propaganda. Was the prime minister going to govern from Fleet Street? A. G. Gardiner defined the explosion in the *Daily News* as "a declaration that the government of this nation is vested in Parliament and not in the Press, in the House of Commons and not in the House of Harmsworth."[62]

February 12 was one of the government's worst days. Lloyd George had even gotten a whiff of a vote of censure. Hankey's conclusion was that the government's flabby response to the *Morning Post* and Robertson's arrogance, coupled with Lloyd George's shaky performance in Parliament, "have had a very damaging effect on the Government." Hankey was surely correct in his view that the prime minister's tergiversation in the face of the opposition of the "soldiers' party" had placed his ministry in jeopardy. Milner and Barnes seemed about to resign in disgust; and Esher reported: "All this indecision is having a bad effect. I hear that the opposition is crystallizing, and that Mr. A. [Asquith] spends hours at Landsdowne H[ouse]. You can realise what this portends. It is far better to make a mistake than to come to no decision."[63]

FEBRUARY 13 (WEDNESDAY)

Matters became even more confused on this day. In full retreat, Lloyd George told Hankey that "he had come to the conclusion that he could not sack Robertson, who was willing to stay on as C.I.G.S. with reduced powers. Lord Northcliffe's attack on Robertson had, he said, made it impossible for him to get rid of him, as all the world would say it was done at Northcliffe's dictation."[64] Milner, when informed that Robertson had forced the government to capitulate, rushed off to see the prime minister. How was the government, he wanted to know, going to explain to the country that it had buckled before the military authorities? At the very least an explanation must be given to Parliament. To keep him from resigning, Lloyd George agreed that Milner and Hankey should draft a paper for Bonar Law to read in Parliament which explained that the Supreme War Council's creation of an Executive War Board necessitated changes; Lloyd George and Derby had consequently agreed to send Robertson to Versailles, but Wully had wrecked this arrangement by turning the offer down. Derby, who along with Robertson would be pictured in an unfavorable light by this explanation, however, refused to go along. Still believing that he could make everything right in the end, he resisted any definitive statement. "I am still hopeful that I may find a satisfactory conclusion, but I can't do it at the point of the bayonet," he wrote the prime minister.[65]

Robertson's supporters then made a fatal miscalculation. After conferring with Wully, who continued to insist that the C.I.G.S. have a seat on the Executive War Board, and the king's envoy, Lord Stamfordham, Derby attempted to return to the first agreement that he had reached with Lloyd George, which would make Wilson the C.I.G.S.'s deputy when the C.I.G.S. was not available to sit on the Executive War Board. "On being asked whether these arrangements were agreeable to me," Robertson writes in his memoirs, "I at once accepted them without qualification of any kind." And why not! It would reestablish Robertson's ascendancy in strategy if Wilson were made his mouthpiece. The secretary of state for war—called a "poor wobbly thing" by Hankey—then put his proposal in the form of a memorandum for the eyes of the prime minister.[66]

Lloyd George gave Derby's fresh proposal to Wilson and told him to discuss it with Milner. Although Derby's proposal was essentially the same arrangement which Milner and Wilson favored if the latter became C.I.G.S., both men were horrified at the prospect of Robertson emerging from this crisis with much of his authority restored. The acceptance of Derby's new position was unthinkable, Milner wrote the prime minister, and it was time "to put your foot down."[67]

For once Milner did not need to prod the prime minister. Lloyd George had only agreed to tie the British permanent military representative to the general staff when it seemed certain that Robertson would not be the C.I.G.S. His astute political instincts told him that the military camp had overplayed its hand this time. It no longer appeared to be a question of the civilians interfering with the military authorities. Rather, it seemed a question more than ever of Robertson's attempting to dictate to the War Cabinet. If Lloyd George adhered to Derby's proposal of the twelfth to retain Robertson as C.I.G.S., insisting at the same time that the British permanent military representative be kept independent of the War Office, he might unite the War Cabinet behind him and appear before Parliament as a reasonable man attempting to implement the policy of the Supreme War Council. As he later told the War Cabinet: "He himself and the War Cabinet had made every possible concession to General Sir William Robertson consistently with adherence to the recent decisions of the Supreme War Council. General Robertson, however, had not yielded an inch."[68]

FEBRUARY 14 (THURSDAY)

In Milner's words, "The game of deliberation, negotiation, and reconsideration began afresh." Shortly after 11:00 A.M. the war Cabinet met without Lloyd George, who was down with his cold. At 12:30 the ministers trooped to the drawing room of the Prime Minister's official residence. Reclining on a sofa, Lloyd George made it clear that he could not accept Derby's latest proposal. Robertson might stay on if he refused to go to Versailles, but Wilson was not going to be put under his thumb. Robertson was then called in to see if he would accept this arrangement.

The blunt-speaking Wully came right to the point. The haggling over the machinery of the Executive War Board tended to obscure the real issue: Did the War Cabinet wish to retain him as its supreme military adviser? He then calmly reiterated his reasons for opposing the division of the C.I.G.S.'s powers which would result from his accepting Derby's February 12 formula. He saw little merit in Lloyd George's contention that his duties at the War Office prevented him from overseeing the general reserve. Hindenburg had no problem in directing campaigns on several fronts. In any event, any problems could easily be overcome by making Wilson his deputy at Versailles when he was not free to attend the sessions of the Executive War Board.

If that were so, Lloyd George inquired, would Wully himself become the deputy at Versailles if Wilson were appointed C.I.G.S.? Caught off balance, Robertson was speechless, asking for a moment to collect his thoughts. But Wilson was "only a temporary general," he finally sputtered. When Robertson left the room he was for all practical purposes finished, although the War Cabinet, now united behind the prime minister, decided to give the rugged warrior another chance to either remain C.I.G.S. on Lloyd George's terms or go to Versailles.[69]

Balfour and Derby were given the unenviable task of attempting to bring Robertson around that afternoon. To no one's surprise he held his ground. How many times, he impatiently asked, must he give his position? He appeared not so much firm as obstinate, and his obvious dislike of Wilson served to undermine his arguments. As Derby and Balfour left Wully's office, they encountered Lord Stamfordham. Would Stamfordham, Derby pleaded, use his influence to break down Robertson's resistance? The king's private secretary agreed to do his best, but he fared no better than Derby and Balfour when he entered Wully's lair. How could he "look anyone in the face," Wully told Stamfordham, if he acquiesced in an arrangement which he deemed dangerous? This said, Robertson made himself appear petty. "If however Sir H. Plumer were to come here as C.I.G.S. he would go to Paris, but certainly not if Sir H. Wilson his Junior was to become C.I.G.S."[70]

After learning Robertson's response, Lloyd George instructed Derby to offer the post of C.I.G.S. to Plumer and gave Hankey the task of making certain that the head of the War Office played it straight. This was a wise precaution because Hankey discovered that Derby's wording of the telegram "was quite calculated to make Plumer refuse."[71] Hankey then redrafted the telegram to Plumer.

The end of the day found Robertson in an untenable position. His view, that "he would be d—— if he would do anything the War Cabinet wanted," angered some of his supporters. The suspicion grew that he wanted a crisis in Parliament, "counting on Squiff & the Labour vote to down L.G."[72]

FEBRUARY 15 (FRIDAY)

With no compromise possible between Robertson and the government, it was obvious that a political brouhaha could not be avoided. Robertson refused to bend, but he placed the government in an awkward position by not resigning or stating unequivocally that he "refused absolutely to take either of the positions offered to him."[73]

Apprehension stalked the halls of Whitehall when Plumer's reply was received. Coached by Robertson, Plumer took his position on the command of the general reserve and refused to head the general staff. Hankey was indeed right when he noted that it "looked suspiciously like a 'rig' by the great General Staff trades union."[74]

Plumer's refusal opened the door of the general staff to Wilson—Lloyd George's first choice as C.I.G.S. Plumer had only been selected because Lloyd George realized that violent opposition to Wilson in the army and Parliament would make the supersession of Robertson more difficult. But, at the same time, Plumer's support of Robertson put the government in a precarious position. Bonar Law and Milner agreed that the government's "position had now become one of great gravity, and that if the Government stuck to its guns, it ran the risk of defeat."[75]

That evening Milner and Wilson talked with Lloyd George at Walton Heath. To their great relief they found the prime minister "in a very fighting humor." As he told them, he now realized "the miserable cowardice and double dealing of Derby and of all Robertson's plots & plans." Although now determined "to catch a hold and govern," he was pessimistic about the results, but at least he would "go down fighting." A hopeful sign was that Asquith seemed unwilling to go to the brink over the government's relations with the military authorities. "Esher tells me that Lansdowne & Asquith have agreed that *you* must be kept in office," Hankey had written that day. Still there were many uncertain elements. Milner and Wilson feared that Curzon, Cecil, Derby, and perhaps even Balfour would resign. And what stance would the powerful Chamberlain take in Paliament?[76]

Haig's position in the end might decide the issue. When in London, he had raised no real difficulties and had even pressured Robertson to go to Versailles. But his position now seemed uncertain. On the fifteenth, Robertson in a private and confidential letter pleaded in so many words for his support. If I agreed to go to Versailles, he firmly told the field marshal, "I would have been a useless tool at Versailles with Wilson here as C.I.G.S." Haig immediately telegraphed Derby that the "only permanent solution of difficulty is that C.I.G.S. should have his deputy at Versailles in same way as French have Foch and a subordinate general at Versailles."[77]

FEBRUARY 16 (SATURDAY)

Lloyd George began to act like the nation's leader. First, on Milner's advice, he visited George V. Combining forcefulness with reasonableness, he told the king "that he could not continue to be responsible unless he and his colleagues were free to take the measures they considered necessary to meet the situation."[78] Robertson would be given yet another chance to either remain as C.I.G.S. or go to Versailles. If he refused, Wilson would be made C.I.G.S., and Haig would be consulted about his replacement at Versailles. When Lloyd George brought this formula before the War Cabinet, Derby attempted to scramble it by asking if Haig, who had been summoned to London and would arrive that evening, were to be consulted about the relationship between the C.I.G.S. and the British permanent military representative. This suggestion was immediately waved down by the War Cabinet. Haig could have his man at Versailles, but he was not about to be allowed to reopen the question that had paralyzed the government for days. But what if Haig refused to go along? The War Cabinet decided that if this occurred the prime minister should refuse to accept his resignation. The only divisive note sounded was Derby's usual threat to quit the government if Robertson were forced out.[79]

After the War Cabinet adjourned Lloyd George summoned Robertson to Downing Street and went through the motions of repeating the government's terms. Robertson asked for time to consider his response and later that afternoon wrote a formal letter of refusal (but not resignation).

Thus ended one of the "most anxious days" of Lloyd George's life. "Have you packed up? We may be out next week," he told one of his secretaries.[80]

FEBRUARY 17 (SUNDAY)

At 9:30 A.M. Robertson paid Haig a visit. The day before, he had impressed upon the field marshal in a letter that the government planned to argue in Parliament that Haig agreed with the new Versailles machinery. "I think you should know this," he pointedly noted. In short, the dagger in Robertson's back would have Haig's name on it. In their conversation Wully emphasized that the machinery of Versailles was not really the fundamental issue. "H. Wilson as C.I.G.S. would get the country into difficulties."[81] Haig, however, believed that he had done all that he could for Robertson through his support of Robertson's position on the command of the general reserve. Unlike Derby, he was not about to be dragged down by Robertson's obstinacy.

Later that day Haig conferred with the prime minister at Walton Heath. To his immense relief, Lloyd George discovered that the field marshal, although he disapproved of the Versailles arrangement which divided the C.I.G.S.'s power, was quite prepared to accept the removal of Robertson and the resignation of Derby without a murmur of protest. "We discussed the whole position for hours," Lloyd George writes. "Haig put up no fight for Robertson. He clearly did not approve of his defiance of a decision come to by the Government." As for Derby's possible resignation, "he sniffed it aside with an expression of contempt."[82]

Derby, in contrast to Haig, had his letter of resignation out of his pocket "for the 28th time about." The prime minister, who was eager to put his man Milner in Derby's place, decided to make an effort to retain his services for the time being. If he resigned, Derby would be free to tell Parliament that both Haig and Plumer agreed with Robertson's criticisms of the Versailles machinery. Hankey was subsequently delegated to see the "flabby jelly" and try to persuade him from quitting the government.[83] That evening Lloyd George sang Welsh hymns, his spirits considerably lifted by Haig's acquiescence.

The enigmatic Scotsman's position, especially his willingness to accept the transfer of Robertson to Versailles, had proven to be Wully's Achilles' heel. What explains the breakdown of the Haig-Robertson alliance that had given the soldiers control of British strategy since late 1915? Was it Haig's sense of duty to his country? His distaste for "squabbling in high places"?[84] His understanding of political realities? Or was it his belief that Robertson, whom he unfairly blamed for the "side show" in Palestine, had outlived his usefulness? Who can speak with certainty about the motives of this distant and paradoxical figure?

The day did not end without a bizzare twist. Derby and Robertson seemed prepared to make a last stand in the War Office. Wully told reporters that he had not resigned; and Derby, when Wilson telephoned him about his new duties, refused to see him.

FEBRUARY 18 (MONDAY)

It was now apparent to Robertson that he stood almost alone. Many of his supporters had talked resignation but everyone stayed in their place. Dependent upon his pay for a livelihood Robertson swallowed his pride and accepted the humiliation of a home command in southeastern England, the eastern command. Was this Lloyd George's final revenge? "Why not the Boy Scouts?" someone asked in Parliament to the accompaniment of laughter when Bonar Law made this announcement.

On the eve of his appearance before Parliament to give the government's case, Lloyd George must have been confident of success. Earlier his government seemed about to fly apart, with some ministers such as Milner and Barnes threatening to resign because he refused to take a firm line against Robertson, and others such as Cecil, Curzon, and Derby threatening to go because they believed that he was ignoring the advice of the military authorities. But in the end they had all been talked around.[85] The origins of the crisis lay in Lloyd George's determination to wrest control of British strategy from Robertson and Haig. Yet when the showdown came the debate within the War Cabinet largely focused on the issue of civilian supremacy. Robertson had been maneuvered by his own obstinacy and by Lloyd George's superior political skills into taking an untenable position. He could not win when it was a question of final authority resting with the civilian rather than with the military authorities. If Parliament were faced with a choice between himself and Robertson on this issue, he would be chosen. Moreover, Robertson could be replaced. But who could replace him? Asquith? Lansdowne? Chamberlain? Henderson? Lloyd George feared Asquith the most. The former prime minister, however, eschewed the fight to a finish which some of his supporters urged upon him. J. A. Spender, his close friend and the editor of the *Westminster Gazette,* told Esher that the Liberal leader "does not mean to push the attack right home. He has no desire to take office now."[86] Even if Asquith had gone all out, his bid for power would surely have fallen short. A headline in the *Daily Mail* perhaps caught the popular mood best: "WHICH WOULD YOU *GO* TIGER HUNTING WITH? ASQUITH OR LLOYD GEORGE?"[87]

FEBRUARY 19 (TUESDAY)

Lloyd George stood before the House with a carefully worded text. A troublesome point was Haig's exact position. Lloyd George had wanted to say that Haig considered the Versailles machinery "workable," but when Haig protested, the wording had been changed to "prepared to work under this arrangement."[88] As for any conflict with Robertson, Lloyd George maintained that his relations with the C.I.G.S. for the past two years have been not merely "friendly, but cordial." When Asquith, who knew better, pressed him on whether he had misrepresented Robertson's position on the creation and command of the general reserve in his statement to Parliament on the twelfth, Lloyd George took considerable liberty with the truth: "I certainly never knew that Sir William Robertson had any objection in principle; quite the reverse."[89] When Asquith refused to accept this statement, he was jeered. The mood of Parliament was to end the squabbling and get on with the war.

With Asquith pulling his punches, the biggest challenge came from Chamberlain, who focused on the press attacks upon the army and navy leadership and the prime minister's relations with the powerful press lords. On the previous day, Northcliffe had joined Beaverbrook and Rothermere in the government as director of propaganda in enemy countries. But this issue was less explosive than the charge of interference with the generals, which Lloyd George had deftly sidestepped.

In later years, Lloyd George gave a lurid account of the crisis over Robertson's dismissal. In his purple prose: "Robertson and his friends meant this time to fight to a finish, and they had every hope of being able to build up a Parliamentary combination drawn from all parties which would reverse the Versailles decision, supplant the Government, and substitute for it one which would make Robertson virtual dictator for the rest of the War, as Hindenburg was in Germany and by the same means." This view has been deemed "nonsense" by Wully's apologist, Victor Bonham-Carter, but there are clearly elements of truth in it. Gwynne even touted a Robertson ministry which included Asquith. Whether Robertson ever considered becoming prime minister is doubtful. But his actions leave little doubt that in a desperate attempt to keep strategy out of Lloyd George's hands he put himself above the government, hoping to destroy either Versailles or Lloyd George in the process.[90] On the other hand, the "soldiers' party" had almost no chance of success. Asquith, although in touch with Robertson and his supporters, would not be a party to such an arrangement, and, more importantly, civilian control of the army was deeply ingrained in the English political and military tradition.

Although Robertson had been squashed, and Versailles saved, Foch still commanded a phantom army. Haig continued to make it clear that he had no divisions to contribute, telling Bonar Law that he would prefer being replaced to turning over any of his troops to the Executive War Board.[91] Haig's position was reprehensible, for he would not really be *losing* divisions by handing them over to Foch. To the contrary, if the Germans massed their troops in his sector, his only hope of fighting on even or near even terms was to receive immediate assistance from the general reserve. Although Lloyd George, despite what he maintains in his memoirs, was surely aware of Haig's stance, he did not make an issue of it, perhaps hoping that the field marshal would bow to pressure applied by the Executive War

Board, Pétain, and Clemenceau. Pétain, however, was just as suspicious and jealous of Foch as Haig and Robertson had been of Wilson when he was the British permanent military representative. The French commander in chief readily agreed with Haig that a personal understanding between them, rather than the creation of the general reserve, was the best way to coordinate the Anglo-French response to a great German offensive. Clemenceau, caught in the middle between Foch and Pétain, tended to favor the latter, telling Haig on February 25 that "he would arrange to 'écarter' (set aside) Foch gradually."[92] Another obstacle to the formation of the general reserve was the position taken by Rawlinson, Haig's choice as Wilson's successor at Versailles. Haig thought that Rawlinson would "play the game honestly" (e.g., support the army against the politicians) and his view was soon confirmed. At lunch with Haig on March 5, Rawlinson assured him that he would "wholeheartedly" support his position on the general reserve.[93] By this time even Foch's paper army was rapidly disappearing. Initially Foch had requested a general reserve of thirty divisions, approximately one seventh of the Allied forces. But Haig, encouraged by Pétain and Clemenceau, clung stubbornly to all of the divisions under his command. Meanwhile, Pétain attempted to reduce the number required of him. Curiously Clemenceau continued to support Pétain, telling Wilson that the general reserve would initially consist of only the British and French divisions withdrawn from Italy.[94] On March 4, seventeen days before the German storm broke, the Executive War Board threw up its hands in despair and in essence turned the negotiations with Pétain and Haig over to the political leaders. Rawlinson's hands, however, were thrown up in glee rather than in despair. "The trouble to my mind is Rawly's attitude," wrote General Sackville-West, Wilson's friend and informant at Versailles. "He thinks *he* can decide what share the British are to take & as he backs D.H. the situation is getting just the same as when Wully always said yes to D.H." In fact, Sackville-West argued that Wilson had helped create a monster in the Executive War Board. "Versailles is to become an appanage or buffer between L.G. & D.H. & you are left out—It wants some thinking over which no doubt you have done."[95]

It all depended on whose ox was being gored. When Wilson was at Versailles, he had steadily worked to undermine the C.I.G.S.'s authority. Standing in Robertson's shoes, he was now unhappy with the role played by Rawlinson. Another concern of Wilson's was Foch's falling star. If Foch's days were "numbered," as he believed, the less influence Versailles had the happier he would be. "If we get in place of him a man of the type of Pétain the less Versailles handles the Reserve the better," he wrote Sackville-West.[96]

When the War Cabinet discussed Haig's attitude on March 6, Wilson defended his actions in the strongest possible terms.

The present situation has arisen largely owing to the delays in settling the composition of the Inter-Allied General Reserve, which was certainly in no sense the fault of the Field Marshal, and were not unconnected with the political crisis which had arisen after the last Versailles Conferences. Field Marshal Haig had now completed his arrangements with General Pétain; he was faced with a possibility of an immediate attack; and he did not like to risk the dislocation of his arrangements at this particular juncture by allocating a portion of his Reserves to the Inter-Allied General Reserve.

The War Cabinet, somewhat taken aback by Wilson's virtual endorsement of Haig's obstructionism, refused to accept the field marshal's position as "necessarily final," although it was admitted that the prospect of an imminent German attack made it awkward to force his hand at the moment.[97]

Lloyd George was unwilling to fight to the last ditch over the general reserve. When Wilson first told him on March 4 that Haig had unequivocally refused to hand over even one division to the Executive War Board, he admitted that he was not prepared to run the risk of Haig's resignation by forcing him to comply with Versailles.[98] He obviously hoped to avoid taking on the army again so soon after surviving his bitter confrontation with Robertson.

On the eve of a meeting of the Supreme War Council in London in mid-March to decide finally the fate of the general reserve, only Foch of those who really mattered was a zealot on the subject. The British government's willingness to capitulate on an issue which it had proclaimed far and wide to be essential, however, was embarrassing. At the very least, Milner argued, the principle of the general reserve must be preserved. More than the security of the Allied forces was involved in Milner's view. "If Haig (or Haig & Pétain?) kill it now, I doubt if it will ever revive. And we shall have once more passed under the yoke of the generals."[99]

On March 14 Lloyd George, Wilson, and Hankey discussed ways of salvaging something of the general reserve. They finally hit upon the idea of considering the British and French divisions in Italy as the general reserve. When this proposal was made at the Supreme War Council, Orlando remarked to Lloyd George, " 'That is very ingenious indeed,' " prompting Clemenceau to add, " 'And if an Italian says that, you may know it is.' " Only Foch, whose preeminent position was being demolished, hotly protested this face-saving device until Clemenceau silenced him with a wave of his hand and the command to "shut up." As for Haig's and Pétain's agreement to assist each other, Lloyd George insisted that this private understanding be immediately communicated to Versailles and that the permanent military representatives work out a common plan to send aid to Italy if the Germans struck south of the Alps.[100]

Although the principle of the general reserve had been preserved, this was an empty and futile gesture. On the day the German blow fell, Sackville-West was correct when he wrote Wilson: "The Executive War Board is dead, dead as a door nail."[101] In its place had been put a personal understanding between the French and British commanders in chief. This suited Haig's purpose because he was determined to destroy Foch's executive authority. Before journeying to London for the Supreme War Council he and Rawlinson agreed that the functions of the Executive War Board "should be *advisory,* not *executive.*"[102] Haig had taken one of the gravest risks of his military career by putting his faith in Pétain, whose previous career had not heightened his reputation for taking bold or risky steps. How prophetic was

Wilson's remark when he told Haig that in a crunch "he would have to live on Pétain's charity & he would find that very cold charity."[103]

Contrary to his memoirs,[104] Lloyd George was partly to blame for the collapse of the general reserve. Fearing the political repercussions of a confrontation with Haig, he did not order him to cooperate with the Executive War Board. If Robertson had retained control of the general staff, the prime minister almost certainly would have been more resolute, attempting to save the Executive War Board and the general reserve as a counterweight to the general staff. In the final analysis, undermining the "Westerners" was always more important to him than the concept of a strategic reserve. Yet even if Lloyd George had fought to save the general reserve, he probably would have failed. The obstructionism of Clemenceau, Haig, Pétain, Wilson, and Rawlinson, not to mention the imminent German offensive, made its demise almost inevitable in March.

NOTES

1. Robertson to Haig, January 12, 1918, Robertson MSS, I/23/78.
2. Haig Diary, January 24, 1918, no. 123.
3. Ibid., October 18, 1917, no. 118.
4. Wilson Diary, December 6, 1917.
5. See David Robin Watson, *Georges Clemenceau: A Political Biography* (1974), p. 296.
6. Wilson Diary, December 17, 1917, and Clemenceau to Lloyd George, December 17, 1917, Lloyd George MSS, F/50/1/27.
7. War Cabinet (301), December 18, 1917, CAB 23/4.
8. War Cabinet Paper G.T. 3343 of January 15, 1918, CAB 24/39, and Hankey Diary, January 22, 1918, 1/4.
9. Milner to Lloyd George, November 3, 1917, Lloyd George MSS, F/38/2/20.
10. *Observer*, December 16, 1917.
11. Esher to Lloyd George, December 12, 1917, Lloyd George MSS, F/16/1/22.
12. Anglo-French Conference, December 23, 1917, CAB 28/3/I.C.-37, and War Cabinet (306), December 26, 1917, CAB 23/4.
13. In January 1918, when Foch first talked with Haig about a generalissimo, the British commander in chief "jumped up like a jack-in-the-box, and, with both hands shot up to heaven, exclaimed: 'Monsieur Clemenceau, I have only one chief, and I can have no other. My King.'" See Clive to Maurice, December 18, 1917, Maurice MSS, 3/5/63, and Georges Clemenceau, *Grandeur and Misery of Victory* (1930), p. 34.
14. Wilson Diary, January 9–11, 1918.
15. Maurice Diary, January 10, 1918, 4/3.
16. Milner to Lloyd George (Wilson to Milner, January 14, 1918, inclosed), n.d., Lloyd George MSS, F/38/3/2.
17. War Cabinet (329), January 23, 1918, CAB 23/5.
18. Robertson (memorandum) to Lloyd George, January 30, 1918, Robertson MSS, I/24/3.
19. Wilson Diary, January 30, 1918.
20. Hankey to Lady Hankey, January 31, 1918, Hankey MSS, 3/23.
21. Wilson to Lloyd George, January 25, 1918, Lloyd George MSS, F/47/7/15.
22. Supreme War Council, January 30, 1918, CAB 28/3/I.C.-39.
23. Wilson Diary, January 30, 1918.
24. Hankey Diary, January 30, 1918, 1/4.

25. Supreme War Council, January 31, 1918, CAB 28/3/I.C.-40.

26. Hankey Diary, February 1, 1918, 1/4.

27. Robertson to Derby, February, 1918 (misdated 1916), Derby MSS, 920 (17).

28. Supreme War Council, February 1, 1918, CAB 28/3/I.C.-41.

29. Supreme War Council, February 1, 1918, CAB 28/3/I.C.-42.

30. Robertson to Lloyd George, February 1, 1918, Robertson MSS, I/24/5/1.

31. See Wilson Diary, January 28 and February 2, 1918, and Hankey Diary, February 2, 1918, 1/4.

32. Captain Peter E. Wright, *At the Supreme War Council* (1921), p. 62, and Supreme War Council, February 2, 1918, CAB 28/3/I.C.-43.

33. Haig Diary, February 2, 1918, no. 123, and Supreme War Council, February 2, 1918, CAB 28/3/I.C.-43.

34. See Supreme War Council, February 1, 1918, CAB 28/3/I.C.-41.

35. Amery to Lloyd George, February 3, 1918, Lloyd George MSS, F/2/1/15, and Hankey Diary, February 3, 1918, 1/4. Milner apparently believed that his appointment as secretary of state for war had been settled and he discussed with Wilson the changes that needed to be made in the personnel of the War Office. See Wilson Diary, February 4, 1918.

36. Robertson to Derby, February 2, 1918, Derby MSS, 920 (17), and Robertson to Stamfordham, February 2, 1918, RA GV F1259/13.

37. Derby (memorandum) to Lloyd George, February 4, 1918, Derby MSS, 920 (17), and War Cabinet (338), February 4, 1918, CAB 23/5.

38. Army Council (242), February 4, 1918 (adjourned to February 6), W.O. 163/23.

39. Esher Diary, February 4, 1918, 2/21.

40. Haig to Lady Haig, February 5, 1918, Haig MSS, no. 149.

41. Derby to Haig and Robertson to Haig, February 7, 1918, Haig MSS, no. 123.

42. Haig to Derby, February 8, 1918, Derby MSS, 920 (17).

43. Repington to Gwynne, February 5, 1918, Gwynne MSS, 21, and Repington, *First World War, 1914–1918,* 2:207–10.

44. The best primary source for untangling the confused events of mid-February is Milner's day-by-day account. Memorandum by Milner (misdated February 14, 1918), Milner MSS, dep. 374. The view from the palace can be found in Stamfordham's memorandum, a running account from February 13 to 18. RA GV F1259/32.

45. Milner to Lloyd George, February 8, 1918, Lloyd George MSS, F/38/3/10.

46. See undated drafts marked "A" and "B" by Milner in Lloyd George MSS, F/38/3/13. Also see memorandum by Milner, Milner MSS, dep. 374.

47. Randolph Churchill, *Lord Derby, "King" of Lancashire: The Official Life of Edward Earl Derby, 1865–1948* (1959), p. 321, and A. M. Gollin, *Proconsul in Politics: A Study of Lord Milner in Opposition and in Power* (1964), p. 482.

48. Memorandum by Milner, Milner MSS, dep. 374, and Wilson Diary, February 9, 1918.

49. Haig Diary, February 9 and 11, 1918, no. 123, and Lloyd George to Milner, February 9, 1918, Lloyd George MSS, F/38/3/11.

50. Wilson Diary, February 10, 1918.

51. Milner Diary, February 10, 1918, Milner MSS, dep. 89, and memorandum by Milner, Milner MSS, dep. 374.

52. Robertson to Derby, February 11, 1918, Robertson MSS, I/24/11.

53. Army Council (243), February 11, 1918, W.O. 163/23, Gwynne to Asquith, February 11, 1918, Gwynne MSS, 14, and Robertson to Derby, February 11, 1918, Derby MSS, 920 (17).

54. Lloyd George, *War Memoirs,* 2:1676.

55. War Cabinet (342–43), February 11, 1918, CAB 23/5. Repington and Gwynne were later prosecuted under the Defence of the Realm Act and forced to pay a nominal fine. But the *Morning Post* was never shut down.

56. Wilson Diary, February 11, 1918.

57. Milner to Lloyd George, February 11, 1918, Lloyd George MSS, F/38/3/12.

58. Haig Diary, February 11, 1918, no. 123.

59. War Cabinet (344A), February 12, 1918, CAB 23/13, Hankey Diary, February 12, 1918, 1/3, and memorandum by Milner, Milner MSS, dep. 374.

60. *Daily Mail* and *Daily Telegraph*, February 13, 1918.

61. *H. C. Deb.*, 5th series, vol. 103 (February 12, 1918).

62. *Daily News*, February 16, 1918.

63. Hankey Diary, February 12, 1918, 1/3, and Esher to Hankey (passed on to Lloyd George), February 13, 1918, Lloyd George MSS, F/23/2/14.

64. Hankey Diary, February 13, 1918, 1/3.

65. Memorandum by Milner, Milner MSS, dep. 374, Hankey Diary, February 13, 1918, 1/3, and Derby to Lloyd George, February 13, 1918, Derby MSS, 920 (17).

66. Robertson, *Soldiers and Statesmen*, 1:235, and memorandum by Derby (shown to prime minister), February 13, 1918, Derby MSS, 920 (17).

67. Wilson Diary, February 13, 1918, and Milner to Lloyd George, February 13, 1918, Lloyd George MSS, F/38/3/13.

68. War Cabinet (347A), February 16, 1918, CAB 23/13.

69. "Statement by General Sir William Robertson," War Cabinet (345A), February 14, 1918, CAB 23/13.

70. Stamfordham Memorandum, RA GV F1259/32, and Robertson to Stamfordham, February 14, 1918, RA GV F1259/23.

71. Hankey Diary, February 14, 1918, 1/3.

72. Wilson Diary, Feburary 14, 1918.

73. Memorandum by Milner, Milner MSS, dep. 374.

74. Robertson to Plumer, February 4, 1918, Robertson MSS, 1/34/45, Plumer to Derby, February 15, 1918, Derby MSS, 920 (17), and Hankey Diary, February 15, 1918, 1/3.

75. Memorandum by Milner, Milner MSS, dep. 374.

76. Ibid., Wilson Diary, February 15, 1918, Esher Diary, February 15, 1918, 2/21, and Hankey to Lloyd George, February 15, 1918, Lloyd George MSS, F/23/2/15.

77. Robertson to Haig and Haig to Derby, February 15, 1918, Haig MSS, no. 123.

78. Stamfordham Memorandum, RA GV F1259/32, and War Cabinet (347A), February 16, 1918, CAB 23/13.

79. Memorandum by Milner, Milner MSS, dep. 374, and War Cabinet (347A), February 16, 1918, CAB 23/13.

80. Entry of February 17, 1918, *Lord Riddell's War Diary*, p. 314.

81. Robertson to Haig, February 16, 1918, Haig MSS, no. 123, and Haig Diary, February 17, 1918, no. 123.

82. Lloyd George, *War Memoirs*, 2:1689, and Haig Diary, February 17, 1918, no. 123.

83. Hankey Diary, February 17, 1918, 1/3.

84. Haig Diary, February 16, 1918, no. 123.

85. Cecil was perhaps the most determined to resign. See Cecil to Bonar Law, February 17, 1918, Bonar Law MSS, 82/9/6, and Cecil to Lloyd George, February 18, 1918, Lloyd George MSS, F/6/5/19.

86. Esher Diary, February 18, 1918, 2/21.

87. *Daily Mail*, February 14, 1918.

88. Davidson to Hankey, February 18, 1918, Bonar Law MSS, 84/7/3.

89. *H. C. Deb.*, 5th series, vol. 103 (February 19, 1918). Robertson had been conspiring with Asquith. See Robertson to Asquith, February 16, 1918, Asquith MSS, 32.

90. Lloyd George, *War Memoirs*, 2:1673, Bonham-Carter, *Soldier True*, p. 333, and Gwynne to Mrs. Asquith, February 18, 1918, Gwynne MSS, 14.

91. Haig Diary, February 18, 1918, no. 123.

92. Ibid., February 24, 1918, no. 123.

93. Haig to Lady Haig, February 21 and March 5, 1918, Haig MSS, nos. 149–50.

94. Wilson Diary, February 26, 1918, and *The Memoirs of Marshal Foch* (1931), p. 241.

95. Sackville-West to Wilson, March 5, 1918, Wilson MSS, file 12 B.

96. Wilson to Sackville-West, March 4, 1918, Wilson MSS, file 12 B.

97. War Cabinet (360A), March 6, 1918, CAB 23/13.

98. Wilson Diary, March 4, 1918.

99. Milner to Lloyd George, March 14, 1918, Lloyd George MSS, F/38/3/19.

100. Hankey Diary, March 17, 1918, 1/3, Supreme War Council, March 14–15, 1918, CAB 28/3/I.C.-47 and 50, and Lloyd George, *War Memoirs*, 2:1720.

101. Sackville-West to Wilson, March 21, 1918, Wilson MSS, file 12 B.

102. Haig Diary, March 10, 1918, no. 124.

103. Wilson Diary, March 13, 1918.

104. Lloyd George, *War Memoirs*, 2:1712–21.

12

The German Offensive and the Maurice Debate

WITH the general staff under Wilson, Lloyd George thought that he had finally gained a controlling interest in British military policy. His critics, on the other hand, now held the prime minister and Wilson directly responsible for any future military failures. "Those who have at last succeeded in getting rid of Sir William Robertson must at least have the courage of their opinions," warned the *National Review*. "They will assuredly be held responsible for anything that goes wrong."[1]

Wilson initially was as popular with the politicians as he was unpopular with the army—"our only military black-leg" was Charteris's bitter comment. "In Sir Henry Wilson the War Cabinet found for the first time an expert adviser of superior intellect," Churchill has written, "who could explain lucidly and forcefully the whole situation and give reasons for the adoption or rejection of any course."[2] Wilson's standing with the ministers, especially Lloyd George, however, declined in the coming months. No British officer spent more time divining German intentions; yet his record of predicting German moves was abysmal. Also, in sharp contrast to Robertson, he was often temperamentally unable to state a definite course of action when he would be held responsible for the results. In Lloyd George's words, "he faced both ways" and "shrank from the responsibility of the final word, even in advice."[3] Lloyd George's harsh appraisal was no doubt colored by the publication of Wilson's diary in the 1920s, which included many unflattering comments about the Welshman; still his characterization of the new C.I.G.S. was not far from the mark. But the glib and supple Irishman was most certainly not Wully, and this explains much of his initial popularity. At no time during the war had the imperial-minded statesmen had a military adviser who took a broader view of the war. Although Wilson might be a closet "Westerner," arguing in March that only in the West could the war be won, he gave every appearance of being an enthusiastic supporter of "Eastern" ventures to expand and protect the British Empire.[4]

Almost unnoticed in all of the excitement during the C.I.G.S. crisis was the quiet burial given to Haig's plan to clear the Flanders coast. On February 8, the War Cabinet authorized the C.I.G.S. to inform Haig that his plan had been canceled by the decisions of the Supreme War Council. Meanwhile, Smuts, after consulting with Allenby in the Middle East, sent his recommendations for future military action in Palestine and Mesopotamia. As the War Cabinet considered a forward policy in the East, which Smuts admitted would put added strain on British shipping, Lloyd George revealed more fully his view of the British role in the war. His strategy was directed less toward the defeat of Germany by British arms than the survival of Great Britain as a world power. No longer would the British army seek victory through a war of attrition. If the German army had to be battered into submission to get a decent peace, the Americans would do the lion's share of fighting and dying. In the event that the war ended in a stalemate, British conquests in the East would serve as valuable bargaining chips at any peace conference. "We might find it possible if Damascus were in our possession," he told the war cabinet on February 21, "to persuade the French to be content with something less than the whole of Alsace-Lorraine in return for compensation in Syria. Fortunately the party in France which was most eager to recover Alsace-Lorraine was also eager to extend French influence in Syria."[5] On March 6, the War Cabinet gave Allenby the green light to advance to the "maximum extent possible, consistent with the safety of the force under his orders."[6]

Allenby's campaign was linked by its advocates to the grand design of containing the Turko-German threat to Britain's Asian position. The triumph of the Bolsheviks in November exposed Britain's Asian flank and prompted deep fears of the enemy's intentions which were certainly not without substance. As they moved above the Black Sea, the Germans began to view South Russia as "the bridge to Georgia, central Asia and India."[7] Meanwhile, the Turks, despite their rickety condition, zealously pursued grandiose dreams of expansion, creating a new "Army of Islam." Their immediate objective was to secure control of all Armenia and create an independent Moslem republic of Azerbaijan. Their long-range objective was to occupy the Caspian coast of Persia and instigate a holy war in Transcaspian and Turkestan which would menace India.[8]

The British response to this twin threat, which bordered on hysteria at times, would have been more balanced if the Middle East had not been so vulnerable after Russia's collapse. Operating from Baghdad, the British realized that they would have great difficulty containing any enemy thrust in southwestern Asia, be it a Turkish-inspired holy war or armed intervention, no matter how poorly supported it might be. In late December, the War Office in desperation ordered a handful of men and officers in forty-one Ford vans and cars to proceed from Baghdad to the Caucasus (about 800 miles) in a quixotic attempt to organize a line of resistance to block the road to India. Major-General L. C. Dunsterville led this tiny convoy, supported by little more than the prestige of the British flag, to Enzeli on the Persian shore of the Caspian. That was as far as he got for the moment. Bolshevik opposition forced him to retreat toward Baghdad. Meanwhile, the Germans reached Odessa, which gave them a route across the Black Sea to Batum and then by rail to Baku on the Caspian.

Believing that the Bolsheviks were in league with Berlin, Milner penned an alarmist note to Wilson on March 5: "I am seriously concerned about the Eastern front. Russia has gone & we must set up a barrier somewhere to stop the Bolshevik flood, carrying German influence with it, or paving the way first, from sweeping right over Asia. . . . We have to draw a line from the Persian Gulf to the Trans-Siberian—nearer west or further east as best we can."[9] Balfour was no less concerned and raised the prospect that the Germans might eventually reach Baku, utilizing it as a base to spread their influence to Central Asia and Afghanistan.[10]

Wilson advocated a mixed bag of moves as a counterpoise to the Turko-German threat to southwestern Asia: Japanese intervention in Siberia, continued pressure in Palestine, an advance from Baghdad into northwestern Persia with the ultimate objective of entering the Caucasus, and the dispatch of military missions from India to Turkestan to counter German agents and propaganda. Unless his suggestions were immediately implemented, he warned, "we run a grave risk of permitting the Germans to establish themselves in a position which will eventually lead to the downfall of our Eastern Empire." Only Wilson's view that Germany would not send an army to that part of the world "for some time to come" offered the civilians any comfort.[11]

To Milner and other ministers, the emerging threat to Britain's Asian position seemed to justify Lloyd George's passionate interest in peripheral operations. "How right was the instinct, wh. led you all along to attach so much importance to the Eastern campaigns & not to listen to our only strategists, who could see nothing but the Western front," Milner wrote the Prime Minister. "If it were not for the position we have won in Mesopotamia & Palestine & the great strength we have developed on that side, the outlook would be black indeed. As it is, the position is *very serious,* but we hold strong cards, if only we play them. . . ."[12]

Milner penned his letter to Lloyd George only hours before the German barrage began to signal the beginning of the titanic German effort to win the war in France before America could make her presence felt in Europe. In retrospect, the government's obsession in March with creating, in Amery's words, "a barrier against the sphere of German power which will sufficiently cover the Suez Canal, Persian Gulf and the frontiers of India in the military sense,"[13] as Germany noisily massed men and equipment in front of Haig, makes curious reading. But it must be noted that even Haig, who rarely looked beyond his own trenches, was, in Milner's opinion, "quite full of this subject [German threat to Persia]! I never saw him so interested."[14] Moreover, Haig was confident that he could "smash" any German assault and seemed more concerned about the possibility that the enemy would not attack.[15]

In part, the relative calm with which the civilians viewed the massive German buildup in the British sector—by mid-March the general staff reported that Germany had ninety-two divisions in a position to strike at

Haig's fifty-seven divisions—was due to Wilson's appreciation of the military situation. According to Wilson, the Allies still enjoyed an overall superiority in rifle strength of 1,500,000 to 1,370,000 men. More importantly, Wilson, who believed that the Germans would only "threaten" in the West and then "fall" on Italy in May or June, encouraged the ministers to believe that Germany was not prepared to stake her last man in an all-out battle in the West. This led to some loose thinking. Perhaps, it was hopefully noted in the War Cabinet, the Germans only planned "to depress the *moral* of the defending forces by a constant but deferred threat of an assault in superior numbers."[16]

Hindenburg and Ludendorff were now virtual dictators of Germany. Hindenburg had the towering reputation, but Ludendorff provided the drive and brains and was the de facto commander in chief despite his position as first quartermaster-general. In November, Ludendorff had made up his mind to seek victory in 1918. Lloyd George, Milner, Amery, Smuts, and others thought it likely that the Germans would maintain an active defensive position in the West in 1918 and consolidate and expand their position in Europe and Asia. This policy would, in all likelihood, have paid greater dividends, but the German high command feared that Germany's allies could not last another year, a state of affairs which would seem to give support to Lloyd George's peripheral strategy. Also, Ludendorff despised the defense and had an overwhelming desire to escape static trench warfare by taking the initiative. Many German military and political leaders hoped that the enemy's morale might be destroyed. Only in this way could Berlin achieve her dream of a vast Eurasian realm which stretched from the Belgian coast to the Russian Pacific coast that would be dominated by Berlin through economic, political, and military means.[17]

Ludendorff's war plan was to deliver a series of smashing blows at the enemy. With German manpower running out, he was quite prepared to risk almost certain defeat if he failed to bring the Allies to their knees before a great American army had been constituted in France. As Correlli Barnett has astutely observed: "It was the Schlieffen Plan again: a gamble under acute pressure of time, making use of a temporary superiority of numbers that in itself was far from overwhelming." The British army was his primary target, with the southern British front between Arras and the river Oise where the British and French joined hands being selected for the first offensive. One consideration for the German high command was its belief that the French might not "hurry to run to the help of their Entente comrades."[18]

The Germans hoped to succeed where the Anglo-French generals had failed by employing tactics which had worked brilliantly at Riga and Caporetto. In opposition to the linear tactics and fixed objectives of the British army, German storm troops were taught the tactics of surprise, speed, and deep and continuous penetration. Instead of predetermined targets, the German infantry was instructed to infiltrate, to bypass strong points, and to take the path of least resistance. Artillery tactics were equally imaginative, with a short but intense bombardment with a high proportion of poison gas to high-explosive shells replacing the long preliminary barrage so typical of British offensives.

Just before five o'clock on March 21 nearly 6,000 German guns began the most awesome display of artillery power that the world had ever witnessed. For the next five hours the skillfully orchestrated barrage continued against the defenses of the Third and Fifth Armies. Then German storm troopers emerged from their trenches and began their assault. A thick ground fog served to cover their movements as they swept across the flattened British defenses. At the end of the day, the German army had captured as much ground as the British and French had during the 140 days of bitter fighting during the Somme battle. Their greatest success was achieved at the expense of Gough's Fifth Army, which had been exhausted by the campaign in Flanders. In Gough's "sector all three zones of the defensive system had been lost. The Germans had in a single day broken clean through into open country."[19]

As the Germans and British were locked in a death struggle, which would not be surpassed in scale until May 10, 1940, when Germany invaded France, Belgium, and Holland,[20] the War Cabinet had its attention fixed on the German menace in Asia. After Wilson suggested that the German attack underway "might only develop into a big raid or demonstration," the War Cabinet discussed Japanese intervention, which, according to Wilson, "was a question of pulling Siberia out of the wreck, in order to save India," and ways of countering the enemy threat to Persia. The Eastern Committee chaired by Curzon was created to serve as a "Vigilance Committee, ready to warn the War Cabinet and furnish advice on the Eastern area of operations."[21]

On the following day, Wilson's tune had changed. He no longer viewed the German attack as a "big raid or demonstration," observing in the War Cabinet that the Germans apparently planned a "long-drawn battle deliberately intended for a trial of strength, in order that a decisive result might be arrived at." Although the reports flowing from the front were often in conflict, Wilson assured the ministers that the information he possessed "gave no cause for anxiety." Lloyd George, however, greeted this news with grave apprehension. It appeared that the Germans, as Maurice and Robertson had forecast, were prepared to gamble their last man in a massive and prolonged battle; and the direction of their bid for victory was through British trenches. To make certain that London was fully and immediately acquainted with the facts, he wanted to establish "liaison officers" between the C.I.G.S. and general headquarters.[22]

By March 23 the magnitude of the British defeat was clear to both the government and general headquarters. The Fifth Army was breaking up. On March 21, Haig had requested three divisions from Pétain; now he asked for twenty divisions!

Staring disaster in the face, Lloyd George was magnificent. With characteristic energy and courage, he postponed the morning meeting of the War Cabinet and took charge in the War Office to locate and rush all available troops to Haig. At 4:00 P.M. he met with the War Cabinet in the War Office. The prospects for the British army could not have been much worse. Figures provided by Macdonogh and Maurice indicated that the Allied superiority in rifles had vanished overnight.[23] More alarming was Germany's concentration against the outmanned British. Wilson reported that "the British Army was now attacked by a large proportion of the German Army, and was menaced with a possible attack by the whole." In short, the British army seemed doomed unless more men were found and the French provided extensive and immediate help. But would Haig's private arrangement with Pétain which had replaced the general reserve, Lloyd George worried aloud, hold up?[24] On the following day, Milner, on Lloyd George's instructions, left London for France to get a firsthand look at the situation.

The anguish and desperation of the ministers was reflected in the War Cabinet minutes of the twenty-fifth. Already the painful decision to send out lads of eighteen and one half years had been made. Now every possible source of manpower was explored. That Britain had few men to spare was demonstrated by the drastic measures considered. Men were to be withdrawn from the munitions industry, coal mines, and dockyards; conscription for Ireland was contemplated; Royal Marines were to be taken from the Navy; Russians living in Britain were to be recruited for labor battalions; the test for eyesight was to be lowered for category "A" men; and even the recall of wounded who had been discharged was discussed, along with the dispatch of conscientious objectors and clergymen to France.[25]

Wilson did not attend this War Cabinet meeting for he had departed abruptly for France hot on Milner's trail because of an alarming telephone call from Haig on the twenty-fourth which portended disaster. Fresh from a conference with Pétain, Haig told Wilson that the Germans were on the verge of driving a wedge between the French and British forces. Pétain, believing that the British were done for, was against committing his reserves to a lost cause. When pressed by Haig, Pétain had informed him that if the Germans continued to press forward, he intended to break contact with the British and fall back southwestwards to Beauvais to defend Paris.[26]

At Doullens on March 26, with shells falling nearby and with the streets clogged with battle-scarred troops, Milner and Wilson conferred with, among others, Clemenceau, Foch, Pétain, and Haig. Pétain's "terrible look" cast a shadow over the conference. Although he now proposed to help Haig hold Amiens, his assurances convinced no one. He had the demeanor of a beaten man. Convinced that his comrade in arms had lost his nerve, Haig played a key role in elevating Foch. When it was suggested that Foch's role be limited to the operations around Amiens, Haig protested, insisting that Foch be given "coordinating" authority over all national armies in France and Belgium. Pétain's apparent reluctance to commit his reserves wholeheartedly to the British front rather than any fundamental change of heart explains Haig's willingness, even eagerness, to be subordinated to Foch. "In my opinion," he wrote in his diary, "it was essential to success that Foch should control Pétain."[27]

Having played an important role at Doullens in creating unity of command and preventing the British and French forces from separating, Milner returned to London to plunge into the agonizing manpower discussions. Many of the desperate measures to raise men discussed on March 25 were either impracticable, devastating to the economy, or politically dangerous. Imposing conscription on Ireland, for example, might do more harm than good, for it would unite the Catholics and nationalists against London, anger the Irish-Americans, and the soldiers produced might be worthless. H. E. Duke, the chief secretary for Ireland, told the War Cabinet that the government "might almost as well recruit Germans." As for the drastic combing out of men from industry, Auckland Geddes, the minister of national service, warned that it would create "tremendous industrial disturbance." On the other hand, any draconian combing out of agricultural workers "would be disastrous to our agricultural policy."[28]

Milner, who now put replacing the army's losses above all else, made his feelings clear to the prime minister.

> If there is a great disaster, we are, as a Govt. "down & out" whatever we do, & we may as well fall gloriously over a big effort to retrieve the situation.
> If, on the other hand, "the plague is stayed," we are in for a long & dragging fight. It must be a year at least before the Americans can make their weight felt. . . . It is simply deluding ourselves to think that the Germans . . . *will not continue to press us for all they are worth.* They are certain to keep on pushing, &, if they do not break us now, they will break us later, unless we can keep on sending substantial reinforcements.[29]

Before the Germans broke right through the Fifth Army, Lloyd George and his colleagues in the War Cabinet had hoped to preserve Britain's staying power and limit British losses by not providing the War Office with all of the fresh recruits it demanded. But, with Ludendorff prepared to accept gigantic losses in an effort to destroy the British army, the British had to do likewise to survive. Yet even if the government strained Britain's manpower to the breaking point, undermining home morale, the economy, and the government in the process, there would still be a delay before these men could be trained and shipped to France. Only America seemed able to fill this perilous gap. On March 29, the British government decided to make a direct appeal to Wilson to send over 100,000 men per month during the next three months "for incorporation by battalions in the British or French armies." The War Office authorities were more blunt. " 'For God's sake, get your men over!' " they told the American military attaché in London.[30] President Wilson responded handsomely to this plea, promising Lloyd George that he would send 120,000 men per month for the next four months. America's apparent willingness to fill the gaps in the decimated British divisions was a tremendous relief to the prime minister because it seemed to give him more latitude in dealing with the manpower crisis, especially with the political quagmire of conscription in Ireland.

It soon became apparent that the Doullens agreement had not sufficiently defined Foch's authority. As soon as Lloyd George awoke on April 2, he was handed a telegram from Churchill, who had been sent by the prime minister to confer with Clemenceau. After personally trying to adjust a misunderstanding among Haig, Rawlinson, and Foch about the responsibility for the defense of Amiens, Clemenceau had decided that Lloyd George must leave for France "at once" to deal with the situation.[31]

When Lloyd George brought the "rumoured" breakdown in Allied cooperation to the attention of the War Cabinet, Pétain, rather than Haig, was singled out for criticism. "The question was discussed as to whether, *in order to secure complete co-ordination in the French command,* it might not be desirable to extend General Foch's powers, so as to give the right of issuing directions or orders, instead of being limited to co-ordination." Wilson, however, opposed any extension of Foch's powers. It was also pointed out that the British public, which had accepted the Doullens arrangement with scarcely a murmur, should perhaps not be disturbed by a further enlargement of Foch's position. In the end, Lloyd George was given the freedom to take whatever action he thought necessary after discussing the situation with Haig.[32]

Wilson's opposition to giving Foch the authority to issue orders deserves further elaboration. Major-General C. E. Callwell and others have attributed a "conspicuous, if not indeed a pre-eminent," role to Wilson in the establishment of a form of unity of command.[33] Personal advancement, rather than the concept of unity of command, however, often seems to have influenced Wilson's actions. Earlier he had vetoed Joffre as supreme commander, in part, because it might undermine his position as the British permanent military representative at Versailles. Now, at the pinnacle of his power, he was strongly opposed to either an increase in Foch's power or an independent British permanent military representative who might compete with him. When Rawlinson was sent to take over the shattered Fifth Army (which was reorganized as the Fourth Army), he was replaced at Versailles by Sackville-West (or "Tit Willow," as Wilson called him).[34] With his ally Sackville-West as British permanent military representative, Wilson now favored strengthening Versailles as a substitute to enhancing Foch's position.[35]

Wilson continued his opposition to giving Foch the power to direct as well as coordinate battles at the Conference of Beauvais on April 3. Before the conference began, Clemenceau showed Lloyd George and Wilson a note which conferred upon Foch the strategic direction of military operations in France while tactics remained in the hands of the commanders in chief. In his diary, Wilson maintains that he opposed Clemenceau's suggestion because it "raised the question of the difference between strategy and tactics, which the C. in C.s might exploit."[36] Given his prior attitude, Wilson's justification of his stand is clearly specious. Although Wilson still clung to the original Doullens agreement, Lloyd George firmly supported giving Foch what he wanted. "Unless he had the necessary power, however, General Foch would prove worse than useless," he told the Allied political and military leaders. Backed by Bliss and Pershing, he got what he wanted. Foch was granted "the strategic direction of military operations," with the important qualification that "each Commander-in-Chief will have the right of appeal to his Government if in his opinion the safety of his Army is compromised by any order received from General Foch."[37]

A disturbing feature of the Beauvais conference for Lloyd George was Pershing's continued opposition to any real incorporation of infantry and machine-gun units with British and French divisions. British frustration over Pershing's preference for building a great American army under his command to parceling out his battalions to the British and French was reflected in an intemperate message from Sackville-West to Wilson. "The man's an ass, I think—he doesn't mean business—what Bliss calls the God-damned American programme is going to f—— up the whole show."[38] Unless Pershing's position softened, Lloyd George would not be able to count on the Americans to replace British losses.

As they walked out of the conference room, Lloyd George asked Foch, "And now which must I bet on, Ludendorff or Foch?" The French general calmly responded, "You can first back me, and you will win. For Ludendorff has got to break through us, and this he can no longer do."[39]

As the first German offensive began to lose its momentum, the government and Haig began to seek reasons for the disaster that had befallen the British army, with each trying to shift the blame to the other. When the king visited the front in late March, he was given a note prepared by Brigadier-General E. W. Cox, the new head of intelligence at general headquarters, which emphasized that the army had not been caught napping; the direction and even the exact date of the German offensive against the Third and Fifth Armies had been known in advance.[40] When he talked with George V, Haig argued that three factors, none of which he had any control over, were responsible for the German breakthrough:

1) British Infantry in France at the beginning of the Battle were 100,000 less than a year ago!
2) We now had 3 times as many Germans on our front as we had last year.
3) We had also extended our line (by order of the British Government) fully ⅕th more than it was last Autumn.[41]

According to the official history, Haig even believed that he and his troops "were at the mercy of an 'Organizer of Defeat.' "[42]

Lloyd George desperately sought to avoid such an epitaph. Conveniently forgetting his own role in the collapse of the general reserve, he told everyone who would listen that Haig was primarily responsible for the Allied failure to match the unity of direction which the Germans possessed. He also bitterly resented the charge that Haig's forces were too weak to withstand the German attack. Robertson, not Lloyd George, had kept the mobile reserves in England because of Haig's assurances that he could hold off any German attack for eighteen days. Moreover, the War Office decided whether or not to allocate men to machine-gun units, the tank corps, etc., rather than to the infantry, where Haig was down. Still, throughout 1917 Lloyd George had resisted giving the army all of the recruits it requested. To a considerable degree his motive had been to force Haig, albeit unsuccessfully, to economize his losses. Hence, if Haig lost because he did not have enough men to defend his longer line, Lloyd George must bear part of the responsibility.

By concentrating their reserves against Haig, the Germans were able to achieve a considerable superiority at the point of their attack. But the British had also been able to do this in 1916 and 1917 without breaking through. Correlli Barnett points out that "in terms of odds and of density of troops within the actual defence system, the British in March 1918 were better placed than the Germans in July 1917, who had succeeded in blunting the first British assault." On the other hand, the Germans were able to call on more reserves in 1917 than Haig had at his disposal in 1918. "Nevertheless," Barnett argues, "the figures alone suggest that the British defence system itself should have been capable of absorbing the German blow for some days; even if paucity of reserves brought about a progressive later collapse."[43] Of course, if the general reserve had been established, Haig might have been able to draw immediately upon French reserves.

Although the Germans only outnumbered the British by about 6 to 4 along their 126-mile front, they had a superiority of 5 to 1 against the Fifth Army. Haig unquestionably followed sound strategic principles by massing his troops in the north, where, with his forces close to the sea, he could not give up much ground without disastrous results. On the other hand, Gough had room to maneuver in the south; and the French reserves were close at hand to give relief. Still Haig was astonishingly complacent, refusing to redistribute his troops, as reports of the German buildup in the south flowed to general headquarters. Gough later told Lloyd George that he believed "Haig's attitude was one of rather welcoming a partial loss of ground on the idea—'that'll larn 'em' (the Govt.) for not doing what he wanted, and for meeting the French wishes."[44] A more balanced explanation of Haig's disposition of his troops is that he expected the Germans to have no better success at breaking through than he had had at Somme and Passchendaele.

As for the question of Haig taking over more of the French line, it must be remembered that Lloyd George, although he accepted the principle of assisting the French by extending the British front, had left the arrangements to Haig and Pétain. To be sure, Haig had probably agreed to extend his line to Barisis because he feared that the Supreme War Council would force him to take over more of the French line. When the permanent military representatives had suggested just that, Lloyd George had fought Haig's battle for him, only acquiescing to joint note 10 after gaining the field marshal's approval. Two points must be emphasized: with the British on the defensive, the French demand that the British take over more of their line was difficult to refuse; and, secondly, Haig never implemented the extension of his line beyond Barisis which the Supreme War Council attempted to impose upon him.

Unfortunately, the French fortifications which the Fifth Army inherited were in frightful condition. Furthermore, general headquarters had paid little attention to defense since 1914 and the defensive tactics it attempted to copy from the Germans were faulty. Too many men (approximately one third of the infantry) were concentrated in the first line of defense, where they were exposed to German artillery. Even then British resistance might have been stouter if the soldiers had had time to dig. But Haig had delayed taking over the French front as long as possible by continuing to attack and by arguing that he needed to maintain his reserves for a resumption of the Flanders attack in the spring.[45] These considerations suggest the conclusion that it is unwarranted to place the blame on Lloyd George and his civilian colleagues for the German success.

In April the *Morning Post* began demanding an explanation of the March

21 disaster, aiming its guns at the government's alleged failure to supply Haig with men. On April 8, Repington wrote: "Why have the reiterated demands of the Army for men remained unanswered? Who but Mr. Lloyd George is responsible for the failure to supply the Army's needs. I think that we shall have to be more ruthless towards Ministers who have failed the country and that our easy tolerance of incompetence is a public danger." Gwynne chimed in with "Hundreds of thousands of men who might have given us victory there in France were squandered upon eccentric expeditions to points of minor consequence." The *Globe* argued that "the present situation is the inevitable result of our national folly in allowing the war to be managed by men who know nothing of war," and the *Daily News* linked German success with "the events which began with the Paris Speech, and ended with the dismissal of Sir William Robertson." To restore confidence in the government, the *Star* demanded the appointment of Robertson as secretary of state for war.[46]

Lloyd George bristled at this criticism, knowing that his government was in danger if Parliament and the public came to believe that the politicians and not the generals were responsible for the German breakthrough. Not surprisingly, he hoped to make scapegoats of the generals, pressuring Haig to remove Gough (which was done) and contemplating the replacement of the field marshal himself. On April 4, the War Cabinet launched into a "wild discussion" about recalling Haig. "There was no doubt that the feeling of the Cabinet was I think unanimously agst. Haig & the whole G.H.Q. There was no question that all confidence is lost," Wilson wrote in his diary.[47]

Haig, who had generally displayed remarkable coolness during the German offensive, nobly offered to step down if he no longer enjoyed the confidence of the government, noting that his conscience was clear for he had "done the best with the means at my disposal."[48] As always, however, the civilians were unable to discover a better general.

After giving an explanation of the German success which amounted to an attack on the army leadership in an unusual meeting with the heads of departments on April 6, Lloyd George appeared before Parliament on April 9 when it reassembled after its long Easter recess. In a combative mood, he was determined to disarm his critics. Unfortunately, as he strove for effect, he made two claims which were to come back to haunt him. The British army, he asserted, was actually stronger at the beginning of January 1918 than it had been the previous January. Then, to protect himself from the charge of meddling in strategy because of his interest in a British offensive in Palestine, he said that in Egypt and Palestine there were only three white infantry divisions "and the rest are either Indians or mixed with a very, very small proportion of British troops in those divisions." The first statement was correct in respect to ration strength which included many noncombatants such as labour battalions; but it was misleading if Lloyd George intended to maintain that Haig's combatant strength was stronger at the beginning of 1918 than it had been at the start of 1917. The second statement was clearly wrong.[49] Allenby, in fact, commanded seven infantry divisions on March 21 which included only a small number of native troops.

Encouraged by Wilson "to try and establish the confidence of the Army and of the nation in some one General"[50] (himself naturally), Lloyd George went out of his way to praise Robertson's replacement, creating the false impression that the new C.I.G.S. had predicted precisely where and when the German storm would break. "I think it is one of the most remarkable forecasts of enemy intentions," he exclaimed, "that has ever been made." The prime minister also used an interesting parallel to defend the government's commitment to "side shows." "There was an Empire which withdrew its legions from the outlying provinces of the Empire to defend its heart against the Goths, and these legions never went back."[51] On the same day, Curzon told the House of Lords that the German success was not due to Haig having insufficient men and equipment.

Just before Lloyd George appeared in Parliament, Maurice had informed the War Cabinet that the Germans had launched an attack in Flanders between the La Bassée Canal and Armentières. Maurice thought that it was only a "demonstration,"[52] but Ludendorff, having failed to destroy the British reinforced by the French around Amiens, had shifted his attention to the north. A weak Portuguese division gave way, opening a gap which the Germans penetrated for more than 3½ miles the first day. When the Germans followed up this success with another attack north of Armentières which forced Plumer to withdraw from Messines and Wytschaete, the situation appeared desperate. On the night of 11–12, Haig wrote his famous "Backs to the Wall" order of the day. By April 12, the Germans had advanced two thirds of the distance they had to go to gain their primary objective, Hazebrouck, a vital railway junction.

The mood in London was not improved by a memorandum prepared by the usually unflappable Macdonogh, who had just returned from the front after assessing the effects of the German March 21 offensive. His every sentence was tinged with panic. "Germany is endeavouring to destroy the British Army and decide the war by concentrating all her available reserves against the British front," he wrote. Britain was faced with "decisive defeat" unless France and the United States gave extensive assistance and all British troops were withdrawn immediately from Italy, the Balkans, and Mesopotamia.[53]

The survival of the British army seemed to hinge on how well the new unity of command would work. With Haig's reserves committed to the battle and with his army losing 70,000 casualties a week since March 21, the British cast covetous glances at the French reserves, their only hope of immediate help. Foch was supposed to be above all national considerations. But, unlike Eisenhower during World War II, he had no machinery for a fully integrated Allied supreme command. With no true counterpart of the Supreme Headquarters Allied Expeditionary Force (S.H.A.E.F.) or Joint Chiefs of Staff, he relied upon his own personal staff. The permanent military representatives offered him the best hope of creating an Allied general staff, but he showed no inclination to use this body, immediately recalling the French permanent military representative, Weygand, after Beauvais to serve as his principal staff officer. As Terraine has pointed out, "His technique was an outdated reversion to the personal command of earlier centuries."[54]

Between Beauvais and the second German offensive, Lloyd George's colleagues in the War Cabinet, encouraged by Wilson, began to have second thoughts about giving Foch the leading role in determining Allied strategy. With no machinery for British input, Clemenceau, who was rightly considered a fanatical French nationalist, might try to use Foch to further French rather than Allied interests. These fears certainly had substance. "Do you know," Foch once told Clemenceau, "that I am not your subordinate?" "No, I don't," Clemenceau retorted. "I don't even want to know who put that notion into your head. . . . I strongly advise you not to try to act on this idea, for it would never do."[55] Alarmed by the news of Weygand's departure from Versailles and fearful that the permanent military representatives where British influence might be felt were going to be allowed to wither away, many British ministers started to dig in their heels. After all, it had been fear of Pétain's apparent defeatism rather than any attachment to the principle of unity of command which had been decisive in the arrangements made at Doullens and Beauvais. Even Lloyd George's previous desire for unity of command was colored by his determination to undermine Haig and Robertson and force the Allies to look beyond the western front. When Clemenceau, almost before the ink was dry on the Beauvais agreement, had suggested that Foch's authority be extended to the Italian front, the War Cabinet, apparently influenced by Wilson, vetoed the idea. Also Lloyd George made it clear to the French premier that he would not tolerate the collapse of the Versailles body. The British leaders also readily accepted Wilson's proposal that a senior British officer (General John P. Du Cane) should be attached to Foch's staff. Foch immediately accepted Du Cane as a member of his staff, but Clemenceau expressed hostility to any British effort to put Foch under the direction of Versailles.[56]

The new German offensive which threatened to drive the British out of Belgium and perhaps into the sea increased anxiety both in London and at general headquarters that Foch might not commit French reserves to the British front soon enough or in sufficient strength. After failing to convince Foch to take over some of the British line on the day before the German attack in Flanders was launched, Haig was convinced that the French meant "to bleed the British to the utmost."[57] Foch's initial response to the German attack seemed to justify this bitter remark. He moved French troops to the north, but he was slow to commit them to battle. Husbanding his reserves for the counterattack, he refused to relieve the exhausted British soldiers while they were engaged in battle. His oft-repeated principle was " 'No reliefs during a battle.' "[58] "General Foch viewed the battle front as one whole; he regarded our army as bearing the brunt to good purpose, namely, in order to keep the Allied reserves, which he did not wish to fritter away, intact," Maurice told the War Cabinet. His "object was to stablise the battle with the least expenditure of reserves."[59] But what if Foch had overestimated the dogged and heroic resistance of the British army as it largely absorbed the sledgehammer blows of the German army? Fortunately he had not.

British resentment of the French, which simmered during this period, was going to boil over during the months ahead and threaten to destroy the new unity of command. For the moment, however, Lloyd George, assured of

Foch's good intentions by Wilson, took the lead in giving Foch a title to match his new position. On April 11, the War Cabinet discussed Foch's desire to be recognized as Allied commander in chief. Opposition was expressed to making Foch "Commander-in-Chief of the Allied Forces in France" because the public had been told that "his function was really that of Strategist-in-Chief." Smuts finally offered the compromise of "General-in-Chief," which was accepted, and Clemenceau and Foch were duly informed.[60] The distinction between general and commander in chief, however, was soon blurred.

Faced with terrible losses which could not be made up from their own sources of depleted manpower, the British civilians became obsessed with the amalgamation of American troops with Haig's forces. After the first German offensive had stalled, Haig had warned his government that his manpower situation would become "critical unless American troops fit for immediate incorporation in my Divisions arrive in France in the meantime."[61] With the Germans employing approximately three of their divisions against the British for every one against the French, the War Cabinet hoped to get the bulk of the American combat troops arriving in France attached to Haig's decimated and battle-worn forces. Pershing, however, remained determined to create an independent American army, resisting pressure from both the British and his own government. Finally, Ludendorff's continued pressure against the Anglo-French forces forced the American commander in chief to bend. On April 24, he concluded an agreement with Milner in London which accepted the temporary attachment of the combat elements of six American divisions scheduled to arrive in May for training and service with the British army.[62]

When news of the Pershing-Milner agreement reached Paris, there was emotional talk of Perfidious Albion. Earlier the permanent military representatives had recommended in joint note 18 that Americans be amalgamated with the French and British forces, and the French wanted their share of the fresh and unbloodied Americans. Quite unfairly, Clemenceau and other French leaders, perhaps encouraged by Repington, believed that the British government was holding back a hidden army of about one million men in Britain.[63] This was nonsense. The British government was scraping the bottom of its manpower barrel and Parliament had just passed a new military act which extended the military age to fifty years, and in a national emergency to fifty-five years.

At the fifth meeting of the Supreme War Council at Abbeville on May 1, Lloyd George discovered that the tiger had his claws out. Why, Clemenceau demanded to know, had the French not been consulted about the Pershing-Milner agreement? "He reminded the Council that General Foch had been appointed to the supreme command in France. This command was not given as a mere decoration. It involved, amongst other things, serious responsibilities, including suitable provision for the future." If the British got 120,000 Americans in May, the French premier insisted, the French must get 120,000 in June.

Lloyd George was conciliatory. The squabbling over the division of American combat troops was bound to arouse Pershing's suspicions. Surely, the American commander in chief grumbled, he was not "to understand that the American army was to be entirely at the disposal of the French and British commands." Also, the prime minister did not want unity of command to break down over this issue. With Clemenceau apparently willing to allow the six divisions arriving in May to be attached to the British army, he accepted Foch's proposal to reconsider the Pershing-Milner agreement in a meeting of Milner, Pershing, and Foch.[64] Subsequently the amalgamation of American combat troops with Allied divisions called for in the Pershing-Milner agreement was allowed to stand for the immediate future, but the six American divisions scheduled to arrive in May were not specifically allocated to Haig. The conflict between Paris and London over the utilization of American manpower was just beginning. In other actions the Supreme War Council dissolved the Executive War Board and extended Foch's authority to Italy, which was now considered as part of the western front.

Although the Allied leaders did not realize it at Abbeville, the German advance in Flanders had reached high tide. Once again Anglo-French resistance had proven too strong, and time was running out on Ludendorff's gamble as Americans in increasing numbers began to arrive in France. Ludendorff's huge losses since March 21 roughly matched Allied losses. Foch's estimate of the military situation which Maurice relayed to the War Cabinet during the dark days of mid-April had proven correct: "If he [Foch] had to choose between playing his own hand or that of Ludendorff, if he had to get to Berlin he would prefer Ludendorff's hand, but as his mission was to check Ludendorff he preferred his own."[65]

Lloyd George returned from Abbeville to face the gravest threat yet posed to his ministry. Following his and Curzon's speeches of April 9 in Parliament, newspapers still favorable to the army had begun to question the truth of their statements. As usual, the *Morning Post* was the biggest thorn in the government's side. On April 17, Repington pointed out that it was not true that there were only three white divisions in Egypt and Palestine on March 21. Elsewhere in the same paper, Gwynne in a leading article accused the prime minister of using "fancy figures" to mask what he alleged was Haig's weakened position on the eve of the German offensive. The following day, Gwynne continued his attack under the heading: "BRING ROBERTSON BACK." The *Globe* seconded this suggestion.

Ominously this rising criticism had its echo in Parliament. On April 18, the Liberal politician Sir Godfrey Baring questioned Lloyd George's statement that Haig was stronger in January 1918 than he had been the previous year. Was not Lloyd George including noncombatant units in his calculation? Ian Macpherson, the under-secretary of state for war, using figures produced in the adjutant general's department for the director of military operations (hereafter abbreviated D.M.O.), asserted unequivocally that British "combatant strength" was stronger in January 1918.[66] Unfortunately the adjutant general's department had erroneously included 86,000 British troops in Italy as part of Haig's army. Maurice's deputy, Colonel Walter Kirke, had given Macpherson these returns without checking them for accuracy.

The press attacks, especially in the War Office's mouthpiece, the *Morning Post,* and Baring's pointed question in Parliament made Lloyd George begin to fear that a military conspiracy was under foot to place unfairly the blame for Haig's defeat squarely on him. Robertson seemed to be involved because Esher reported that the former C.I.G.S. was seeing Repington every day. In an effort to neutralize Wully, Lloyd George was quite prepared to support Haig's suggestion that Robertson go out to France as his second in command. Robertson, however, refused, writing Haig that Lloyd George was just trying to get him out of London. "My job is C.I.G.S. or nothing,"[67] he suggestively noted. Did Wully really believe his own press and contemplate a comeback atop the wreckage of Lloyd George's government? Whatever Robertson's motives, Lloyd George thought that he perceived Wully's hand at work when his eyes fell on the most recent weekly summary, which he thought was the work of Maurice, Robertson's alter ego on the general staff. To the prime minister's dismay the weekly summary prepared by the office of the D.M.O. claimed that the Germans now had a superiority in rifle strength of approximately 333,000, which, if true, would make a mockery of Lloyd George's previous comparisons of Allied to enemy rifle strength in Parliament. When the weekly summary was brought to its attention on the twenty-second, the War Cabinet was incredulous. How could a shift of this magnitude take place almost overnight? The new figures "appeared to be utterly inconsistent" with the War Office's previous calculations, it was noted.[68]

With the *Morning Post* at this very moment calling for "A CHANGE OF GOVERNMENT," Lloyd George believed that the War Office's new numbers were "all part of Robertson's campaign."[69] In an angry letter to the secretary of state for war, Lloyd George pointed out what he considered were discrepancies and omissions in the weekly summary, concluding: "From any point of view this document is extraordinarily slipshod, and I suggest that a thorough investigation be made as to how it came to be prepared and who is responsible for editing and issuing it."[70]

Maurice, who had been in France from April 14 to April 17 and was about to be replaced by Major-General P. de B. Radcliffe as D.M.O. as part of Wilson's housecleaning in the War Office, argues that he had no part in producing the new figures in the weekly summary which was dated April 18.[71] Maurice nonetheless later attempted to defend the calculations in the weekly summary against Lloyd George's contention that they were "cooked." After an internal investigation within the War Office, new figures were produced that lowered the Allied inferiority in rifle strength to 262,000.[72] The revised figures, however, still did not take into account the new muscle the British army now possessed in areas like artillery, tanks, aircraft, machine guns, etc. But the awkward fact remained: Germany had attained a clear, though temporary, superiority in rifle strength by transferring divisions from Russia to France.

Another pointed arrow being fired at Lloyd George in the press concerned Haig's extension of his line, which Haig's defenders claimed had been forced upon him and was largely the cause of the collapse of the Fifth Army. After George Lambert gave notice that he planned to ask a question in Parliament on this subject on April 23, the War Cabinet discussed the government's response and decided that a reply should be given in the sense that there was not the smallest justification for the suggestion that this portion of the line [defended by the Fifth Army] was taken over contrary to the judgment of Sir William Robertson and Sir Douglas Haig; the arrangements in the matter were made entirely by the British and French military authorities.[73]

That afternoon Bonar Law put the government's case to Parliament. When asked by George Lambert if Haig and Robertson had been overruled by the government on the extension of the British line in Barisis, Bonar Law responded that "the arrangement was a military arrangement, made between the two military authorities [Haig and Pétain]." When another member of the House, Mr. Pringle, asked, "Was this matter entered into at the Versailles War Council at any time?," Bonar Law replied, "this particular matter was not dealt with at all by the Versailles War Council."[74]

What Bonar Law said was essentially correct. Although Haig and Robertson had raised objections, especially about Clemenceau's demand that the British take over French trenches beyond Barisis, the government had left the actual arrangements to Haig and Pétain. The Supreme War Council, of course, had not acted on the extension of the British line to Barisis that Haig and Pétain had agreed upon prior to its meeting in early February; and it was this extension to Barisis to which all the questions in Parliament were directed. Technically, then, Bonar Law was right in asserting that the Supreme War Council had not forced Haig to take over the additional line which he defended on March 21.[75]

To Maurice, Bonar Law's response was just one more incident of the government's attempt to shift all blame to Haig and the army for the German breakthrough. Consequently, he moved closer to challenging publicly the government's statements in Parliament. Before taking such a drastic step, however, he consulted his friend Robertson. Wully, practical as always, cautioned Maurice to get his facts right and expressed doubts that "the days of L.G. are numbered." But he clearly approved of Maurice's decision to write a letter for publication in the press. "You are contemplating a great thing—to your undying credit," he wrote.[76]

Maurice agonized for some time about violating the king's regulations by contradicting the government in the press. It would end his military career and many would accuse him of rank insubordination. He even wrote a letter to Wilson on April 30, suggesting in so many words, that the government should set the record straight. Wilson, as Maurice probably expected, made no reply. Instead the C.I.G.S. noted in red on his letter that Maurice had never brought this to his attention while he was still D.M.O.,[77] and it was a valid comment. According to his one-sided account, "Intrigues of the War," Maurice maintains that he was too preoccupied with the German offensive to read Lloyd George's and Curzon's speeches on April 9. Yet he writes in his diary on that day: "Curzon made a number of absolutely untrue statements in H of L."[78] Although Maurice later went to the trouble of reading Lloyd George's exact words in *Hansard* and noted in his diary that the newspaper accounts had not revealed to him Lloyd George's misstatements, this would appear to be a rationalization for his failure to speak out while he was still D.M.O. The press, for example, paid particular attention to Lloyd George's claim that Haig's forces were stronger in January 1918 than they had been in January 1917.[79]

John Gooch has suggested that Maurice's underlying motive was to spark a national discussion which would result in the creation of a more efficient machinery to conduct the war.[80] Others have argued that he hoped to salvage the honor of the army and prevent the government from sacking Haig.[81] Lloyd George, of course, believed that Maurice was involved in a military conspiracy against the government. In truth, Maurice, a soldier of the old school, found the idea of consorting with the military and especially the civilian enemies of Lloyd George distasteful. He thought of involving Asquith, but quickly dropped the idea. When he took his letter to the *Morning Post* on May 6, he emphasized to Gwynne and Repington that he "had shown the letter to no soldier."[82] In his own mind this kept his hands clean. Yet, even if he had not actually shown his letter to Robertson, he had certainly discussed its contents with the former C.I.G.S. Also, he had to be aware of the ramifications of publicly attacking the government. The War Cabinet's ability to run the war, not its veracity, was the central issue. With some papers pressuring Asquith to demand an investigation of the cause of the virtual destruction of the Fifth Army,[83] any public stand on his part might give Lloyd George's opponents the necessary ammunition to destroy him. Gwynne immediately sent Asquith a copy of Maurice's letter, noting: "It is primarily an affair for the House of Commons, since there is ample evidence in the letter that the Ministers of the Crown have lied to the House of Commons."[84]

On the morning of May 7, Maurice's sensational letter appeared on the streets in the *Morning Post, Times, Daily Chronicle,* and *Daily News.* Maurice challenged the truthfulness of the government on three major points: Bonar Law's statement of April 23 that the Supreme War Council had not been involved in the extension of Haig's line; Lloyd George's assertion that the British army was stronger in January 1918 than in January 1917, and his claim that Allenby commanded only three white divisions in Egypt and Palestine.

The initial reaction of the press to "GEN. MAURICE'S BOMBSHELL," as the *Star* called it, reflected the seriousness of the situation. If the government had really let Haig down as Maurice implied, the *Daily Chronicle* warned, "the country could not view the Cabinet's responsibility leniently." The *Westminster Gazette,* the primary organ for Asquith and his supporters, asserted: "It is now for the House of Commons to assert itself and insist on a searching inquiry into General MAURICE's allegations, whatever the consequences to him or to the Government." Investigation or not, the *Morning Post* had already made up its mind about Lloyd George's fitness to retain power: "He has presumed to drive the chariot of war. He would have been wiser to have left the management of those fiery steeds to stronger and more experienced hands. If he had succeeded he would have had the credit! As he has failed he must abide the consequences." Many papers such as the *Times* and the *Manchester Guardian* which had previously supported the government made it clear that Lloyd George must not attempt to dodge Maurice's serious allegations.

The skirmishes the government had fought with its critics over the March 21 disaster were over. Now the battle had begun. The government was convinced that Maurice's letter was part of a military conspiracy despite his denials and its apprehension was fueled by some truly fantastic rumors. On May 8, Hankey recorded the following in his diary:

> Mark Sykes called before the War Cabinet and told me in confidence "from one Chinovnik to another" that Robertson had lunched with Asquith on the previous day. Later I learned from Davies, who got it from Ll. G's valet (!) that a few days ago Robertson gave a dinner to Trenchard [the chief of air staff who had created a stir in mid-April when he had resigned], Repington & Gwynne . . . & Maurice, & that after dinner the party were joined by Asquith & Jellicoe; that the Maurice letter was discussed, and that at the end Robertson said he would have nothing to do with it.[85]

One would not have been overly surprised to learn that Kitchener had returned from the depths of the sea to add his name to this list of the "outs" of the military establishment. Robertson, as a matter of fact, had lunched with Asquith on the day Maurice's letter was published, but the rest of this story was pure fantasy. Maurice, having taken the plunge, retired into the background, making no real effort to work with Lloyd George's political enemies.[86]

For any revolt in Parliament to succeed, Asquith had to give his wholehearted support to it. As Esher had written Wilson a week earlier: "There is nothing to fear so long as Asquith shrinks from office."[87] Although Gwynne was now prepared to accept Asquith over Lloyd George,[88] the former prime minister did not want to return to power by destroying the government during this perilous period. On the eve of the debate in Parliament about Maurice's allegations, the *Westminster Gazette,* which probably spoke for Asquith, made a remarkable overnight switch in its position.

> As for the House of Commons, its duty is plain. General MAURICE's letter is merely an opportunity for those whose real object is the overthrow of the present Government. That is the real issue which members will have before them tomorrow. The unity which has hitherto been preserved in the face of the enemy is threatened, and at a moment of unparalled danger we look like being involved in a storm of internal dissension. It is a situation which must give every patriotic man occasion for the most severe self-examination and discipline.[89]

Still, Asquith wanted answers and he supported the appointment of a select committee to investigate Maurice's charges.

After lengthy discussion within the War Cabinet about the best method of dealing with Maurice's allegations, Lloyd George decided against a select committee. On May 8 he told the War Cabinet that such a committee would be "perfectly useless" and would only lead to a "Party wrangle."[90] His method of handling the Maurice letter was through a statement to the House. A considerable advantage for Lloyd George in following this course was that he would force the House to make a choice between himself and Asquith. In truth, the violent opposition to Asquith and the "Old Gang" in many quarters was Lloyd George's greatest strength. A campaign had already been launched in Fleet Street against what the *Evening News* unfairly called "THE ASQUITH OFFENSIVE."[91] With no justification, Asquith's enemies in the press continued to associate all of Lloyd George's opponents with the "pacifists." This tended to divert attention from the fundamental issue. Maurice's serious charges, which implied that the government was incompetent, not Asquith's political fortunes, were the issue. Another reason for Lloyd George's willingness to make his stand in the House was that he was reasonably confident that he could parry Maurice's allegations. The indefatigable Hankey had prepared a superb brief during the afternoon and early evening of May 7 which gave Lloyd George a plausible defense with the exception of the obvious mistake concerning the number of white divisions in Egypt and Palestine.[92]

Although certainly not suggested by Hankey, Lloyd George had decided to build his defense around Under-Secretary for War Macpherson's response to the Baring question on April 18. Macpherson's incorrect returns, which had been produced in the adjutant general's department and given him by Maurice's deputy, were as follows[93]:

	Combatant Strength in France	Ration Strength in France
January 1, 1917	1,253,000	1,530,000
January 1, 1918	1,298,000	1,832,000

Since these figures had passed through Maurice's department, Lloyd George appeared to have an iron-clad case against the former D.M.O. Maurice's most explosive charge that the government had failed to support Haig could be shown to be false using the figures furnished by his own department. There was only one thing wrong with this defense. P. de B. Radcliffe, the new D.M.O., sent corrected figures from the adjutant general to Lloyd George's secretary, Philip Kerr, on May 8 which painted a quite different picture of Haig's situation at the beginning of 1918. The new returns read as follows[94]:

	Fighting Troops		Nonfighting Troops	
	British	Coloured (Indian Cavalry)	British	Coloured
January 1917	1,069,831	8,876	217,533	2,704
January 1918	969,283	11,544	295,334	2,256

	Labour (Labour corps did not exist until mid-1917)		Total Effectives
	British	Coloured	
January 1917	——	——	1,298,944
January 1918	190,197	108,203	1,576,817

This was actually the second copy of the adjutant general's revised returns on British troop strength in France to reach the government before Lloyd George's speech to Parliament. On May 7, the adjutant general sent the above returns to Hankey; and the secretary of the War Cabinet relied on these revised statistics which corrected Macpherson's mistaken returns when he prepared Lloyd George's defense on May 7, noting: "I frankly admit that the rifle strength of the Army [in January 1918] had been decreased by [figure omitted by Hankey] bayonets."[95]

The whole episode becomes curiouser and curiouser because of what has been called the "lost box" by Beaverbrook in his *Men and Power, 1917–1918*. On October 5, 1934, Miss Stevenson, who was assisting Lloyd George in the writing of his memoirs, wrote the following in her diary:

> Have been reading up the events connected with the Maurice Debate in order to help D. with this Chapter in Vol. V, and am uneasy in my mind about an incident which occurred at the time & which is known only to J. T. Davies & myself. D. obtained from the W. O. the figures which he used in his statement on April 9th in the House of Commons on the subject of man-power. These figures were afterwards stated by Gen. Maurice to be inaccurate. I was in J. T. Davies' room a few days after the statement [she must mean the May 9 Maurice debate], & J. T. was sorting our red dispatch boxes to be returned to the Departments. As was his wont, he looked in them before locking them up & sending them out to the Messengers. Pulling out a W. O. box, he found in it, to his great astonishment, a paper from the D.M.O. containing modifications & corrections to the first figures they had sent, & by some mischance this box had remained unopened. J. T. & I examined it in dismay, & then J. T. put it in the fire, remarking, "Only you & I, Frances, know of the existence of this paper."[96]

One theory is that Davies destroyed the adjutant general's report sent to Hankey on May 7 rather than any paper from the D.M.O. as Miss Stevenson thought.[97] But this cannot be correct, for Hankey obviously received the revised statistics and made use of them. The D.M.O. report Miss Stevenson refers to must have been Radcliffe's note to Kerr (with the adjutant general's most recent returns), which was the first communication from the department of the D.M.O. to the government correcting Macpherson's April 18 statement to Parliament. A copy, not the original, of Radcliffe's correspondence with Kerr exists in the Lloyd George Papers today.

The "lost box" mystery is actually of little significance because it is now known without question that Lloyd George knew that Macpherson's figures were wrong when he used them to discredit Maurice in Parliament on May 9. After listening to Lloyd George's speech, Hankey made this comment in his diary: "While he had figures from the D.M.O.'s Dept. showing that the fighting strength of the army had increased from 1 Jan. 1917 to 1918, he had the Adjutant General's figures saying the precise contrary, but was discreetly silent about them."[98]

In Lloyd George's defense, he no doubt smelled a rat when the revised returns were produced by the adjutant general on the very day that Maurice lit his political bomb in the press. Why, he must have asked himself, had the adjutant general waited until this moment to admit his department's error and supply the government with information which seemed designed to support Maurice's allegations? Lloyd George surely placed as much faith in the new returns as he did in the often distorted statistics furnished by the War Office in the past. After all, the adjutant general had done more than subtract 86,000 troops in Italy which had been incorrectly added to Haig's strength in January 1918. If this alone had been done, Haig's corrected "combatant strength" was 1,212,000 in January 1918, down 41,000 from January 1917. However, by placing artillerymen, machine-gunners, tankers, etc. with Haig's "nonfighting troops," it now appeared that Haig had only 969,383, "fighting" troops in January 1918, down approximately 100,000 men from January 1917. Adjutant General Macready's distinction between Haig's "non-fighting" and "fighting" (or infantry) strength was dubious, to say the least. Fighting for his survival against what he thought was a military conspiracy which had been brewing for some time, Lloyd George chose to suppress the adjutant general's new returns of May 7 and stick to the numbers supplied by his department in mid-April to Macpherson for his statement in Parliament. He might have made a strong case by challenging the War Office's narrow interpretation of Haig's "fighting" strength. But a serious flaw in the Welshman's character was that he was often devious when forthrightness would have served him just as well if not better.

After rehearsing his speech in front of Milner, Austen Chamberlain, who had recently joined the War Cabinet, Hankey, and Kerr, Lloyd George put his case to Parliament. At a little before 4:00 P.M. Asquith opened the debate. Instead of focusing on Maurice's charges, Asquith chose to explain why he wanted a select committee in a long and lifeless speech. Then it was time for Lloyd George to stand up and do some rhetorical prizefighting. Taking the offensive, he rained blows upon Maurice, using almost every trick he knew to discredit him. His most devastating point was that the government's comparison of Haig's strength at the beginning of 1917 and 1918 had been handed to Macpherson by Maurice's own department.

Lloyd George made it clear that he considered the motion for a select committee a vote of censure. If the motion carried, Asquith would be returned to power. The prime minister finished his brilliant, though distorted, speech with a passionate appeal for national unity and an end to the bickering.

> I have just come back from France. I met some generals and they were telling me how now the Germans are silently, silently, preparing perhaps the biggest blow of the War, under a shroud of mist, and they asked me for certain help. I brought home a list of the things they wanted done, and I wished to attend to them. I really beg and implore, for our common country, the fate of which is in the balance now and in the next few weeks, that there should be an end of this sniping.[99]

The stunned opposition was virtually speechless. When the bell rang for a division of the House on the motion for a select committee, Lloyd George was assured of his greatest triumph in Parliament; when the votes were tallied, he had won by the wide margin of 293 to 106. There would be no select committee and no investigation of Maurice's charges.

A few days after this momentous debate, Lloyd George talked with Riddell about the political intrigues against him. "I can play that game as well as, if not better than, they can—in fact I have done so. . . I don't know about the wisdom of the dove, but I have some of the craftiness of the serpent."[100] No one would have agreed with this more than Maurice. The end, rather than the means, mattered most to Lloyd George; and there can be no question that Lloyd George lied to the House to destroy Maurice's credibility. What must not be forgotten, however, is that the thrust of Maurice's charges was that the government was responsible for the setbacks of the army. This was based on the crude and one-sided view that the Germans broke through because Haig did not have enough men to defend his sector. If Maurice's version became accepted as fact by the public, it would mean the ruination of Lloyd George's government.

Far from being weakened by the Maurice affair, Lloyd George emerged from his smashing success in Parliament politically more secure than ever before. For the rest of the war he had little to fear from Parliament or Asquith. During the next few days he attempted to consolidate his ascendancy in British military policy. Before the Maurice debate, he had eased Derby, the army's friend, out of the War Office, sending him to Paris as the British ambassador in mid-April.[101] Now, with Milner as secretary of state for war and Wilson as C.I.G.S., the door of the War Office was wide open to him, and he moved to exploit the broken defenses of the army. On May 14, he told his colleagues that the examination of military questions took up too much of the time of the War Cabinet; consequently he proposed to meet with Milner and Wilson and the appropriate military authorities to make inquiries into military questions, reporting when necessary the facts to the War Cabinet, which would now begin thirty minutes later than in the past.[102]

The first of the secret meetings of the so-called "X" Committee took place in the War Office.[103] How symbolic of Lloyd George's intentions. At long last he seemed to be in a position to play the captain of war. Although later meetings took place at 10 Downing Street, the primary purpose of the "X" Committee, which served to exclude the other members of the War Cabinet from military policy, was to examine the existing military situation and chart future British strategy.

One change which Wilson urged upon Lloyd George, the recall of Haig, was not implemented. Although French had been sent to Ireland in preparation for the appointment of Haig as commander in chief of the home forces, Lloyd George apparently hoped to avoid another controversy so soon after the Maurice debate. At the second meeting of the "X" Committee, it was decided to inform Parliament that no change was contemplated in the command of the British Expeditionary Forces.[104]

The massive German onslaught in the West, although it had forced the government to withdraw troops from the periphery, had not converted the "Easterners" into "Westerners." To the contrary, Ludendorff's offensives, which had failed to break down Allied resistance but had resulted in huge losses to attacked and attacker alike, reinforced the belief of Lloyd George and many of his colleagues that a great offensive by Haig's declining forces was impossible in 1918. Amery, who often assisted Hankey in his secretarial duties at the "X" Committee meetings, wrote a memorandum, "Future Military Policy," dated May 22, which suggested that the government must not ignore the East even though Allenby's offensive had been canceled and many of his white troops transferred to the West. "For the next eighteen months at least the only theatre in which the Allies can take the strategical initiative is in the East," he argued. Once the situation in the West had been stabilized, Amery wanted British divisions sent to Palestine from France to enable Allenby to launch his offensive.[105] Despite the great German effort in France, many ministers kept a watchful eye on the enemy in the East. Even though the general staff was confident that India was safe for the moment,[106] the Germans seemed determined to exploit their position in Russia. To keep Russia's manpower, wheat, and oil from falling into the hands of Berlin, the British looked to America and Japan for assistance in stopping the field-grey tide from flowing across the old tsarist empire.

On May 27, Wilson seemed ready to put the authority of the general staff behind this peripheral strategy. The Allies had approximately four more anxious months in France, he told Milner and Lloyd George, while American reinforcements gradually tipped the scales in their favor. By late 1918 or early 1919, however, the Allies would not yet possess sufficient strength to attempt a decisive battle. "We must indulge in no operations of the Passchendaele type in this period," he said to the immense satisfaction of Lloyd George. "Consequently, between the time when our anxieties had been relieved and we would be able to strike a decisive blow in the Western front, a long period must exist. He was examining the situation on the basis that this period might be employed for striking a blow in one or other of the outlying theatres."[107]

As Wilson, Milner, and Lloyd George plotted future strategy, the Germans launched their third great offensive. This time they drove through French trenches on the Chemin des Dames where five exhausted British divisions had been sent to this supposedly "quiet" sector to recuperate. Like a tired heavyweight boxer behind on points in the last round, Ludendorff was swinging wildly attempting to deliver a knock-out punch. On a twenty-five-mile front, the Germans once again surged forward, covering an astonishing ten miles the first day.

The German offensive confronted the Anglo-French forces with their greatest crisis since the Germans were bearing down on Paris in 1914. Victory seemed further away than ever. "Writing now, before breakfast," Wilson recorded in his diary on June 1, "I find it difficult to realize that there is a possibility, perhaps a probability, of the French Army being beaten. What would this mean? The destruction of our army in France? In Italy? In Salonika? What of Palestine and Mesopotamia, India, Siberia and the sea? What of Archangel and America?"[108] During the next anxious weeks, Lloyd George never abandoned hope of winning an overwhelming victory over the enemy. As usual, however, he wished to travel a different road to victory from that of the British high command.

NOTES

1. *National Review* 71 (March 1918): 33–34.

2. Churchill, *World Crisis*, 4:110.

3. Lloyd George, *War Memoirs*, 2:1688 and 1715.

4. Wilson, like Lloyd George, saw no hope of breaking through the German defenses in 1918. His formula for success in 1919 was a massive tank assault rather than human-wave attacks. Cabinet Paper G.T. 3969 of March 19, 1918, CAB 24/45.

5. War Cabinet (351A), February 21, 1918, CAB 23/13.

6. Ibid. (358A and 360A), March 4 and 6, 1918, CAB 23/13. This order was canceled when the German offensive began.

7. Fischer, *Germany's Aims in First World War*, p. 550.

8. Richard Ullman, *Anglo-Soviet Relations, 1917–1921*, vol. 1: *Intervention and the War* (1961), p. 304.

9. Milner to Wilson, March 5, 1918, Wilson MSS, file no. 11. Also see the alarmist "Weekly Report on Turkey & Other Moslem Countries," Cabinet Paper G.T. 3836 of March 6, 1918, CAB 24/44.

10. Cabinet Paper G.T. 3840 of March 7, 1918, CAB 24/44.

11. Memorandum by Wilson, n.d., W.O. 106/982. Also see War Cabinet (362), March 8, 1918, CAB 23/5, and Amery to Lloyd George ("Notes on policy in Persia and Transcausia," March 14, 1918, inclosed), March 15, 1918, Lloyd George MSS, F/2/1/16.

12. Milner to Lloyd George, March 20, 1918, Lloyd George MSS, F/38/3/20.

13. Amery, "Unity of Operations in the East," March 20, 1918, CAB 25/72.

14. Milner to Lloyd George, March 20, 1918, Lloyd George MSS, F/38/3/20.

15. Wilson Diary, March 18, 1918, Haig to Lady Haig, March 20, 1918, Haig MSS, no. 150, and Haig Diary, March 2, 1918, no. 124.

16. War Cabinet (363–65), March 11–13, 1918, CAB 23/5, and Wilson Diary, March 16 and 20, 1918.

17. Fischer, *Germany's Aims in First World War*, pp. 429–624, and Hajo Holborn, *A History of Modern Germany, 1840–1945* (1969), pp. 487–94.

18. Correlli Barnett, *The Swordbearers: Studies in Supreme Command in the First World War* (1963), p. 279, and Brigadier-General James E. Edmonds, *A Short History of World War I* (1951), p. 281.

19. Barnett, *Swordbearers*, p. 309, and Martin Middlebrook, *The Kaiser's Battle 21 March 1918: The First Day of the German Spring Offensive* (1978).

20. Middlebrook, *Kaiser's Battle*, pp. 308–22. According to Middlebrook, German dead and wounded on this day were more than double the British dead and wounded. When 21,000 British prisoners are added, however, the losses suffered by the British and Germans were almost identical.

21. War Cabinet (369), March 21, 1918, CAB 23/5.

22. Ibid. (370), March 22, 1918, CAB 23/5.

23. Lloyd George believed that the 88,000 troops (10,000 from the Fifth Army) on leave in Britain were not counted by the War Office. Lloyd George, *War Memoirs*, 2:1730. On the other hand, the rifle strength of the Allies included Americans (49,000), Belgians (58,000) and Portuguese (26,000). The Germans now had 191 divisions to 165 for the Allies. Given the superiority of German soldiers to the Belgians, Portuguese, and untried Americans, it is difficult to accept Wilson's contention at this time that "for purposes of calculating, the present forces might be reckoned as approximately equal." War Cabinet (371), March 23, CAB 23/5.

24. War Cabinet (371), March 23, 1918, CAB 23/5.

25. Ibid. (372), March 25, 1918, CAB 23/5.

26. Haig Diary, March 24, 1918, no. 124.

27. Ibid., March 26, 1918, no. 124, Wilson Diary, March 26, 1918, and "Memorandum by

Lord Milner on his Visit to France, including the Conference at Doullens, March 26, 1918," CAB 28/3/I.C.-53.

28. War Cabinet (375–76), March 27–28, 1918, CAB 23/5.

29. Milner to Lloyd George, March 28, 1918, Lloyd George MSS, F/38/3/22.

30. War Cabinet (377), March 29, 1918, CAB 23/5, and Robertson, *Soldiers and Statesmen*, 1:331.

31. Churchill to Lloyd George, April 2, 1918, Lloyd George MSS, F/8/2/18, and *Memoirs of Marshal Foch*, pp. 272–73.

32. Author's italics. War Cabinet (380), April 2, 1918, CAB 23/6. Repington, for example, gave his wholehearted approval to the elevation of Foch. *Morning Post*, April 1, 1918.

33. Major-General C. E. Callwell, *Field-Marshal Sir Henry Wilson: His Life and Diaries*. 2 vols. (1927), 2:84.

34. War Cabinet (377), March 29, 1918, CAB 23/5.

35. Maurice Diary, April 1–2, 1918, 4/3.

36. Entry of April 3, 1918, *Wilson: Life and Diaries*, 2:86.

37. Allied Conference, April 3, 1918, CAB 28/3/I.C.-55a.

38. Ibid., Sackville-West to Wilson, April 8, 1918, Wilson MSS, file 12 B, and War Cabinet (387), April 9, 1918, CAB 23/6.

39. *Memoirs of Marshal Foch*, pp. 276–77.

40. Cox, "Note on the German Offensive," March 31, 1918, Haig MSS, no. 124.

41. Haig Diary, March 31, 1918, no. 124.

42. *Military Operations, France and Belgium, 1918*, 1:vii.

43. Barnett, *Swordbearers*, p. 297.

44. "Talk with Lloyd George and General Sir Hubert Gough," November 28, 1935, Liddell Hart MSS, 11/1935/107. Also see Liddell Hart, *Fog of War*, pp. 272–76.

45. Barnett, *Swordbearers*, pp. 297–99, and Liddell Hart, *Fog of War*, pp. 274–75.

46. *Daily News*, April 9, 1918, *Globe*, April 8, 1918, and *Star*, April 8, 1918.

47. War Cabinet (382A), April 4, 1918, CAB 23/14, and Wilson Diary, April 4, 1918.

48. Haig to Derby, April 6, 1918, Derby MSS, 920 (17).

49. Wilson freely accepted responsibility for this mistake in his diary entry of May 8, 1918. On March 23, War Cabinet (371), CAB 23/5, he told the ministers that the British had three white divisions in Egypt—not in Egypt *and* Palestine. On March 27, War Cabinet (374A), CAB 23/14, however, he asserted that Allenby "had under his command three Divisions of white troops," two of which should be withdrawn from the line to send to France if necessary. On the other hand, there is a letter in the Lloyd George Papers (F/47/7/20) from the prime minister to Wilson, dated March 29, 1918, requesting information on the number of white infantry in Egypt and Palestine. It is minuted "Not seen by C.I.G.S." A statement, "Rifle Strength of White Infantry—Egyptian Expeditionary Force—Egypt and Palestine," dated March 29, 1918, giving the number of white infantry in the Egyptian Expeditionary Force (96,135, including 1,764 French and 398 Italians), was returned. Hence, Lloyd George almost certainly had the correct figures when he gave his speech, allowing Wilson, who did not know that the War Office had furnished Lloyd George with the facts, to take the blame.

50. Hankey to Lloyd George, April 8, 1918, Lloyd George MSS, F/235.

51. *H. C. Deb.*, 5th series, vol. 104 (April 9, 1918).

52. War Cabinet (387), April 9, 1918, CAB 23/6.

53. Memorandum by Macdonogh, April 10, 1918, W.O. 106/982.

54. Terraine, *Haig: Educated Soldier*, pp. 426–27.

55. Jere Clemens King, *Generals and Politicians: Conflict between France's High Command, Parliament and Government, 1914–1918* (1951), p. 219; Esher warned Lloyd George: "I urge you not to put your faith in Clemenceau. He will always put France before England: and he cannot be blamed." Esher to Lloyd George, April 13, 1918, Lloyd George MSS, F/16/1/24.

56. War Cabinet (383 and 386), April 5 and 8, 1918, CAB 23/6, Lloyd George to Clemenceau,

April 4 (and via British Section, Versailles), April 5, 1918, Lloyd George MSS, F/50/2/18–19, and Clemenceau to Lloyd George, April 7, 1918, Lloyd George MSS, F/50/2/24.

57. Haig Diary, April 8, 1918, no. 125.

58. Cruttwell, *History of the Great War*, pp. 519–20.

59. War Cabinet (393), April 17, 1918, CAB 23/6.

60. Ibid. (389A), April 11, 1918, CAB 23/14, and (391), April 15, 1918, CAB 23/6. Also see Lloyd George, *War Memoirs*, 2:1749–50.

61. Haig to Derby, April 7, 1918, War Cabinet (388A), April 16, 1918, CAB 23/14.

62. Memorandum by Milner, April 29, 1918, Lloyd George MSS, F/210/2/31.

63. Derby to Balfour, May 1, 1918, Lloyd George MSS, F/52/1/31.

64. Supreme War Council, May 1, 1918, CAB 28/3/I.C.-57.

65. War Cabinet (393), April 17, 1918, CAB 23/6.

66. *H. C. Deb.*, 5th series, vol. 105 (April 18, 1918).

67. Wilson Diary, April 20, 1918, and Esher Diary, April 18, 1918, 2/21.

68. War Cabinet (396), April 22, 1918, CAB 23/6. It should be noted that the general staff had been keeping the War Cabinet fully and accurately informed of the new German divisions as they arrived on the western front from the East.

69. Wilson Diary, April 22, 1918.

70. Lloyd George to Milner, April 24, 1918, Lloyd George MSS, F/38/3/25.

71. There is some confusion about when Maurice officially gave up his duties as D.M.O. He asserts that he left the War Office on the twentieth to go on leave that he had accumulated, but Hankey still lists him as D.M.O. in the War Cabinet minutes as late as April 23.

72. The student who desires to probe this controversy of numbers in more depth should consult Lloyd George, *War Memoirs*, 2:1781–84, War Cabinet (396), April 22, 1918, CAB 23/6, and Maurice, *Maurice Case*, pp. 164–68.

73. War Cabinet (397), April 23, 1918, CAB 23/6, and Hankey to Lloyd George ("Summary of proceedings of the War Cabinet & Supreme War Council in regard to the extension of the British line in France," April 22, 1918, inclosed), April 22, 1918, Lloyd George MSS, F/23/2/31.

74. *H. C. Deb.*, 5th series, vol. 105 (April 23, 1918).

75. Derby and Haig certainly did not accept the excessive subtlety of Bonar Law's response in Parliament. Haig gave Milner a note when he visited general headquarters on April 28 which emphasized that he had always opposed the principle of extending his line. Also, Derby, who incorrectly believed that the Supreme War Council had been forced to order Haig to extend his line to Barisis, fired off an angry letter to Milner, accusing the War Cabinet of attempting to shift all responsibility to Haig and Pétain. See Haig Diary, April 28, 1918, no. 126, and Derby to Milner, May 7, 1918, Milner MSS, C. 696/2.

76. Robertson to Maurice, May 4, 1918, Maurice MSS, 4/5/24.

77. Wilson Diary, May 7, 1918.

78. "Intrigues of the War" first appeared in a series of articles in *Westminster Gazette* and later in a pamphlet (1922). See Maurice Diary, April 9, 1918, 4/3.

79. See, for example, *Times* (London) and *Morning Post*, April 10, 1918.

80. John Gooch, "The Maurice Debate 1918," *Journal of Contemporary History* 3 (October 1968): 211–28.

81. Maurice, *Maurice Case;* and Timothy Crandall Sullivan, "The General and the Prime Minister: Henry Wilson and David Lloyd George in War and Peace, 1918–1922" (Ph.D. diss., University of Illinois at Urbana-Champaign, 1973), p. 110.

82. Repington, *First World War, 1914–1918*, 2:296.

83. See, for example, the leading article, "THE RESPONSIBILITY OF MR. ASQUITH," in the *Nation*, April 27, 1918.

84. Gwynne to Asquith, May 6, 1918, Gwynne MSS, 14.

85. Hankey Diary, May 8, 1918, 1/3.

86. Following the debate Maurice did, however, try to justify his actions to A. G. Gardiner, the editor of the *Daily News*, who was waging a vendetta against the prime minister. Stephen Koss, *Fleet Street Radical: A. G. Gardiner and the Daily News* (1973), pp. 239–40.

87. Esher to Wilson, May 1, 1918, Lloyd George MSS, F/47/7/24.

88. Gwynne to Asquith, May 8, 1918, Gwynne MSS, 14.

89. *Westminster Gazette,* May 8, 1918. Beaverbrook's pen slips when he writes that the *Westminster Gazette* called for the overthrow of Lloyd George's ministry on this date. See his *Men and Power, 1917–1918,* p. 254.

90. War Cabinet (406–7), May 7–8, 1918, CAB 23/6.

91. *Evening News,* May 8, 1918.

92. "Copy extracted from Hankey's magnum opus," May 8, 1918, Lloyd George MSS, F/235. See also Roskill, *1877–1918,* pp. 540–42.

93. War Cabinet (407), May 8, 1918, CAB 23/6.

94. P. de B. Radcliffe to Kerr (adjutant general's statement, May 7, 1918, inclosed), May 8, 1918, Lloyd George MSS, F/235.

95. "Copy extracted from Hankey's magnum opus," May 8, 1918, Lloyd George MSS/F/235.

96. Entry of October 5, 1934, *A Diary by Frances Stevenson,* p. 281.

97. Maurice, *Maurice Case,* pp. 171–75.

98. Hankey Diary, May 9, 1918, 1/3.

99. *H. C. Deb.,* 5th series, vol. 105 (May 9, 1918).

100. Entry of May ?, 1918, *Lord Riddell's War Diary,* p. 330.

101. See Hankey Diary, April 17, 1918, 1/3, Derby to Lloyd George, April 16, 1918, Lloyd George MSS, F/14/5/16, Milner to Lloyd George, April 13, 1918, Lloyd George MSS, F/38/3/23, and Amery to Lloyd George, April 14, 1918, Lloyd George MSS, F/2/1/17.

102. War Cabinet (411), May 14, 1918, CAB 23/6.

103. "X" Committee (1), May 15, 1918, CAB 23/17.

104. Ibid. (2), May 16, 1918, CAB 23/17, and Wilson Diary, May 10, 1918.

105. Amery, "Future Military Policy," May 22, 1918, Milner MSS, dep. 372.

106. Wilson, "Security of India," April 30, 1918, W.O. 106/314, and Eastern Committee (7), May 6, 1918, CAB 27/24.

107. "X" Committee (4), May 27, 1918, CAB 23/17.

108. Entry of June 1, 1918, *Wilson: Life and Diaries,* 2:103.

13

The Uncertain Road to Victory

THAT Germany could not be defeated in 1918 was an article of faith in London in the spring and summer of 1918. This belief, along with imperial considerations, the worsening manpower crisis, and the consequent fear that Haig's army might be reduced to a second- or third-class military force by the end of the year, played a decisive role in shaping the civilians' strategic views and determining their attitude toward both the British high command and the new generalissimo.

The French continued to believe that Britain was hoarding her manpower. Within days after he had deflected the serious charge in the Maurice debate that he had placed the army in danger by starving Haig of men, Lloyd George received a letter from Clemenceau demanding that the British divisions broken up since March 21 be reconstituted. The fierce-tempered French premier held in contempt the "A" and "B" categories used by the British War Office ("a mere sailor's notion"), mistakenly believing that category "B" men were restricted to service in the United Kingdom when, in fact, they had been used abroad as clerks, in labor battalions, etc., and Haig was about to commit them to battle in certain circumstances.[1] To allay French suspicions, Lloyd George at the Supreme War Council at Abbeville had allowed a French officer, Colonel Roure, to come to London to investigate Britain's utilization of men in khaki. The Frenchman's visit apparently destroyed once and for all the French notion that the British were holding back a vast army in Britain. Many soldiers in Britain were in training units; others were in hospitals or recovering from wounds. Derby reported to London that he had learned from private sources that Clemenceau "now believes our figures and that it has disturbed the Government very much as they were under the impression that we had lied to them and that we had a large reserve which they now find to be non-existent."[2] Clemenceau, however, remained convinced that more could be done to maintain Haig's army by withdrawing men from civil life. Lloyd George continued to stress British contributions in shipping and in the production of coal and war material, but the French, who had mobilized more men despite a smaller population to draw upon, refused to accept this argument. Yet French manpower policies in 1918 were not that different from the British. When Pétain requested the release of 200,000 men from the 1,200,000 withheld for industry to maintain his forces, the French War Ministry, supported by Clemenceau, gave him only a fraction of the men he demanded, although the French commander in chief maintained that the drafts provided him between April and October would leave him short 154,000 men by the beginning of November.[3]

With France's ability to continue the war in question, Lloyd George was prepared to go quite far in satisfying Clemenceau about British manpower policies, as the extraordinary mission of Roure demonstrates. But he thought intolerable what he considered was the War Office's continued intrigue against him on this question. In mid-May, Macready, perhaps in retaliation against Lloyd George's refusal to use the corrected figures supplied by his department in the Maurice debate, wrote a memorandum which could have come from Repington's pen. In no uncertain terms, the government's past manpower policies were blasted. Coming on the heels of the Maurice debate, Lloyd George saw a sinister motive in its production. The adjutant general maintained that the weakened and perilous state of Haig's army was due to the failure of the government to heed the Army Council's incessant demands for fresh recruits throughout 1917. He also emphasized that the War Office's calculations of Haig's wastage in 1918, which had been rejected by the Manpower Committee, had been completely vindicated by events. There was even a dig at the government for pushing a forward policy in Palestine when Haig's present and future need for riflemen was so apparent.[4]

Auckland Geddes, the minister for national service, immediately rushed to the government's defense, taking the adjutant general to task for statistical errors ("I would suggest that the War Office Statistical Department be reinforced") and emphasizing that the army had increased in size since January 1, 1917. Many men, of course, had been allocated to the new arms (tanks, machine-gun units, etc.) rather than to the infantry. But whose responsibility was this?[5]

On Lloyd George's instructions, Hankey then expanded on Geddes's theme to rebut the adjutant general. Calling Macready's memorandum a "laconic and one-sided document," the secretary of the War Cabinet noted: "It is the business of the Army to get the best value that it can out of the men. If it considers that better fighting value is obtained from artillery, machine-guns, aeroplanes, trench motors, tanks, poison gas, and other mechanical adjuncts, than by devoting the same personnel to infantry, the Army is no doubt right to make this allocation." Hankey also emphasized that Lloyd George and the War Cabinet had throughout the latter half of 1917 underlined the growing manpower crisis to the military authorities and cautioned them against excessive losses. Yet the high command had treated these warnings "with disdain". "They were always ready to ask the Government for men, and to warn the Government of the danger of not providing them, but never to adopt a policy of husbanding their man-power."[6] This last argument actually came very close to reflecting Lloyd George's true position on manpower. As shown elsewhere, he had resisted the extreme combing out of vital occupations, not only to maintain Britain's staying power, but to force Haig to economize his losses. This policy had come to grief during the battles of Passchendaele and Cambrai. Whatever one thinks of this policy, it cannot be said that Haig had not been repeatedly warned about the number of new recruits available to him.

Macready's paper made Lloyd George more anxious than ever to shake up the War Office personnel. Milner, in this regard, was a great disappointment. Although Milner often agreed with Lloyd George about the larger issues of the war, especially grand strategy, his allegiances shifted when he moved to the War Office. Never was this so clear as when the prime minister, after Macready was eased out of the War Office by being appointed commissioner of metropolitan police in early September, proposed merging the departments of the adjutant general and quartermaster general and placing them under a civilian in an apparent attempt to gain control of the army's production of at times questionable statistics.[7] This plan naturally provoked bitter resentment from the professionals, and Milner came down very strongly on the side of the military authorities in fighting what he called a *"retrograde step."* Milner also angered Lloyd George by putting forward Macdonogh, a Robertson appointee, as Macready's replacement. There was much unpleasantness over this, but, when Milner made it a question of Lloyd George's confidence in him, the prime minister relented. There was no merger and Macdonogh suceeded Macready.[8] Milner's different perspective as secretary of state for war probably best explains the widening gulf between him and the prime minister during the last months of the war.

On the eve of the third German offensive of 1918, Foch's leadership came under increasing attack by Henry Wilson. By mid-May three British soldiers had been lost since March 21 to every one French soldier. Yet the French seemed unwilling to recognize the gigantic losses suffered by or the dominant role played by British arms. Wilson even feared that Foch sought the amalgamation of the French and British forces and the destruction of an independent British army. After the generalissimo succeeded in dispersing part of Haig's army by transferring some battered British divisions to supposedly "quiet" French sectors to relieve French divisions from the trenches, Wilson, who had opposed this move, concluded that "the French mean to take us over body and soul." On May 15, the Army Council considered a paper by Wilson addressed to Milner. As he had warned three weeks earlier, Wilson asserted, the British army was disappearing "into scattered fragments impossible of control by our General Headquarters." Moreover, this *roulement* was contributing to French domination of Allied transportation and the pooling of Allied resources. The Army Council, no less than Wilson, was opposed to any amalgamation of the British and French armies or the loss of British control over their supply services. When Milner forwarded Wilson's paper to the prime minister, he noted: "[We should] make it clear to the French now at once, that, when we agreed gladly to strategic unity of control, we never contemplated the *administrative unification* of the French & British Armies, & that it is quite impossible for us to agree to it."[9]

At first, Lloyd George resisted challenging Foch's new authority, telling Milner and Wilson that "the first consideration was to win the battle; nothing must be done which handicapped General Foch in this respect."[10] Lloyd

George obviously hoped that the new unity of command would encourage the French to expend more of their men and material in the battles ahead to ease the pressure on Haig's forces. But French actions after the German attack against the Chemin des Dames ridge hardened him against Foch and Clemenceau. The German high command had planned this attack as a diversionary offensive to draw off the Allied reserves from the north before attacking the British again. But its success encouraged Ludendorff to continue it. By the beginning of June the Germans had driven to the Marne and were within less than fifty miles of Paris, where panic reigned.

The continued German inroads on Allied manpower, with the war-weary French bearing the brunt of the attack this time, was the catalyst for a nasty confrontation between Lloyd George and the French on June 1 during a meeting at Versailles of a committee of the Supreme War Council which included only British and French leaders. Foch began the meeting by reading a memorandum which charged that the French were making every effort to maintain their number of divisions while the British allowed their divisions to dwindle away without sending adequate reinforcements from the home forces or from British forces "operating in distant countries."

When Foch's paper was discussed, Milner made the obvious point that the Germans, not the policy of the British government, were responsible for the reduction of British divisions in the West from sixty-one to fifty-three despite the transfer of two divisions each from Italy and Palestine to France. After all, the British had suffered approximately 350,000 casualties since March 21. With Paris itself threatened, Clemenceau brushed these and other British arguments aside.

> *M. Clemenceau* said that the fundamental question was that put by General Foch, namely: how many combatant divisions could be maintained? The French had lost 2,000,000 men in this war, and had been obliged to reduce divisions. Nevertheless, they intended to maintain 100 divisions, even if they had to fill them up with niggers.
> *Mr. Lloyd George* said he thought we could keep up our divisions if we incorporated niggers in them.
> *Mr. Clemenceau* said he did not mind how we did it. . . . the fact remained that the country with a smaller population had given more men to the army.

This highly emotional discussion came to an abrupt end when Lloyd George suggested that the French send a representative to London to "show us where and how to find more men." This proposal, Clemenceau exclaimed, gave him "extraordinary satisfaction."[11] Lloyd George felt that he had nothing to hide, and he hoped that a visit by a Frenchman (it was to be Colonel Roure again) to the British War Office would force the soldiers to make better use of men in the home forces, including men of the "B" category, and behind Haig's lines. When Roure showed up at the War Office, the professionals practically slammed the door in his face. Robertson, who was now commander in chief of the home forces, even told the government that he would refuse to be responsible for the defense of the United Kingdom if the forces under his command were further reduced in strength.[12]

Although the German offensive against the French had lost its momentum by early June and Paris was in no immediate danger, relations between London and Paris continued to deteriorate. Wilson reckoned that the Germans still had forty-eight reserve divisions in a position to attack British trenches, and the C.I.G.S. and Haig were concerned that Foch was denuding the British army of reserves available to it. The reserves of the French divisions in Haig's sector were withdrawn by Foch, along with the five American divisions training in his sector, and sent south. Then, on June 4, Haig received a telegram requesting him to place three British divisions astride the Somme to be used either on the French or the British fronts. Haig complied with this demand, but not without issuing a formal protest.[13]

Wilson was even more alarmed than Haig by Foch's deployment of Allied reserves. Foch was going to lose the war he bluntly told Lloyd George and Milner on June 5 by taking away Haig's reserves and by rejecting Wilson's suggestion that Haig's line be shortened at its northern end by the sea. "He was absolutely convinced that we were not in a position to hold the present line against the attack that Prince Rupprecht, who still had 48 divisions in reserve, could deliver against us."[14] During a second meeting of the "X" Committee on this day, it was decided to dispatch Milner and Wilson to France to confront Foch and Clemenceau.[15]

On June 7, Haig, Foch, Milner, Wilson, and Clemenceau, among others, attempted to reach an understanding about Foch's authority at the French Ministry of War. It was a delicate matter, with the French naturally fearing for the safety of Paris and the British for the security of their army. The British government's support of Haig made the French tread warily. Foch promised to consult Haig (which implied common agreement) before moving troops from his front.[16] Future relations between Haig and Foch were actually to be better than between the British government and Foch.

Unknown to the French, their British ally was anticipating at this very moment the utter ruin of the French army. These frightening thoughts were not confined to the British civilians. According to Wilson, Haig believed that the reserves being sent south were being committed to a lost cause because the French were "beaten."[17] In London, the civilians even considered the possibility that the British forces might have to be evacuated from the Continent.[18]

Avoiding defeat rather than total victory was uppermost on the minds of the leaders of the empire as they gathered in London to participate once again in meetings of the Imperial War Cabinet. On the eve of this meeting to plan and coordinate the military effort of the empire, Milner in a letter to the prime minister discussed British military policy and strategy in the event that Germany overran France and Italy.

It is rather fortunate, that you have all the Dominion people here at this critical time. It will give you a chance of telling them what they really are up against & finding out, whether they are prepared for all that is involved in "seeing it through."

We must be prepared for France & Italy both being beaten to their knees. In that case the Germano-Austro-Turko-Bulgar bloc will be master of all Europe & Northern & Central Asia up to the point, at wh. Japan steps in to bar the way, if she does step in. . . . In any case it is clear that, unless the only remaining free peoples of the world, America, this country & the Dominions, are knit together in the closest conceivable alliance & prepared for the maximum of sacrifice, the Central bloc, under the hegemony of Germany, will control not only Europe & most of Asia but the whole world. . . . The fight will now be for Southern Asia & above all for Africa (the Palestine bridge-head is of immense importance) & success may largely depend on what supplies we can get from India & Australia, instead of having to send everything from this country by routes increasingly dangerous & perhaps very much lengthened.

Another concern for the British were reports that the Germans were moving across the Black Sea to the Caucasus to establish a base for the penetration of central Asia and had preparations underway to send reinforcements to the Turkish theater.[19]

German pressure had forced the civilians to pour all available men and equipment into France, but their minds were obviously never far from the periphery. A German victory on the Continent would be the end for France and Italy; but if the British Empire clung to its position in Mesopotamia and Palestine and forged stronger ties with Japan and especially the United States, the rim powers might still be able to contain or even defeat Germany and her allies.

> You asked me [Amery wrote the prime minister] the other day to say what I thought of the situation, and I ventured to sum it up by saying that as soon as this "little side show" in the West is over, whether the line gets stabilised or disappears altogether, we shall have to take the war for the mastery of Asia in hand seriously, and that in that quarter we can call a New World into being to redress the balance of the Old—if the Old should go wrong, which I am not yet prepared to admit.[20]

Despite the gloomy military situation, Lloyd George had abandoned any idea of buying a favorable peace in the West by allowing Germany to expand eastwards and gave no thought to anything less than victory. The all-out enemy effort convinced him that the German leaders were unprepared to consider any peace which the British Empire could accept. "They would be selling out at the top of the market,"[21] he told the dominion leaders. Even if France collapsed, he told Wilson, he was prepared to fight on "if America will stick to it."[22]

America, more and more, exerted a powerful influence on Lloyd George's approach to the war. Since 1916 the British army had assumed the major burden in fighting the German army. More confident of the fighting ability of the American army than Haig, he was determined to shift this responsibility to the "Yanks" as soon as possible and concentrate British military in the outlying theaters. His indirect strategic views, which had been strengthened rather than weakened by recent military developments, were bound to bring him into conflict with Haig and the French; and he hoped to enlist the support of the dominion leaders to strengthen his hand. On June 11, he spoke at length in the Imperial War Cabinet about past battles and future prospects. Taking pains to link his "Eastern" strategy to Britain's ability to continue the war if France and Italy went under, he discussed Allenby's capture of Jerusalem.

> We have captured a very considerable part—perhaps the most important part—of Palestine. That is important, not merely from the point of view of the great historical associations which attach to that country but from the point of view also of possible future developments, because Palestine is the great bridge-head in that part of the world. . . . This means that if we were to be thrown back as an Empire upon our old traditional policy of utilising the command of the sea in order to cut off our enemies from all the sources of supply and from all possible means of expansion, north, east, south, and west, Palestine would be invaluable, as would also be Mesopotamia.

Lloyd George clearly saw no way of achieving decisive results in the West in 1918. Any victory over the German army would have to wait at least until 1919 and then much would depend upon the ability of the Americans to fulfill their promise of sending 100 divisions (or about 2,700,000 men) to Europe. Still, the German breakthrough had demonstrated that the fortifications in the West were not impenetrable. "There is no doubt that they [the Germans] have shown what can be accomplished on the Western Front by troops properly trained and skilfully handled."[23] This amounted to an attack on the British high command; and the competence of Haig and other British generals was the topic of the second meeting of the Imperial War Cabinet.

Apparently egged on by Smuts, Robert Borden, the Canadian prime minister, delivered a bitter tirade against the generals, concentrating on the last phase of Haig's Flanders offensive. "The gain was not worth the candle [and] . . . the result was not worth the loss," General A. W. Currie, the commander of the Canadian corps, had told him in respect to the capture of the village of Passchendaele. W. F. Massey, the prime minister of New Zealand, added his voice to this criticism. At Passchendaele, he asserted, New Zealanders "were asked to do the impossible" and were "simply shot down like rabbits."[24]

On June 14, Smuts attempted to clear the government of all responsibility for Passchendaele, pointing out that Lloyd George had pleaded with the military authorities to limit their attacks in the West and concentrate on Germany's war-weary allies. This was not quite fair, for the ultimate responsibility for the Flanders offensive rested with the civilian authorities. Smuts also discussed past difficulties between the government and its military advisers. The focal point of the conflict was how the war should be won, not intrigue of the ministers against the army, he ingeniously explained.[25] The government's conduct of the war thus defended, Lloyd George and his fellow "Easterners" then carried on a well-coordinated campaign to keep the dominion leaders out of the camp of the "Westerners."

On June 15, a memorandum by Amery was circulated to the members of the Imperial War Cabinet. Britain's first objective had to be holding the line in France, Amery stressed. However, even if the German drive stalled in the

West, the Allies had "no reasonable prospect" of "acquiring a definite military ascendancy over the Germans till the autumn of 1919 or spring of 1920." Only in the East might the British Empire take the initiative during the interim. Its goal should be "to keep the German menace in the East at arm's length." The Turk must be ejected from Palestine, Syria, and Mesopotamia, Persia secured, part of the whole of the Caucasus and Armenia taken, and a line drawn in Russia "at the Urals or bent back from the Caspian to the Yenisei or even to Lake Baikal." With a great American army eventually giving the Allies military superiority in the West and with the German and Turkish threat contained in the East, the empire would have reason to be confident about obtaining a "tolerable" peace settlement, whether it came at the peace table or on the battlefield.[26]

On June 18, Wilson gave his support to Amery's "Eastern" sentiments. Standing before the dominion prime ministers in the War Office, armed with a map and pointer, the C.I.G.S. talked for seventy minutes on past and future strategy. Although the Germans considered the West the decisive front, this had not prevented them from picking off Britain's allies one by one. As he condensed the strategy of the war for the benefit of the "frocks," his pointer beat a tattoo on the map. He had not had such a moment since his famous lecture that had dazzled the ministers during the meeting of the Committee of Imperial Defence on August 23, 1911.

> It is very nearly fair, and it is very nearly true to say . . . when we took Bullecourt, a little village, at the end of the Somme fight, the Boche took Roumania; when we took Messines, they took Russia; and when we took Passchendaele, they very nearly knocked out Italy in the same months. And our decisions, or attempts at them were *here,* all theirs being out on *that* side. . . . As regards the future—I am speaking as a soldier—I want to see us established along the Rhine; but it seems to me that if we do get ourselves into that pass, that is not getting a real decision on this front. It seems to me we have to get a position on this side (the East) as well as on the west. If that is so, we have got to get everybody to help, and we must get the Japanese. I can see no other way out of it. No military decisions, as far as I can see, that we can get *here* now will settle the east. It is for that reason that I think that between the days when all anxiety is past, this autumn, and the time when we throw down the glove *here* for a final clinch, we ought to exploit the outside theatres as much as we can, so that at the Peace Conference we, the British anyhow, will not be so badly off.[27]

Finally, on June 25, Curzon, the chairman of the Eastern Committee, weighed in with a lecture on the importance of the much derided "side shows."

> It may very well be that those whose eyes are almost exclusively concentrated on the West—because of the magnitude of the forces there engaged, because of the peril to our shores, because of its greater proximity to our lives—are somewhat mistaking the real proportions and focus of the case with which we have to deal, and that as time goes on, they may realise that the Eastern is not less important than the Western theatre of war.

At great length he talked about the danger of Germany advancing through the door which Russia's collapse had flung open.

> Let us, representatives of the British Empire who are here, realise fully that Germany is out in this war to destroy the British Empire. That is the first and foremost of her objects, and one of the methods of destroying the British Empire is not merely the destruction of her forces at Calais or Boulogne, but it is by rendering her position in the East insecure. She sees that the power of Great Britain is built upon her overseas strength.[28]

The dominion prime ministers could not help being influenced by this wave of "Eastern" sentiment, and Massey, according to Hankey, remained "the only out and out Westerner." A clear reflection of the mood of the imperial leaders can be found in the discussion over whether or not to transfer more of Allenby's force to France. Pressed by Wilson, the civilians reluctantly decided to recall the 54th Division, retaining, however, the Australian Mounted Division in Palestine. Once the Italian front seemed secure, which would enable the British divisions there to be sent to the West if necessary, this decision, however, was first provisionally and then finally reversed.[29] (Later the 54th Division played a key role in Allenby's successful offensive in September and October.) An important consideration for the civilians was that, once a British division was sent to France, it might never be extracted from that theater. As Smuts put it, "He doubted if General Foch would ever agree to sending the troops back to Palestine."[30]

Smuts touched upon a delicate question which was uppermost on Lloyd George's mind in June. On June 6, exactly twenty-six years before "D" Day, U.S. troops went into action at Belleau Wood near Château-Thierry. Although their inexperience resulted in heavy casualties, the Americans fought with determination. "If the Americans concentrated a great Army on the Western front next year," Lloyd George noted in a meeting of the "X" Committee, "it might be possible for our Army to follow its traditional *rôle* of operating on the outskirts of the war area."[31] Gaining support for a policy so favorable to imperial interests, however, was certain to tax Lloyd George's ingenuity to the utmost. In an attempt to escape the domination of the British high command, Lloyd George had worked towards unity of command. But Foch, like Haig and Robertson, wanted the British to concentrate their military power in the West. Lloyd George hoped to place Americans in the British sector and use the British divisions thus freed for operations in other theaters. But Foch, determined that Britain maintain all of its divisions in the West, was wrecking this policy by stationing most of the Americans in the French sector. In his distribution of American troops, Lloyd George believed that "Foch had, intentionally or unintentionally, 'done' us in the matter."[32] Determined to get all of the ten divisions originally allocated to the British sector for training in the Pershing-Milner agreement, he was prepared to challenge the authority of the generalissimo. Also, to give the British more influence he hoped to breathe new life into the body of Allied permanent military representatives at Versailles. As for Foch's own small staff, although it obviously needed strengthening, he wanted it to reflect the

British as well as French view. When Wilson suggested that Foch take over Pétain's staff for his own, Lloyd George objected, arguing that Foch's staff would then be "biased in the interests of General Pétain's Army. We were entitled to ask Monsieur Clemenceau that General Foch should have an independent Staff."[33]

The Supreme War Council meeting at Versailles in early July gave Lloyd George an opportunity to ventilate his opposition to any French attempt to dominate Allied war policy. First, on July 2 he took on André Tardieu, the high commissioner for Franco-American affairs, for meddling in British shipping arrangements with the Americans. Shipping, of course, was Britain's ace in the hole in any quarrel with the French; and the Welshman was determined to keep it independent from any French interference or control. In an attempt to hasten the arrival of American soldiers to France, Tardieu had undertaken unilateral discussions with Washington, only bringing in Joseph Maclay, the British minister for shipping, the previous day. Lloyd George demanded to know why the British authorities had only been "casually consulted." The question was one solely for the Americans and the British to decide.[34]

On the following day, July 3, there was an even more violent explosion by the volatile Welshman. This time his anger was directed toward the French government, which had, without consulting its allies, changed the standing orders for the multinational Eastern Army in the Balkans from a defensive to an offensive posture. The preemptory behavior of the French placed the supreme command in jeopardy. "It was evident that the moment General Foch came to be considered merely as the servant of the French Government trouble would arise," he thundered. "At the present moment they trusted him absolutely, but if it was thought that he was taking instructions from one Government more than from another, this feeling of complete confidence would disappear."[35] In short, if the machinery of the Supreme War Council, especially the role of the permanent military representatives, was similarly ignored in the future, it might mean the ruination of unity of command. Hankey and probably Lloyd George, too, suspected the French of having ulterior political and financial motives in the Balkans.[36] Lloyd George's violent outbursts and his threat to explode the unity of command put the French exactly where he wanted them—on the defensive. On the prime minister's initiative, a resolution was passed which instructed the permanent military representatives to study military operations for 1919. When Foch learned of this infringement on his authority, he was enraged and threatened to resign. When he made known his intentions to Lloyd George, the latter was unmoved. Turning to Clemenceau, he said within Foch's hearing, "There was a d—— sight too much of these Generals threatening to resign & that if they were private soldiers they would be put up agst. a wall & shot."[37] In the end the wording but not the substance of this resolution was changed.

Although Lloyd George made his point that British interests must not be ignored, he had much to answer for himself. What the British delegation dared not tell the French in open council (although Wilson wanted to make a clean breast of it) was that they planned to transfer British divisions to other theaters as soon as the Allied line in the West was secure.[38] Such were the rubs and tensions of the generalissimo experiment in mid-1918.

The conclusion of the "angriest" Supreme War Council yet, as Wilson called it, was a prelude to another incident which threatened to wreck the unity of command. On June 9, the Germans had launched a second diversionary offensive, near Compiègne, the Battle of Matz, which ground to a halt on June 14 with no dramatic results and with German reserves further depleted. As Corelli Barnett has written, "Thresh about how he might, the situation was now closing darkly round the German field commander. Clemenceau had been quite unshaken by the German advance to the Marne. The decisive battle—in Flanders still—had yet to be fought. However, German strength was melting."[39] What is apparent today about the declining strength of the German army, however, was not so obvious to the weary Allied soldiers as they anxiously waited and wondered where the next German blow would fall. Wilson even told the British ministers on July 8 that "the Germans could now put in a bigger attack than they did on the 21st March."[40] As late as mid-June, the German high command thought of attacking Flanders next, but the enemy still seemed too strong there to achieve decisive results. Hence, Ludendorff turned once again to a diversionary attack against the French to draw Allied reserves away from the north. Soon after the beginning of this offensive, planned for July 15 around Rheims, he hoped to drive through British trenches toward Hazebrouck. Aircraft and artillery, in fact, were transferred northwards to participate in this attack against the British almost as soon as the Second Battle of the Marne began in mid-July.[41]

On the eve of this attack, there was near panic in London that Foch, who was unfairly thought to be Clemenceau's puppet, was prepared to leave Haig in the lurch as he massed Allied reserves in front of Paris. On July 11, the War Cabinet discussed "the danger that the French, for political reasons, might endeavour to safeguard Paris at grave risk to the British front." Smuts expressed concern that "French reserves were being moved much too far South, bringing about a distribution of reserves, as far as the British front was concerned, not dissimilar to that existing before the attack of March 21st." The War Cabinet decided that Lloyd George should write Clemenceau "pointing out that General Foch was an Allied and not merely a French Commander-in-Chief, and that he must treat the Allied interests as a whole, making his dispositions on this basis and not mainly from the point of view of French interests."[42] Lloyd George also continued to express concern about the French monopolization of American divisions. More than the defense of Paris was involved in this, he believed. "Clemenceau had more than hinted that he was getting hold of the American divisions in order to compel us to re-fill our own," he told Bonar Law, Milner, and Wilson on July 12. "This was an unjustifiable attempt to put pressure upon us."[43] To press the "queer tempered old gentlemen" on the distribution of American troops, he thought of dispatching Smuts and Borden to France, believing that these dominion leaders were more likely to "prevail over Clemenceau" and would "have special influence with Pershing."[44]

Much has been written about Haig's allegedly broad view of the military situation in July in contrast to the narrowness of the British government. Yet his view of Foch's direction of Allied reserves often mirrored that of the British civilians. On July 13, he wrote the following in his diary: "Foch has made up his mind that the *main* attack will fall on the French East of Rheims. Our information does not bear this out. We fear that the enemy is preparing to put in a small attack against the French, while his main blow is delivered elsewhere."[45]

On July 14, the tension between the British and French reached a climax. Foch ordered four British divisions from Haig's reserves to proceed south and four more divisions to be held in readiness to move in the same direction. Previously the generalissimo had moved the remaining six French divisions of the Détachment de l'Armèe du Nord (the French army group in Flanders) southwards, positioning them at Beauvais, where they could reinforce the British front in an emergency. As soon as Lloyd George learned of Foch's orders, he convened an emergency council of war in Sussex, where he was the guest of Riddell at Hurstpierpoint. It was late evening when Milner, Wilson, Radcliffe, the D.M.O., Borden, Hankey, Kerr, and Smuts gathered around the prime minister. Both Haig and Wilson still expected the main German offensive to take place against the British. Fearing a disaster for British arms worse than March 21, Lloyd George threatened to countermand Foch's transfer of the four British divisions south "unless Haig could give a guarantee that Rupprecht would not attack him!" Although Smuts's anxiety matched Lloyd George's, Milner and Wilson supported Foch's actions, and their steadying influence served the prime minister well. Before attempting to overrule Foch's orders, Lloyd George agreed to dispatch Smuts to general headquarters to get Haig's view of the situation. Smuts was also expected to pressure the French to replace the British divisions sent south with American divisions. Apparently Smuts's mission was not enough to satisfy Lloyd George because as soon as the meeting broke up Wilson telephoned Haig, instructing him to appeal to his government under the Beauvais agreement if he thought Foch was "not acting solely on military considerations" or if he believed that his front was "endangered."[46]

On July 16, Smuts reported his findings to the Imperial War Cabinet. Haig, he said, had initially thought that Foch had momentarily "almost lost his head in his alarm at this situation"; consequently he had written him that he was "not inclined to fall in with General Foch's views until he had had a personal interview." When this meeting took place, German intentions were no longer a matter of conjecture; they were attacking the French along a front of some fifty-five miles. After Foch assured Haig that he planned to place the British divisions he received in a position to return quickly to the north if the Germans attacked there, the field marshal agreed to deliver the requested divisions. Haig also informed Smuts that his most recent intelligence indicated that as many as nine of Rupprecht's divisions had been moved to the French front, and seven had already been identified in the recent offensive. With only twenty-three fresh German divisions in a position to attack him, he was much less anxious about the security of his army. Haig also defended Foch's distribution of the American divisions because their presence "had had a remarkable effect in stimulating the French moral, without which . . . [he] doubted if the French Army should have had any offensive spirit left."[47] To his undying credit, Haig, under immense pressure, acted correctly when the facts were known to him. Two days later, however, he began to have second thoughts. Believing that a German attack of between sixteen and eighteen divisions was imminent on both sides of Kemmel, he attempted without success to retrieve two of the divisions he had committed to the French.[48]

Although Haig shared Lloyd George's concern that Foch's actions might endanger the British front, his conduct during this critical test for the supreme command was certainly more admirable than Lloyd George's. Wilson told the prime minister that he was far from certain that the German offensive underway was the main attack; and Macdonogh took exception to Haig's estimate of the reserves available to Rupprecht, counting thirty-three fresh enemy divisions instead of twenty-three.[49] Confronted with this military advice, it is not surprising that Lloyd George continued to believe that the British had been badly served by Foch. "If it should turn out that he had let us down in this matter," he told Wilson and Milner, "it would wreck the unity of command."[50] Happily, a successful French counterattack on the eighteenth derailed the German plan of attacking the British and saved unity of command.

During these trying days, Lloyd George had difficulty finding a general whom he could trust. He continued to hold Haig's leadership in contempt and he wanted to sack him. After criticism of the military authorities had surfaced during the first meetings of the Imperial War Cabinet, Lloyd George had immediately moved to establish a committee of the dominion leaders, the Committee of Prime Ministers, which included Wilson and Milner. If he had his way, this committee would serve as a hanging jury to remove Haig.[51] His motives were many and complex. If he pushed a policy of protecting and expanding the empire in the East, he knew that Haig would join with the offensive-minded Foch in opposing a limited role for the British army in the West. He also believed that Haig was not making the best use of men behind his line.[52] Moreover, Haig now seemed disinclined to assist him in forcing Foch to station more American divisions in his sector which might free British divisions for use away from France. General Cavan, the commander in chief of the British forces in Italy, was scheduled to arrive in London soon, and Lloyd George, apparently believing that his service away from the western front had given him the proper perspective, contemplated putting him in Haig's place. When the prime minister discussed the removal of Haig with Milner, the secretary of state for war was "not yet clearly convinced that a better substitute could be found." This infuriated Lloyd George. If Milner did not understand how important it was to give the army new leadership, he told Hankey, he would find someone who did. That someone, Hankey realized to his dismay, was himself.[53]

When Cavan arrived in London, he was pressed very hard by the Committee of Prime Ministers on July 23 about the possibility of achieving decisive results against the Austrians. W. M. Hughes, the Australian prime minister, emphasized the importance of "getting some hold on Austrian territory before the Peace Conference." Hughes, like the other imperial leaders, it must be emphasized again, saw no hope of defeating the German army in the near future. "On the Western front," he argued, "it was evident that it would be a very slow business to drive the Germans back to the Rhine. It did not appear possible to do this in the present year, or next year, even with the American assistance, although, perhaps, it might be accomplished the year after."

Cavan generally went along with Hughes's pessimistic forecast of military operations in France and favored an Allied offensive in Italy. He was, however, vague and uncertain about its results. Allied forces might penetrate Austria in the direction of Trent, but they were unlikely to get very far because of the "difficult mountain country." On the other hand, Cavan would not fall in with Lloyd George's desire to deliver a decisive blow against the Austrians by an offensive across the Piave into the plains. Such a movement, Cavan argued with some justification, would expose Italian communications to a counter blow from the north.[54] Cavan's inability to promise a decisive victory in Italy almost certainly lowered his standing in the eyes of the prime minister.

Another disappointment was in store for Lloyd George when he talked with Francesco Saverio Nitti, the Italian minister of the treasury, and Marquis Imperiali, the Italian ambassador in London. It quickly became obvious that the Italians, who had a wildly exaggerated view of Austria's strength, were primarily interested in receiving Allied assistance for defensive purposes. Although they made no immediate demand for French or British soldiers, they expressed the desire to get their hands on a few American divisions in the near future. When Wilson noted that Foch and Pershing would be hostile to such a suggestion, Lloyd George, perhaps to enlist Italian support against the generalissimo, "pointed out that one of the difficulties of a united front arose from the fact that a General-in-Chief of one nationality or another had to be chosen, and in the present case he was of French nationality. He thought that perhaps too much advantage was being taken of this fact, and that the whole scheme of a united command was thereby to some extent weakened."[55]

This statement was indicative of Lloyd George's mounting impatience over Foch's utilization of American divisions. (Pershing, of course, had his own ideas about the use of American troops: he made clear his intentions of placing newly arrived American divisions under his command in their *own* sector.)[56] On July 26, at a meeting of the "X" Committee, Lloyd George

drew attention to the latest telegrams which indicated that the French were intending to get the whole of the American Army into their sector. He was convinced that this was part of the political game which General Foch was playing at M. Clemenceau's instigation. The whole object of it was, by depriving us of the support of the American troops, to force us to keep up our present total of 59 divisions regardless of the effect upon our industries and national life generally. It was intolerable that the French should attempt to put the screw upon us in that way and he was determined that if this continued he would ask the authority of the Cabinet to refuse the French any ships for the conveyance of American troops to France.[57]

LLOYD GEORGE AND THE GENERALS

Later that day the War Cabinet gave Lloyd George the authority to use Britain's "shipping position, if necessary, as a lever to secure a fair redistribution of Allied forces in the line on the introduction therein of the American divisions."[58] On August 2, a letter was duly sent to Clemenceau, threatening the French with the reduction of British tonnage devoted to transporting Americans.[59]

By this extreme policy Lloyd George hoped to gain the freedom of action to reduce Haig's force in the future and use Britain's "surplus strength elsewhere—in Italy, Salonica, Turkey, or Persia."[60] As he schemed and plotted, the generals in the West were moving in another direction. The Second Battle of the Marne, which wrested the strategical initiative from Ludendorff, was an unmitigated disaster for the Germans. The ground gained in their offensives in March, April, and May proved to be a serious liability now that they were thrown back on the defensive. The huge salients they had punched in the Allied front extended their line, requiring an additional sixteen divisions for defense, and their troops in this conquered territory "were lying out in open positions with no facilities for defence."[61] Although hardly anyone thought that Germany was beaten, the initiative had now shifted to the Allies, reinforced by fresh Americans. Both Haig and Foch had long hankered for a return to the offensive. In great secrecy, they now took these plans seriously in hand. In late July, Foch, with the French army having carried the heaviest burden recently, assigned Haig the leading role in the Allied offensive planned for August 8.[62]

Astonishingly the British civilians and even the C.I.G.S. were kept in the dark about these plans.[63] Consequently, the discussion in London focused on military operations in 1919 or even 1920. On July 25, Wilson completed a long and rambling memorandum, "British Military Policy 1918–1919." The Allied military position now seemed much more favorable. The Germans were stalled in the West and the East seemed secure for the immediate future. Germany was withdrawing rather than sending troops to the Turkish theater; and the swirling chaos of Russia made it impossible for Berlin to take hold in that country. Hence, although Wilson had much to say about the importance of the East, his gaze was firmly set on the desolate, shell-pocked battlefields of France, where he favored military operations in 1918 to place the Allies in a position to fight a decisive battle in 1919. Lloyd George's desire to launch great attacks in either Italy or Palestine was given a cold douche and an offensive in the Balkans was generally opposed.[64]

When Lloyd George's eyes fell on this memorandum, he was "bitterly disappointed" at its "purely 'Western front' attitude." It was "simply 'Wully redivivus,'" he grumbled to Hankey.[65] On July 31, the Committee of Prime Ministers took up Wilson's memorandum in a discussion notable for its pessimism.[66] Milner led off the attack on Wilson's thesis that Germany might be defeated in 1919 in the West: "In his view the Western front was a candle that burned all the moths that entered it." Milner's strategy for the future, even more than Lloyd George's, was political in nature. Convinced that Britain, even if she strained her remaining manpower past the breaking point, could only play a secondary role on the western front, he favored reducing Haig's forces to thirty-five divisions, utilizing the surplus thus created in other theaters where the British role in the war might be magnified. If Britain gambled her last man in a bid for victory in 1919, he argued, the result would almost certainly be a stalemate. Even if the Germans agreed to talk peace, the voice of the empire would be reduced to a whisper at any peace conference.

America would have an Army equivalent to 120 divisions, France perhaps 40, and the British Empire perhaps 23. When Australia said she wanted the Pacific Islands, or Palestine, President Wilson would look down his nose and say: That he had entered the War with quite different ideas in view, he would say he had his 120 divisions ready to continue the War, and he would ask what assistance we could give. Before we decided to put our Army on the table next year and get it smashed to pieces he thought that this consideration ought to be very carefully weighed.

Smuts agreed with Milner that it was hopeless to seek to defeat Germany in the West: "He did not question that the Western front was the decisive front, but from the beginning of the War it had always proved the fatal front." The South African general even maintained that "a purely military decision was not possible in this war." His strategy, like Milner's and Lloyd George's, was to concentrate British military power "where the crust of the enemy's resistance was thinnest. . . . instead of pressing for a purely military decision we should use our military strength where we might exploit the economic and diplomatic position. . . . When Germany saw her Allies being broken up she would probably make peace. In short, he would depend as much on the moral and diplomatic as on the military factor."

Lloyd George took exception with Smuts's view that a good peace might be obtained through negotiation. "He believed that a military victory was even more important than the securing of the terms of peace we desired." In no other way might German militarism be smashed once and for all. The dilemma facing the author of the "knock-out blow," of course, was: Where could Germany be knocked out? As a perplexed Hughes expressed it, where might "the Achilles' heel of the enemy be found"? Lloyd George made it clear that he was looking toward the Italian theater once again, and he read from a secret report which indicated that Austria-Hungary was a "doomed Empire."[67]

When these discussions resumed the next day, the civilians received their first hint that an Allied offensive was about to be launched when Borden reported that he had learned of secret movements of Canadian troops to participate in an attack. When Wilson admitted that "he knew nothing of any forthcoming operation," Lloyd George was greatly agitated. Milner defended Foch by arguing that he had the authority to plan and execute "minor operations" to rectify the line. But Lloyd George, fearing another Passchendaele over the horizon, would not hear any defense of Foch's actions. "It was, he said, the business of the Government to weigh up its resources. If they found that their forces were being reduced too low, it was their business to exercise restraint on their Generals." Weighing heavily on his mind were the ominous recruiting figures for next year (Geddes maintained that there would be only 170,000 recruits for the army for the whole of 1919) and the dangerous situation being created by the withdrawal of skilled men from the munitions industry for the army.[68] Foch, he continued, "had always been somewhat reckless of human life. . . . He always seemed to proceed on the assumption that the numbers of men were inexhaustible. Only in February of the present year he had produced a calculation, according to which Great Britain still had a reserve of 2,000,000 men." More than this particular battle was at issue. What if Foch ignored the British government in plotting strategy for 1919? A Somme or Passchendaele style offensive was just as unpalatable under Foch as it was under Haig.

The imperial leaders talked about "their constitutional position *vis-à-vis* General Foch." It was noted that the Beauvais agreement prevented the civilians from interfering with the conduct of the war unless Haig, believing that his forces were endangered, appealed to the government. Had Beauvais, then, destroyed any influence the civilians might have over the generals? Such a situation could not be allowed to stand. "It was pointed out that Field Marshal Haig was bound to submit any big operation to the Government, that is to say, any operation of the magnitude that would involve heavy casualties. . . . It was generally agreed that, if General Foch were to decide on a plan such as that proposed by the Chief of the Imperial General Staff, the British Government would not be *functus officio*." In reality, the unity of command gave Haig considerable latitude in the series of offensives he launched in the summer and fall of 1918. If it had not been for the protective shield of the generalissimo, Lloyd George who wanted "to limit our strategy to our income" might have stopped him in his tracks, arguing that the British army must conserve its strength.

At this meeting of the Committee of Prime Ministers, Lloyd George asked Wilson if he "really thought in his heart that, with the means at their disposal, the Allies could get a decision on the Western front next year, taking into consideration the rate at which the American Army could be developed, and without assuming the collapse of Austria?" Wilson, sensing that his head was on the block, began to backpedal. A few minutes earlier, he had argued that he only approved of "advances of a few thousand yards" to improve the Allied position in 1918, assuring the ministers that "it was often a relatively cheap and easy matter to advance a short distance." Now, in response to Lloyd George's direct question, he said that he only proposed making *preparations* for a great offensive in France in 1919. "As the time approached we should be able to judge as to whether we had any real chance of success. Otherwise, we could postpone." Lloyd George had heard this too many times in the past to be reassured; "he was in the position of one, who, once bitten, was twice shy," he grumbled.

But was it possible for the anti-German coalition, propped up by America, to last until 1920? Lloyd George continued to argue that the collapse of Austria would mean the end for Germany. But was this certain? Furthermore, would the Italians, even if assisted by her allies, fight with determination? As a matter of fact, there was grave concern that Italy might have a slight lead over Austria in the race to drop out of the war. Despite the many imponderables about Britain staking everything on a successful offensive in Italy, Wilson was instructed by the imperial leaders to "report as to the possibility of knocking out Austria."[69]

To make certain that Wilson got the message, Lloyd George dispatched Hankey to talk with him. The prime minister, Hankey bluntly told Wilson, believed that he "was too much like Robertson. 'It is Irish instead of Scotch, but it is still whisky.' " Wilson weakly responded that "he was dominated by the idea of not quarrelling with our allies & more especially with Foch." To get in the good graces of the prime minister once again, he "explained a scheme he had for concentrating 12 divisions this winter on the Italian front."[70] A few days later, however, Wilson told the civilians that "unless Marshal Foch was in a position to set free the required number of divisions at once or in the near future, no important attack could be made [against Austria] before the snow fell." In sum, although Wilson "regarded the Italian theatre as a most promising one," he "was afraid it was too late to do anything this autumn."[71]

As Lloyd George and Wilson began to fall out over strategy, the Battle of Amiens began. As the British army turned once again to the offensive, many soldiers in the trenches were filled with apprehension. A young British staff officer, Cyril Falls, who was later to become one of the most authoritative historians of the war, wrote in the midst of the massive preparations for the assault: "So the old tricks are coming out of the conjurer's box. I have seen it too often before—the Somme, Messines, Ypres, Cambrai—to be fully confident of a great success on this occasion. But one thing is sure: if we take the knock this time after Ludendorff has shown us how it is done, we may as well give up. On the whole I am hopeful."[72] With dominion troops given the leading role, Rawlinson's Fourth Army, assisted on its right by the French First Army, left its trenches on August 8. Supported by over 400 tanks and a swarm of aircraft, the infantry followed a creeping barrage into the enemy's fortifications. Caught completely by surprise, the German center south of the Somme gave way. When dusk fell an advance of from six to eight miles had been made with relatively small losses; many prisoners and big guns had been captured.

German spirits had been lowered as much as British spirits were raised. The psychological impact of the lumbering and menacing tanks, which were impervious to machine guns and rifles, was especially devastating to German morale. There is much truth to Ludendorff's famous description of the events of August 8 as "the black day of the German army." German morale began to crack for the first time in the West. Reserve divisions being pushed forward were called "Black Legs" and "War Prolongers" by German troops in retreat. One German soldier even yelled at the reinforcements: "We thought that we had set the thing going; now you asses are corking up the hole again."[73]

Churchill's account from the front was ebullient in its praise of Haig and his troops. "There is no doubt," he wrote Lloyd George, "Haig has won a very great success which may well be the precursor of further extremely important events. . . . It seems to me this is the greatest British victory that has been won in the whole war, and the worst defeat that the German Army has yet sustained."[74]

Haig's splendid victory in no way altered Lloyd George's dark view of offensives in the West. Over lunch with Hankey on August 13, he admitted that he did "not take a very sanguine view of our military prospects, in spite of recent successes." Intensely suspicious of the French, he told Wilson later that day that he "was determined that our Army shall not be ruined by fighting instead of the French."[75] One result of this British success was that Haig's position was now secure. On behalf of the Imperial War Cabinet, Lloyd George sent him a message of congratulations.[76]

The reader, with the knowledge of hindsight, should not be too hasty to condemn Lloyd George for his pessimism. The breakthrough of August 8 was no greater than that achieved at Cambrai; and the Allied forces could not maintain their momentum in the face of stiffening German resistance. The tanks, as John Terraine has demonstrated, were not "war-winners" in their infant stage. They were slow, often unreliable, and easy to knock out by artillery. By August 10, out of the 414 tanks committed to the battle, only 85 were still in action.[77] Of course, as the official history admits, general headquarters might have made better use of this promising instrument of war through more imaginative tactics.[78]

The Germans had lost nothing strategically vital in this attack and they still occupied more Russian and French territory than they held in 1917. Their forces numbered over 2,500,000 men and a formidable defensive system protected Germany from attack. Moreover, the French and British "were incapable, morally and physically, of a massive and shattering breakthrough like that of March 21."[79] The growing American forces seemed to hold the key to the total destruction of the German army. In the opinion of Germany's military and civilian leaders, as Correlli Barnett has written: "It was not the present that was impossible; it was the future."[80]

No imperial leader took a more pessimistic view of the military situation than Smuts. Wilson had estimated that the Allies might launch a war-winning offensive in 1919 with seventy reserve divisions because of the ever-increasing strength of the American forces. But were these numbers really sufficient for a decision in 1919? "I do not think so," Smuts asserted in the Imperial War Cabinet on August 14. Believing that neither side could force a decision in the West, Smuts feared that the Germans would direct their attention to the East in 1919. The thrust of Smuts's remarks was that Britain, with her Asian interests, had the most to lose by continuing the war. Taking up where Lansdowne had left off, he argued:

> It may well be that, by the indefinite continuance of the war, we shall become a second or third-class Power, and the leadership, not only financially and militarily, but in every respect, will have passed on to America and to Japan. Europe will have fought itself out to a finish, and she will have been utterly smashed, and not even the roots of future progress would be left in her. . . . I am very much against fighting it to the absolute end, because I think that, although that end will be fatal to the enemy, it may possibly be fatal to us too.

Opposed to the Foreign Office's definition of a sound peace in Europe which assumed the total defeat of Germany, Smuts's strategy continued to be that of concentrating on "the weakest points of the enemy's armour" to force the Germans to accept a compromise peace.[81]

On the following day, Smuts's position was attacked from all sides during a meeting of the War Cabinet that included the dominion prime ministers. Curzon, whose zeal for the empire was unsurpassed, argued that Smuts exaggerated when he painted a picture of "a great tide of invasion rolling against our Eastern Empire while our efforts were being sterilized in the West." It was his view "that it was essential to go on hammering till Germany was definitely beaten and brought to a different frame of mind, so that we could secure a peace which Germany would keep and not have the strength to break." Lloyd George accepted Smuts's thesis that the Allies might not be strong enough to defeat the German Army in 1919. But he continued to insist that total victory over the enemy was essential to a lasting peace. "He was convinced that we ought to go on until we could dictate terms which would definitely mark the view taken by humanity of the heinousness of Germany's offence, and which would be the effective starting-point of a League of Nations."[82]

The reader might ponder this irony. Lloyd George, the exponent of indirect strategy, favored what amounted to imposing unconditional surrender on Germany. Haig, whose strategy was designed to ruin the German army, was now moving towards Smuts's camp, arguing during the later discussion of armistice terms that it was unwise to demand severe terms from Germany. A continuation of the war might not be worth the price in blood the British would have to pay and a harsh peace would leave Germany humiliated and longing for revenge.[83]

By mid-August, the Committee of Prime Ministers had a preliminary draft report on future military policy and strategy before them. Lloyd George's position on the manpower situation of the empire held center stage, with the preliminary draft report prepared by Hankey emphasizing:

> At the present stage of the War, man-power has become the controlling factor on the handling of which victory or defeat may depend. . . . the husbanding of our man-power has become a consideration on which the whole future of our Empire depends. . . . Consequently, it is not only the right but the duty of the Government to assure itself that operations involving the probability of heavy casualties are not embarked on unless they give a probability of producing commensurate results on the final issues of the War and without wrecking the future of the Empire. . . . The Government, indeed, is in the position of a Board of Directors who have to insist that before committing the resources of the company in some great enterprise they shall be fully apprised of its prospects, cost, and consequences.[84]

After breakfasting with the prime minister on August 16, the dominion prime ministers discussed the conclusions of this paper. The difficulties involved in Lloyd George's scheme of delaying a bid for victory in the West until 1920 and reducing Haig's army (the figure was now thirty-six divisions which included the dominion forces and five divisions of category "B" men) in order to maintain Britain's war plant and fight in other theaters were highlighted. Once again it was emphasized that, even if the Allied armies held together until 1920, public support for the continuation of the war might have collapsed by then. Also, how could the British Empire defend itself against the charge that it was letting its allies down by limiting its role in the bloody trenches in France? "MR. HUGHES said it was obvious that the position would be very delicate as regards our Allies. It would be difficult to tell France and our other Allies that we now preferred to look after ourselves and to draw the line as to the number of troops we would place at stake." Exactly how difficult such an imperial strategy would be was indicated most forcefully to Lloyd George in a letter he received two days later from Clemenceau, which accused the British Empire of admitting, in so many words, that it had "arrived at end of sacrifices which it could make in common cause."[85]

In the end, the imperial leaders were forced to admit that there was little likelihood that they could escape Britain's commitment to the costly Continental war without seriously damaging the anti-German coalition. Wilson's principle that Britain should make preparations for a supreme effort in the West in 1919 was accepted, but final approval of any offensive was withheld. On the other hand, Lloyd George remained determined to reduce Haig's forces, and he made it clear that he only acquiesced in this decision because he "held the view that the Western front included Italy," where he, Milner, Smuts, and Borden believed that Allied prospects were far more promising than in France. The imperial leaders also refused to accept the General Staff's position that nothing big should be attempted in Palestine or that an autumn offensive in Italy was not feasible.[86]

This draft report was never signed because the course of the war in the West and East very quickly made the discussions of the Committee of Prime Ministers academic. How fortunate! The continued strong interest of Lloyd George and others in military operations away from France and their desire to limit the British commitment to France to thirty-six divisions, filling the gaps in the British line with Americans, might have destroyed the concept of a generalissimo, if not the alliance.[87]

Following the success of British arms at Amiens, there was a pause in the offensive. To keep the pressure on the enemy, Foch urged Haig to keep pushing Rawlinson's Fourth Army and the French First Army forward on the Roye-Chaulnes front. Haig, when informed by Rawlinson that the position Foch wanted to attack was strongly defended and casualties were bound to be heavy, ignored this order. On August 15, he drove to Foch's headquarters for a showdown. When Foch at first persisted, Haig informed him that he *was responsible to my Government and fellow citizens for the handling of the British forces.*[88] Haig's successful stand against Foch made it abundantly clear thereafter that the commander in chief of the British army was not a compliant instrument of the generalissimo. When the offensive resumed on August 21, it was Haig's strategy which prevailed over Foch's. Foch desired a series of frontal assaults to drive the Germans back to the

Hindenburg Line as rapidly as possible. Haig, however, favored a great turning movement.

In opposition to the general staff and civilians, Haig wanted the British to do their "utmost to get a decision this autumn,"[89] a policy that put him on a collision course with the prime minister who now thought victory impossible in the West until 1920, and then only with the Americans doing most of the fighting. At this very moment, Macdonogh was telling the members of the War Cabinet and the dominion prime ministers that he did not think that Foch and Haig "had any big objective in view." Their military operations "were more a tapping of the enemy's weak points than anything else."[90] As the Allied forces continued to advance along a broad front, Wilson did everything possible to assure the ministers that the British armies "were now confronted with a different situation from that which had obtained at Passchendaele." British losses "were remarkably slight, the fighting having been of the nature of advance-guard and rear-guard fighting, and not a general battle attack."[91]

As Haig approached the formidable Hindenburg Line, anxiety grew in London that the period of "cheap" advances was coming to an end. On August 31, Lloyd George, Bonar Law, Milner, and Wilson discussed Foch's desire to continue the offensive. Although Wilson pointed out that Haig "did not mean to press his operations if they involved heavy casualties," the politicians were skeptical. Haig had displayed little interest in economizing his losses in 1916 and 1917 and they feared that he would continue his attacks with little or no regard for the cost. Concern was also expressed that he would misuse the American divisions still under his command, thereby discouraging Pershing from sending any more troops to the British sector. On Lloyd George's initiative, Wilson was instructed to telegraph immediately "Field Marshal Haig warning him that the War Cabinet would not approve of attacks on the Hindenburg line involving heavy casualties whether to British or American troops."[92]

When Haig received this message marked "H. W. Personal" on the morning of September 1, he was infuriated. Was this his reward for a superbly conducted campaign? "It is impossible for a C.I.G.S. to send a telegram of this nature to a C.-in-C. in the Field as a 'personal one'," he noted in his diary. "The Cabinet are ready to meddle and interfere in my plans in an underhand-way, but do not dare openly to say that they mean to take the responsibility for any failure though ready to take credit for every success!"[93] In his memoirs, Lloyd George denies all responsibility for this telegram: "As to the casualty warning, Sir Henry Wilson acted entirely on his own initiative on this occasion. . . . I cannot account for Sir Henry Wilson's letter [*sic*] to Haig."[94] This, alas, was incorrect as the minutes of the "X" Committee conclusively prove.

Lloyd George's attitude toward an offensive against Bulgaria was quite different from any attempt to storm the Hindenburg Line. Although the War Office was unenthusiastic about an offensive by the Eastern Army, now reinforced by the Greeks, Paris favored an attempt to knock Bulgaria out of the war.[95] General Guillaumat, who had been replaced by the capable Franchet d'Espèrey as commander in chief of the Eastern Army, arrived in London in early September to win British support for a Balkan assault. After listening to a glowing report by Guillaumat concerning the potential of the Eastern Army, Lloyd George gave his approval.[96] Hankey, who was not present, has written that "this was one of the rare cases in which Lloyd George actually overruled his own military adviser."[97] This is incorrect. Although Wilson was not very enthusiastic about the proposed offensive, he agreed that it should be attempted.[98]

September was the most encouraging month of the war yet for the Allies. On the fifteenth, Franchet d'Espèrey's Eastern Army attacked, cutting the Bulgarian forces in half and putting them to flight. Four days later "Bull" Allenby, his white infantry lost to France replaced by two Indian divisions from Mesopotamia, began an attack which has been called by Liddell Hart "both one of the most quickly decisive campaigns and the most completely decisive battles in all history."[99] Enjoying a superiority of perhaps 2 to 1 in infantry, 8 to 1 in cavalry, and 3 to 2 in guns, Allenby implemented the plan he and Smuts had devised in early 1918.[100] His major departure from the South African's strategy was that he broke through along the sea rather than inland. The Turkish forces in front of him were rapidly destroyed and he was off to Damascus, reaching that city by October 1. Not surprisingly, Lloyd George was determined to gain maximum exposure for these twin triumphs in theaters so dear to his heart. Wilson was instructed to make certain that the War Office's lecture to the press about these "Eastern" successes " 'must not be given by an unbalances [sic] orientalist, who does not know that there is more than one point to the compass.' "[101]

In France, the month began with the Germans continuing to fall back to the Hindenburg Line. Each new battle report by Wilson to the War Cabinet seemed more optimistic. On September 3, he noted: "Captured documents showed that the Germans were in a bad condition." After the British penetrated the outer defenses of the Hindenburg Line, the C.I.G.S.'s enthusiasm was unrestrained: "The evidence of the last few weeks all tended to show that no line could now be regarded as impregnable. Previously all soldiers had been agreed that no real advance could be obtained on a narrow front, and that such an advance must be made on a front of at least 20,000 yards, yet the Hindenburg Line had been broken on a front of 3,000 yards."[102] A great victory by the American First Army at the St. Mihiel salient south of Verdun on September 12–13, which resulted in the capture of 15,000 prisoners and 450 guns, was another encouraging omen. An area held by the Germans for four years had been overrun in thirty hours.

In an effort to convince the civilians that the nature of the fighting had changed and victory was within his grasp, Haig, on his own initiative, made a trip to London to talk with Milner. Brimming over with enthusiasm and confidence, he told the secretary of state for war: "Within the last 4 weeks we had captured 77,000 prisoners and nearly 800 guns! There has never been such a victory in the annals of Britain, and its effects are not yet apparent. . . . *It seems to me to be the beginning of the end.*"[103]

With only 170,000 recruits available for the army for all of next year, Milner was dubious. To see the war up close he left London for a ten-day tour of the front. When he visited Foch, the generalissimo praised Haig, arguing that he had abandoned his "abominable" methods of the autumn of 1917 and had grown considerably as a strategist and tactician. "Instead of hammering away at a single point, we [the British] made a series of successive attacks, all more or less surprises & all profitable" with an economy of losses.[104] Despite this picture of a "new" Haig, Milner remained fearful that the British army might melt away by the end of 1918 without decisive results. The last year of the war was, in fact, the most costly—and successful—year for the British Expeditionary Force, with casualties exceeding 800,000.[105] When Milner visited general headquarters he did not like the gleam in the field marshal's eyes. Although he warned Haig "that if the British Army is used up now there will be no men for next year," he returned to London "with grave doubts whether he had got inside of D. H.'s head." Haig was "ridiculously optimistic" he told Wilson, who agreed. "I must watch this tendency & stupidity of D. H.," the C.I.G.S. wrote in his diary. "The Man Power is the trouble & D. H. & Foch & Du Cane *can't* understand it."[106]

Lloyd George, who greeted each new casualty list with dismay, was just as determined as Milner to prevent the British army from assuming the primary role in attempting to break through the German defenses. The British had carried the greatest burden in the battles of 1918; yet Haig had only two American divisions on his front, although well over a million and a half American troops were now in France, over one half of them having been transported in British ships. Desirous of reducing Haig's divisions during the winter and forcing the Americans to make up the difference in the British sector, he continued to use shipping as a weapon. With the Turks and Bulgarians on the run, he was now primarily concerned with giving British soldiers a respite from the horrors of the West and protecting British industry. On the day that the British army broke through the Hindenburg Line, September 29, he made it clear to Maclay, the minister of shipping, that the British would in the future refuse to convey American soldiers to France "until this situation has been *cleared* up."[107]

Picking a fight with the Americans and French over the distribution of American divisions was clearly a shortsighted policy with victory so near. But it should be remembered that in mid-October after the Germans began their quest for peace Haig no longer believed that the German army could be broken up in 1918. On October 19, alarmed by the stiffening of German resistance on the seventeenth, he told the civilians that

the German Army is capable of retiring to its own frontiers and holding that line against equal or superior forces. . . . If the French and American Armies were capable of a serious offensive *now,* the Allies could completely overthrow the remaining efficient enemy divisions before they could reach the line of the Meuse. They are not. We must reckon with that fact as well as with the fact that the British Army alone is not sufficiently fresh or strong to force a decision by itself. . . . So we must conclude that the enemy will be able to hold the line which he selects for defense for some time after the campaign of 1919 commences.[108]

Although Haig believed that the German army was not yet destroyed, the German political and military leaders desperately wanted peace. Ludendorff's war-winning offensive had turned out to be a war-losing offensive. As he used up Germany's last reserves in one desperate attack after another, American reinforcements at the rate of 10,000 a day streamed across the Atlantic; over 2,000,000 American troops had arrived when the guns were silenced. Having lost the initiative after the Second Battle of the Marne, the German army was pushed back across the blood-soaked battlefields to the Hindenburg Line, which was breached in late September and early October. As the Hindenburg Line began to crumble, Bulgaria suddenly collapsed, severing Germany's link to Turkey and opening up a southern invasion route of Austria and Germany. The tottering of her allies and the capitulation of Bulgaria had a profound impact on Ludendorff and the civilian leaders. If an armistice were not quickly concluded, there was concern that the Allies would have a new front close to the borders of Saxony and Bavaria.[109]

The collapse of Berlin's allies made Lloyd George more confident than Haig that the anti-German coalition could treat Germany as a beaten country in drawing up armistice terms. He also now took a more favorable view of Foch because of the latter's desire to finish off Turkey and invade Germany through Bavaria.[110] On the prime minister's initiative, Foch was given strategical control of all military operations against Germany.[111] No invasion was necessary. With its allies flying the white flag and its army decimated, although still intact, Germany signed an armistice on November 11. After 1,563 days the terrible carnage finally came to an end.

Lloyd George emerged from the war with a reputation larger than life. His most recent biographer entitles his chapter on his wartime premiership, "THE MAN WHO WON THE WAR."[112] Others have ranked him with the earl of Chatham and Churchill as a war leader. Certainly, there seems to have been no one else on Britain's political stage who could have been better cast than Lloyd George as prime minister when the strain was so great in every quarter. His courage, independent mind, ability to inspire and extraordinary political skills served the nation well. His dynamic energy coursed through the veins of the government, acting as the nation's life blood. But the historian's duty is to separate the man from the myth.

In understanding Lloyd George's strategy, one must first recognize the importance that he attached to the political ramifications of military operations. He never looked upon strategy solely in terms of interior vs. exterior lines, logistics or the topography of the land. The impact of military operations on home morale, manpower, existing or potential allies, and the security and advancement of the British Empire were uppermost in his mind. This emphasis on political factors often meant that he and most of the British generals spoke a different language. Wilson was an exception. His frequently geopolitical analysis of the war map helps explain why he and Lloyd George were in harmony for a time.

Humanitarian considerations also played an important part in his opposition to the costly western offensives. In Lloyd George's mind, it would seem, British generals such as Haig represented his prewar enemies, the squirarchy and capitalists; the rank and file of the British army represented the oppressed he had championed before the war. The common soldiers, no less than the poor and sick of industrial Britain, deserved protection against forces beyond their control. "Haig does not care how many men he loses," he once told Stevenson. "He just squanders the lives of these boys. I mean to save some of them in the future. He seems to think they are his property. I am their trustee."[113] The unprecedented casualties, which in truth were more a result of the nature of the conflict than general headquarters' frequently unimaginative tactics, strengthened Lloyd George's resolve to give the civilians a greater voice in the conduct of the war.

Lloyd George failed to have the decisive impact on the higher strategy of the war he sought. In Asquith's government, although he helped set the Salonikan venture in motion, his plan for a great Balkan offensive was frustrated, more by Balkan politics, divisions among the Allies, and limited British military resources than by blundering on the part of the military authorities and his civilian colleagues. As prime minister, despite his frantic efforts to give Allied strategy a new direction, he, like Asquith before him, bowed ultimately to the government's military advisers on almost all major strategic questions. The Calais arrangement and the creation of the Supreme War Council and the Executive War Board were not really exceptions to this rule, because they were concerned directly with questions of command and organization rather than strategy. These decisions, moreover, were made under the protective shield of Allied councils. Only on the question of a Turkish offensive did Lloyd George overrule Robertson. Even then, he worked through the Supreme War Council. When Lloyd George gained a measure of control over the general staff with the replacement of Robertson by Wilson, the Germans had the strategical initiative.

Lloyd George's political insecurity and the limitations imposed by coalition warfare restricted his authority. Also, his imagination, flexibility, and boldness—qualities which served him well in politics—did not always inspire confidence about his judgment in military matters among his civilian colleagues. He was inclined to push grandiose schemes without fully taking into consideration the difficulties, logistical and otherwise, of implementing them. Opposed to his "political" strategy and unreservedly committed to the extreme "Western" view, Robertson was unwilling to tell him how his plans might be made to fit actual conditions. Rather, Robertson kept from the civilians his doubts about Haig's strategy and tactics and "cooked" the advice the War Cabinet received about a Turkish offensive. The basic dilemma confronting Lloyd George was that the peripheral strategy he favored, although politically attractive from the standpoint of detaching Germany's allies, expanding the empire, and raising home morale while undermining the enemy's, could not by itself destroy the German army. If Lloyd George had favored a compromise peace rather than total victory his indirect strategy would have been easier to defend. Yet, despite his profound pessimism about the ability of the British army to achieve decisive results in the West, he adhered to the policy of the "knock-out blow" except for a brief flirtation with a compromise peace based on the sacrifice of Russian territory to Germany. Smuts, who did not believe in either the possibility or wisdom of total victory, made a more logical connection between military and political objectives. His "Eastern" strategy in late 1917 and early 1918 was directed toward improving Britain's negotiating position. The only way Lloyd George could square this circle in 1918 was to look to the Americans to deliver the decisive blows in 1919 or 1920—and suffer the resulting casualties. In attempting to substitute American for British troops and trying to restrain the "Westerners," Lloyd George came into conflict with the supreme command which he had worked mightily to create. His attitude toward Foch demonstrates once again that he was motivated more by a desire to influence higher strategy than by any strong attachment to the principle of unity of command.

The reader should not be too hasty in condemning Lloyd George for his reading of the military situation in late 1917 and early 1918. He was right in opposing the resumption of the British offensive in Flanders, which, in all likelihood, would have demoralized the British forces. Also, given the failure of the great western attacks to achieve decisive results from 1914 to 1917, he was justified in believing that Haig could defend his front. And it must be recalled that Robertson—not the War Cabinet—was responsible for holding back the general reserves in Great Britain before March 21. If Germany, as Lloyd George and other imperial-minded statesmen feared, had remained on the defensive in the West and concentrated on consolidating and expanding her position in Russia and the Middle East, with the ultimate objective of reaching a negotiated peace with the Allies, the East would have been of paramount importance to the British in 1918. Instead, Ludendorff exhausted his forces in a gamble for victory in France. After the Second Battle of the Marne, the German army was fatally weakened and beyond its formidable defenses. The Allies were then able to launch a series of limited attacks, none of them approaching the scale of Somme or Passchendaele. Haig deserves credit for his skillfully conducted campaign. No one in Britain was more surprised by his success than Lloyd George. But can anyone seriously argue that the "Westerners" could have achieved the same results in 1918 if the Germans had remained on the defensive, protected by the Hindenburg Line with their reserves intact?

The waves of panic unleashed within the German high command by the destruction of its allies, especially Bulgaria, were viewed by Lloyd George and his supporters as vindication of their "Eastern" strategy.[114] Haig's sympathizers have just as forcefully argued that the field marshal's campaign from August 8 onwards brought Germany to her knees.[115] In reality, Germany's defeat was caused by many factors: the blockade, propaganda, the entrance of America into the war, the collapse of Germany's allies, and the defeats suffered by the German Army in the West. Germany's surrender did not really settle the "Easterner"-"Westerner" debate conclusively one way or the other. German nerve cracked when both "Eastern" and "Western" strategy succeeded at the same time. Even then, it was Ludendorff's bankrupt "Western" strategy that set the stage for Germany's defeat.

NOTES

1. Clemenceau to Lloyd George, May 16, 1918, quoted in Clemenceau, *Grandeur and Misery of Victory*, pp. 93–96.
2. Derby to Balfour, May 18, 1918, Lloyd George MSS, F/52/1/33.
3. *The Australian Imperial Force in France*, 6:170.
4. Cabinet Paper G.T. 4598 of May 21, 1918, CAB 24/51.
5. Cabinet Paper G.T. 4618 of May 22, 1918, CAB 24/52.
6. Cabinet Paper G.T. 4598 of May 28, 1918, CAB 24/52. Lloyd George put his name to this paper authored by Hankey, and it was circulated during the second week of June. Hankey Diary, June 11, 1918, 1/3.
7. For Lloyd George's desire to put the production of War Office statistics in new hands, see "X" Committee (5), May 29, 1918, CAB 23/17. The Welshman also believed that a civilian administrator could make more efficient use of the services behind the lines.
8. See Milner to Lloyd George, September 6, 1918, MSS Milner, c. 696/2, Milner to Lloyd George, September 10, 1918, Lloyd George MSS, F/38/4/16, and Wilson Diary, September 3, 1918.
9. Entry of May 12, 1918, *Wilson: Life and Diaries*, 2:99, and Wilson to Milner, May 15, 1918 (Army Council conclusion, May 15, 1918, and Milner's minute attached), Lloyd George MSS, F/38/3/32. It was noted in the War Cabinet that shipping was Britain's ultimate weapon in any conflict over control of the supply services. War Cabinet (419), May 28, 1918, CAB 23/6.
10. "X" Committee (2), May 16, 1918, CAB 23/17.
11. Anglo-French Conference, June 1, 1918, CAB 28/3/I.C.-63 B.
12. See Wilson Diary, June 8 and 12, 1918, "X" Committee (3 and 10), May 17 and June 10, 1918, CAB 23/17, and Tom Jones to Hankey, June 13, 1918, Lloyd George MSS, F/23/2/38.
13. The five American divisions, however, were soon replaced by an equal number of Americans. Haig Diary, June 4, 1918, no. 128, and Edmonds, *Short History of World War I*, pp. 323–25.
14. "X" Committee (7), June 5, 1918, CAB 23/17.
15. Ibid. (8), June 5, 1918, CAB 23/17.
16. Wilson Diary, June 7, 1918, and Haig Diary, June 7, 1918, no. 128.
17. Wilson Diary, June 6, 1918.
18. "X" Committee (8), June 5, 1918, CAB 23/17, and Hankey Diary, June 5, 1918, 1/3. Subsequently the Admiralty reported that shipping was available to embark from 300,000 to 400,000 men daily. See "Arrangements for Evacuation from France," June 25, 1918, Milner MSS, dep. 374.
19. Milner to Lloyd George, June 9, 1918, Lloyd George MSS, F/38/3/37. For British alarm about German designs in the East, see War Cabinet (425 and 429), June 4 and 10, 1918, CAB 23/6, and "X" Committee (5), May 29, 1918, CAB 23/17.
20. Amery to Lloyd George, June 8, 1918, Lloyd George MSS, F/2/1/24.
21. Imperial War Cabinet (15), June 11, 1918, CAB 23/43.
22. Wilson Diary, June 8, 1918.
23. Imperial War Cabinet (15), June 11, 1918, CAB 23/43.
24. Ibid. (16), June 13, 1918, CAB 23/43.
25. Ibid. (17), June 14, 1918, CAB 23/43.
26. Amery, "War Aims and Military Policy," June 15, 1918, Lloyd George MSS, F/2/1/25.
27. Imperial War Cabinet (18), June 18, 1918, CAB 23/43. Yet another example of how British minds were moving is the position taken by Esher. Previously the staunchest of "Westerners," he told Wilson that the "outside theatres" were Britain's "most promising sphere" when the Americans had a great army in France. Wilson Diary, June 14, 1918.
28. Imperial War Cabinet (20), June 25, 1918, CAB 23/43. At this time there was great anxiety within the Eastern Committee about German penetration of the Caucasus. To right

what Curzon called an "almost hopeless position," Wilson and others, against the opposition of the Foreign Office, considered bribing Persia and Afghanistan into an alliance with Britain by encouraging them to take territory from the former tsarist empire. See Eastern Committee (14 and 16), June 18 and 24, 1918, CAB 27/24.

29. Hankey Diary, June 21, 1918, 1/3, Cabinet Paper G.T. 4837 of June 13, 1918, CAB 24/54, and Committee of Prime Ministers (19A and 20A), June 21 and 26, 1918, CAB 23/44. Significantly, the decision to keep the 54th Division in Palestine was made final on the day after the Second Battle of the Marne began when the final outcome of the struggle in the West was still very much in doubt. War Cabinet (446), July 16, 1918, CAB 23/7.

30. Committee of Prime Ministers (19A), June 21, 1918, CAB 23/44.

31. "X" Committee (19), July 1, 1918, CAB 23/17.

32. Ibid. (14), June 17, 1918, CAB 23/17.

33. Ibid. (12, 14, and 18), June 13, 17, and 28, 1918, CAB 23/17. Lloyd George also thought of replacing the lightweight Sackville-West with Du Cane to beef up the British section at Versailles. Wilson Diary, July 10, 1918.

34. Supreme War Council, July 2, 1918, CAB 28/4/I.C.-69.

35. Ibid., July 3, 1918, CAB 28/4/I.C.-70.

36. Hankey Diary, July 3, 1918, 1/3.

37. Wilson Diary, July 4, 1918.

38. Ibid., July 3, 1918.

39. Barnett, Swordbearers, p. 334.

40. War Cabinet (442), July 8, 1918, CAB 23/7.

41. See Edmonds, Short History of World War I, pp. 328–30, and Liddell Hart, Real War, p. 420.

42. War Cabinet (444A), July 11, 1918, CAB 23/14. In his message Lloyd George argued that Britain had a "special claim" to American divisions because British ships had transported many of them to France since the beginning of May. If the British were overwhelmed by "superior numbers" because of Foch's distribution of troops, he warned, "it would undoubtedly be fatal to the continuance of the arrangement [generalissimo]." When Clemenceau was slow in responding, a second note was sent. Lloyd George to Clemenceau, July 13, 1918, and Balfour (via Derby) to Clemenceau, July 18, 1918, Lloyd George MSS, F/50/3/7–8. Haig at this time also expressed a desire to get more American divisions behind his lines. By the end of July there would be about 30 U.S. divisions in France, but unless the present distribution was altered, 25 of these divisions would be in the French sector. Wilson Diary, July 12, 1918, and Committee of Prime Ministers (24A), July 15, 1918, CAB 23/44.

43. "X" Committee (20), July 12, 1918, CAB 23/17.

44. Lloyd George to Milner, July 14, 1918, Lloyd George MSS, F/38/4/1.

45. Haig Diary, July 13, 1918, no. 129, and The Australian Imperial Force in France, 6:453–54.

46. Wilson Diary, July 14, 1918, Hankey Diary, July 14, 1918, 1/3, Committee of Prime Ministers (24A), July 15, 1918, CAB 23/44, and Wilson to Haig (by telephone, 12:25 A.M.), July 15, 1918, Haig MSS, no. 129.

47. Committee of Prime Ministers (24B), July 16, 1918, CAB 23/44.

48. See Wilson's comment in "X" Committee (22), July 17, 1918, CAB 23/17.

49. War Cabinet (447), July 17, 1918, CAB 23/7; Wilson Diary, July 15 and 17, 1918.

50. "X" Committee (23), July 18, 1918, CAB 23/17.

51. For the establishment of this committee, see "X" Committee (13), June 14, 1918, CAB 231/17, and Imperial War Cabinet (19), June 20, 1918, CAB 23/43. The first meeting of the Committee of Prime Ministers took place on June 21, 1918.

52. Lloyd George told the War Cabinet that "not less than four Departments" in addition to Colonel Roure (who maintained that from 200,000 to 300,000 more combatants could be found among men already mobilized) had criticized the army's use of manpower. "We could not

continue taking men from industries," he continued, "and practically raising a mutiny in this country in the rural districts, and among the tribunals until we were convinced that the best use was being made of the men we had taken." Milner attempted to defend Haig's utilization of men by emphasizing the difference between the organization of an army fighting on its own soil with "quiet" sectors and one fighting abroad on an active front as was the case with the British. "I am not prepared to deny that there may be some truth in the charge that our methods tend to err on the side of 'eclecticism' and lavishness of organisation. But it is equally dangerous to err in the opposite direction," he wrote in reference to Roure's report. For Roure's report and Milner's response, see Cabinet Paper G.T. 5277 of n.d., CAB 24/59, and Cabinet Paper G.T. 5532 of August 28, 1918, CAB 24/62. Also see War Cabinet (449), July 19, 1918, CAB 23/7, and "X" Committee (21), July 16, 1918, CAB 23/17.

53. "X" Committee (21), July 16, 1918, CAB 23/17, and Hankey Diary, July 16, 1918, 1/3.

54. Committee of Prime Ministers (26A), July 23, 1918, CAB 23/44, and Hankey Diary, July 23, 1918, 1/5.

55. Anglo-Italian Conference, July 24, 1918, CAB 28/4/I.C.-73.

56. Frank E. Vandiver, *Black Jack: The Life and Times of John J. Pershing.*, 2 vols. (1977), 2:926. Pershing chose the French over the British front, in part, because of logistics. The rail lines running from his main bases made the northeast much more accessible than the British front. Foch, of course, welcomed the relief that the Americans gave the war-weary French army. The growing French control over Allied transportation was another irritant to Anglo-French relations. The centralization of transportation in France under Albert Claveille in July, Eric Geddes warned the prime minister, gave Foch more control over "the detailed strategy of the Allied Armies' Commanders than any number of Conventions." See *Military Operations, France and Belgium, 1918*, 1:36, and Geddes to Lloyd George, August 8, 1918, Lloyd George MSS, F/18/2/18.

57. "X" Committee (25), July 26, 1918, CAB 23/17.

58. War Cabinet (452), July 26, 1918, CAB 23/7.

59. The American plan to have 100 divisions in France by 1919 was already in serious trouble according to Reading, the British ambassador in Washington. "X" Committee (25), July 26, 1918, CAB 23/17. In his letter to Clemenceau, the prime minister warned that even a program of eighty divisions was not now possible because the British could not increase their shipping tonnage and might even be unable to maintain present levels. Lloyd George to Clemenceau, August 2, 1918, Lloyd George MSS, F/50/3/9. Lloyd George also asked the king, who was about to depart for France, to urge Haig to put in a request to the War Office that he have at least ten American divisions. "Of course this is not cricket," Wilson noted when he discovered the prime minister's machinations. Wilson Diary, August 5, 1918. There can be no question that Parsons misses Lloyd George's primary motive when he writes "that the British reduced the flow of American troops to France in order to advance their own economic interests and to constrict Wilson's power to forge the armistice and peace terms." Edward Parsons, "Why the British Reduced the Flow of American Troops to Europe in August–October 1918," *Canadian Journal of History* 12 (December 1977), pp. 173–91.

60. Hankey Diary, August 1, 1918, 1/5.

61. Wynne, *If Germany Attacks*, pp. 322–23.

62. Terraine, *To Win a War*, p. 106.

63. Apparently Foch was just as close-mouthed with his own government, with the French ministers usually receiving only a few hours' advance warning of an attack. Wilson Diary, October 4, 1918, and Guinn, *British Strategy and Politics*, p. 85.

64. Wilson, "British Military Policy 1918–1919," July 25, 1918, CAB 25/85. Despite its "Western" slant, Haig was unimpressed by Wilson's broad view of the war. "Words! Words! Words! lots of Words! and little else. *Theoretical Rubbish*. Whoever drafted this stuff will never win any campaign," was his acid notation on this memorandum. Haig MSS, no. 129.

65. Hankey Diary, July 30, 1918, 1/5.

66. Lloyd George later attempted to rewrite history, picturing himself as the optimist and the British generals as the pessimists about the course of the war in the West. See, for example, Lloyd George, *War Memoirs*, 2:1857–67.

67. An extreme example of Lloyd George's violent opposition to attacks in the West is found in his response to Hughes's criticism during this meeting of the Salonikan venture, which had locked up many Allied troops with little result thus far. "The Salonican diversion," Lloyd George countered, "had probably saved hundreds of thousands of men from being engulfed in the mud of the Western front." Committee of Prime Ministers (27A), July 31, 1918, CAB 23/44.

68. See Committee of Prime Ministers (27B), August 1, 1918, CAB 23/44, and Churchill to Lloyd George, July 7, 1918, Lloyd George MSS, F/8/2/25.

69. Committee of Prime Ministers (27B), August 1, 1918, CAB 23/44.

70. Hankey Diary, August 2, 1918, 1/5.

71. Committee of Prime Ministers (29A), August 8, 1918, CAB 23/44.

72. Falls, *Great War*, p. 374.

73. Ibid., p. 376.

74. Churchill to Lloyd George, August 10, 1918, Lloyd George MSS, F/8/2/30.

75. Hankey Diary, August 13, 1918, 1/5, and Wilson Diary, August 13, 1918.

76. This message gives the lie to the legend that Lloyd George refused to recognize Haig's achievements. Still, it is equally true that the prime minister unfairly tried to give most of the credit to Foch (or unity of command). Committee of Prime Ministers (29B), August 12, 1918, CAB 23/44, and War Cabinet (457), August 13, 1918, CAB 23/7.

77. Terraine, *To Win a War*, pp. 115–16.

78. *Military Operations, France and Belgium, 1918*, 4:156–57. Also see Liddell Hart, *Real War*, pp. 436–37, and Barrie Pitt, *1918: The Last Act* (1963), pp. 199–206.

79. Barnett, *Swordbearers*, pp. 353–54.

80. Ibid., p. 354.

81. Imperial War Cabinet (31), August 14, 1918, CAB 23/43. Smuts was especially concerned at this juncture that the Germans might join hands with the Turks in Persia and threaten India. Macdonogh, however, emphasized that the Germans only had the 5th Caucasian Corps, "which was not of high fighting value," in the Caucasus. Eastern Committee (23), August 8, 1918, CAB 27/24.

82. War Cabinet (459), August 15, 1918, CAB 23/7. Amery wrote Smuts that he agreed with much of what he had told the imperial leaders, but he argued that Britain must fight on to 1920 if necessary to gain "the essentials of security," i.e., dominant position in the East. As for the West, Amery believed that it was "enough to secure military superiority without actually carrying it out to its conclusion in the physical expulsion of the Germans from France and Belgium." Amery to Smuts, August 16, 1918, Smuts MSS, 684.

83. For Haig's position, see Terraine, *To Win a War*, pp. 215–20. In early 1918, it should be remembered, Haig had informed Smuts and Hankey that Britain might as well make peace because she had already gotten a great deal out of the war overseas.

84. See "Report of the Committee of Prime Ministers. Preliminary Draft as a Basis for Consideration," August 14, 1918, CAB 23/44.

85. Clemenceau insisted that the United Kingdom had a pool of 2,000,000 men between the ages of nineteen and forty-two even after the essential industries had been provided for from which sufficient men could be drafted to maintain fifty British divisions (in addition to ten dominion divisions) in France. As shown elsewhere, Lloyd George had been pleased with Colonel Roure's criticism of the army's utilization of manpower; now Clemenceau was using this Frenchman's calculations against him. See Clemenceau (via Derby) to Loyd George, sent August 17, received August 18, 1918, Lloyd George MSS, F/50/3/15. Lloyd George's response was to call Roure's report an "unscientific, misleading and fallacious document." Lloyd George to Clemenceau, August 31, 1918, Lloyd George MSS F/50/3/17.

86. Committee of Prime Ministers (32B), August 16, 1918, CAB 23/44.

87. After Pershing, with Foch's approval, took three of the remaining five American divi-

sions from Haig and put them under his own command in late August, Lloyd George became more determined than ever to resist the French (and now apparently American) effort to force the British to maintain their existing number of divisions in France. On August 26, he wrote an explosive letter to the British ambassador in Washington: "Clemenceau and Foch mean to compel us to keep up our numbers on the British front by refusing to take over the line. This policy would be fatal to the British Empire as we have no reserve of men here which would enable us to keep up anything approximating to the number of divisions we now maintain in the field, and if we endeavoured to keep up that number until the summer of next year we should be left with no army at all for the rest of the war. I cannot conceive of a more disastrous plan from the British point of view. I mean therefore to fight it with every available resource. Shipping is one of those resources and until the French and Americans come to terms with us on the question of the line I do not propose to give any further assistance in the matter of shipping." Lloyd George to Reading, August 26, 1918, Lloyd George MSS, F/43/1/15.

88. Haig Diary, August 15, 1918, no. 130. Also see Terraine, *To Win a War*, p. 120.

89. Haig Diary, August 21, 1918, no. 130.

90. War Cabinet (461), August 20, 1918, CAB 23/7.

91. War Cabinet (462 and 464), August 21 and 27, 1918, CAB 23/7.

92. "X" Committee (27), August 31, 1918, CAB 23/17. Wilson would have been more accurate if he had written the Drocourt-Quéant Line, Haig's next objective.

93. Haig Diary, September 1, 1918, no. 131.

94. Lloyd George, *War Memoirs*, 2:2030.

95. A likely reason for the War Office's lukewarm attitude toward an offensive was that d'Espèrey made his plans without consulting Milne, the commander of the British forces, and never even visited the British sector. "One cannot help feeling here that the French are playing their cards in this theatre solely for their own purposes," Milne informed Wilson. Milne to Wilson, July 27, 1918, Lloyd George MSS, F/47/7/35.

96. Anglo-French Conference, September 4, 1918, CAB 28/5/I.C.-74.

97. Hankey, *Supreme Command*, 2:837. This is also Lloyd George's version in *War Memoirs*, 2:1918–19.

98. Wilson Diary, September 4, 1918.

99. Liddell Hart, *Real War*, p. 439.

100. *Military Operations: Egypt and Palestine*, vol. 2, part 1, p. 35, and W. K. Hancock, *The Sanguine Years 1870–1919* (1962), p. 472. The magnitude of Allenby's victory, of course, now made the British position secure in the East. On the eve of his attack, there had been concern, especially on Smuts's part, about the loss of Baku even though the War Office assured the ministers that Germany would not be "able to take advantage of the comparative cessation of military operations on the Western front during the winter months to indulge in any big campaign in the East." Smuts, however, believed as late as September 18 that "the initiative appeared to be passing to the Turks." See Eastern Committee (30 and 32), September 11 and 18, 1918, CAB 27/24.

101. J. T. Davies to Wilson, September 24, 1918, Lloyd George MSS, F/47/7/44.

102. War Cabinet (468 and 472), September 3 and 13, 1918, CAB 23/7.

103. Haig Diary, September 10, 1918, no. 131.

104. Milner to Lloyd George, September 17, 1918, Lloyd George MSS, F/38/4/17.

105. *Statistics of the Military Effort of the British Empire During the Great War, 1914–1920*, p. 362.

106. Haig Diary, September 21, 1918, no. 131, and Wilson Diary, September 23, 1918.

107. Lloyd George to Maclay, September 29, 1918, Lloyd George MS, F/35/2/82. Also see Lloyd George to Milner, September 29, 1918, Lloyd George MSS, F/38/4/20. As the Americans increased their share of the fighting, the French decreased theirs. By November 11, the French "held only 40 miles of active front." *Military Operations, France and Belgium, 1918*, 5:584.

108. "X" Committee (29), October 19, 1918, CAB 23/17.

109. See Ralph Haswell Lutz, ed., *The Fall of the German Empire, 1914–1918.* 2 vols. (1932), 2:460–63. Also see Lutz's *The Causes of the German Collapse in 1918,* trans. W. L. Campbell (1934), pp. 266–67, and Ludendorff's reaction to Bulgaria's collapse, *Ludendorff's Own Story,* 2:365–72.

110. See, for example, his comments in War Cabinet (489A), October 21, 1918, CAB 23/14. Wilson pleased the Welshman by drawing up a plan for a great invasion across the Danube and through Rumania during this period. Wilson Diary, October 22, 1918.

111. Allied Conferences, October 5, and November 2 and 4, 1918, CAB 28/5/I.C.-76, 89 and 93. Franchet d'Espèrey's strategy, however, made the prime minister's blood boil. The French general, without consulting Milne, made a plan for the conquest of Constantinople which largely excluded the British. "He and his colleagues," Lloyd George bluntly told Clemenceau on October 7, "did not consider that General Franchet d'Espèrey in acting like this had behaved as an Allied Commander-in-Chief. His plan was mainly political and not military." The irony of Lloyd George's accusing someone else of being motivated by political rather than military considerations in formulating strategy should not be lost on the reader. Allied Conference, October 7, 1918, CAB 28/5/I.C.-79, and Hankey Diary, October 7, 1918, 1/6.

112. Rowland, *Lloyd George: A Biography,* chapter 11.

113. Entry of January 15, 1917, *A Diary by Frances Stevenson,* p. 139.

114. See, for example, Hankey, *Supreme Command,* 2:836–52.

115. See especially Terraine, *To Win a War* and *Haig: Educated Soldier.*

Bibliography

1. GOVERNMENT RECORDS (PUBLIC RECORD OFFICE, LONDON)

Files of International Conferences
Files of the War Office
Files of the Supreme War Council
Files of the Foreign Office
Files of the Cabinet Office, including:
    War Council
    Dardanelles Committee
    War Committee
    War Cabinet
    Imperial War Cabinet
    Committee of Prime Ministers
    "X" Committee
    Sub-Committee of Imperial War Cabinet on Territorial Desiderata
    Eastern Committee
    Russia Committee
    War Policy Committee
    Man-Power Committee
    Cabinet Memoranda ("G." and "G.T." series)
    Committee of Imperial Defence

2. MANUSCRIPT COLLECTIONS

Public Record Office (London)
    Balfour MSS
    Hankey MSS
    Grey MSS

Kitchener MSS
Macdonogh MSS
British Library (London)
Balfour MSS
Cecil MSS
Murray-Robertson MSS
Northcliffe MSS
House of Lords Record Office (London)
Lloyd George MSS
Bonar Law MSS
India Office and Records (London)
Curzon MSS
Liddell Hart Military Archives, King's College, University of London (London)
Kiggell MSS
Liddell Hart MSS
Maurice MSS
Robertson MSS
Spears MSS
University Library (Cambridge)
Smuts MSS
Bodleian Library (Oxford)
Asquith MSS
Gwynne MSS
Milner MSS
National Library of Scotland (Edinburgh)
Haig MSS
Imperial War Museum (London)
Wilson MSS
Churchill College Archives (Cambridge)
Hankey MSS
Rawlinson MSS
Royal Archives (Windsor)
George V MSS
Liverpool Record Office (Liverpool)
Derby MSS

3. SERIAL PUBLICATIONS

The *Daily Chronicle*
The *Daily Mail*
The *Daily News*
The *Daily Telegraph*
The *Evening News*
The *Evening Standard*
The *Globe*
Manchester Guardian
The *Morning Post*
The *Nation*
The *National Review*
The *Observer*
Parliamentary Debates (Hansard)
The *Star*
Sunday Times
The *Times*
The *Westminster Gazette*

4. BOOKS, THESES, AND ARTICLES (INCLUDING AUTOBIOGRAPHIES, BIOGRAPHIES, AND WORKS CONTAINING SOURCE MATERIAL)

*Adams, R. J. Q., *Arms and the Wizard: Lloyd George and the Ministry of Munitions*. College Station, Tex., 1978.

Amery, L. S. *My Political Life*. Vol. 2: *War and Peace, 1914–1929*. 1953.

Ash, Bernard. *The Lost Dictator: A Biography of Field-Marshal Sir Henry Wilson*. 1968.

Asquith, Earl of Oxford and. *Memories and Reflection, 1852–1927*. 2 vols. Boston, 1928.

Barnett, Correlli, *The Swordbearers: Studies in Supreme Command in the First World War*. 1963.

Bean, C. E. W., gen. ed. and principal author. *The Official History of Australia in the War of 1914–1918*. 12 vols. Sydney, 1921–1943.

Beaverbrook, Lord. *Men and Power, 1917–1918*. 1956.

———. *Politicians and the War, 1914–1916*. 1960.

Blake, Robert, ed. *The Private Papers of Douglas Haig, 1914–1919*. 1952.

———. *The Unknown Prime Minister: The Life and Times of Andrew Bonar Law, 1858–1923*. 1955.

*Place of publication is London, Cambridge, or Oxford unless otherwise indicated.

Bonham-Carter, Victor. *Soldier True: The Life and Times of Field-Marshal Sir William Robertson, 1860–1933.* 1963.

Boraston, Lieutenant-Colonel J. H., ed. *Sir Douglas Haig's Despatches: December 1915–April 1918.* 1919.

Callwell, Major-General C. E. *Field-Marshal Sir Henry Wilson: His Life and Diaries.* 2 vols. 1927.

Cassar, George H. *Kitchener: Architect of Victory.* 1977.

———. *The French and the Dardanelles: A Study of Failure in the Conduct of War.* 1971.

Chamberlin, William Henry. *The Russian Revolution.* Vol. 1: *1917–1918, From the Overthrow of the Czar to the Assumption of Power by the Bolsheviks.* Paperback edn., 1965.

Chambers, Frank P. *The War Behind the War, 1914–1918: A History of the Political and Civilian Fronts.* New York, 1972.

Charteris, Brigadier-General John. *At G.H.Q.* 1931.

———. *Field-Marshal Haig.* 1929.

Churchill, Randolph. *Lord Derby, "King" of Lancashire: The Official Life of Edward Earl Derby, 1865–1948.* 1959.

Churchill, Winston, S. *The World Crisis.* 4 vols. 1923–1928.

Clemenceau, Georges. *Grandeur and Misery of Victory.* Engl. trans., 1930.

Cook, Edward. *The Press in War-Time with Some Account of the Official Press Bureau.* 1920.

Cook, George L. "Sir Robert Borden, Lloyd George and British Military Policy, 1917–1918." *The Historical Journal* 14 (March 1971).

Cooper, Duff. *Haig.* New York, 1936.

Cooper, John Milton, Jr. "The British Response to the House-Grey Memorandum: New Evidence and New Questions." *Journal of American History* 59 (March 1973).

Creiger, Don M. *Bounder from Wales: Lloyd George's Career Before the First World War.* Columbia, Missouri, 1976.

Cross, Colin, ed. *Life with Lloyd George: The Diary of A. J. Sylvester,* New York, 1975.

Cruttwell, C. R. M. F. *A History of the Great War, 1914–1918.* 1936.

———. *The Role of British Strategy in the Great War.* 1936.

David, Edward., ed. *Inside Asquith's Cabinet: From the Diaries of Charles Hobhouse.* New York, 1977.

Davidson, Major-General John. *Haig: Master of the Field.* 1953.

Dutton, D. J. "The Calais Conference of December 1915." *The Historical Journal* 21 (March 1978).

Edmonds, Brigadier-General James E. *A Short History of World War I.* 1951.

————, compiler. *British Official History, Military Operations: France and Belgium*. 13 vols. of text. 1922–1948.

Esher, Reginald Viscount. *Journals and Letters*. Maurice V. Brett, ed. 4 vols. 1934–1938.

Falls, Captain Cyril, and MacMunn, Lieutenant-General Sir G. *British Official History, Military Operations: Egypt and Palestine*. 2 vols. 1928–1930.

Falls, Captain Cyril. *British Official History, Military Operations: Macedonia*. 2 vols. 1933–1935.

————. *The Great War*. Paperback edn. New York, 1959.

Ferris, Paul. *The House of Northcliffe: A Biography of an Empire*. New York, 1972.

Fischer, Fritz. *Germany's Aims in the First World War*. Eng. trans., paperback edn. New York, 1967.

The Memoirs of Marshal Foch. Engl. trans. New York, 1931.

Fraser, Peter. *Lord Esher: A Political Biography*. 1973.

Fry, Michael G. *Lloyd George and Foreign Policy*. Vol. 1: *The Education of a Statesman: 1890–1916*. Montreal, 1977.

Gilbert, Martin. *Winston S. Churchill*. Vol. 3: *The Challenge of War, 1914–1916*. 1971.

————, ed. *Winston S. Churchill*. Vol. 3: *Companion, Part 1, Documents July 1914–April 1915*. 1972.

————, ed. *Winston S. Churchill*. Vol. 3: *Companion, Part 2, Documents May 1915–December 1916*. 1972.

Gollin, A. M. *Proconsul in Politics: A Study of Lord Milner in Opposition and in Power*. New York, 1964.

Gooch, John. "The Maurice Debate 1918." *Journal of Contemporary History*. 3 (October 1968).

————. *The Plans of War: The General Staff and British Military Strategy c. 1900–1916*. New York, 1974.

Gough, General Sir Hubert. *The Fifth Army*. 1931.

Grey of Fallodon, Viscount. *Twenty-five Years 1892–1916*. 2 vols. New York, 1925.

Guinn, Paul. *British Strategy and Politics, 1914–1918*. 1965.

Hanak, Harry. "The Government, the Foreign Office and Austria-Hungary, 1914–1918." *Slavonic and East European Review* 47 (January 1969).

Hancock, W. K. *Smuts: The Sanguine Years 1870–1919*. 1962.

————, and Van Der Poel, J., eds. *Selections from the Smuts Papers*. vol. 3. 1966.

Hankey, Lord. *The Supreme Command, 1914–1918*. 2 vols. 1961.

Havinghurst, Alfred F. *Radical Journalist: H. W. Massingham, 1860–1924*. 1974.

Hazelhurst, Cameron. *Politicians at War July 1914 to May 1915: A Prologue to the Triumph of Lloyd George*. New York, 1971.

The History of the Times, Vol. 4: *1912–1920*, part 1. New York, 1952.

Holborn, Hajo. *A History of Modern Germany, 1840–1945*. New York, 1969.

Howard, Michael. *The Continental Commitment: The Dilemma of British Defence Policy in the Era of the Two World Wars. The Ford Lectures in the University of Oxford*. 1972.

Jenkins, Roy. *Asquith: Portrait of a Man and An Era*. Paperback edn. New York, 1966.

Jones, Thomas. *Lloyd George*. 1951.

Kennedy, Paul, ed. *The War Plans of the Great Powers, 1880–1914*. 1979.

Keegan, John. *The Face of Battle*. Paperback edn. New York, 1976.

Kernek, Sterling J. *Distractions of Peace During War: The Lloyd George Government's Reactions to Woodrow Wilson December, 1916– November, 1918*. Philadelphia, 1975.

King, Jere Clemons. *Generals and Politicians: Conflict between France's High Command, Parliament and Government, 1914–1918*. Berkeley, Calif., 1951.

Kitchen, Martin. *The Silent Dictatorship: The Politics of the German High Command under Hindenburg and Ludendorff, 1916–1918*. New York, 1976.

Koss, Stephen. *Asquith*. New York, 1976.

———. "The Destruction of Britain's Last Liberal Government." *Journal of Modern History* 40 (June 1968).

———. *Fleet Street Radical: A. G. Gardiner and the Daily News*. Hamden, Conn., 1973.

Lennox, Lady Algernon Gordon, ed. *The Diary of Lord Bertie of Thame, 1914–1918*. 1924.

Liddell Hart, Captain B. H. "The Basic Truths of Passchendaele." *Journal of the Royal United Service Institution* 104 (November 1959).

———. *The Real War, 1914–1918*. Paperback edn. Boston, 1930.

———. *Through the Fog of War*. 1938.

Lloyd George, David. *War Memoirs of David Lloyd George*. 2 vols. 1938.

Lloyd George, Frances. *The Years That Are Past*. 1967.

Louis, Wm. Roger. *Great Britain and Germany's Lost Colonies, 1914–1919*. 1967.

Lowe, C. J., and Dockrill, M. L. *The Mirage of Power*. Vol. 2: *British Foreign Policy 1914–1922*. 1972.

———. *The Mirage of Power*. Vol. 3: *The Documents British Foreign Policy 1902–1922*. 1972.

Ludendorff, General Erich von. *Ludendorff's Own Story: August 1914– November 1918*. Engl. trans. 2 vols. New York, 1919.

Lutz, Ralph Haswell. *The Causes of the German Collapse in 1918.* Engl. trans. 1934.

———. ed. *The Fall of the German Empire, 1914–1918.* 2 vols. 1932.

McEwen, J. M. "The Press and the Fall of Asquith." *The Historical Journal* 21 (December 1978).

McGill, Barry. "Asquith's Predicament, 1914–1918," *Journal of Modern History* 39 (September 1967).

Magnus, Philip. *Kitchener: Portrait of an Imperialist.* 1959.

Marder, Arthur, Jr. *From the Dreadnought to Scapa Flow.* Vol. 4: *1917: Year of Crisis.* 1969.

Maurice, Nancy, ed. *The Maurice Case from the Papers of Major-General Sir Frederick Maurice.* With an appreciation by Major-General Sir Edward Spears. 1972.

Middlebrook, Martin. *The Kaiser's Battle 21 March 1918: The First Day of the German Spring Offensive.* 1978.

Middlemas, Keith, ed. *Thomas Jones Whitehall Diary.* Vol. 1: *1916–1925.* 1969.

Morgan, Kenneth O. *Lloyd George.* With an introduction by A. J. P. Taylor. 1974.

———, ed. *Lloyd George Family Letters, 1885–1936.* 1973.

———. "Lloyd George's Premiership: A Study in 'Prime Ministerial Government.'" *The Historical Journal* 13 (March 1970).

Nicolson, Harold. *King George V: His Life and Reign.* 1952.

O'Brien, Terence H. *Milner: Viscount Milner of St. James's and Cape Town, 1854–1925.* 1979.

D'Ombrian, Nicholas. *War Machinery and High Policy: Defence Administration in Peacetime Britain 1902–1914.* 1973.

Owen, Frank. *Tempestuous Journey: Lloyd George His Life and Times.* New York, 1955.

Parsons, Edward. "Why the British Reduced Flow of American Troops to Europe in August–October 1918." *Canadian Journal of History* 2 (December 1977).

Painlevé, Paul. *Comment J'ai Nommé Foch et Pétain.* Paris, 1923.

Pershing, John J. *My Experiences in the World War.* 2 vols. New York, 1931.

Pitt, Barrie. *1918: The Last Act.* 1963.

Pound, Reginald, and Harmsworth, Geoffrey. *Northcliffe.* 1959.

Repington, Lieutenant-Colonel C. à. Court. *The First World War, 1914–1918.* 2 vols. 1920.

Robbins, Keith. *Sir Edward Grey: A Biography of Lord Grey of Fallodon.* 1971.

Robertson, Sir William. *From Private to Field-Marshal.* New York, 1921.

————. *Soldiers and Statesmen, 1914–1918*. 2 vols. 1926.

Roskill, Stephen. *Hankey Man of Secrets*. Vol. 1: *1877–1918*. 1970.

Rowland, Peter. *David Lloyd George: A Biography*. New York, 1975.

Lord Riddell's War Diary 1914–1918. 1933.

Rothwell, V. H. *British War Aims and Peace Diplomacy, 1914–1918*. 1971.

Rudin, Harry R. *Armistice 1918*. Reprint edn. Hamden, Conn., 1967.

Ryan, Michael, W. "From 'Shells Scandal' to Bow Street: The Denigration of Lieutenant-Colonel Charles à Court Repington." *The Journal of Modern History*. On Demand Supplement, 50 (December 1978).

Sanders, Liman von. *Five Years in Turkey*. 1927.

Sixsmith, E. K. G. *Douglas Haig*. 1976.

Spears, Brigadier-General E. L. *Prelude to Victory*. 1939.

Statistics of the Military Effort of the British Empire During the Great War, 1914–1920. 1922.

Steiner, Zara S. *Britain and the Origins of the First World War*. Paperback edn. New York, 1977.

Sullivan, Timothy Crandall. "The General and the Prime Minister: Henry Wilson and David Lloyd George in War and Peace, 1918–1922." Ph.D. diss., University of Illinois at Urbana-Champaign, 1973.

Stone, Norman. *The Eastern Front, 1914–1917*. New York, 1975.

Swartz, Marvin. *The Union of Democratic Control in British Politics during the First World War*. 1971.

Sylvester, Albert James. *The Real Lloyd George*. 1947.

Tanenbaum, Jan Karl. *General Maurice Sarrail 1856–1929: The French Army and Left Wing Politics*. Chapel Hill, N.C., 1974.

Taylor, A. J. P. *English History, 1914–1945*. 1965.

————. *Essays in British History*. Paperback edn. Harmondsworth, Middlesex, 1976.

————, ed. *My Darling Pussy: The Letters of Lloyd George and Frances Stevenson*. 1975.

————. *The First World War: An Illustrated History*. Paperback edn., New York, 1972.

————. ed. *Lloyd George: A Diary by Frances Stevenson*. 1971.

————, ed. *Lloyd George: Twelve Essays*. New York, 1971.

Taylor, H. A. *Robert Donald*. 1934.

Terraine, John. *Douglas Haig: The Educated Soldier*. 1963.

————. "The Impact of Mons, August 1914." *History Today* 14 (August 1964).

————. *Impacts of War, 1914 and 1918*. 1970.

————. *Mons: The Retreat to Victory*. New York, 1960.

———. *The Road to Passchendaele: The Flanders Offensive of 1917, A Study of Inevitability.* 1977.

———. *The Western Front, 1914–1918.* 1965.

———. *To Win a War, 1918: The Year of Victory.* 1978.

Toland, John. *No Man's Land: 1918, The Last Year of the Great War.* New York, 1980.

Torrey, Glen E. "Roumania and the Belligerents 1914–1916." *Journal of Contemporary History* 1 (July 1966).

———. "Roumania's Entry into the First World War: The Problem of Strategy." *The Emporia State Research Studies* 26 (Spring 1978).

Trask, David F. *Captains & Cabinets: Anglo-American Naval Relations, 1917–1918.* Columbia, Missouri, 1972.

———. *The United States in the Supreme War Council: American War Aims and Inter-Allied Strategy, 1917–1918.* Middletown, Conn., 1961.

Turner, John. *Lloyd George's Secretariat.* 1980.

Ullman, Richard. *Anglo-Soviet Relations, 1917–1921.* Vol. 1: *Intervention and the War.* Princeton, N.J., 1961.

Vandiver, Frank E. *Black Jack: The Life and Times of John J. Pershing.* 2 vols. College Station, Tex., 1977.

Watson, David Robin. *Georges Clemenceau: A Political Biography.* New York, 1974.

Watt, Richard, M. *Dare Call It Treason.* 1963.

Wavell, Field-Marshall Viscount. *Allenby: Soldier and Statesman.* 1946.

Wheeler-Bennett, John W. *Brest-Litovsk: The Forgotten Peace, March 1918.* 1938.

Williams, M. J. "Thirty Per Cent: A Study in Casualty Statistics." *Journal of the Royal United Service Institution* 109 (February 1964).

Williams, John. *The Home Fronts: Britain, France and Germany 1914–1918.* 1972.

Williamson, Samuel R., Jr. *The Politics of Grand Strategy: Britain and France Prepare for War.* Cambridge, Mass., 1969.

Wilson, K. M. "The War Office, Churchill and the Belgian Option: August to December 1911." *Bulletin of the Institute of Historical Research* 50 (November 1977).

Wilson, Trevor. *The Downfall of the Liberal Party 1914–1935.* 1966.

———. ed. *The Political Diaries of C. P. Scott 1911–1928.* 1970.

Woodward, David R. "Britain in a Continental War: The Civil-Military Debate Over the Strategic Direction of the Great War of 1914–1918." *Albion* 12 (Spring 1980).

———. "The British Government and Japanese Intervention in Russia During World War I." *Journal of Modern History* 46 (December 1974).

————. "'Brass Hats' and the Question of a Compromise Peace, 1916–1918," *Military Affairs* 4 (April 1971).

————. "David Lloyd George, A Negotiated Peace with Germany and the Kuhlmann Peace Kite of September, 1917." *Canadian Journal of History* 6 (March 1971).

————. "Great Britain and President Wilson's Efforts to End World War I in 1916." *The Maryland Historian* 1 (Spring 1970).

————. "The Origins and Intent of David Lloyd George's January 5 War Aims Speech." *The Historian* 34 (November 1971).

Woodward, Sir Llewellyn. *Great Britain and the War of 1914–1918.* 1967.

Wright, Captain Peter E. *At the Supreme War Council.* 1921.

Wrigley, Chris. *David Lloyd George and the British Labour Movement: Peace and War.* New York, 1976.

Wynne, Captain G. C. *If Germany Attacks: The Battle in Depth in the West.* 1940.

————. "The Development of German Defensive Battle in 1917, and Its Influence on British Defence Tactics, Part 1." *The Army Quarterly* 34 (April 1937).

Young, Kenneth. *Arthur James Balfour: The Happy Life of the Politician Prime Minister, Statesman and Philosopher, 1848–1930.* 1963.

Zeman, Z. A. B. *The Gentleman Negotiators: A Diplomatic History of World War I.* New York, 1971.

Index

Abbeville: Robertson-Foch conference at, 170 n. 50; S.W.C. at, 295–96

Aitken, Sir Max (later first Baron Beaverbrook), 99–101, 131, 181, 275; on L G's exploitation of "shells scandal," 51 n. 13; and "soldiers' party," 100; plots with L G to reorganize government, 121, 123 n. 37, 126–27; appointed minister in charge of propaganda, 269; his error, 300 n. 89; on "lost box," 302

Allanson, Lieut.-Col. C. J. L.: on retention of general reserve in Britain, 238

Allenby, Gen. Sir Edmund H. (later first Viscount), 223, 231, 316, 318; in collusion with Robertson, 199, 206, 211, 231 n. 51, 241–42; thinks Smuts's offensive plan workable, 245 n. 110; offensive approved by War Cabinet, 283; his number of white divisions, 292 n. 49, 296, 299; Amery wants his forces reinforced, 305; overwhelming victory, 332

Allied general reserve. *See* Unity of command; General reserve, inter-Allied

American Expeditionary Force (A.E.F.), 171–72, 177, 210, 235, 328; British high command's view of offensive capacity of 238–39, 245–46, 333; suggestion to brigade with British forces, 236 n. 74, 257–58, 293–95; L G looks to for decisive blows in West, 283, 315–16, 336; British request greater help from, 288; Pershing's desire for independent force, 289–90, 323, 330 n. 87; Pershing-Milner agreement, 295–96, 318; L G wants to substitute American for British soldiers in the West, 318, 322, 324, 330, 333; L G angry over Foch's utilization of, 323–24 n. 59, 476 n. 87, 333 n.

107; British concern about future dominant role, 325, 328; concern that Haig might misuse, 331; St. Mihiel, 332

Amery, Leopold S.: on strategy, 166–67, 221–22, 242–43, 284–85, 305, 316–17, 329 n. 82; on role of S.W.C., 227 n. 26; role at Versailles, 243; on Smuts, 244; wrongly accused of being source of Repington's information, 246 n. 120; warns L G about War Office's use of press, 260

Amiens, Battle of, 327, 330; L G's pessimism about, 328

Arras, Battle of, 142–155

Asquith, Arthur, 119

Asquith, Herbert H. (later first earl of Oxford and Adquith), 15–17, 34, 40, 62–63, 65, 78, 86, 110 n. 69, 111, 116–17, 122–23, 133, 163, 186, 203–4, 209, 215, 224, 226, 335; calls council of war, 18–19; L G requests review of war policy, 27; Balkan operations, 30, 33; L G critical of, 44, 59, 64, n. 77, 69; appoints cabinet committee on munitions, 50; opinion of Kitchener, 52–53, 64–65, 67, 69; shakes up Imperial general staff, 61, 74, 78–80; critical of Allied military planning, 86; on compulsion, 87–88; American mediation, 90; L G's appointment as secretary of state for war, 98–102; concern about generals' conduct of war, 119; supports Robertson against L G, 120–21; on L G's instability, 121; Paris conference (November 1916), 121–22; L G in conflict with over reorganization of government, 124–29 n. 63 passim; resignation, 129; favors Flanders offensive, 130, 137; L G sus-

353